The Wreck of the *San Francisco*

ALSO BY JOHN STEWART
AND FROM McFARLAND

*Jefferson Davis's Flight from Richmond: The Calm Morning,
Lee's Telegrams, the Evacuation, the Train, the Passengers, the Trip,
the Arrival in Danville and the Historians' Frauds* (2015)

The Acrobat: Arthur Barnes and the Victorian Circus (2012)

Antarctica: An Encyclopedia, 2d ed. (2011)

*Byron and the Websters: The Letters and Entangled Lives
of the Poet, Sir James Webster and Lady Frances Webster* (2008)

*Confederate Spies at Large: The Lives of Lincoln Assassination
Conspirator Tom Harbin and Charlie Russell* (2007)

Broadway Musicals, 1943–2004 (2006; paperback 2014)

African States and Rulers, 3d ed. (2006; paperback 2014)

Italian Film: A Who's Who (1994; paperback 2012)

Moons of the Solar System: An Illustrated Encyclopedia
(1991; paperback 2012)

The Wreck of the *San Francisco*

Disaster and Aftermath in the Great Hurricane of December 1853

JOHN STEWART

McFarland & Company, Inc., Publishers
Jefferson, North Carolina

For Gayle Winston

LIBRARY OF CONGRESS CATALOGUING-IN-PUBLICATION DATA

Names: Stewart, John, 1952 March 5– author.
Title: The wreck of the San Francisco : disaster and aftermath in the great hurricane of December 1853 / John Stewart.
Description: Jefferson, North Carolina : McFarland & Company, Inc., 2018 | Includes bibliographical references and index.
Identifiers: LCCN 2018014112 | ISBN 9781476674100 (softcover : acid free paper) ∞
Subjects: LCSH: San Francisco (Steamship) | Steamboat disasters—United States—History—19th century. | Shipwrecks—North Atlantic Ocean. | Voyages to the Pacific coast.
Classification: LCC G530.S254 S74 2018 | DDC 910.9163/6—dc23
LC record available at https://lccn.loc.gov/2018014112

BRITISH LIBRARY CATALOGUING DATA ARE AVAILABLE

ISBN (print) 978-1-4766-7410-0
ISBN (ebook) 978-1-4766-3263-6

© 2018 John Stewart. All rights reserved

No part of this book may be reproduced or transmitted in any form or by any means, electronic or mechanical, including photocopying or recording, or by any information storage and retrieval system, without permission in writing from the publisher.

Front cover artwork of the wreck of the steam ship *San Francisco* by Currier & Ives, 1854 (© 2018 PicturesNow)

Printed in the United States of America

McFarland & Company, Inc., Publishers
Box 611, Jefferson, North Carolina 28640
www.mcfarlandpub.com

Table of Contents

Preface • 1
Prologue • 3

General Orders No. 2 • 9
Picking the Right Ship • 16
The U.S.S. *San Francisco* • 23
Will She Ever Sail? • 26
Trial Runs • 33
Departure Day Minus One • 43
Ship's Log • 52
Thursday, December 22, 1853 • 55
Friday, December 23 • 62
Saturday, December 24 • 71
Sunday, December 25 • 97
Monday, December 26 • 106
Tuesday, December 27 • 111
Wednesday, December 28 • 116
Thursday, December 29 • 135
Friday, December 30 • 140
Saturday, December 31 • 142
Sunday, January 1, 1854 • 148

Monday, January 2 • 151
Tuesday, January 3 • 153
Wednesday, January 4 • 157
Thursday, January 5 • 159
Friday, January 6 • 162
Saturday, January 7 • 166
Sunday, January 8 • 168
Monday, January 9 • 170
Tuesday, January 10 • 174
Wednesday, January 11 • 176
Thursday, January 12 • 177
Friday, January 13 • 180
Saturday, January 14 • 186
Safe • 190
The Voyage of the *Antarctic* • 194
The Inquiry • 198
The *Falcon* and the Trial of Major Wyse • 213

Epilogue • 217
Appendix: Those Aboard the San Francisco • 229
A Note on Sources • 239
References • 241
Four Previous Books • 245
Index • 247

Preface

On the morning of December 22, 1853, a brand new steamship left New York Harbor on its maiden voyage. The length of a football field, the *San Francisco* was arguably the best-made ocean-going vessel built up to that time, and had been chartered by the United States Government to carry most of the men of the Third Artillery to the Pacific Coast. The Army was badly needed out there in the far west. The State of California was only a few years old, and the Gold Rush had brought with it not only a fantastic influx od people, but a corresponding amount of lawlessness. On top of that, the Indians were playing up.

Only two days out of New York, 300 miles off the coast of Delaware, the *San Francisco* ran into one of the great hurricanes of maritime history. Her sails and masts were blown away, the engine was wrecked, and scores of human beings were washed overboard. With no power of her own, the ruined steamer became a floating coffin as cholera broke out on board. With people dying fast, and with the ocean constantly threatening to drag the ship down at any moment, the men battled frantically with the pumps to keep afloat. Other vessels began to pass by, but with the seas so high they could be of little help. Finally, with the storm abating, three ships in succession managed to take off the survivors and bring them back to civilization. After two weeks, the nightmare was over. But the drama continued. Two of the three rescuing vessels had been so damaged by the storms that they were hardly in a position to take on such a large number of unexpected passengers, let alone the threat of cholera, and it wasn't long before water and provisions began to run out. Facing death at every turn from thirst, starvation, exhaustion, exposure, and even a mutiny, they barely made it back to land. But they did. As for the Third Artillery, it had been decimated.

Then came the aftermath, the accusations, the denials, the shocking revelations of ineptitude and gross negligence by the Government, the cover-up, and finally the Inquiry and the price to be paid.

This book consists basically of a prologue, the story of the wreck, and an epilogue. The prologue gives the background to what led up to the adventure. The middle section is a day by day account of what happened between the time the San Francisco left New York Harbor until the day the survivors made it back to New York, i.e., from December 22, 1853, to January 14, 1854. The Epilogue tells what happened afterwards. There is also an appendix, listing all those on board the ship.

Prologue

It would never have happened if it hadn't been for Padre Hidalgo. Not that he's to blame; it's just that when he shouted he precipitated a chain of events that culminated inexorably in one of the greatest disasters in maritime history.

September 16 marks the day in 1810, in the little Mexican town of Dolores, when Miguel Hidalgo's first revolutionary grito—"shout"—was heard around the world. It wouldn't be for another 11 years and 11 days, and only then after a long war with Mother Spain, that the Mexicans would win freedom in deed as well as in proclamation. But one thing is certain; if El Grito de Dolores had been a mere whisper, the steamer *San Francisco* would not have been wrecked 43 years later.

In 1821 Mexico included a good portion of what today goes to form much of the western and southwestern United States of America, including California and Texas, both thinly settled back then. Just prior to Mexican independence, a few Americans had secured permission from the Spanish authorities to establish settlements in Texas, and the new government would, as it turned out, honor that agreement. By 1836 there were roughly 25,000 people living in Texas, about 85 percent of whom were non–Hispanic. Presuming upon the confidence of such ethnic weight, the Texans declared their independence from Mexico, the Mexicans objected, and the Alamo happened. Later that year the Republic of Texas was created, and duly recognized by other countries as a sovereign state. Mexico declined to send an ambassador.

By 1845 there were 6,220 Mexicans, 680 foreigners, and perhaps 15,000 Indians living in California, a total of probably no more than 23,000 individuals in the same space that today squeezes in almost 40 million. Although not Mexico's fault, California held little attraction for potential immigrants. There was nothing there. It was dull as dishwater. It would take a yellow mineral to change all that.

As for what was happening farther to the east, at the end of the year, December 29, 1845, Texas became the twenty-eighth star on the American flag. Although this annexation, along with the acquisition of the Oregon Territory six months later, greatly expanded the frontiers of the U.S.A., it immediately led to trouble with Mexico, who were still under the impression that it was they who owned Texas. They thought they still owned California too, and in that they were equally mistaken. Ownership of land goes to those who can prove it, and the best proof of all is a big stick. Mexico had a small stick.

With very definite prejudice, the U.S. Army marched, rode and sailed in force into the land of their southern neighbor. The army was divided into three basic arms: The Infantry, Cavalry, and Artillery, each being subdivided into regiments, and each regiment into companies. The regiments were numbered in order of precedence, for example, the First Infantry, the Second Cavalry, the Third Artillery. The companies were given letters, in order of seniority: Company A, Company B, and on down the alphabet to Company M, missing only J, that letter being too easily confused with a capital I. Of the Third Regiment of Artillery, to take but one case, all but two of the companies fought in Mexico. California too became, though to a much lesser extent, a theatre of this war, with Company F of the Third Artillery, among other army units, going out to protect the growing American interests on the Pacific coast. For Company F, going around the Horn as they did, it was like going to a distant country, an expedition into the unknown. But, on January 26, 1847, 198 days out of New York, the steamship *Lexington* finally nosed her way into the harbor of the California capital of Monterey. Although they were not the first American troops on the West Coast, Company F, with its 113 men—mostly recruits enlisted the previous spring—did establish, the very day after the Monterey landing, the first U.S. Army post in California. In the meantime the *Lexington* carried the rest of the troops north up the coast to San Francisco.

Among those just arrived at Monterey were First Lieutenant William Tecumseh Sherman, who was about to celebrate his 27th birthday; Lieutenant Henry Wager Halleck of the Engineers; and a 28-year-old second lieutenant from Pennsylvania named Lucien Loeser. A notable visitor to the post in April and May of 1847 would be Major Thomas Swords, quartermaster of the Army of the West, then aged 40.[1]

The war ended just outside Mexico City with the signing of the Treaty of Guadalupe Hidalgo on February 2, 1848, and with it the map of the mainland U.S.A. came to look, for the first time, much as it does today, stretching from Maine to San Diego, from Puget Sound to Key West. The world came to comprehend, with startling clarity, the full meaning of a term that had been coined just three years earlier—Manifest Destiny. Another expression just starting to come into vogue was "land grab."

Manifest destiny or land grab? If there was ever any dispute over terminology it was settled by the gods. Nineteen days before the Treaty of Guadalupe Hidalgo, and almost 2,000 miles to the north of the Mexican capital, a New Jersey man, James Wilson Marshall, unearthed a yellow nugget in the debris at the bottom of a millrace he owned with a Swiss named Jacob Sutter, about 200 feet from the South Fork of the American River, in a California community called Coloma. Talk of Marshall's discovery spread locally like wildfire, and by the beginning of April 1848, as word of the ground-breaking event was starting to make its way into the territory's newspapers, people were flocking to Sutter's Mill for the easy pickings. The military governor of California went to the diggings to confirm the strike. Accompanying him on his mission was Lieutenant Sherman. The Gold Rush was on.

---

1. Army post returns.

News of the massive, earth-shattering find had to be transmitted to the U.S. Government, a world away in Washington, D.C., and Lucien Loeser, still stationed at Monterey, was the right man for the job of courier, having just been promoted to first lieutenant and thereby entitled to go home on a long furlough. Carrying Marshall's nugget among other things, Lieutenant Loeser left Monterey on a southbound steamer heading for the city of Panama, which at that point in history was an outpost of the country of Colombia. Here he climbed on the back of a horse, made the dangerous crossing of the isthmus in a few days, and finally arrived in the United States on November 28, 1848.

As soon as word got out in the Eastern press that there was gold in Californ-eye-ay, a mass movement of people took place larger than any other since the time of the Crusades.

In those days, transcontinental rail travel was still in the planning stage; it would be another two decades before they drove home the Golden Spike that would make a coast-to-coast train trip possible. So, in the late 1840s, there were five basic ways a Forty-Niner could get from the east to the promised land. To cross overland by wagon, using the old California Trail, could take a year or more, depending on disease, Indians, accidents and a host of other eventualities. Or he could take ship and go all the way down to the tip of South America and then up the other side. This voyage could take up to six months, that is if he made it around the notorious Cape Horn. Another way was to ship down to Vera Cruz and cross Mexico by land. But in 1849 you didn't really want to be wandering around down there south of the border if you were a "gringo," not after what you and your fellow Yanquis had just done to the Mexicans. Finally, Central America offered two main crossing places, the Isthmus of Panama and Lake Nicaragua, both of them much quicker than any other route, but fraught with hazards, if not danger. None of these considerations stopped thousands upon thousands of argonauts from venturing out in search of the Golden Fleece.

As far back as 1847 the U.S. Government had recognized its responsibility for assuring postal delivery to that small but ever increasing number of Americans settling on the west coast. To help fulfill their commitment, the government awarded contracts to three private parties, a certain amount of compensation going along with each contract. The first party, a shipping company, would run steamers down the Atlantic coast from New York City to the Panama Isthmus. The conveying of the mail by land across the isthmus, from the Atlantic side to the city of Panama on the Pacific coast, was entrusted to the dubious care of local contractors. The third group, another shipping firm, would carry the mails from Panama up the west coast to San Francisco. The two shipping companies, the one handling the east coast and the other the west, would maintain the right to carry passengers as well as the mails.

When William Henry Aspinwall founded the Pacific Mail Steamship Company on April 18, 1848, to fulfill his 10-year contract with the U.S. Government to carry the mails between the cities of Panama and San Francisco, many thought he was crazy, a victim, perhaps, of an over-indulgence in big dreams. There was absolutely nothing they could see out there in that part of the world that could possibly interest this giant New York merchant and shipbuilder. But W.H. Aspinwall was a lot more than just a dreamer; he was lucky. And he had a crystal ball. Although no one in the east would know of Sutter's Mill for some months yet, Aspinwall could obviously see quite clearly in his glass orb the desperate madness that was already sweeping California. That insanity would soon have millions of people rushing headlong to the west coast, and a good number of them would, sooner or later, have to make use of W.H. Aspinwall's steamers.

The first P.M.S.S. steamer, the *California*, set out from New York on October 6, 1848, went around the Horn, up the west coast of South and Central America, to the territory she was named for, and arrived in San Francisco Harbor on February 28, 1849, bringing with her several early and well-paying Forty-Niners whom the ship had picked up along the way.

On April 1, 1849, the second Aspinwall steamer, the *Oregon*, arrived at San Francisco, and, on June 4, the *Panama* pulled in after a voyage of four months. The ship's purser on the *Panama* was a New Yorker named Theo Schell. At only 22, he was the best purser to be found on any ocean-going vessel, his attention to his passengers already legendary.

Soon, with the argonauts pouring across Central America and searching desperately for a steamer, any steamer, to take them up the west coast to California for the free gold, Mr. Aspinwall and his Pacific Mail Steamship Company became rich indeed. The Gold Rush was very definitely on.

In 1850 the company transferred Purser Schell to the *Unicorn*, and at that very moment the *Panama* acquired a new skipper, a Maryland man who, although he had just started with Aspinwall's line, was experienced enough at sea to be able to claim that he had visited San Diego as early as 1832, and that was certainly saying something. For another few years Captain James Thomas Watkins would ply the seas unknown to the world at large, just another skipper. But his time would come. Out of the blue, for reasons far beyond his control, in the last three weeks of January 1854 he would become, for a brief while, one of the most famous men in the world.

Howland & Aspinwall decided to add a couple of steamers to their Pacific fleet, and in June 1850 contracted with two of the great New York City shipyards—Messrs. Smith & Damon, and William H. Webb.[2] It was the one taken on by Webb that three and half years later would dominate newspaper headlines around the globe.

The impact of the Gold Rush upon California was such that, virtually overnight, it transformed that territory from a sleepy backwater that held no interest for anyone but a few intrepid pioneers into the fastest growing place the world had ever seen. The Mexican War was over, Manifest Destiny had wrested California from the defeated enemy, U.S. military outposts had begun to proliferate there—Benicia and San Diego Barracks were established in April 1849—and in 1850 a thirty-first star appeared on the American flag.

In addition to all his other ventures, W.H. Aspinwall saw great possibilities for

---

2. *North American and United States Gazette* (Philadelphia), June 21, 1850.

Panama. The village of Chagres, at the mouth of the river of the same name, had long slumbered on the Atlantic side of the isthmus, and by 1848 had deteriorated into a virtual ghost town. Then news of the California Gold Rush broke in the East, and almost instantaneously a boom town exploded into being on the opposite bank of the Chagres River. Yankee Town, they called it, or Yanqui Chagres, full of gold-seekers on their way up river by steamer and across the hazardous isthmus to the land of purchased dreams. Mr. Aspinwall had no use for Yanqui Chagres, not for what he had in mind, and so he founded another, completely new town 10 miles up the coast to the east, and they called it Aspinwall. From here the New York mogul would build a railroad across the isthmus to the Pacific coast, and millions of people would pay to use it. The 47-mile project was begun with the laying of the first length of rail in May 1850. But it wouldn't be until January 28, 1855, that the first successful run all the way from Aspinwall to Panama City would be made, and that was two years too late for the Third Artillery.

Another fantastically wealthy American, Cornelius Vanderbilt, perhaps the greatest tycoon of his age, also caught the strong whiff of gold in Central America. In those days, whenever a ship made the voyage from New York to the Isthmus of Panama, it would pass by the Mosquito Coast of Nicaragua. There was a town on this coast named San Juan del Norte, built at the mouth of the San Juan River. If one were to go 135 miles up this river into the interior, one would emerge into Lake Nicaragua. On the other side of that giant body of water was Virgin Bay, separated from and connected to the Pacific Coast by a strip of land a mere 12 miles long. So, Vanderbilt established a route that shaved a week off the time taken to cross the Panama Isthmus, and which also had the advantage of avoiding the awful jungles. However, primarily as a result of internal warfare within Commodore Vanderbilt's own company—waged notably by his treacherous partner Charles Morgan—the route folded.

W.H. Aspinwall's Panama Railroad and the Vanderbilt initiative across Nicaragua were simply examples of commercial evolution at work, entrepreneurs supplying a demand. There was money to be made here. But one had to be a big player, or things would probably go wrong. There were always lesser men prompted by half-baked dreams to search for quicker, better routes from the Atlantic to the Pacific, those who wondered why they had to go all the way down to Nicaragua, or even worse, to Panama, when staring them in their relatively-speaking face, on their back doorstep, was the Isthmus of Tehuantepec, the slimmest portion of Mexico. This, and similar potential Mexican land routes had been fruitlessly explored for years, but by 1853, with the lure of the glittering metal out there in California and the coming of Aspinwall's railroad, and with the humiliating sting of the late war fading from the collective Mexican memory, these adventurers were spurred on to fever pitch. It might have seemed, to the interested observer, that every tenth Yank south of the border was trying to get an exclusive grant from the Mexican Government to run an overland route. One of these men, Albert C. Ramsay, former colonel of the 11th Pennsylvania Volunteer Infantry during the Mexican War, even got as far as making an arrangement with the Pacific Mail Steamship Company to link up with their new steamer about to be completed in New York—the *San Francisco*, which would soon be making her way out west to take her place in the P.M.S.S.'s line of ships plying between the cities of Panama and San Francisco.

But Ramsay's dreams, like those of all the others, contained insufficient starch to compete successfully with the obstacles and difficulties thrust in their way: The financing of such an enterprise, the complexities of dealing with the Mexican Government, and the fact that Lady Luck was not looking their way. Mexico never happened.

As for Theo Schell, the purser, come early 1853 he was still working for the Pacific Mail Steamship Company, plying the West Coast on their steamer *Tennessee*, when he got word from Howland & Aspinwall that their most magnificent vessel to date, the *San Francisco*, was nearing completion. For their best ship the P.M.S.S. needed their best purser. They also wanted their best skipper, James T. Watkins.[3]

The Mineral Springs Hotel in Lynn, Massachusetts, was quite famous back in 1833, when it was run by Major Jabez Ward Barton. On November 17 of that year, a new Barton was born—Charles Frederick. When Charles was still an infant, they all moved to the Maverick House, in Boston, where the young fellow grew up. In 1841 the Major moved on to the Albion, and eight years later young Charles Barton went to sea. On February 12, 1853, the new clipper *Golden Light* sailed from Boston, bound for San Francisco. Ten days into her voyage she was struck by lightning and set afire. Five boats managed to get off, but only three were picked up by the British ship *Shand* and returned to Boston. Charles Barton, the second mate, was lucky. Lady Luck favors men of 19. Shortly after his narrow escape, Mr. Barton was posted to the *San Francisco* as third officer.

By July 1853 the Forty-Niners and the Indians were acting up out west, and so, in order to provide a semblance of law and order, the War Department was endeavoring to collect together, from several states in the East, a considerable detachment of recruits to be sent as soon as possible to the state of California and to the Oregon Territory, in order to reinforce the various army units already there. The depot for the collection and instruction of recruits—boot camp, as it would be called today—had been moved the previous year from Fort Wood, on Bedloes Island to Fort Columbus, the castle on Governors Island, both dots of land being situated in New York Harbor. On July 1, 1853, Lieutenant Colonel John J. Abercrombie, of the Second Infantry, replaced Colonel Joseph Plympton, of the First Infantry, as superintendent of the depot. The recruits, as soon as they had been instructed, were sent off to the different regiments on the Pacific coast.

---

3. *New York Herald*, April 4, 1853; *New York Times*, May 26, 1853.

General Orders No. 2

General Orders No. 2 were issued from U.S. Army Headquarters in New York, on September 26, 1853, in the name of Secretary of War Jefferson Davis, and signed by Lieutenant Colonel Lorenzo Thomas, an assistant adjutant general, by command of Major General Winfield Scott, the general in chief.[1] These orders had to do with the movement of troops. According to Paragraph 5, six companies of the Third Regiment of Artillery were to leave their respective forts on the New England coast and make their way to New York Harbor, to concentrate there, at Fort Columbus, to await their ship, and thence to proceed via Cape Horn to the Pacific Division. In other words, to California and Oregon.

What this meant was that almost an entire regiment was to be transported from one coast of the United States to the other. A monumental and unprecedented job of logistics. But the army was up to the task, at least in theory.[2] They had the money, the expertise, the experience, the will, and the power to see it through, and of course, they would have the right ship. Yet this voyage would entail at least four months at sea, maybe six, and so one other element was required, and without that particular element, no matter how thorough and painstaking the planning of the overall operation might be, the men would never reach their destination. Throughout history, soldiers had been routinely marched once a week by their superiors to a place of worship in order to beseech the relevant deity to look down favorably upon one military enterprise or another. The United States War Department was no exception. However, as it turned out, this time they were praying to the wrong god.

The order contained the notice "The Colonel of the Regiment will receive further instructions for his government from these headquarters." These were words that, in hindsight, bode as ill as the ultimate bad card dealt out of a Tarot deck, for the Colonel of the Third Artillery was William Gates.

Officers of the affected companies who were at that moment on leave of absence

---

1. Report of the Secretary of War, Jan. 30, 1854.
2. Although this was indeed an unprecedented job of logistics as far as taking a whole regiment out to California by way of the Horn, very much alive in the War Department's memory was the disaster of July 1852, when the Fourth Infantry, which included Lieutenant Ulysses S. Grant, was sent out west, via the Isthmus of Panama. This involved shipping more than 700 persons from New York to Aspinwall on the steamer *Ohio*, transferring them across the isthmus, and then embarking them on a steamer for the trip up the Pacific Coast to San Francisco. The trouble lay in hopeless management of the Panama crossing and in cholera, which ravaged the regiment.

or under orders to join the regiment were to make their way to Fort Columbus forthwith.

"The necessary supplies and transportation will be furnished by the proper departments."[3]

―※―

First Lieutenant William T. Sherman had received his captain's brevet in 1850, for "meritorious service" performed as he languished bravely in California while the Mexican War was raging elsewhere.[4] A brevet was the traditional reward given by the army to an officer for Sherman's sort of service or for gallantry in the field, or both. Even though the brevet brought no additional pay, authority, or responsibility, and despite the fact that his substantive rank was still first lieutenant, he could now call himself Captain Sherman. At least that was something. But what Sherman really wanted was a conspicuous record of gallantry, and severely chagrined that he couldn't, in all conscience, number himself one of the Gay and Gallant Third who had earned that nickname while facing actual enemy fire in Mexico itself, and keenly aware of the limitations of a peace-time army career, he resigned his commission in Company I of the Third Artillery on September 6, 1853, and became a banker in San Francisco.

Sherman's decision set in motion a chain of events that would prove disastrous for Richard Hamilton Smith and his wife Elizabeth. In those days, during eras of peace, an officer was promoted according to strict seniority, a very clear and rigid pecking order. Whenever a vacancy occurred for one reason or another, a vacuum was created in the Army List, and the War Department had no tolerance for a vacuum. So the vacancy had to be filled by promotion from below. In this case, when Sherman left the army the space he had once occupied became a gap in the list of active first lieutenants, and that gap was automatically and immediately filled, by Second Lieutenant Richard H. Smith. As was customary, Smith was given leave upon his promotion, and when he went back to work on September 13, 1853, he was transferred from Company I to Company A, who were stationed at Fort Trumbull, in New London Harbor, Connecticut.[5] Lieutenant Smith didn't know it then, but it would be the last furlough he would ever get in his life. Another thing the young Tennessean was blissfully ignorant of was that he had just over two months to live.

At that time, Fort Trumbull was commanded by Colonel Francis S. Belton, and in his absence by Captain George Taylor, a veteran of the Seminole War, and former assistant professor of mathematics at West Point, who had won his major's brevet during the Mexican War. On September 27 Major Taylor went on leave, and the newly promoted First Lieutenant Smith found himself in charge of the post. It was Smith who, the very next day, received General Orders No. 2 from army headquarters in

---

3. The orders were published in various newspapers, including the *North American and United States Gazette*, Philadelphia, Sept. 30, 1853.
4. This is not to say there was no fighting in California during the Mexican War; there was, but it was all over by the time Sherman got there.
5. Army post returns.

New York. Company A was to head down to New York Harbor as soon as possible. They were going to California.[6]

Just two weeks before Richard Smith's promotion, another vacancy had unexpectedly occurred in the list of first lieutenants. A man named Brown had died on August 22, 1853, and nine days later Second Lieutenant William Andrew Winder was officially bumped up to fill his place. On that same day, therefore, an opening was created for a new second lieutenant, and next in line was James Van Voast, a native of Schenectady, now aged 26, who stepped into Winder's old place on the Army List. What had hitherto been merely a brevet for Van Voast now became a substantive rank. Three weeks later, on September 23, Second Lieutenant James Van Voast transferred from Company G of the Third Artillery to Company D of the same regiment, and arrived at his new company's permanent post, Fort Independence, which was situated in Boston Harbor and commanded by another veteran of the Mexican War, Major Francis Octavius Wyse. F.O. Wyse, then 42, was a graduate of West Point in the same Class of 1837 that produced not only such future illuminati as Jubal Early, Braxton Bragg, and Fighting Joe Hooker, but also—and more relevant to the story of the *San Francisco*—George Taylor. The post surgeon at Fort Independence, Horace Raguet Wirtz of the Medical Department, would be described by the *New York Times* of January 16, 1854, as "a young man of energy and vivacity," and the young Philadelphian was certainly that, having fought in Mexico with General Sterling Price. Major Wyse received General Orders No. 2 on September 28, 1853, instructing him to take his company down to New York Harbor.[7] Three days later Dr. Wirtz celebrated his thirtieth birthday.

Fort Preble was situated in Portland Harbor, in Maine, and was the home station of Company G of the Third Artillery. By August 1853 Major Charles Spencer Merchant was in command there. A veteran of several wars—with Britain in 1812–15, with Mexico in 1846–48, and with various Indian tribes—Major Merchant was now 58, and still bore the scars of a severe wound in a skirmish with the Comanche. The other two officers at Preble were Captain Charles L. Kilburn and Second Lieutenant William Andrew Winder. Bill Winder got his promotion to first lieutenant on the last day of August, and his week's leave started the following day. Major Merchant left with him, and Captain Kilburn assumed temporary command of the post. Winder was back at his post on the eighth of September, but Major Merchant's leave was extended to the twenty-eighth. On September 15 Kilburn relinquished command of the company to Lieutenant Winder, and left the post on the twentieth, whereupon Winder took command of the whole place. In times of both peace and war, an officer's load is much lightened by the help of a good sergeant, one he can trust. For Bill Winder, Elijah R. Brown was such a man, and, inasmuch as an enlisted man could be, a friend. Only four and a half years before, Brown had been a clerk in a retail grocery store in his home village of West Troy, New York, but now, at 31, he was the valued first sergeant

---

6. Army post returns.
7. Army post returns.

of Company G. On September 28 Major Merchant returned to Fort Preble to find that General Orders No. 2 had arrived that day from army headquarters in New York.[8]

William A. Winder had a second cousin once removed, Second Lieutenant Charles Sidney Winder, six years younger than Bill but on a faster track, although no one knew it yet as Charlie had only been promoted to his current rank two years earlier. As things would turn out, Bill's track may have been slower than Charlie's, but it would be longer, a lot longer. By July 28, 1853, the brave and amiable Charlie Winder of Company H, always cheerful and very popular with his men, had been pasturing for some time as post adjutant at Fort Adams, Rhode Island, where his company and Companies B and L were stationed, each, of course, under the command of an officer, but all under the umbrella command of William Gates, the colonel of the Third Regiment of Artillery, whose base this was. On that day in late July, however, Captain and Brevet Lieutenant Colonel Edward J. Steptoe relinquished command of Company H to Charlie Winder.[9]

Life at Fort Adams might have been somewhat bucolic, but there were moments of excitement, some quite embarrassing to the army. In November 1852, for example, three young privates from Charlie Winder's company went into the nearby town of Newport on a spree and were arrested for riotous behavior and beating up a city policeman. Edward Eylsom, from Taunton, Massachusetts, was 22, and had been a boatman when Lieutenant Sewall Fremont enlisted him at Providence, Rhode Island only a few months before. Now he and his two pals, Lorenzo A. Phelps and Bernard Gannon, were behind bars. Their trial came up in early March of '53, and they were sentenced to six months in the county jail. By June the army was desperately trying to get them out, for it looked as if there might pretty soon be a massive troop movement to the West Coast.

For his bravery at Buena Vista, Major John MacRae Washington, a Virginian and a graduate of West Point in 1817, was awarded a brevet lieutenant colonelcy, and immediately after the Mexican War was made military governor of New Mexico, which, at that time included most of the land that today comprises the states of New Mexico and Arizona plus parts of Kansas, Oklahoma, Texas, Colorado, and Utah. On July 26, 1853, orders were issued to the effect that Colonel Gates was to relinquish command of Fort Adams to Colonel Washington. However, Colonel Washington, by now 56, was on leave until October 21, so Captain Henry Judd, of Company L stepped up to take over when Gates left the post on the first of August. Judd was in command less than two months when, on September 27, he left the post to go up on detached service to Fort Sullivan, in Eastport, Maine, and First Lieutenant Sewall Lawrence Fremont, also of Company L, and the regimental quartermaster, as well as being a distinguished veteran of the Mexican War, took command of Fort Adams, ably assisted by Charlie Winder and the fort's surgeon, Richard Sherwood Satterlee,

---

8. Army post returns. It was noted by the commanding officer in that month's post return for Fort Preble that 33 recruits were required to bring the fort up to strength.
9. Army post returns.

another old hand from Mexico, and who held the rank of major. It was Lieutenant Fremont who received General Orders No 2 on September 28, 1853.[10]

Company I of the Third Artillery were stationed at Fort Sullivan, in Eastport, Maine, out of the six companies the farthest away from New York City. Captain and Brevet Lieutenant Colonel Martin Burke commanded company and post. A Marylander by birth, Colonel Burke had been in the army since 1820, and in the Third since 1823. Now, still suffering from a disease he had contracted during the Mexican War, he was supported at Fort Sullivan by First Lieutenant and Brevet Captain Horace B. Field—who had been transferred from Company K on August 10—and the spruce young brevet second lieutenant, John G. Chandler, as well as three sergeants, three corporals, a musician and 26 privates.[11]

A couple who happened to find themselves guests at Fort Sullivan for a month were Sergeant Horace Fox and a man named George Washington May, both of whom belonged to Company K and were now working as recruiters under Captain Dawson in the actual town of Eastport. Dawson had been temporarily called away from his recruiting duties and so left his two men at the fort until he could come back to collect them on September 11.[12] Mr. May had been enlisted on May 10 of that year, in New York, by Captain Dawson himself. He was the perfect recruiter's recruit: 6 foot 1 tall, a clerk, 31 years old, and an Englishman to boot, from Croydon, Surrey. Better yet, May was the son of a well-known Dutch Reformed minister now working in New York, and brother of a famous artist in Paris and of an accomplished poetess in Philadelphia. Well, perhaps even better than that was the fact that this was not Mr. May's first enlistment. Back in '44, Lieutenant Sherman had recruited him in Boston, and during the Mexican War, Private May had performed spectacularly enough at Palo Alto, Resaca de la Palma, Monterrey, Veracruz and Cerro Gordo to get a field commission in the Ninth Infantry. He had left the army in 1849, but by 1853 he was back. From now on, no matter what rank he held at any given time—usually private, but occasionally temporary sergeant—everyone called him "Lieutenant May." He should have stayed out of the army after Mexico. If he had, he wouldn't have been on board the *San Francisco* on December 22, 1853, when the Third Artillery nosed out into the Atlantic for its rendezvous with the Devil.

On September 29, 1853, Colonel Burke received special War Department orders telling him that Captain Judd, of Company H, was on his way up from Fort Adams, and on the thirtieth he received General Orders No. 2, informing him that he and Company I were to make their way without delay to New York Harbor, where they would be taking a ship that would carry them to California.[13]

---

10. Army post returns. On September 30, 1853, First Lieutenant and Brevet Captain Hamilton L. Shields joined the post at Fort Adams. Although Shields would not be on the *San Francisco*, he would play a significant part in the court of inquiry held in New York in the wake of the tragedy.
11. John Gorham Chandler, from Lexington, Mass., was 22, had graduated from West Point that year, and only since July 1 had been a brevet second lieutenant. According to the Army post returns, there was one desertion from Fort Sullivan that September, and 16 recruits were required to bring the company up to scratch.
12. Army post returns.
13. Army post returns.

First Lieutenant Ambrose Everett Burnside was in command of Company K, at Fort Constitution, on New Castle Island, in Portsmouth Harbor, New Hampshire, but he went on six-months leave beginning in June 1853, and while away, in October, he resigned from the army. So, by September 1853, the man actually in command of the post at Portsmouth was Brevet Major William Austine, supported by First Lieutenant Lucien Loeser, the man who had brought back the nugget from Sutter's Mill. General Orders No. 2 reached Fort Constitution on September 29, 1853. As for Lieutenant Burnside, he would be back years later to leave a great mark in the history books.[14]

The six companies moved fast from their posts, and within a few weeks were duly assembled at their new home in New York Harbor.[15] All they were waiting for now was the ship that was going to carry them all to the land of gold.

—⚙—

Fort Columbus, as the home of a permanent force of the U.S. Army, housed, as a general rule, between 150 and 200 men, most of them spending their five-year term in what was called general service, in other words, not attached to any regiment. However, sometimes the number of men at the fort was increased to as many as 500 through the intake of recruits or West Point graduates who would usually spend some time on Governors Island before joining their respective regiments. The permanent force was under the command of Captain and Brevet Major John T. Sprague, Company E, Eighth Infantry, while Colonel Abercrombie had authority over the recruiting side of things.[16] One of the young officers under Major Sprague was Brevet Second Lieutenant John Bell Hood, then 22, fresh out of West Point, and soon to go to California with Company B of the 4th Infantry. Indeed, he was scheduled to go out on the *San Francisco*, but, at the last moment, was ordered to stay behind. He would eventually end up going via the Panama Isthmus and thus avoid the disaster that was soon to take place in the Atlantic. General Hood would become famous some years later during the Civil War.

There were 170 guns mounted on Governors Island: 18-, 24-, 32- and 42-pounders. Attached to the fort was an arsenal of ordnance to which stores of every description would be sent from the different manufactories, and thence shipped to every part of the United States. A fundamental element of station life was the school for the sons

---

14. Army post returns.
15. The Army post returns confirm various histories of the Third Artillery in regard to the whereabouts of the other companies at the time, and to the re-formation of Companies B and L around this time. Company C, under the command of Colonel Braxton Bragg, and Company E, under Major Tim Sherman, both companies by now having been equipped as light artillery, were stationed at Fort Gibson, in the Cherokee Nation, and at Fort Snelling, Iowa, respectively, while Companies F and M had been in California since 1848. As for Companies B and L, they had been in Texas since April 1853, and now General Scott ordered that the privates in these two companies should be transferred to the First Artillery, and that the raw recruits who were at that moment being trained at Fort Columbus with a view to putting them into the First Artillery should now, along with recruits of the general service, be sent to California on the *San Francisco*, to reorganize there the two companies B and L of the Third Artillery.
16. *New York Times*, Dec. 5, 1853.

of soldiers, which provided an excellent education in the English courses and in the fife and drum. By October 1853 there were 90 boys all under 15 years of age. The command also had a select library of 700 volumes at their disposal. An Episcopal church was attached to the station, and was under the pastoral care of the Rev. Dr. John McVickar, of the U.S. Army, who was also the schoolmaster; he had been at the post for just over three years. In connection with the church was a Sunday school, which was largely attended.[17]

It was here, at Fort Columbus, that the officers and men of the Third Artillery rendezvoused in October 1853. On their first Sunday morning, mustered in their best regimentals, the entire command, numbering well over 400 men, were marched to the church. Upon reaching the entrance to the place of worship they were informed that those having scruples of conscience against taking part in the services may retire, and would be marched, without prejudice, to their quarters, where the rules and articles of war would be read to them. Some took advantage of this option. The rest entered the church—all 15 of them.[18]

---

17. *New York Times*, Dec. 5, 1853.
18. *Weekly National Intelligencer*, Oct. 29, 1853.

Picking the Right Ship

Behind the scenes, things were happening with the thoroughness and speed for which the army was justly well-known. Four days after the issuing of General Orders No. 2, Thomas S. Jesup, the army's quartermaster general in Washington, wrote to Thomas Swords, the quartermaster of New York—the same Swords who had been quartermaster of the Army of the West during the Mexican War, and who was now a lieutenant colonel—instructing him to provide transportation for the companies of Artillery recently ordered to the Pacific via Cape Horn. "You will consult with Major General Scott, or such officer as he may designate, as to the amount of transportation necessary to be provided." Colonel Swords received this letter the same day it was sent—October 1.[1]

Also that day, Lieutenant Colonel Lorenzo Thomas, assistant adjutant general, acting on behalf of General Scott, wrote from U.S. Army headquarters in New York to Colonel Gates, regimental commander of the Third Artillery.[2] Although Gates couldn't possibly have known it at the time—indeed, no one else could have known it either—this letter would start a ball rolling that would roll right over him.

William Gates was originally from Gloucester, Massachusetts, the son of a Revolutionary War veteran. He had been one of the very first batch of graduates from West Point, in 1806, and had fought in the War of 1812 and various Indian wars. A notable blip in his career, and one that would come back to haunt him years later, occurred in 1836, when he was court-martialed for cowardice. Notwithstanding this momentary setback, in 1845 he assumed command of the Third Artillery and took the regiment to the Mexican War. Now, come late 1853, he was 65, and for seven years had been married to Harriet Louise Carter, who was only 32. Dr. Buel, who would be the surgeon on the *San Francisco*, describes Louise as a "Newport belle."[3] Colonel Gates had already been in the army for 20 years before his second wife was born, and therein lay at least part of the problem that would, before long, manifest itself—an old man under the thumb of a young wife. This weakness on the part of the reg-

---

1. Report of the Secretary of War, Jan. 30, 1854.
2. Report of the Secretary of War, Jan. 30, 1854.
3. Buel, 1872. William Peter Buel was a civilian, originally from Sheffield, Massachusetts. Son of a physician, he had graduated from Yale in 1826, practiced in New York City for twenty years, and then, his health failing, had moved to California, where he joined the Pacific Mail Steamship Company as a ship's surgeon.

imental commander would help to ruin his career and his life, and to kill hundreds of his men, including his own son.

Colonel Gates was, of course, to have the run of Governors Island for as long as he was there, and he would arrange for the accommodation of the officers and men under his command while they waited to embark on the vessel that would take them to California. As for the recruiting side of Fort Columbus, a lot of men were being enlisted for the Third Artillery at this time, in recruiting stations all over the country, primarily Harrisburg, Pennsylvania, and Boston, Massachusetts. Of the 84 recruits who were finally put into Company B, 39 had joined up at Harrisburg, while of the 51 who went into Company L, 32 were enlisted at Boston. The army would be bringing them all to Governors Island, where Colonel Abercrombie would be supervising their basic training, under the direction of the adjutant general, and so it was impressed upon Gates to disturb Abercrombie and his staff as little as possible. Sooner or later, however, as a matter of course, Abercrombie would turn the recruits over to Gates, who would then assign them to companies. All men presently under the command of Colonel Gates who had nine months or less to serve, would be left behind and transferred to the Fourth Artillery, unless they wanted to re-enlist, in which case they would be discharged right there at Governors Island and, just before sailing, be re-enlisted for another five years. The officers going around the Horn would be allowed six months pay in advance. If the winds were favorable, Gates was instructed to touch in at San Diego, where he would find orders from the general commanding the Pacific Division, for the disposition of the Third Artillery, and this would govern Gates's further movements. If San Diego were to prove out of the question, then Gates was to proceed up to San Francisco, where he was to report to the general.[4]

Colonel Gates was in New York City on October 1 when he drew up the obligatory formal written requisition to Colonel Swords for a vessel to be chartered to take his regiment to the West Coast. He would require not only a ship, but provisions for nine months at least. Although this was a voyage that usually took four months or so, that was only an average, and so it was better to be safe than sorry with the provisions, as anything might happen during the upcoming trip. So Gates ordered nine months of subsistence—three months flour and six months hard bread—and should the capacity of the vessel admit, he would estimate for and take 12 months subsistence of all articles except breadstuffs. He would see that the necessary fixtures for cooking, and particularly for baking bread, were provided for all the command. As for protection, each company was going to take with them 2,000 rounds of ball cartridge.[5]

In his letter to Swords, Colonel Gates estimated that there would be 25 officers and 450 men going along, plus women belonging to the six companies. Gates had no idea how long it would be before he might sail, but he was going to try to have everything ready so that they could leave New York Harbor on the fifteenth of that

---

4. Orders to Gates.
5. Report of the Secretary of War, Jan. 30, 1854.

very month, October. That gave everyone just two weeks. As for the voyage itself, Colonel Gates stressed to Colonel Swords the need for a clipper ship, as a clipper would be much faster than the packet ships then generally in use for transporting this number of persons.[6]

On receipt of the letters from Quartermaster General Jesup and Colonel Gates, Colonel Swords went to visit General Scott's office personally, to take orders from the Great Man. Scott told him that it was immaterial what kind of vessel the troops went in—steamer, clipper, or full ship, it didn't matter. What was important was that the men had plenty of room and were able to make the voyage comfortably.[7] General Scott put back the time of sailing from the fifteenth to the twentieth of October.

On October 3, Swords advertised that proposals would be received at the quartermaster's office in New York "until Friday, the 7th inst., at 12 o'clock, noon, for the transportation hence to San Francisco via Cape Horn, of about 30 officers and 475 men and laundresses, by steamer, clipper, or full vessel."[8]

Never let it be said that the War Department didn't look after its boys. Married officers and enlisted men were allowed to take their wives and children if they chose. As for those who were unmarried, both officers and men, army tradition allowed for each company to take four camp women or "laundresses," who belonged to the regiment.[9]

"The men are to be provided with berths, water, and means of cooking," continued the advertisement, "with ample room in the hold for their stores and luggage, and about 1,500 barrels of extra provisions. The officers to be furnished with cabin fare and accommodations. The vessel or vessels to sail on or about the 20th inst. Proposals will also be received, as above, for the transportation from New York Harbor to Benicia, of about 10 tons, and 1300 lbs. bulk of ordnance stores, now ready."[10]

Now the army needed a competent general to oversee the embarkation at New York Harbor of literally hundreds of artillery men, as well as women and children and miscellaneous persons. On the same day that Colonel Swords placed his advertisement, October 3, Colonel Lorenzo Thomas wrote to Brigadier General John Ellis Wool, then commanding Eastern Division, in Troy, New York, bringing him up to date on what was happening with the troop movement to California. "I am instructed by the General in Chief [i.e., General Scott] to request that you will please accept the command, and superintend their embarkation, which is to take place on the 20th inst." He sent a copy of this letter to Colonel Swords.[11]

Swords got several responses to his advertisement, and on October 7 he and Colonel Gates opened the replies, from this batch bringing the choice down to the four vessels that had the carrying capacity for the job: The brand new Pacific Mail

---

6. Report of the Secretary of War, Jan. 30, 1854.
7. Report of the Secretary of War, Jan. 30, 1854.
8. Report of the Secretary of War, Jan. 30, 1854.
9. Buel, 1854; Fremont.
10. Report of the Secretary of War, Jan. 30, 1854.
11. Report of the Secretary of War, Jan. 30, 1854.

Steamship Company steamer *San Francisco*, and the three clippers, *Westward Ho*, *Eagle*, and *Lightfoot*. The steamer, which had been constructed with a view to her occasional employment in the transportation of troops, was not yet ready for sea; certainly there was no way she was going to make General Scott's October twentieth embarkation deadline. If October 20 were truly to be the departure date, then that left the three clipper ships. The 1,650-ton *Westward Ho*, built by the great Bostonian shipbuilder, Donald McKay only the year before, was what they called an extreme clipper, one sacrificing cargo capacity for speed, and she had already made the trip from New York to San Francisco in 105 days; the *Eagle*, under the command of Captain Farren, had made the same run in 111 days only that April; and finally there was the 1,996-ton clipper *Lightfoot*, which had just been built by Jackson & Ewell for Howes & Co., of Boston, for $140,000.[12]

Swords met General Wool in New York City on October 10, and submitted to him all the proposals he had received from the advertisement, bringing to the old general's attention particularly the four vessels that Swords and Colonel Gates had selected as the most promising. It was not long before the choice came down to two: The steamer *San Francisco* and the clipper *Lightfoot*.

General Wool favored the *San Francisco*, but wouldn't commit, partly because that vessel wouldn't be ready in any time even close to October 20. Wool advised Swords to ask General Scott's advice on this issue. Scott couldn't make his mind up either, and referred Swords to Quartermaster General Jesup, a suggestion Swords followed up on by telegraphic dispatch that same day, October 10. Meanwhile six companies of artillery were converging upon New York Harbor for what they all thought would be a stay of only a few days. Partly to keep alive the possibility of the *San Francisco*, there was a new departure date being proposed now, November 15.[13]

On the morning of October 11, Jesup, then in Washington, answered Swords's dispatch with one of his own. "Is there any certainty that the steamer will be ready by the fifteenth of next month? and if so, can we get the whole vessel? Without a positive order from the General in Chief or the Secretary of War, I will never again allow citizen passengers to go in the same ship with troops. Report in detail in regard to Mr. Aspinwall's offer. Will his steamer be able to take the supplies—say for nine or twelve months—for the command, and does he offer the whole ship for $75,000?"[14]

Quartermaster Jesup had reservations about the *Lightfoot*, indeed about clipper ships in general, at least for this sort of expedition. "I am under some apprehension that troops would be subjected to great inconvenience, if put on board of a clipper ship. They would be either smothered by the closeness of the vessel, if it be close as

---

12. *New York Times*, Jan. 14, 1854.
13. *New York Herald*, Oct 18, 1853: An ad says: "For San Francisco. The new double-engine steamship, *San Francisco*, will be dispatched for the above port via Rio de Janeiro and Valparaiso, on Tuesday, November 15, by the Pacific Mail Steamship Company, 54 and 55 South street." This ad would run in the *Herald* until Nov. 14, by which time it was clear that the *San Francisco* was not going to make that sailing date.
14. Report of the Secretary of War, Jan. 30, 1854.

I understand those vessels necessarily are, or be constantly wet, if it not be kept with closed hatches." He instructed Swords to inquire into this matter "particularly and minutely." Jesup was under the impression that the insurance offices demanded higher insurance on the cargoes of clipper ships to the Pacific than on those of ordinary ships because they were so much more liable to damage, in consequence of the closeness of the vessel. He wanted Swords to investigate this matter as well. "Time is an important matter in all military movements," he said, "but the health and comfort of the troops are more so." He asked if only one ship—as opposed to clippers—had been offered, having supposed that public notice would have produced a wide competition and that the army would have had many vessels to select from. He wanted to know the time estimated for the voyage to San Francisco by the steamer, by the clipper, and by the best packets, and what the cost would be. "Report fully and speedily."

Swords received Jesup's letter the following day, October 12, and immediately set out to report fully and speedily to his superior. The first thing he did was write a letter to W.H. Aspinwall, President of the Pacific Mail Steamship Company, and owner of the steamer *San Francisco*. The letter was brief and to the point—five points actually:

> 1. "Can you give a positive assurance that the steamer *San Francisco* will be ready to take the troops on board and commence the voyage by the 15th of next month?" The next month being November, of course.
> 2. "What part of the vessel will be appropriated for the accommodation of the troops, and what space to the baggage and stores—including fifty wagons?"
> 3. "Will the vessel take any citizen passengers or private freight?"
> 4. "At what points will the steamer touch for coaling, etc.?"
> 5. "What is the probable time it will take to reach San Francisco?"[15]

Colonel Swords also set out to draw up a report on the *Lightfoot*. He went to the marine insurance offices, and found that, despite the impression Quartermaster Jesup was under, the insurance for a clipper was the same as that for a full ship. He also discovered that a clipper was not considered to be a better vessel than an ordinary sailing ship. And finally, he learned that the average time from New York to San Francisco by clipper, around the Horn, was between 106 and 112 days, whereas by full ship the average was 130 days. In fact, just at the time Swords was investigating speeds, the clipper *Mischief*, which had left New York on May 20, was making its way up the Pacific coast and would arrive in San Francisco on November 9, after 133 sailing days. News of that statistic would not reach the War Department in time to influence their decision, but if it had, the primary issue of speed, when considering a clipper over a steamer, would have been rendered largely irrelevant.[16]

Aspinwall received Swords's letter that same day, and replied immediately, answering the five questions point by point. He had been assured by the machinists

---

15. *New York Times*, Feb. 8, 1854.
16. *New York Times*, Feb. 8, 1854.

that the engines would be ready for a trial by steam by November 1, which would allow ample time to meet the army's new November fifteenth deadline. However, Aspinwall did not write "15th November"; he wrote "15th December." This was an error, yes; he should have written "November," but he had been hearing things, something to do with the engines, and he was already beginning to suspect that there was no way he could meet the army's deadline of November 15. In the privacy of his mind—and he was keeping this very quiet—he felt that the departure date would be more like December 15 than November 15, and this slipped out in the letter. If anyone noticed the mistake, they don't seem to have mentioned it. Mr. Aspinwall wrote that the entire steamer would be at the disposition of the government, excepting only a few berths for personal friends of the steamer's skipper, Commodore James T. Watkins. These friends would be lodged in parts of the second cabin that were not occupied by the officers and their families. However, Aspinwall bent over backwards so far as to say that if the officers commanding the troops objected to this arrangement, then Commodore Watkins's friends simply would not be on board when the time came. The saloons and their state rooms were to be allotted exclusively to the officers and their families, and Aspinwall assured his potential client that no citizen passengers or private freight would be taken. The steamer would call in for coal at Rio, Valparaiso, and Acapulco.[17]

Apropos of these foreign ports of call, the War Department had given orders that the soldiers were not to be exposed to civilian life there, for fear that they might get into trouble or contract some disease; meaning, of course, of the venereal variety.

Mr. Aspinwall then addressed Colonel Swords's fifth and final point: "Taking the voyage of the [John L. Stevens] as a standard for estimating the probable time between New York and San Francisco, and without allowance for the superior qualities and better promise of the *San Francisco*, I presume 80 (eighty) days is the period in which we expect to accomplish the voyage." Given the speed records set by clippers up to that time, this was an amazingly optimistic presumption on the part of Mr. Aspinwall. Besides, the *San Francisco*'s cylinders were of small size—65 inches in diameter with an eight-foot stroke—only three-fifths the capacity of, say, Collins steamers. And when one considers that the tonnage of an average Collins steamer was only 25 percent greater than that of the *San Francisco*, Aspinwall couldn't have expected a great rate of speed for his new steamer, even at her load line, much less at the heavy draft at which she was doomed to leave port.[18]

The last thing Swords mentioned in his speedy reply to the quartermaster was that the *Stevens*, "which they say is smaller than the *San Francisco*, measures 3931 superficial feet on her upper deck, 4713 superficial feet on her main deck, 5201 superficial feet on her lower deck, and is entitled by law to carry 1316 passengers, and has ports on each deck." Swords was not particularly pushing the *Stevens* on Jesup, and

---

17. *New York Times*, Feb. 8, 1854; Fremont.
18. Franklin Institute; Partridge; *New York Times*, July 5, 1853; *New York Tribune*, Jan. 23, 1854.

certainly that steamer had not been one of the vessels mentioned in any of the replies he had received from his advertisement. It was just a "for your information" item for Jesup.

Jesup, of course, would have liked more options to choose from, and keenly aware that time was of the essence, he weighed that up against the safety and comfort of the men and chose the *San Francisco*.

The U.S.S. *San Francisco*

The 2,272-ton *San Francisco*, was a steamship of superlatives. It was easy to brag about her, and so they did. "One of the most magnificent ocean steamers afloat." This "new and splendid vessel," 281 feet 5 inches long, with a deck length of 276 feet and concave lines at each end, had been three years in the building at Webb's shipyard at the foot of Sixth Street in lower Manhattan, and only this past June 17 had been launched from that very yard into New York Harbor, waters that led directly down the bay and from there into the Atlantic Ocean, graveyard for many a ship just in case anyone present on this happy occasion happened to reflect upon that gloomy subject. The maximum amount of human thought possible had gone, and was still going, into the *San Francisco*. As $350,000 worth of massive ocean-going supremacy slid into the sea, the mere cost of the enterprise would have dispelled any negative thoughts, except perhaps those of the company that had insured this leviathan for six-sevenths of its value.[1] Mr. Webb himself, William Henry Webb, New York's most celebrated builder of such vessels, was two days short of his 37th birthday as he watched with considerable pride the birth of his new Titan infant. Unfortunately, no matter how much brain work went into this monarch of the waves, it would not be enough.

Modern-day readers picturing an elegant steamship the length of a football field might see in their mind the *Queen Mary*, but, strictly speaking, the *San Francisco* was a foretopsail schooner with two masts carrying foresail, topsail and jibs to propel it through the water, in much the same way as vessels had always harnessed the power of the winds. Columbus had crossed the Atlantic using sails. But sails have their limitations. If the wind stops, so does the ship, unless you care to get out the oars. In fact, it was that very idea—oars—that changed everything. In the early 1800s the steamer was invented, with a steam engine supplying power to paddle wheels, also known as side-wheels, water wheels, or side-paddles. Situated at both sides of the ship, each wheel turned constantly, acting like 14 enormous canoe paddles. But whereas canoe paddles depend on the strength and endurance of the human arm, these steamer paddles were untiring, and very, very fast. Now ocean-going vessels

---

1. *Boston Daily Atlas*, June 3, 1853; Partridge; *New York Herald*, July 5, 1853; *New York Tribune*, Jan. 16, 1854. The *Herald* says the *San Francisco* had a 41-foot breadth of beam, and was 24½ feet deep, although Partridge says she had 23 feet 6 inches depth of hold and 39 feet 10 inches molded breadth.

had not only sail power but steam power as well, and need never stop, unless, of course, the engine broke. If that were to happen then the vessel would simply lie in the water, essentially immobile, until the wind picked up and filled the sails, which it inevitably did, sooner or later. But if, heaven forefend, the ship were to run into an extremely violent Atlantic hurricane which both tore all the sails away and wrecked the engine, then you were just about as unlucky as a sea-going passenger could be. You would be floating in the middle of the ocean with no power to go anywhere except where the wind and waves took you, and hoping to hell that the ship's hull would hold up under the pressure. If your hull wasn't up to riding out a hurricane, then you would sink.[2]

The *San Francisco*'s hull, made of the best Maryland oak, was remarkable for its immense strength, and was up to any challenge. Its bottom, filled with massive keelsons running the length of the vessel, was solid timber out to the turn of the bilges, and had been caulked before planking. They made a big deal of that, boasting that it would guarantee the steamer's safety.[3] And, as it turned out, they were right; it did. Unfortunately, there would be no such guarantee for the safety of the passengers.

Although comparatively speaking the hull of the *San Francisco* was not heavily timbered, as an additional security for the frame it was strengthened by double diagonal iron braces running from the floor heads to the upper or spar deck, all bolted to the frame and riveted together at each intersection, and still further secured by a large horizontal belt of iron plate which ran fore and aft the whole length of the ship under the waterways and over the upper ends of the diagonal braces. Furthermore, the fact that the ship's engine and boiler space was narrow—104 feet by 15 feet, including passages—allowed for the introduction of another method of strengthening the vessel, one that had never before been adopted. Two cross-planked bulkheads, 15 feet apart, extended the whole length of the ship, fore and aft, from the timbers at the bottom of the hull up to the spar deck, one on each side of the engine and its two round shelled, drop-flued boilers, secured to the bottom and the middle deck beams, and diagonally braced with iron the whole length, which rendered it impossible for anything much less than a complete wreck to throw a timber out of its socket. By virtually enclosing the engine and boilers, this arrangement therefore had the added benefit of greatly protecting the steamer's vital machinery. What all this meant was that the *San Francisco*—the basic ship—was able to withstand an uppercut from Neptune himself. She was classed as A-1 at Lloyds.[4]

The *New York Herald* of July 5, 1853, was able to report that the *San Francisco*'s

---

2. Partridge; Franklin Institute; Partridge; *New York Herald*, July 5, 1853.
3. Partridge; Franklin Institute; *New York Herald*, July 5, 1853.
4. Partridge; Franklin Institute; *New York Herald*, July 5, 1853; *New York Tribune*, Jan. 23, 1854. Each boiler was 13 feet 8 inches in diameter by 34 feet long, and had its own separate funnel, while the engine frames were made principally of boiler plate. The ship's fire-rooms, placed fore and aft, were air-tight, the air for combustion being forced in by fan-blowers, driven by separate engines. The danger from fire was well provided against by having two independent fire pumps with separate boilers attached, seven tier keelsons and three engine keelsons.

machinery was now being completed at the Morgan Works.⁵ It really meant something in those days for a ship to have its engine and boilers constructed by the Morgan Iron Works, especially if the designer was Morgan's own famed engineer Miers Coryell. But there was a problem with Mr. Coryell. Genius as he may have been, he was only 27. It was his engine and his boilers that went into the *San Francisco*. It was his engine that would fail even before the steamer sailed; four unsatisfactory trial runs in the placid waters of New York Harbor where even a row boat would perform well. It was his engine that would, when the awful moment of truth arrived out there in the Atlantic, give out the very first moment it was put to a true test. And, by the engine giving out, the *San Francisco*, and scores of human beings, were doomed. To condemn a man for his youth is, of course, unfair, and no one ever condemned young Mr. Coryell; nobody ever even wondered if the engine might have been better if the designer had had more experience.

The *San Francisco*'s paddle-wheels, driven by the ship's steam engine, were of somewhat unusual construction, although not by any means untried. Variously known as Morgan's Feathering Paddle-Wheels, Morgan's Eccentric, and the "feathering float," they were constructed upon a scientific principle lately discovered in England, and similar wheels were running on the West India Mail steamers from Great Britain. Twenty-eight feet in diameter, with a face of eight feet, and a dip of five feet, they were fitted with feathering buckets. The object was to maintain the faces of the paddles in a nearly vertical position, and thus avoid the plunging and lifting of the water attending the ordinary construction when subjected to any considerable amount of dip. The *San Francisco* was the first instance of their employment on any extensive scale in the U.S.A., and, despite rumors that their complex mechanism would make them liable to derangement, the wheels in this instance would fail in no particular when the true test came out in the Atlantic, and were ascertained by the chief engineer, Mr. Marshall, only a few hours before the abandonment of the vessel, to be in every respect as perfect as when they left the hands of their constructors.⁶

And so they bragged about the science that had gone into this beautiful new ocean-going wonder, this monster that could lawfully take 1,600 crew and passengers. Hinges and oscillators everywhere, wheels and paddles. To top it all off, the ship's wheelhouse sported a gilt phoenix. Despite all that, although embodying several peculiarities, the *San Francisco* was not in a much greater degree than many other steamers an experimental ship.⁷ What made it different was not its past, nor its present, but its future.

---

5. *New York Herald*, July 5, 1853; *San Francisco Daily Alta*, July 17, 1853. It was actually Messrs. Quintard, Merritt & Co., a division of the Morgan Iron Works, who constructed the engines for the *San Francisco*. In 1844, at the age of 22, George William Quintard had married Charles Morgan's daughter, and in 1850 became one of the proprietors of the Morgan Iron Works.

6. Tredgold; Partridge; *New York Herald*, July 5, 1853; *New York Tribune*, Jan. 23, 1854. Morgan, the inventor, was an Englishman, and not connected in any way with Charles Morgan, an American, who made ships' engines, the same Morgan who had once been a partner of Commodore Vanderbilt in the Nicaragua route to California.

7. Southworth; Partridge; Buel, 1872; *New York Tribune*, Jan. 23, 1854.

Will She Ever Sail?

Now, in October, with the correspondence flying between Colonel Gates and the two army quartermasters, Mr. Webb was putting the finishing touches to his latest masterpiece. As a further feather in his cap, and therefore something to enhance his reputation with the U.S. War Department, the great ship builder was, at the very moment, wrapping up a deal with the Tsar to build a battleship for the Russian Navy.

And there could be no better skipper than Commodore Watkins who, on November 20, would be celebrating his forty-fifth birthday, hopefully at sea.

They were already touting this new seagoing marvel as the "Queen of the Pacific," because that ocean is the one she would be plying as a career once this maiden voyage was over. But in order to get from New York to her work station in the Pacific, she would have to go around Cape Horn, and that meant first venturing out of New York Harbor into another ocean. If you think the Pacific can be a rough place, wait until you get into the Atlantic.

On October 13, Quartermaster General Jesup instructed Colonel Swords to accept Aspinwall's offer of the *San Francisco*, if General Scott or General Wool approved. Wool did approve, and so, on behalf of the War Department, Swords chartered the magnificent new vessel on October 15, at a rental of $75,000.

Quartermaster General Jesup had been hearing rumors that the owners of the *San Francisco* were meaning to stow on board three years' supply of stores and subsistence for the captain and crew, in other words for 130 persons. He couldn't believe these rumors, but he could feel his indignation rising nonetheless. "Such an attempt would be a fraud," he said. No vessel going to a port on the Pacific usually took more than 12 months' supply, which is what the troops would be taking. And if that was the amount the troops were taking, then the ship's crew must be limited to the same, no more. Rumor or not, it was the Quartermaster's duty to look into it, see if there was any truth behind it. On November 5, from Washington, D.C., he wrote a letter to Colonel Swords asking him to investigate the matter. In his letter, Jesup stressed that the decks of the *San Francisco* must not be cumbered with freight, but there should be room for the men to exercise. If the wagons couldn't be taken in the hold, then they would have to be shipped out to California in some other vessel. Oh, and one other thing, Colonel Swords, there should not be more coal shipped than the quantity required to reach the first point at which the vessel is to coal, in other words

Rio de Janeiro. Oh, and one other thing; sufficient room should be reserved for the stores of the officers and men. "Look closely to all these matters, and have the provisions of the contract so specific as not to admit of dispute."

Swords didn't get the letter until the morning of November 8, at which point he dashed off a note to Mr. Aspinwall, the ship's owner, who in his speedy reply to Swords that same day, refuted the rumor that Jesup had heard. Swords then wrote back to Jesup that day, enclosing a copy of Aspinwall's reply.

Meanwhile something quite embarrassing had happened at Fort Columbus. It was Horace Field. On October 10, just a few days after Company I had come down from Fort Sullivan, they found Captain Field somewhat under the influence of the poppy. If that wasn't bad enough, he was on duty at the time, as officer of the day. He should have known better, being a married man, a West Point graduate, a veteran of the Indian wars in Florida and a promising young officer who had won his brevet captaincy for gallant and meritorious conduct during the Mexican War, but, at 35, Horace Field was fast approaching that stage of life when dreams become the demons haunting an unfulfilled life. The court-martial held at Governors Island found him guilty as charged, and he was sentenced to be cashiered. However, the case went to the President for consideration, and word came down from Franklin Pierce on November 7 that the disgraced officer was to resume his sword, as if the incident had never happened.[1] But it had happened. If Horace Field had been just that little higher on opium, he could simply have floated off to that green and pleasant land where awful things don't happen. It was his innate temperance that doomed him. Within six weeks Captain Field would be gurgling away his last seconds in the tumultuous waters of the Atlantic Ocean.

The law required that whenever a vessel was chartered by the U.S. Government, it must be inspected by highly qualified personnel from the Navy Department, to make sure it had been built in strict conformity to the necessary legal specifications, and, in the case of vessels such as the *San Francisco*, to ascertain its fitness for government mail service. There was a third reason, common to all vessels chartered by the government, and that was to see that they were suitable for war purposes, if hostilities were to break out during the life of such a charter. So, on November 2, 1853, the Department constituted a board for the purpose of making a careful examination and survey of the *San Francisco*. But, for the government, in this particular case, it was more than just a question of meeting basic lawful standards. They were keenly aware of how much was riding on this project. If something were to go wrong during the voyage, if some part of the machinery were to prove defective, say, and break during a hurricane, then there was a possibility that the steamer might be wrecked, and hundreds of lives might be lost, a good portion of them the Third Artillery. This,

---

1. Washington *Evening Star*, Nov. 23, 1853; *Weekly Herald*, Nov. 26, 1853.

of course, would be a nightmare for all concerned, so it obviously behooved the government to make sure the ship was as safe as it could be. They took their legal, practical and moral responsibilities very seriously, and cheered themselves on for so doing. But the din of self-congratulation was so loud they failed to hear the warning bells.

The steamer now being ready for inspection, the board was ordered to proceed forthwith and then report their findings to the Navy Department. No deadline was imposed upon the board, partly because at that point of time, in early November, two sailing dates had already been put back in consequence of the steamer not being quite ready yet, and now no one could tell exactly what the new departure date was going to be. However, because everyone knew, or at least was hoping, that the big day was reasonably imminent, someone really should have given the inspecting board a deadline. Perhaps they assumed the board would carry out their mission with reasonable speed.

The board consisted of four men. Commodore Lawrence Kearny, of the U.S. Navy, would, at the end of the month, be celebrating his sixty-fourth birthday. The Commodore was a man of whom the gods would say, "Yes, he lived a life." He had taken part in the War of 1812, had fought pirates and slave traders in the West Indies and the Gulf of Mexico, and had completely and spectacularly eliminated the Greek pirate problem in the Mediterranean. Down in Galveston, while skipper of the *Enterprise*, he had forced pirate Jean Lafitte out of his base without a shot being fired. He took on opium smugglers in China and paved the way for that country's trading relationship with the U.S.A. He helped thwart a British takeover of Hawaii, in 1848 became mayor of Perth Amboy, New Jersey, and in 1852 was appointed Superintendent of the Atlantic mail ships.

Commander Charles Henry Bell, also of the U.S. Navy, had just turned 55. Like Kearny, he was a native of New Jersey, had fought in the War of 1812 and in the Mediterranean, and had taken on more than his own share of pirates and slavers around the world. Bell knew what it was like to go down at sea during a violent storm. In 1825 his schooner, the *Ferret*, capsized beneath him off the coast of Cuba, and he was in the water for a whole day. Five men died. So he knew the importance of a sound ship. Bell knew. But, after 30 years, did he remember?

The great wooden gates of Dartmoor Prison swung inwards on their creaky hinges, and a young man emerged into the dense fog of freedom. Like the other boys coming out with him, Will Skiddy had just survived the notorious massacre of April 6, that awful moment when the guards had fired on the American prisoners. Now, shoeless but hopeful, they were made to march the 16 miles to Plymouth, where a ship was waiting to take them home. After three years, the War of 1812 was over. Will Skiddy was still 19, yet he had had more adventure in those few years than most men have in a whole lifetime.[2] Back in the States he became a naval architect and ship

---

2. Another prisoner who made the march from Dartmoor to Plymouth was Thomas Smith. Two of his granddaughters were the sisters Lucia and Sarah Eaton, both of whom were on the *San Francisco* when it wrecked.

builder of great renown and some considerable wealth, and by 1853, as a Navy constructor for U.S. mail steamships, Captain William Taylor Skiddy, now 62, was appointed to the board of inspection for the *San Francisco*.

At age 32, Chief Engineer William Henry Shock was not only by far the youngest member of the board, he was of a different generation entirely from the other three. A Marylander through and through, he had risen through the U.S. Navy engineer grades, had seen much action in Mexico, and by 1853 had been appointed inspecting engineer of all ocean-going steamships carrying the U.S. mails. The *San Francisco* was soon going to be leaving New York carrying the Third Artillery, yes, but once she arrived on the West Coast she would be added to W.H. Aspinwall's Pacific Mail Steamship Company's fleet plying between Panama and San Francisco. So, naturally, Shock was appointed one of her examiners.

These, then, were the four men who formed the board of inspection, and with no firm deadline to press them, they took their time at the job. It wouldn't be until December 19 that Mr. Shock finished his report, and the board would not submit that report until two days later. It wouldn't be for another couple of days that the Navy Department received the report, and by that time it was too late. The *San Francisco* had sailed.

If the well-intentioned events had, indeed, come to pass the way they were meant to, if the whole inspection report business had not been so mismanaged, then one of the great tragedies of the nineteenth century might have been avoided. But that was in the future, a future that held death and untold misery on a large scale. It was a future that shouldn't have happened, wouldn't have happened if the authorities had been on the ball.

On Monday, November 21, 1853, Howland & Aspinwall wrote a letter to U.S. Secretary of State William L. Marcy, requesting a passport for George Woolsey Aspinwall, the tall, slightly graying, and very pleasant owner of the Aspinwall Steam Transportation Line. In another three days, with his colored servant in tow, George would be pulling out of New York Harbor on his brother's brand new steamer, heading for California. Those were the days when a passport could arrive the next day, and on the twenty-second, with two days to spare, Howland & Aspinwall duly received the awaited package from Washington.

George Aspinwall would have applied for the passport himself but he was too sick at home in Philadelphia even to write the letter. It was not just a temporary sickness that George was going through; he was dying. At 39, married with five young children, he knew that the odds were very much against his seeing a fifth decade, so on November 23 he summoned up the energy to revise his will.

But George would not be boarding the *San Francisco* on November 24. No one else would either. That Thursday came and went, and still the troops languished at Fort Columbus, their baggage and camp equipage all ready for shipment to California. However, there was good news. It would only be a few more days now. As the Washington *Evening Star* of Friday, November 25, 1853, put it: "The Third Regiment of Artillery are expected to sail from New York for California tomorrow, in the steamer *San Francisco*, going around the Horn. They should arrive in eighty or ninety days."

In their estimate of the steamer's speed, the *Evening Star* had obviously been infected by Mr. Aspinwall's enthusiasm of six weeks earlier. And, as for the new departure date, that Saturday did indeed see Major General Wool at New York Harbor, in the early stages of supervising the departure of the troops, but in the end it didn't lead to much in the way of the ship sailing.

However, the chain of command on the voyage was now clear. Colonel Gates would be in charge of all the military personnel aboard, as well as the women and children; or perhaps one might be tempted to say the real officer in charge was his wife, Mrs. Colonel Gates. Major Wyse was second in command of the regiment. He was also officer commanding Company D, and in that role was assisted by Second Lieutenant James Van Voast. Charles S. Merchant, being the senior major of the regiment after Wyse, was the third officer in command, but because he was detailed for logistics duty, his company—G—was given to First Lieutenant Bill Winder.[3]

Company A was under the command of 37-year-old Brevet Major George Taylor, whose wife, Emeline Everitt, of Smithville, North Carolina, was also scheduled for the trip.[4] Taylor was to be assisted on the voyage by First Lieutenant Richard H. Smith, who was traveling without benefit of wife and infant daughter.

Bill Winder's cousin, Second Lieutenant Charlie Winder, was running Company H; and Company I was commanded by Colonel Martin Burke, assisted by First Lieutenant and Brevet Captain Horace Field and Second Lieutenant J.G. Chandler.

Company K was normally under the command of Captain and Brevet Major William Austine, but he went on leave and so didn't make the trip. Taking his place was First Lieutenant Lucien Loeser, the acting assistant regimental commissary, and the man who had brought the gold nugget back from Sacramento five years earlier. Loeser was bringing his wife, Sarah, as well as Sarah's sister, Miss Lucia Eaton, and the ladies' maid.

The recruits would be under the command of Captain Henry B. Judd, whose wife was traveling with him. It was Judd who was partly responsible for forming this detachment of green men into Companies B and L once they arrived in California, but suddenly new orders came in that the two companies were to be formed immediately, before and during the voyage. This created a bit of a difficulty. All existing non-commissioned officers belonged to other companies, and there were none spare to oversee the great number of new recruits. Judd solved the problem by taking a few of the more talented or experienced privates out of those other companies, and in some cases from the new batch of recruits, and giving them temporary sergeant or corporal rank.[5]

---

3. Merchant.
4. Emeline, born on June 23, 1823, was first cousin to the wife of Lieutenant Sewall Fremont.
5. Army enlistment records; Army post returns.

One such man was Edward Eylsom of Company H, whom the army had busted out of that Newport jail after the little fracas the year before in which he and his two pals had assaulted a local cop. Now Mr. Eylsom was being given two stripes as he boarded the *San Francisco* for the trip of a lifetime. His partners in crime, Gannon and Phelps, didn't make the voyage, instead being placed on general duty at Fort Columbus.

Lieutenant S.L. Fremont, who had changed his name from Fish in 1843, was to go out with the force as regimental quartermaster, accompanied by his wife, the former Mary Elizabeth Langdon, of Smithville, North Carolina, and their three children. Ellen Mae was the oldest. The plan was for her to celebrate her fifth birthday somewhere off the Pacific Coast of South America in March 1854. Richard Langdon, the Fremonts' only son at that time, would, with a bit of luck, have already arrived in California when he turned four on April 29, while Mary Lawrence, the youngest, had just completed her first full year on this earth on November 13.

First Lieutenant James A. Hardie, of Company H, being regimental adjutant, was scheduled to go on the voyage, but as things turned out he left his position and Fort Adams on December 1 to become aid (as they spelled it then) to General Wool the following week. So, as such, he never made the trip. Fremont wound up doubling as acting adjutant.

Meanwhile, the departure date of November 26 came and went. Men were deserting in droves. Desertion was an everyday fact of life in the army, of course, brought about by boredom, fear, or just the sheer realization that "This ain't for me." The prospect of a four-month voyage in an untried steamer provided a new reason for hightailing it out of the Third Artillery. A number of men got clean away from Fort Columbus, never to be seen again, but those who were apprehended or surrendered themselves were brought back and placed in confinement, some awaiting a general court-martial, others simply being restored to duty without trial.

Much farther south, on November 29, 1853, the brig *Napoleon*, of Portland, Maine, under the command of Captain William Strout, left Matanzas in Cuba bound for Boston. Almost four weeks later, she would have a minor brush with fate.

One day after the *Napoleon* left Cuba, the largest iron ship then afloat eased out of the Clyde under the command of Captain Robert Crighton who, at over six feet tall epitomized the rugged Glasgow skipper. The *Three Bells*, built in 1850 by William Denny & Bros., at Dumbarton, for Glasgow butchers William and Finlay Bell and their cousin John Bell, was 29 years younger than her master.[6] Right from the start of her voyage, the *Three Bells* had bad weather, with one gale after another assailing her in her westward crossing of the Atlantic. "During one of these, her binnacle light and compass were carried away."

---

6. Burnside. The three-masted 649-ton *Three Bells* was 171 feet long on deck, with 30 feet breadth of beam, and 17 feet depth of hold. She had a clipper bow.

On December 5, 1853, Lieutenant Bill Winder of Company G celebrated his thirtieth birthday, and the following day Dr. Satterlee turned 57. Both men were the sons of army officers, Winder's father an insufferable martinet whose time would come during the Civil War, and Satterlee's father a patriot, whose time had long gone, during the Revolutionary War.

This from the *New York Times* of Monday, December 5, 1853: "The Third regiment of Artillery, now stationed at Fort Columbus, Governor's Island, will sail this week in the new steamship *San Francisco*, for California, by way of the straits of Magellan. A part of the command will disembark at San Diego, and the remaining portion will be stationed at such other points as the emergencies of the case may require. This regiment is one the finest in the service, and numbers 450 men, rank and file."

The *National Intelligencer*, of Washington, D.C., in their issue of December 9, 1853, was just as optimistic about the departure date of the Third Artillery, letting their readers know that the regiment "will move out to California this coming week in the *San Francisco*." They didn't know it then, but General Scott had put back the date of departure yet again, from December 15 to December 21. Meanwhile, some of the officers and their families were staying at the Astor House, in New York City, waiting for the great moment, at an expense they could ill have afforded if the Pacific Mail Steamship Company hadn't been gracious enough to pick up the tab.[7]

---

7. Buel, 1872.

Trial Runs

In a perfect world, the *San Francisco* should have remained in New York and the army should have given more thought to chartering the *Lightfoot* because that clipper, snub notwithstanding, left New York Harbor on Monday, December 12, 1853, under the command of Captain Reuben Snow, and would duly arrive at San Francisco on March 25, 1854, after a passage of 114 days. So, if the Artillery had only taken the *Lightfoot* they would have made it, all things being equal.[1]

Bound for New York under the command of Captain Charles Babbitt Pendleton, the *Lucy Thompson* sailed out of Liverpool on December 16, 1853. The two-year-old packet ship could accommodate 400 passengers over and above the number of ship's personnel, but on this trip she had only 206 aboard, men, women and children, all British immigrants, almost all of them laborers. This left a lot of berths vacant, a factor that would, before too long, prove to be of tremendous importance and comfort to a great many people. For the first half of her regular transatlantic crossing the *Lucy Thompson* had a fair run, despite the occasional heavy weather, but when she got into the western portion of the ocean things changed. Captain Pendleton had gone to sea as a young lad from Dighton, Massachusetts, and in his 37 years of life so far and his five years as skipper of the *Lucy Thompson*, he had never experienced a storm as bad as the one he and his ship found themselves in now.[2] Soon, the gallant little packet would stumble into a situation that would raise an otherwise journeyman vessel to the status of a footnote in world history.

The people of New York City awoke on the morning of Saturday, December 17, to find a dense fog enshrouding not only the island of Manhattan but the two rivers that ran down each side of it—the East River and the lower portion of the Hudson, which at that point in time and in geography was called the North River. The entire harbor was invisible. Vessels of all sorts were in the bay, carefully picking their way along their designated routes, sounding their warning bells to alert others to their presence. As she did on a regular basis, the steamer *Eagle*, out of Keyport, New Jersey, had left Shoal Harbor earlier that morning, carrying a considerable quantity of truck and market produce, as well as a crowd of passengers and their belongings. She passed close by Sandy Hook and then up into the Lower Bay of New York Harbor, to The

---
1. The *Lightfoot* would be wrecked off Calcutta on June 29, 1855.
2. Huston; Ship's manifest.

Narrows—that aptly named passage of water that separates Brooklyn from Staten Island—where she pulled in at Fort Hamilton, on the Brooklyn side, to take on more passengers.[3]

Among the baggage taken on at the fort were three trunks belonging to a corresponding number of ladies whose Brooklyn home was a couple of miles inland, at New Utrecht. As one of the trio, Lucia Eaton, says, "As I live a short distance from the City of New York my luggage must be taken up in a ferry boat, thence transferred to the *San Francisco*." Another of the trunks belonged to Miss Eaton's sister, Sarah Loeser, and the third, the largest, to their servant. All three, trunks and females, were the responsibility of Sarah's husband, Lieutenant Lucien Loeser, who had thought it best to get his party's baggage on board the *San Francisco* a day or two before the steamer sailed, so from time to time their chests and some few trunks had already been sent up to the city and stowed aboard the ship. The three women would get to New York City later, but right now, following Lieutenant Loeser's strict instructions, they had made sure the remaining three trunks were ready to be picked up by the *Eagle* to be taken to the *San Francisco*, which was anchored in the stream of the North River, a short distance by steam-tug from one of the several piers jutting out into the water from Lower Manhattan.[4]

By 9:30 that morning, now fully laden, the *Eagle* was making her way gingerly north through the Upper Bay toward the city. The fog was as impenetrable as ever as the heavily loaded vessel passed between Bedloes Island and Governors Island, and that's when, without any warning at all, it happened.[5]

The crash was horrendous and so violent that the *Eagle* was cut down to water's edge and immediately sank forward of the wheelhouse, which is where all the passengers' belongings were stored. The people themselves were in complete panic—fog, crash, vessel sinking, couldn't see a thing. What had happened was that the Staten Island ferry, the steamer *Sylph*, had been going down the bay, too fast for the conditions, and had plowed right into the *Eagle*. The ferry took off all the *Eagle*'s distressed passengers and crew, and carried them to Pier No. 1, East River.[6]

On December 18, Lucia Eaton was at her home in Brooklyn, getting ready for church, when she happened to glance through her window and see the steamer *Eagle* out in the bay. This was the very vessel that had been hit by the Staten Island ferry only the previous morning. She was able to make out that the bow was under water, "the stern being perfectly strong." The *Eagle*'s curtains were blowing in and out of the window, and the whole of the promenade deck was filled with Christmas greens. "Thus she looked as she passed down the bay at the mercy of the tide." Miss Eaton then made her usual Sunday morning pilgrimage, but was unable to focus on the service due to the horrible forebodings she was experiencing.[7]

---

3. *Boston Daily Atlas*, Dec. 19, 1853; *New York Times*, Dec. 19, 1853, and April 17, 1854; Eaton.
4. *Boston Daily Atlas*, Dec. 19, 1853; *New York Times*, Dec. 19, 1853, and April 17, 1854; Eaton.
5. *Boston Daily Atlas*, Dec. 19, 1853; *New York Times*, Dec. 19, 1853, and April 17, 1854; Eaton.
6. *Boston Daily Atlas*, Dec. 19, 1853; *New York Times*, Dec. 19, 1853, and April 17, 1854; Eaton.
7. Eaton.

Lucia Eaton, like so many survivors of the wreck of the *San Francisco*, claimed later to have suffered premonitions about the upcoming trip to California. Of the many first-hand accounts of the tragedy, hers is by far the most extensive, longer even than the ship's log or the so-called "journal" of Second Officer Gretton. Written six months after the event, "The Narrative of Miss Lucia Eaton," while it certainly contains countless historical gems that can be found nowhere else and therefore contributes magnificently to our overall story, does, for a good portion of its length, rely heavily upon hindsight as well as other people's personal accounts that appeared in the newspapers soon after their safe return to land. As for this earlier incident involving the *Eagle*, Miss Eaton's memory was jogged by newspaper clippings from that time, but her skills as a researcher couldn't come close to matching her enthusiasm for telling a good story.

The next morning, Lucia Eaton saw the wreck again, this time lying at the wharf. Her servant went over to what remained of the vessel and learned what had happened. The good woman might have saved herself the trouble by reading the newspapers, which were already out. A little later that day, Miss Eaton was back at her window, busily engaged in sewing, when she again took a look out of her window. Once more she saw the wreck of the *Eagle*. "It had left the wharf and since lying on the flats, far off in the distance near Staten Isle." The *Eagle* had indeed been towed to the Jersey Flats, about a mile north of the lighthouse at the northern tip of Staten Island, to await repairs.[8]

The *Eagle* wasn't the only thing of interest Lucia Eaton saw in the water that morning. There, right in front of her, passing down the bay very slowly, was, of all things, the *San Francisco*, undergoing her fourth and last trial trip before the voyage. Mr. Eaton got up and went out to look at his daughter's future floating home as it passed into The Narrows, approaching Fort Lafayette, the tiny island 200 yards out from Fort Hamilton. "I do not wish my family to go out in that steamship if she is not perfectly safe," he remarked, with a triteness that afflicts all retired majors from time to time. The family watched the great ship with a deal of curiosity. "She stopped just back of Fort Lafayette, and after a while started down the bay again." She made two or three turns, then directed her course for the city, being towed up by a tug. It seemed to Miss Eaton and her family that all was not right, that the *San Francisco* ought to have gone out as far as Sandy Hook.[9]

It being extremely unlikely that the Eaton family were more expert in nautical affairs than, say, Mr. Shock, the naval inspector who was aboard the steamer as it made that particular run up and down the bay, and given that no one, at the time,

---

8. *Boston Daily Atlas*, Dec. 19, 1853; *New York Times*, Dec. 19, 1853, and April 17, 1854; Eaton.
9. Eaton. The Bar of Sandy Hook, commonly referred to as "the Bar," is a series of shoals running roughly south from Long Island to the northern tip of the New Jersey spit known as Sandy Hook, and acts as just that, a bar, separating and shielding New York Harbor from the deep and rough waters of the Atlantic. Being shoals, they are dangerous to incoming and outgoing vessels, and so experienced pilots were needed to guide sea-going traffic through them. These men would go out ahead in a pilot boat, basically saying "Follow Me." Once the vessel had cleared the Bar, the pilot was discharged.

ever questioned the manner in which the *San Francisco*'s trial runs were conducted, Miss Eaton's worries that those trials were not being managed properly were almost certainly prompted by what she read in the newspapers in early 1854, after the nightmare of the famous wreck was over.

"Justice," one of the survivors of the wreck of the *San Francisco*, had a letter published in the *New York Times* of January 19, 1854, parts of which, he claimed, represented the views of one of the ship's engineers.[10] "The steamer, we believe, never made a trial trip at sea, and her engines had never been sufficiently tested before she was sent upon her long voyage." And this is quite true. It is also inexplicable. The four trials were all merely runs down the safe and calm New York Bay. The ship would never actually go out beyond the Sandy Hook Bar, and into the ocean, until the real departure. But by then it was too late.

Other people would, over the years to come, have things to say about those trial trips, the first of which had taken place in early December, over a month later than originally scheduled. George Gretton, for example, the *San Francisco*'s second officer, says, in his "journal," that "her trial trips had been successful, and everything looked favorable." One has no way of knowing whether Gretton believed that or if he was just toeing the company line for the sake of his job. The opinion of the *New York Times* of January 16, 1854, as understated as it was, was quite opposite to Mr. Gretton's: "[T]he *San Francisco* had not been remarkably successful in her two or three short trial trips." Miss Eaton says: "She had been out once or twice before but each time was towed back by two steam tugs."[11]

Lieutenant William A. Winder, reminiscing in 1883 for a reporter from a San Diego newspaper, recalled that there were two trial trips, with the ship breaking down both times, "and then, without any further trial, sailed with several hundred human beings on board." He added that these failures, "together with the fact that two other ships of the same line had come to grief," caused uneasiness in those about to sail on the *San Francisco*. "The citizen passengers, fortunately for them, knew nothing of her failures." As is the case with Miss Eaton's concerns, one has no difficulty in appreciating the post-facto wisdom of Bill Winder.

Colonel Samuel Cooper, the adjutant general, when called to the stand during the second day of the court of inquiry, on February 7, 1854, remembered that there were three trials. "The last was reported by Mr. Aspinwall as entirely satisfactory." When asked by the court, "What was the result of the other trial trips? Did the ship go to sea in either of her trials, or below Fort Hamilton?," Cooper, replied, rather lamely, that he didn't know; he hadn't been on board.[12]

Colonel Cooper's somewhat hollow statement was echoed a week later by Mr. Mellus, the *San Francisco*'s first officer, the keeper of the log. Apparently the steamer stood a pretty hard trial before making the voyage, she made several trips down the

---

10. "Justice," as he called himself in this letter, remains unidentified despite attempts at analysis.
11. Franklin Institute; Gretton; Eaton.
12. Cooper.

bay, and the last one was satisfactory to the officers of the ship. They all thought she would be the fastest ship in the world.[13]

The truth is that on the first trial the vacuum obtained in the condenser was very poor, and it was absolutely necessary to maintain a tolerable vacuum in the condenser. The condenser, located directly beneath the shaft, and in the angle formed by the frames of the engine, was a large, strong, cast-iron cylinder, its purpose being to condense the steam. But on this first trial, the *San Francisco*'s condenser proved of insufficient power to condense all the steam, and was amended. On the second and third trials it put up a better show, but it was still not good enough, and was therefore amended again. And then the steamer made its fourth and final trial run, the one seen by Miss Eaton from her home in Brooklyn.[14]

Again, the survivor known to history as "Justice," wrote, from New York: "It may not be known to the public generally, but it is known to the officers who formed a part of the command on this ship, that her engine had never worked well—even here in smooth water." The *San Francisco* had been originally furnished with a patent condenser. "That condenser was a total failure. It was tried thrice, and failed each time." The part that constituted the patent was removed, and the same cylinder retained. The working of the engines continually threw into the condenser large quantities of water and steam, the steam being mostly condensed and adding to the sum of the water, and all of it had to be constantly pumped out against the pressure of the air through a series of tubes, or pipes, placed within the cylinder of the condenser. The large pumps employed for this purpose were termed air-pumps. In a steam engine the air-pump first removed the injection and the condensed water, which was its chief duty. Next it pumped out or exhausted from the whole shell, or cylinder, including the condenser, air which entered through leaks, or came over from the boilers, or entered mechanically, mixed with the injection water; and lastly it exhausted a quantity of vapor. The amount of work the air-pump had to perform depended, therefore, first, upon the quantity of steam condensed, and consequently the amount of injection water used; and secondly, upon the quantity of air that entered through leaks in the exhaust pipes, water valves, condenser joints, and so forth, and its duty was not dependent at all upon the size of the condenser.[15]

It was usual in double-engine steamers, such as the *San Francisco*, to have two air-pumps, either of which could, on occasion, work alone. The *San Francisco* had only one, placed horizontally, but it was made double-acting and was driven by direct attachment to an independent steam cylinder, placed fore and aft between the frames, and was thus worked by a separate, auxiliary engine. This was a novel, and as later became plainly apparent, injudicious contrivance.[16]

---

13. Mellus testimony.
14. Franklin Institute; *"Engineer;" New York Tribune*, Jan. 23, 1854. One of the trials, either the second or the third, took place on December 14, according to the *New York Post* of the following day.
15. "Justice;" *New York Tribune*, Jan. 23, 1854; "Engineer." As "Engineer" reminds us, the breaking down of an air-pump was a common occurrence, even when engines were not strained by a violent gale.
16. *New York Tribune*, Jan. 23, 1854; *New York Herald*, July 5, 1854.

The air-pump in the *San Francisco*'s engine, after the removal of the tubes, had less duty to perform, as the condenser then required less water to condense the same quantity of steam than it did when the tubes were in place. There was, therefore, also less vapor and less air to remove, so that the air-pump was relieved, rather than, say, being overloaded. After the tubes were withdrawn, the pump performed satisfactorily.[17]

Engineers were aware that one of the main objections to an oscillating engine system was the inconvenience of working the air-pump. In such double engines this procedure was accomplished by cranking the center shaft, adding to its expense and weight, thus making the shaft the part most likely to break. And if the center shaft were to break, the condensing apparatus might become disabled. And if there were an eccentric on the center shaft, as there was on the *San Francisco*'s, this was even worse, on account of its enormous friction.[18]

"Justice" continues, with a growing sense of outrage: "This engine was never properly tested until the night of our disaster, when it failed—the ship became unmanageable—fell off into the trough of the sea, which boarded her, and destroyed more than two hundred human lives at one dash. Was not this tampering with life? Was there no criminality in sending a ship to sea that had never been so far out of New York on a trial trip as Sandy Hook?"[19]

According to "Engineer," an otherwise anonymous man, in a letter he wrote to the *New York Times*, there "were … four trials instead of one, as is usually the case, and on the last, all the steam was condensed, and the engines, with the same amount of steam, did a greater duty than is usually performed."[20]

Said the *New York Tribune* of January 23, 1854: *"This unfortunate steamship made several rather unsatisfactory trial trips."* The difficulty was not in the boilers or in the engines, but in the want of vacuum, and this was due to the incapacity and bad arrangement of the air-pump. The ship was furnished at first with a patent condenser—J.P. Pirsson's patent—*"to which the difficulty has been most complacently ascribed,"* apparently without considering that the same principle had been successfully employed on the *Keystone State* and the unfortunate *Albatross*, and that a precisely similar construction of condenser, made under the inspection of the same patentee, was, at that moment being employed on the *John Hancock* during the Ringgold expedition, on the *Augusta*, and on the *John L. Stevens*. "But whatever may be the merits or demerits of this condenser, which consists of tubes in which the steam is cooled without mixture with salt water, it is worthy of especial remark that the tubes were entirely removed in a vain attempt to remedy the difficulty, and the ship went to sea with a plain injection condenser of the usual old-fashioned and orthodox description."[21]

---

17. "Justice;" *New York Tribune*, Jan. 23, 1854; "Engineer."
18. *New York Herald*, July 5, 1853.
19. "Justice." His figure of 200 is an exaggeration.
20. *New York Times*, Jan. 23, 1854.
21. The main difference between Pirsson's condenser and others was the freshwater. All other types of condenser used seawater. Freshwater helped preserve the boilers and saved fuel, perhaps 59 tons of coal per day. George Woolsey Aspinwall, brother of the owner of the *San Francisco*, had Pirsson's on three of his own steamers, and said, "I can only say I never would send a ship to sea without the Pirsson condenser."

The very same day that Lucia Eaton witnessed the last trial run of the *San Francisco*—December 19, 1853—Chief Engineer Shock finally completed his examination of the engines, boilers and machinery, and his enclosed report, dated that day, finished by saying, "The small air-pump did not perform its work with that regularity of motion which was desirable; but its adoption being new—in fact the whole arrangement being different to what has preceded it in a great many points—ask for and claim an indulgence until time shall familiarize the engineer with the best system of management for his charge, which differs in fact, if not in detail, with every new steamer now constructed."

Why wasn't Shock worried about this problem with the air-pump? Well, he was, but not to the extent of warning the Navy Department that it might pose a threat to the safety of the ship. He just hoped things would get better as the long voyage proceeded. As for his expressed hope that the passage of time would serve to familiarize the engineer of the ship with this new piece of machinery, did it not occur to Shock that out there in the notoriously dangerous Atlantic was not the place for a first real trial run? Instead, he was bound by his mandate—inspect and report. And that is just what he did. His findings were enclosed with a letter sent by Commodore Kearny to the Department on the twenty-first of December. Wasn't the board aware that the twenty-first was the new scheduled sailing date for the *San Francisco*? Everyone else was. Despite the never-ending postponements, come December 20 or thereabouts, the general public knew the departure date to be within a day or two, or at least they thought they did, which amounts to the same thing when examining the passage of Shock's report. The proof of this is not hard to find. The *New York Times* of December 20, 1853, reported an incident that had happened on Governors Island about six o'clock the evening before, the evening of the very day Mr. Shock was finishing his report. The bored men of the Third were waiting, and waiting, at least those who were not deserting, when the "alarm of fire … was occasioned by the burning of the straw beds and other rubbish belonging to the Third Artillery, USA, which sails in the new steamship *Yankee Blade* for California today." All right, the *Times* got the wrong ship, but they had certainly been led to believe that the departure of the troops was about to happen, immediately, "today," the twentieth."

As it happened, the *San Francisco* didn't sail until the twenty-second, but that isn't the point. The report didn't reach the Navy Department until after the ship had gone. The report, therefore, was useless. The commissioning of the report was to no purpose at all. And the ship was wrecked.

The same day that Miss Eaton witnessed the *San Francisco*'s last trial run down the bay, her brother-in-law, Lieutenant Loeser, sent word to her to come up to the

---

22. *New York Times*, Dec. 20, 1853. The *Yankee Blade*, built by Messrs. Perrine, Patterson & Stack for the Opposition Line, did, indeed, sail from New York on December 20, 1853, with 300 passengers. She reached Aspinwall on the 28th, picked up passengers coming from Panama, and made it back to New York on January 10, 1854. On February 2, 1854, she left New York bound for California, to take up her duties on the West Coast, but was wrecked that November.

city the following morning, Tuesday the twentieth. The three Eaton trunks, last seen floating in the harbor after the *Eagle* was hit, had been rescued and replaced by new ones. All 280 pieces of clothing had been washed and dried in a day and a half, so, on the appointed day, full of feelings of impending doom about the trip to California, Miss Eaton traveled up to Manhattan, accompanied by her sister and father, and booked into a hotel. They went down to the pier, where they were met by Lieutenant Loeser, who confirmed that the *San Francisco* would, indeed, be sailing the next day, Wednesday. If one believes Miss Eaton's "Narrative," her father had learned quite a lot about the last trial trip of the *San Francisco*, so much so that he was able to inform his daughter that the condenser, which had been the problem, had been taken out since the ship's return to the city the day before, at the end of her last trial run. If one doesn't believe her, then it is fairly obvious that she took her information from the article written by the mysterious "Justice." Either way, her fears now somewhat assuaged, the rest of the day was spent in her hotel room getting her clothes well and truly dried and packed. That evening, while it was still light, Sarah Loeser and Mr. Eaton left, telling Lucia they would be back the next day, the father to see both ladies off.[23]

Meanwhile, also in New York, Colonel Gates's instructions from the War Department on Monday, December 19, included taking nine months provisions for his men; three months flour and six months hard bread. But it came down to space. When General Wool examined the ship that day with Colonel Swords, he ordered three months supplies taken off. Swords felt that the ship was loaded too deep for speed, but he never for a minute contemplated danger as a consequence. No one did. The ship's owner, Mr. Aspinwall, was also of the opinion that the ship was too deeply loaded, and some of the *San Francisco*'s officers voiced that opinion too. Aspinwall went so far as to make his objections known to General Wool. In the end, when the steamer finally sailed, she was drawing 16 feet instead of her normal 12. In fact, so deep was the vessel in the water, and so heavily-laden, that Captain Watkins expressed the hope that they might escape a hurricane for at least for five days so that they could burn off some of the coal to lighten the load.

The *San Francisco* had, in her hold, about 3,500 barrels of stores, rations, etc., which would weigh in the region of 600 tons, and, despite Quartermaster General Jesup's injunction to Colonel Swords, she was carrying about 750 tons of bituminous coal, 250 more than her full complement. Even then, the amount of coal was probably understated, as a voyage to Rio would require at least 35 days of coal, which, if the figure of 750 were correct, would give but 22 tons a day. The capacity of the coal bunkers was 500 tons, so the extra had to be stored on the main deck and between decks, a good deal of it in the space alongside of and on both sides of the engine and boilers, a space that was normally used for luggage. The putting of coal there forced them to find a new place to store the luggage, and they chose lower steerage. These logistical decisions, which were made by the ship-owners and the officers of the *San*

---

23. Eaton.

Francisco and not the army, posed a new problem. The only instructions Lieutenant Fremont, being the regimental adjutant, got about the arrangement of the baggage was from Colonel Gates, who told him to arrange it so that the men who were going to get off in San Diego could get theirs first. But there was so much baggage. It was everywhere. Lieutenant Fremont estimated that the officers alone brought on board 1,000 barrels of it, and that didn't include their personal stuff, such as trunks, which went into their cabins. Lower steerage could have, and should have, accommodated 217 enlisted men, but it was now so full of baggage that the men had to be billeted somewhere else. Adding to this chain of problems, baggage and supplies for the troops now filled the hold. Because of the sheer unexpected volume of things aboard, nothing was where it was meant to be, and men were constantly involved in the pointless labor of moving barrels of quartermaster's stores from one place to the next, replacing subsistence stores with baggage. Bearing in mind that P.M.S.S. steamers ordinarily carried little heavy freight, the *San Francisco* was probably 600 tons overweight.[24]

A further aggravation came when General Wool wanted to know if 50 dragoons could be taken aboard as well. He upped that to 80, but it didn't really matter what the figure was, Colonel Gates wouldn't allow it. There simply wasn't enough room. When the contract had been made between the government and Mr. Aspinwall, it was for six companies of men, a number later increased to eight when taking into account all the new recruits who would soon be forming into Companies B and L. Colonel Swords and Colonel Abercrombie, the superintendent of Governors Island, went aboard the steamer just to see if there might be space for the dragoons, but, again, it didn't make any difference. Swords had heard there was smallpox among the dragoons, so there was no way he was going to allow such a thing. In fact, only one dragoon wound up going on the trip, and he would turn out to be one of the principal players in the story.

Originally from a town in Maine that bore his surname, John William Tudor Gardiner of the First Dragoons had been in the same class at West Point with William T. Sherman and George H. Thomas. Earlier in 1853, Captain Gardiner had been a member of Governor Stevens's surveying expedition of the northern route for the Pacific Railroad, and now, at 36, he was heading out to California to join his regiment.[25]

Up until the time the *San Francisco* actually sailed, on the morning of December 22, 1853, there had been many false alarms concerning her departure date. And, as time would tell, for years after the wreck, survivors who wrote about it, newspapers that published their own articles on it, and historians who have made mention of it to one degree or another, have more often than not erred on this critical point. And

---

24. Franklin Institute; Partridge; Fremont; *New York Tribune*, Jan. 16, 1854; *New York Herald*, July 5, 1853; Mellus testimony. The engine and the boilers ran up from the steerage deck to the main deck above (Partridge). The army food and provisions had not been insured.
25. Fremont; *New York Weekly Herald*, Dec. 24, 1853.

that may be because, in the few days before the steamer did sail, it was extremely rare to find a newspaper item reporting the real departure of the *San Francisco*. But there was one, the *Boston Daily Atlas*, of Wednesday, December 21, 1853: *"New York. Cleared 20th, steamer San Francisco, Watkins, San Francisco."* If only that had been true.

Departure Day Minus One

General Wool was still in New York City that Wednesday, and it was by his orders that the troops of the Third Artillery were to be embarked that day onto the steamer *San Francisco*. The embarkation, not only of the soldiers and their families, but also of the citizen passengers, was to take place in two stages, one in the morning and the other in the afternoon.

"On the morning of Wednesday, the 21st ... we were informed that Mr. Aspinwall had everything in readiness for a departure."[1]

The *San Francisco*, by now to all intents and purposes completely laden, and with her crew all aboard and ready to go, was still lying at anchor off the piers in the North River, simply awaiting her guests. Livestock and poultry thronged the forward deck. This was of course, food. Major Merchant was on deck to supervise all human logistics from the moment the first passenger's footsteps echoed on the planking.[2]

Early in 1853 the Emperor of Brazil founded the Maritime Hospital of St. Isabel, in Rio de Janeiro, for the express purpose of treating, free of charge, any foreigner—passenger or sailor—who arrived at the port carrying, or being suspected of carrying, a contagious disease. Official news of this magnanimous imperial gesture was promulgated in New York on April 7, 1853, by the Brazilian consul general, Antonino Jose de Miranda Falcão, who had been appointed to his position in 1852. Now aged 55, this typographer and journalist, and founder of the famous newspaper *Diario de Pernambuco*, was aboard the *San Francisco*, about to head back to Rio, accompanied by his servant. Traveling with them was Senhor Abrio, a member of the Brazilian Government, and wife.[3]

As it was for most of the other voyagers, the twenty-first was the big day for the Loeser party. After all the delays, the moment was finally here. Early that morning Lieutenant Loeser, his wife, Sarah, and Sarah's sister, Miss Eaton, were obliged to go

---

1. Mrs. Gates.
2. Fremont; Buel, 1854; Buel, 1872; Southworth; Eaton.
3. The name of the consul general will usually be seen misspelled, and even worse, seen as Jacinto Derwanz. Captain Watkins came up with this name Derwanz—where from is anyone's guess. He also has "Derwanz" aboard with his lady, which is doubtful. As for Senhor Abrio, his name is variously seen as Alrio, Abico, Albran, C.W. Albrao, and even Dr. Labrade. He is occasionally referred to as being of the Brazilian Navy. Watkins calls him "Capt. Battie" of the Brazilian Army. But, no matter the spelling, the man himself remains elusive. I have arbitrarily settled for Abrio.

out to the great ship in a small steam tug, accompanied by friends who were there to say their adieux. Mr. Eaton did not get down to the pier until just before this little boat started off, and was therefore obliged to shake hands and say his farewells to his daughters over the side of the vessel. When the party got aboard the *San Francisco*, they took their seats in the upper saloon, near the stove, as it was a very cold and disagreeable day, too unpleasant to remain on deck. "We saw all the arrivals," writes Lucia Eaton. "Several ladies and some of the officers came on board during the morning." Like the Loeser group, these people came over from the pier by tug.[4]

For those who chose to explore their new surroundings rather than remain in the comfort of the saloon, the *San Francisco* presented a new world of magnificence and sheer size. The huge vessel had four levels, all running fore and aft pretty much the whole length of the ship. The lowest was the hold, at the bottom, and directly above that was the main deck. Next, still going upwards, came the spar deck—otherwise known as the upper deck—running from the forward hatch to the rear of the wheels and engine-room. This deck measured eight and a half feet in height from its floor to its ceiling, and was as wide as the top and projecting guards. Resting on top of the officers' cabins on the spar deck was the hurricane deck, also called the upper spar deck or promenade deck, a light joiner's deck running from the top of the ship's bulwarks and, with nothing projecting above it, being there simply as a splendid promenade on which the passengers could stroll and get an incomparable view of what was out there. The main and spar decks, forming part of the ship's hull, each had a spacious and superbly fitted saloon and an extra-large cabin, with state rooms around the sides thereof. Everywhere there were walkways, passageways, and utility rooms, and there would ultimately be other miscellaneous ad hoc places on board that would, under the stress of circumstances, reveal themselves as nooks of accommodation, not as salubrious as the state rooms but nevertheless the difference between life and death.[5]

Both the main and spar decks had their own sub-levels amounting to what might be called mezzanines. The lower levels of the main deck, for example, contained the store room, hospital, wash room, ice house, kitchen and bakery, officers' mess room, water closets and bathroom, porter's room, barber shop, and the steerage quarters.[6]

There were two levels of steerage, upper and lower, and together they could take 1,000 passengers. In most ocean-going vessels of the day, to travel steerage meant spending weeks or months on end, at least during the sleeping hours, in conditions that were so disgusting as to be barely comprehensible to twenty-first–century sensibilities. Steerage was a nightmare not merely to be tolerated, but to be survived. However, none of this on the *San Francisco*. Four hundred seventy-five berths for the enlisted men, and their women and children, had been arranged around the

---

4. Eaton; Buel, 1854.
5. *Daily Alta*, Aug. 12, 1853; Buel, 1872; Partridge; *New York Herald*, July 5, 1853; Fremont; *Daily National Intelligencer*, Jan. 9, 1854.
6. *Daily Alta*, Aug. 12, 1853; Buel, 1872; Partridge; *New York Herald*, July 5, 1853; Fremont; *Daily National Intelligencer*, Jan. 9, 1854.

upper steerage cabin and the lower steerage cabin, and these quarters vied in neatness with the more expensive cabins of the finest sailing packets then plying the seas. Steerage on the *San Francisco* was a pleasant dream. That was the plan, anyway. But it wouldn't work out that way.[7]

There was great activity at Fort Columbus, down the bay at Governors Island. Major Wyse was getting together the first four companies of artillerymen who would be making the short trip by steam tugs to the waiting *San Francisco*.

Being not only regimental quartermaster but also, in Lieutenant Hardie's absence, acting adjutant, Lieutenant Fremont still had accounts to settle in New York City before departure. Today he would be making several last minute trips back and forth between there and Governors Island. The first was early that morning. He arrived at Fort Columbus at 7:30, and within an hour was back in Manhattan, where he ran into Dr. Satterlee, who pressed into his hand two separate and distinct pieces of paper, and told him to find Colonel Gates in the city and personally hand him these papers. The first paper consisted of orders from General Wool to the effect that those soldiers who had smallpox were to separated from those who didn't, and those not already vaccinated from those who had been. The second was an official letter Satterlee had written to Fremont that very morning. It concerned measles.[8]

On a ship at sea, measles was worse than smallpox in that, to some degree the smallpox vaccination offered protection against contagion, whereas there was no such safeguard against measles. The doctor had heard that some of the officers had children with measles. Fremont, as acting adjutant, must, under no circumstances, allow measles to be brought aboard the *San Francisco*.[9]

But, as it would turn out, it was going to be very difficult for Dr. Satterlee to enforce his edict. The very young Mrs. Colonel Gates says: "We had delayed going on board on account of my children having the measles." As a matter of fact, only Ida, the youngest, actually still had the measles. Julius was just getting over it at that point, which was perhaps just as bad as having it. Loulie, the eldest, had not contracted the disease.[10]

Fremont, carrying the two letters from Dr. Satterlee, ran into Colonel Gates at Judson's Hotel before ten o'clock that morning, and duly handed them to him. The colonel kept General Wool's orders, but, as for Satterlee's order about the measles, he read it and handed it back to Fremont, telling the acting adjutant that as the measles were a trifling matter the children would go; they must go anyway.[11]

With Colonel Gates still in the city, Fremont and Dr. Satterlee traveled together to Fort Columbus, arriving there about 1 p.m. It was only then that they discovered

---

7. *Daily Alta*, Aug. 12, 1853; Buel, 1872; Partridge; *New York Herald*, July 5, 1853; Fremont.
8. Fremont; Satterlee. Fremont would later give this letter to Lieutenant Hardie, but before he did that he made a copy. That copy would be lost in the wreck, along with all the official records of the regiment. By the time the court of inquiry convened in New York in February 1854, the original could not be produced, as Lieutenant Hardie was by then in California.
9. Satterlee.
10. Mrs. Gates; Fremont.
11. Fremont.

for the first time that they were to go on board that very day, and that four companies of men, under the command of Major Wyse, had already left Governors Island by steam tug that morning for the North River and were now safely on board the *San Francisco*.[12]

While Fremont and Satterlee were at Fort Columbus, processing all this new information, Lieutenant Francis Key Murray, of the U.S. Navy, was getting off a steam tug in the North River, and climbing aboard the *San Francisco*. Murray, who just five days earlier had celebrated his 33rd birthday, was going only as far as Rio, and so now would, for a while, at least, find himself in the unfamiliar role of passenger as he voyaged down to Brazil to join his squadron. He would find a few others going only as far as Rio. One of them was a man with a distinctly unsavory past.[13]

In 1839, young Frederick Hamilton Southworth, originally from Utica, New York, was making a living as an unemployed inventor in Baltimore when he married Emma Dorothy Eliza Nevitte, who was then just 18. They moved to St. Louis, and two years later to Wisconsin, where they had a son. With another child on the way, they took up residence at Washington, D.C., where Emma's grandmother continued to support them. But this support was cut off, and Fred deserted them for Brazil. In late 1853, now 38 years old, he was returning to Rio on the new steamer *San Francisco*.

Soon after Frank Murray boarded at one o'clock, the *San Francisco* upped anchor and dropped down the bay, heading past Governors Island to the Quarantine ground, where she was to take on board the second and last complement of troops, as well as some additional stores.[14]

The Quarantine station was the name given to the New York Marine Hospital at Tompkinsville, on the northeast side of Staten Island. Here, all vessels coming into New York Harbor were inspected for infectious diseases which might be on board. It was off Quarantine that the *San Francisco* docked in mid afternoon, ready to receive two more companies of the Third Artillery, as well as all the new recruits. It was here that the steamer would anchor for the night.[15]

That afternoon, Lieutenant Fremont, still engaged in last minute bureaucratic business, left Governors Island to return to the city. At the same time the last detachment of troops left what had been their home for the last three months, and, under the command of Lieutenant Colonel Washington, steamed out of Governors Island

---

12. Fremont.
13. Frank Murray became a midshipman at the age of 15. A lieutenant since 1849, his experiences in life thus far had been varied. He had been in a fight with the Seminoles, with only a few sick men to aid him; he had ridden out a gale off Cape Hatteras on the brig *Washington*, where his commander, Lieutenant George Bache and a number of men were washed overboard and drowned; he was in command of the Coast Survey steamer *Jefferson* when it was shipwrecked off the coast of Patagonia; and during the Mexican War he had been acting master on the bomb vessel *Vesuvius*.
14. Murray; Partridge; Southworth; Buel, 1854. Fred Southworth and Dr. Buel both say that the *San Francisco* arrived at Quarantine that morning; they are wrong. Lucia Eaton says it was evening. She is wrong. It was the afternoon.
15. Murray; Buel, 1854.

by tug, and made their way down to Quarantine, where they were embarked by Washington and Captain Gardiner, the dragoon.[16]

Captain Gardiner, in his testimony of February 11, 1854, during the court of inquiry, was asked by the judge advocate: "What part of the troops that went on board the *San Francisco* did you embark?," to which he replied, "The part that got on board at Quarantine ground in the afternoon."

Question: "The afternoon of what day?"

Answer: "Of the 21st December 1853."

Question: "What troops were they?"

Answer: "A portion of the 3rd Artillery."

Question: "Do you recollect the size of the detachment?"

Answer: "I do not. I have no idea; they were taken in a small tug, and that was crowded."

Question: "So far as you saw the embarkation of the troops, was it conducted in military order?"

Answer: "I thought not."

Major Merchant, when questioned at the court of inquiry, on February 15, 1854, said: "The decks of the steam tug in which the troops came were very crowded; the men, in my opinion, could not be formed in companies and marched on board the boat; they came aboard as well as the case admitted of."[17]

Lucia Eaton says: "In the afternoon all of the troops [came aboard] and, with some exceptions, most of the passengers. At three o'clock we were called to dinner."[18]

In New York City, Lieutenant Fremont found Colonel Gates and then the two of them, along with their families, took the steam tug together for Quarantine, where they boarded the *San Francisco* just as it was getting dark. So, despite Dr. Satterlee's strict orders, Mrs. Gates and her children "hurried on board Wednesday afternoon, in anticipation of an immediate departure."[19]

Colonel Gates later tried to justify his children's presence on board the *San Francisco*: "The Surgeon's protest was sent to me only a few hours before the steamer was to sail, thus leaving me no opportunity of finding a home for a child convalescent from an attack of measles." He considered all danger of contagion passed, and admitted without reserve that, although a soldier, he could not forego his duty as a father. "I could scarcely then have consented under such circumstances to abandon my sick child to the care and protection of strangers." He then used the statements of Doctors Satterlee, Buel and Wirtz to validate his actions: "Not a solitary soldier was attacked by this disease."[20]

And that was true, as far as it went. None of the soldiers did, in fact, contract

---

16. Judd; Gardiner.
17. Merchant.
18. Eaton.
19. Mrs. Gates.
20. Gates's written statement to the court of inquiry on Feb. 24, 1854. Because he was indisposed that day, the statement was read aloud to the court by his counsel, Captain Shields.

the disease. However, young Ida Gates did communicate it to one of Lieutenant Fremont's children, Richard, as well as to one of the Reverend Cooper's brood and to other boys and girls on board.[21]

That the measles did not spread further than it did was pure luck. And no thanks to Colonel Gates. He tried to wiggle out of it, of course, by pretending that his child was merely convalescent, in other words implying that that the measles was no longer active. But it was active, otherwise the other children wouldn't have contracted it, something the colonel conveniently omitted to mention in his statement to the court of inquiry.

There can be no question, and there was none then, that Colonel Gates behaved in a completely irresponsible manner over the measles issue. On the one hand he had a wife and children to think about, and on the other he had hundreds of passengers to look after, including all the men of his regiment. He could, and should have, simply ordered his wife to stay behind on Governors Island with the children, where they would have been well taken care of by the army. There would have been no need to abandon his sick child to the care of strangers, as he plaintively put it. That was ridiculous. What governed his motives was clearly Louise, his young wife, who wanted to go with him to California, at all costs.

One of the passengers bound for Valparaiso was Edward Jarvis Tenney, of Methuen, Massachusetts, who had lost his father just a few months earlier. A Harvard man, still only 20, Ned had been corresponding for four years with his half-cousin, Lizzie Andrews, a girl he was desperately in love with. But Ned needed to prove himself, get himself fixed up in life before they could get married, and so he signed on to the *San Francisco* as a clerk, to work his passage to Valparaiso where he would set up in the mercantile business, make his pile, and return for Lizzie. Unfortunately, things were to go horribly wrong with Ned's plans.

The Rev. William Henry Cooper, Doctor of Divinity, of the Protestant Episcopal Church, was originally from Stonehouse, in Devon. While resident chaplain at Malaga, he acquired not only the Spanish language but a wife, Josefa Maria Magdalena Jauregui de Avila. He was subsequently rector of various parishes in the U.S., and a missionary to South America and then, in October 1853, on the invitation of the Foreign Committee of the Board of Missions, he agreed to undertake a mission to Rio de Janeiro. He would never, in fact, get to Rio.[22]

Most of the officers were now aboard; however, Colonel Washington had gone to the city to collect his wife, and would be back soon, while others, due to a misapprehension over sailing time, were running late, and wouldn't arrive on board until after dark. There was also the case of Major Taylor, the commander of Company A.

---

21. Satterlee.
22. The Reverend Cooper's wife and six children went with him on the *San Francisco*. The children were: Ellen, 12; Sofia, 8; Josefa Maria Magdalena, 6; William Henry Cranmer, 4; Isabella, 2; and James Warburton, 7 months.
"Most of the officers were now aboard..." Fremont; Gardiner; Merchant; Eaton.

"When we reached the *San Francisco* ... we found that Major Taylor and his lady were not on board," wrote Mrs. Gates. It seemed that the major and his lady were lost. "We waited for their arrival, in hopes that they would come in the remaining boats, but they did not.... Colonel Gates felt unwilling to wait any longer for them."[23]

"We all sat around the stove," reported Lucia Eaton, "and as we were acquainted with many who were present, our time passed very pleasantly."[24]

On this day, December 21, the inspection report of the Navy Department's constituted board of examiners was sent to Washington. Not a moment too soon, and perhaps too late, as December 21 was meant to be the day the ship sailed from New York. From an external examination, they said, everything seemed reasonable. "Her motive power consists of two oscillating engines with sixty-five-inch cylinders and eight feet stroke, with an independent engine to work the air pumps." These powerful engines, oscillating as they did with a new adjustable cut-off arrangement, were of the totally suitable capacity of 1,000 horsepower each, and, with their frames being made principally of boiler plate, were ranged in line opposite one other fore and aft, each one inclined toward the other 45 degrees from the vertical line, like the sides of the letter A, and both being connected directly to the same crank pin and fired up by two boilers, one placed forward and one abaft the engines, instead of side by side as in a normal steamship. Thus this arrangement left a clear run on each side of the main deck from bow to stern. "As these are peculiar engines," the report continued, "we beg leave to transmit the accompanying report from Mr. Shock, Chief Engineer, who is associated with us on the Board. The *San Francisco* is a substantial vessel of her class, measuring about 2272 tons, and with suitable war appointments and additions could be readily converted into a war steamer."[25]

Actually, although the structure of the engine was entirely new, the novelty was in the arrangement alone, not in the actual engine. Oscillating cylinders, each with two piston-rods, were free to vibrate, like field-pieces, on trunnions being made hollow to permit the ingress and escape of the steam. The necessity for connecting rods, working beams and other arrangements, was thus completely avoided, so, owing to the diminution of the number of the working parts, the engine was rendered lighter, more compact, and less liable to accident. For all these reasons, the oscillating engine would later, with modifications dictated by the tragedy of the *San Francisco*, be adopted, in preference to the side lever, as the way of the future.[26]

---

23. Mrs. Gates.
24. Eaton.
25. Partridge; Franklin Institute; *New York Herald*, July 5, 1853; *New York Tribune*, Jan. 23, 1854.
26. Partridge; Franklin Institute; *New York Herald*, July 5, 1853; *New York Tribune*, Jan. 23, 1854. The use of two piston rods in oscillating engines was a novelty, and, as far as could be judged without trial, an improvement. They passed like cap-bolts through the journal block of the crank pin, and for additional security, the journal block was confined within guides bolted to the cylinder cover. The valves were poppets with vertical stems, arranged in a simple and compact manner, steam and exhaust channels diverging from the trunnions to each chest. In starting or stopping, the engineer stood on a platform moving with the cylinder (Franklin Institute).

However, the way of the future envisaged by America's shipbuilders in 1853 was just a nebulous swirl in their crystal balls and of no real use to the *San Francisco*. By the time the Navy Department received the board's report, the object of the exercise was fighting for her very life 300 miles out in the Atlantic. And as for the possibility of converting the brand new vessel into a war steamer, she would never be converted into anything but a floating coffin. It wouldn't be until the twenty-seventh of December, after scores of human beings had been washed overboard from the deck of the doomed steamer, that the Navy Department wrote back to the four-man inspection board saying that their report had been received. "The Department instructs you to advise with the officers associated with you in the inspection of the steamer *San Francisco* on the defects pointed out by Chief Engineer Shock, and to state whether they are such as will materially impair her efficiency as a war steamer." Note the word "defects," and the hopeful use of the future tense. Note that the Navy's concern was with how those defects might affect the steamer's performance if she had to be turned into a warship. Note the total lack of concern with how those defects might affect the safety of the ship while transporting hundreds of soldiers through a vicious Atlantic Ocean.

Unbelievably, it would not be until January 5 of the following year, when Mr. Shock was on leave and confined to a sick bed in Baltimore, that Captain Kearny, U.S.N., replied to the Navy Department on behalf of the board. "In the meantime, may I be permitted to suggest to the Department that the engineer in charge of the engine on the *San Francisco*—now at sea—upon arriving at the port of destination, and such others as may be appointed to examine into the merits of the new principle and value of the small air pumps, be directed to report thereon from thence." What Captain Kearny was suggesting through the veil of his "thences" and "thereons" was that upon the *San Francisco*'s arrival in California, Mr. Marshall, the chief engineer, and any other qualified appointees who just happened to be out on the west coast at that precise time, should let the Navy Department know how the air-pumps had performed during the voyage.

—⚋—

On the *San Francisco* that evening of the twenty-first of December, soon after nine o'clock, Colonel Gates, who was sitting with the two Eaton sisters aft, declared that he had to go up on deck and "look after my boys." The ladies, assuming he was talking about his sons, suggested it was a little late for them to be still up. "I mean my men," he laughed. "I must go up and see if they are comfortably fixed for the night." It wasn't long afterwards that Miss Eaton retired to her state room in the lower cabin.[27]

—⚋—

---

27. Eaton.

The impending tragedy of the *San Francisco* should not have been unforeseen. For a month shipping in the Atlantic had suffered most severely from hurricanes and storms of unusual violence, and there had been no moderation in the weather by the time the brand new steamer sailed. The marine reports in New York would record that at the end of December 1853 about 60 vessels went ashore in the neighborhood of Cape Cod and the adjacent coast.[28]

---

28. *San Francisco Call*, June 12, 1898.

Ship's Log

The official log book of the *San Francisco* was kept by First Officer Edward Mellus. Originally from Dorchester, Massachusetts, Mr. Mellus had been at sea for 20 years, and was now 33, with a wife and five-year-old son at home. However, there was a sizable blot on Mr. Mellus's Pacific Mail Steamship Company copybook. At the beginning of the year he had been skipper of one of the firm's steamers, the *Tennessee*, plying up the West Coast, but on March 6 he managed to run her aground at San Francisco. The company then put him in command of the *Columbus*, and from there he was transferred to the *San Francisco*, but this time as first mate under Commodore Watkins. The *San Francisco*'s immediate mission, her first ever, was to transport the Third Artillery to California, but once having done that, she was to replace the *Tennessee* on the West Coast.[1]

The log of the *San Francisco* covers the dates December 22, 1853, to January 5, 1854, inclusive; in other words, from the time the ship left New York Harbor to when the last of the survivors of the wreck were rescued and the steamer was scuttled. The log book was the property of the Pacific Mail Steamship Company, and was destroyed in the San Francisco earthquake of 1906.

Fortunately, enough extracts from the log were published in the three great New York newspapers—the *Herald*, the *Times*, and the *Tribune*—for us to have a very good overall view of what it contained. William Hull Wickham, the ship's 21-year-old storekeeper, had, until just before the ship sailed, been a ticket agent for the P.M.S.S., working out of Howland & Aspinwall's office. On January 13, 1854, when he and Mr. Mellus arrived back in New York after the incident, the two men, with the ship's log in front of them, were interviewed by reporters from the *Herald* and the *Times*. On the morning of January 14, 1854, the *Herald* offered their readers both interviews, side by side, naming both men as sources. There was so much in common between the two accounts that the other two papers felt that to reproduce both would be redundant. Mr. Wickham's version being far and away the more extensive of the two, the *Times* and the *Trib* quite naturally picked that one, cryptically referring to Wickham merely as "one of the officers."

Thirteen years before the *San Francisco* was launched, George Gretton had been

---

1. Mellus testimony.

one of the most able manufacturing jewelers in the city of Albany, New York. But then he got the sea fever, and with Peter Leddy and Stephen Hutchins went off on a whaling voyage. Being unable to free their nostrils from the stench of blubber, that was enough maritime experience for the other two lads, but George stayed at sea. By late 1853 he was 35, unmarried, and had been selected by the Pacific Mail Steamship Company as Second Officer for the *San Francisco*'s maiden voyage.

During the short but eventful voyage of the new steamer, Gretton made copious notes. After the wreck, and safely back in the U.S.A., he used these notes, along with Mr. Mellus's log, to write up his own account, which took the form of a journal, or even, indeed, a log. Gretton later married, moved to California, and died in San Francisco on March 5, 1888, leaving his book to his daughter. In 1907 the daughter, by now Mrs. Ann Hoogewout, of Alameda, felt that the famous San Francisco newspaper, the *Call*, might be interested in taking a look at this small book which, by now, yellowed and stained and worn on the corners, had not seen the light of day since Mr. Gretton wrote it over 50 years earlier. Ida L. Brooks wrote an article on the Gretton book for the September 22, 1907, edition of the *Call*, after which the book itself went back to the family. At some point later in time, the family donated the book to the Golden Gate National Recreation Area, and they in turn transferred it to the San Francisco Maritime National Historical Park Research Center, where *Copy of the Log of the San Francisco from New York to San Francisco in Dec. 1853* remains to this day, described in the Center's finding aid as a 42-page engine room log book. Despite its title, this book is not a copy of the log, nor is it anything to do with the engine room. It is a post facto journal, guided by Mr. Mellus's log, that's all.[2]

Unfortunately, although not tragically, Gretton's book, as we see it today, is not quite complete. The opening paragraph is to do with the ship sailing, on December 22, 1853, yet the *Call* article of 1907 refers to things happening before that moment. For example, the article quotes Gretton as saying that the steamer was "hove short" off Staten Island. This is nowhere to be found in the book as we know it now. The paper also says, about the steamer, that *"her trial trips had been successful, and everything looked favorable."* Again, this relates to information which precedes the opening entry in the book. Without question, then, one or more of the first pages—probably only one—of Gretton's book have been lost over the years since 1907.

Mr. Marshall, the chief engineer on the *San Francisco*, also relied to some extent on the ship's log when it came time for him to be interviewed by the press in January 1854.[3] And it is clear too that certain other witnesses—for example, Lieutenant William A. Winder—dipped into the log from time to time when writing their accounts.

The log was, as most other ships' logs were in those days, compiled according to "sea time," otherwise known as "nautical time." This is confusingly different from

---

2. San Francisco *Daily Evening Bulletin*, March 6, 1888; San Francisco *Call*, Sept. 22, 1907.
3. John Woolsey Marshall was 34, a native of Westchester County, New York. His third child had been born on January 24 that year.

"land time" or "civil time." In civil time, the one most of us reckon time by, the day begins at midnight. However, at sea in the mid-nineteenth century, the day began 12 hours earlier, i.e., at noon the previous day. To make things more difficult, ships' logs would use civil time when they were in port, and nautical time when they were at sea. At least they would most of the time. But not always.

So, the log of the *San Francisco*, kept by Mr. Mellus, the first officer, begins with the steamer leaving New York at 9 a.m. on December 22, 1853. That was land time. However, three hours later, at noon, because they were now on sea time, the log passes over into December 23. Still, 1 p.m. is one p.m., no matter which system you're on, "p.m." meaning post meridian, and "meridian" being another word for "noon."

In this book everything has been converted to civil time.

Thursday
December 22, 1853

Everyone aboard the *San Francisco* arose in good spirits this morning. Surely, unless something else were to go wrong, today was the day. And what a day it was! The sun was shining very bright, the air was clear and cold, and the sea was smooth. No better way to start a winter voyage.[1]

However, unbelievably, there was yet another delay. Major Taylor and his wife had still not shown up, and Colonel Gates was getting more and more upset about it. While Gates was fuming over the missing Taylors, Commodore Watkins sent him word that the *San Francisco* was ready to leave port. All he needed was the command from the colonel. So Gates gave it. To hell with Taylor. He had given him every possible chance, even put off the sailing for an entire night and much of the following morning, so now the dilatory major and his lady were on their own. But Lieutenant Fremont stepped in and asked Colonel Gates to reconsider. If George Taylor missed the boat he would have to make his own way out to California via the Isthmus of Panama, and so would be put to a large expense. Reluctantly, the regimental commander ordered the ship's captain to wait a little longer.[2]

Finally the major and his wife made it on board, and at precisely nine o'clock that morning the steamer left its anchorage off Quarantine, and stood down the bay, with clear weather and a light breeze from the southwest.[3]

Major Taylor had previously commissioned a third party to secure a state room for himself and his wife, but when the couple made their way to what would be their home for at least four months they found that it was in the lower cabin, in the saloon on the main deck. Off this cabin were about 20 small state rooms, not particularly well-lighted, and most of them containing three berths each. That situation was

---

1. Eaton.
2. Mrs. Gates.
3. Mellus account; Wickham; Gretton. Fred Southworth, the passenger bound for Rio, says the ship departed at 8:30 a.m.; Dr. Buel, in his 1854 statement, offers 10 a.m. Lucia Eaton, copying from Buel, says that the Taylors finally came aboard at 10 a.m., which, of course, would mean a departure after that time. However, it must be acknowledged that both Wickham and Gretton were copying from the ship's log, which had been written by Mr. Mellus. Bearing in mind Mr. Mellus's obligation to be accurate—after all, what use is a log unless it is accurate?—and given the fact that the moment of departure was the first really important event of the actual voyage, it is hard to believe that the first officer got the time wrong.

acceptable, perhaps, for Colonel Gates and his family, but for a Southern gentleman such as George Taylor it simply wouldn't do, even if he had been traveling alone. Aside from everything else, the room was too far aft. And so the major made a fuss, pulled rank, and got two or three occupants kicked out of their billets upstairs on the spar deck aft the wheel houses, where several of the officers and a few citizen passengers were housed in the large, elegant, airy state rooms that surrounded the upper saloon. The vacated state room in the lower cabin was then allocated to Mrs. Sarah Loeser and her sister, Miss Lucia Eaton, who now joined Commodore Watkins, who had his quarters here, and the one or two families who were not as privileged as the Taylors.[4]

If only the Taylors had been on time, the entire history of the world would have been different. Certainly the personal lives of Major and Mrs. Taylor, and those of hundreds of others, would have been immeasurably enriched, by not coming to an end.

While it is true that this is looking through the convenient retroscope of hindsight, Mrs. Colonel Gates had this to say of Major Taylor only a few weeks after the wreck: "It will be seen from these circumstances that each step that was taken seemed to conspire to lead him on to his fate. Had the vessel not waited for him he would have been saved; and had he occupied the state-room designated for him he would not have been swept overboard when the saloon went over."[5]

Colonel William Gates, animated by the consciousness of having faithfully discharged his duty, left "these shores for the distant scene of my future labors with buoyant hopes and a happy heart." As the old colonel stood on the deck of the ship, looking back toward an ever shrinking New York Harbor, he couldn't help feeling that his destiny was linked with that of his comrades in arms, which, of course, it was. What that destiny was turned out to be very different from what he had imagined. "There was promise of a speedy and propitious voyage."[6]

"The morning of Thursday was lovely," wrote Dr. Buel, supposedly in his journal; "the sea calm and smooth, with gentle breezes from the northwest. Whatever gloomy forebodings might have existed seemed quieted by so fair a presage. All was bright and cheerful. We began to calculate the days that were to elapse before reaching Rio Janeiro, where we were to make our first port."[7]

"We soon left Quarantine," wrote Lucia Eaton, "and proceeded down the bay rather slowly, but this did not alarm us as we heard the speed would be increased by degrees."[8]

It wasn't every day that the grandson of one of the signers of the Declaration of

---

4. Buel, 1854; Mrs. Gates; Eaton; Fremont; Marshall, Jan. 14, 1854; Southworth. Each of these state rooms on the spar deck had two doors, one into the general cabin and the other leading directly onto a spacious walk out on deck (*Lewis County Republican*, New York, Jan. 25, 1854, taken from the *New York Tribune*).
5. Mrs. Gates.
6. Gates testimony.
7. Buel, 1872. It is quite clear, from Buel's wording, that his "journal" was not written in time, as he claimed.
8. Eaton. Here Lucia Eaton is taking from newspaper coverage of the ship's log.

Independence struck up the band for a passing ship, but that's just what happened as the *San Francisco* was making her way south through The Narrows, with Fort Hamilton on her left. Major William Walton Morris, of the Fourth Artillery, might not have been the most pleasant individual, or the most popular with his own men at the fort, but he certainly managed to establish an instant rapport with hundreds of strangers heading into the unknown that morning. This untypically generous gesture from the notoriously unfriendly fort commander delighted Colonel Gates, who went up to his troops standing on deck and said, "My men, give them three cheers." So the soldiers of the Third cheered, and Morris's men of the Fourth cheered. Everyone cheered. Why not? It was a beautiful day. For scores of human beings on board the passing steamer this would be the last act of kindness they would ever experience outside their own little floating world.[9]

"Continues with light breezes and pleasant weather," reported the ship's log at precisely noon that first day out, December 22, 1853, and at 20 minutes past 12 the officers of the *San Francisco* discharged the pilot outside the Bar, "light ship bearing N.E. by compass; distance four miles; course by after compass S.E." As soon as they passed Sandy Hook to head out into the Atlantic, the ladies went below into the first saloon.[10]

The term "ship's log" has two definitions. One is, of course, the book kept by a ship's officer to record the day-to-day events of the voyage. The other refers to a mechanical instrument, towed astern, used to measure the speed of a ship as it travels through the water; an odometer, in effect. Also called a "patent log," this object—until the time of the Civil War, anyway—had to be hauled out of the water every hour in order to read the distance traveled in that time. "At 1 P.M. put over the patent log, 2 P.M. took it in found the ship had run 3½ miles. At 3 put it over again."[11]

The weather being chilly, the ladies and children gathered around the stove, and at three o'clock that afternoon the passengers experienced their first Atlantic fine-dining aboard the world's newest and perhaps most magnificent steamer, the ladies being called down first so as to prevent confusion. "Every delicacy of the season was to be found upon the table, and everything in perfect order." Commodore Watkins was in good spirits, pleased with himself and everything and everyone around him. Major Taylor's wife sat beside Lucia Eaton, and talked about her ill health, and hoped the sea voyage would be of service to her. "She had been obliged to hurry very much to get ready to accompany the major." After dinner, Miss Eaton and her friend, Mrs. Sallie Chase, went up to the spar deck, where they took a promenade.[12]

As the two ladies were soon to find out, they were not the only ones on the spar deck that cold afternoon. There were between 300 and 350 men camped out there,

---

9. Eaton. Major Morris's grandfather was Lewis Morris.
10. Wickham; Mellus account; Gretton; Eaton. The quote is from Gretton.
11. Gretton.
12. Buel, 1854; Eaton. The quotes are from Eaton. Of course one could always take a promenade on the spar deck if one wished, as Miss Eaton and Mrs. Chase did in this instance, but the usual place for such a stroll was the promenade deck.

50 to 75 of them aft the paddle wheels. For about half the length of the ship the spar deck had rooms on it, while the other half had canvas curtains hanging down three and a half feet from the hurricane deck above, their bottom fringes being attached to the bulwarks. The six already-formed companies of troops had been assigned by Lieutenant Fremont to the open gangway space on either side of the engine, to the guards on either side of the upper saloon, and to the vacant space at the rear of the saloon not occupied by baggage. This couldn't be called quartering, as such, for no man had a fixed place or position and was constantly liable to be moved about and separated from his effects by the necessary duties of the ship. But it was the only place aboard for them. Here during the night, double rows of standard movable berths called standees, of three tiers each, were erected and then removed during the day. In addition, from the engine to the rear of the saloon were small standees over the guards on both sides. However, there were not quite enough standees for all the soldiers; at least 15 men at any one time had no option but to creep under the sails or lie on the baggage. For the first two nights at sea, although the hurricane deck above and aft the wheels kept out the worst of the weather, all of these troops suffered intensely from cold, especially those sleeping along the guards. Captain Judd's state room opened out along the guards, thus giving him the opportunity to hear what the men there were saying during the night. The following morning they complained to him that they hadn't slept, having been up all night stamping their feet and trying to keep their blood circulating. As Judd says, "Of all beds, the coldest is a sacking bottom, as these were without mattresses; ice is warmer. I will add that these nights were very cold; we suffered intensely in the cabin; mattresses were procured by some of these men in the standees, but the captain of the steerage took them away, as they were liable to be injured there from the wet."[13]

The two ladies, walking up and down, couldn't help watching the soldiers on their part of the spar deck. "They were a wretched looking set as they were nearly all new recruits." Some were standing by the smoke stacks trying to keep warm, others jumping up and down and clapping their hands to prevent them from freezing. "It was very hard and they looked so miserable that I could not help pitying them. The officers did all in their power to make them comfortable." The plan was, as the ship proceeded south into warmer climes, to have the men pitch their tents on deck, at which time it would be much more pleasant for them.[14]

---

13. Judd; Fremont; Eaton; Mellus testimony; Buel, 1854; Partridge; *New York Herald*, July 5, 1853. Behind the upper saloon were luggage, arms chests, and some coal in bags below the luggage. The putting of the men on the side of the saloon over the guards was intended for a temporary arrangement, and expected to ease in almost a week, or as soon as enough coal and provisions were consumed to enable the men to remove the luggage from before the forward hatch. No standee berths for the men were over the guards (Fremont).

14. Buel, 1854; Eaton. Miss Eaton's assertion that these men on the spar deck were nearly all new recruits seems to be at variance with the fact that it was the six already formed companies—A, D, G, H, I, and K—who were quartered there, not the recruits of Companies B and L, who were being housed on the main deck below, in upper steerage, where they had permanent berths such as were normally provided for steerage passengers. But perhaps, at that moment, the majority of the men she was looking at were, indeed, recruits who just happened to be up there on the spar deck (Fremont; Buel, *American Journal*).

The officers and soldiers were busily employed in getting the baggage in order, men were being detailed for guard, and officers of the day were being chosen, as was an officer of the guard by night. "Order was established, and all was going on very well."[15]

By four o'clock that afternoon the patent log had just completed its latest hourly drag in the water. The men heaved it in, and they found that the ship was making 7⅝ knots.[16]

As Frederick H. Southworth says, "The noble ship glided through the waters, as if she had long known old ocean, and her engine and machinery, together with her new middle wheels, worked well, and called forth the admiration of all on board. Her motion was easy..." Or as Lieutenant William A. Winder, the commander of Company G, put it: "The day was beautiful and everything promised a pleasant and prosperous voyage. The ship was well provided with everything which could render us comfortable, and every luxury that could be procured was placed on board. All these things, together with the gentlemanly and efficient officers of the ship, and pleasant company in the cabin, served to render us happy and contented."[17]

Dr. Wirtz intimated, with a hint of something in his tone that could only have come from the convenience of hindsight, that due to the magnificence of the ship, and to the aggressively positive publicity she had received, every man on board felt assured of a safe and agreeable voyage.

He continues, obviously taking from Bill Winder's account: "The sky was bright and the sea was smooth on the day of our embarkation. Our ship was stocked to repletion with everything that could supply our wants or administer to luxury; the ship's crew was numerous and well chosen, and the seamen in command were tried and gallant mariners; gentlemanly officers of United States Army and Navy were on board, and a large party of agreeable ladies graced and enlivened the society of the cabins. What more could we ask to inspire us with the most agreeable anticipations of our voyage?"[18]

Lucia Eaton says: "All anticipated much pleasure on the trip," which was all well and good, but on that first day out no one noticed the slow speed and the wallowing paddle wheels, no one, that is, except the captain and his main officers. Something was not quite right. It was the engine.[19]

"Unfortunately, the reliance they placed in their strong ship, and the security

---

15. Eaton.
16. Mellus account; Gretton. Today, the knot is a unit of speed—one nautical mile per hour, the nautical mile being 6090 feet as opposed to 5280 land feet—and therefore to say "knots per hour" is like saying "miles per hour per hour." One must say just "The ship was doing seven knots," not "seven knots per hour." But back in 1853 the term knot usually meant just the distance, i.e., a nautical mile, and the term "knots per hour" was used by every sailor.
17. Southworth; Winder, Jan. 6, 1854.
18. Wirtz account.
19. Eaton; Partridge.

with which all sought their snug berths on the night of the 22nd of December, was to be awfully dispelled within a few brief hours."[20]

The *San Francisco*'s professional crew were there to please. Mrs. Catherine Evelina Livingston, one of the Pacific Mail Steamship Company's stewardesses, was, in many ways, a woman out of the ordinary. Her introduction to the peculiar world of shipwrecks came in 1837, on the very vessel in which she was immigrating to the New World from England at the age of 14. She subsequently married a ship's steward, Hudson Livingston, a much older man, a colored man as a matter of fact, and she had naturally drifted into his line of business, surviving a second wreck during her career. It would therefore have come as no particular surprise to her as she went about her work on the *San Francisco* this first day out in the Atlantic, that within a few short hours she would have a third.[21]

Alexander Auchinleck, the First Engineer, and Edward Osier, the ship's quartermaster, had been brothers-in-law for eight years, ever since Alex had married Mary Osier in her home town of Buffalo. Mr. Auchinleck, himself from Philadelphia, was now 35, and had been an engineer at sea for some years, both U.S. Navy and merchant. That first evening out on the *San Francisco*, "We sat in the mess room, joking and talking with one another."[22]

During their first two days at sea the crew were amply employed in clearing the decks of the various articles displaced in the hurry of departure, and the troops, with their vigilant officers, were also busy in setting things to rights. "The ladies felt the first motion and freshness of the sea, and even many of the gentlemen manifested an unusual love of retirement, but upon the whole good humor and cheerfulness prevailed throughout the vessel." New acquaintances were formed, "and some of older date cemented." Friends strolled about the decks together, admiring the proportions and model of their floating home, or leaned idly over the bulwarks, contemplative cigar poised between fingers, watching the dip and flash of the billows, "and interchanging the expression of their future hopes and plans." At table all was mirth and ease. Among the soldiers, cooped up as they were, the jest and laugh went around, "and the sailor's song kept time, frequently in the night, to the beat of the engine."[23]

One of those who retired quite early that evening was Lucia Eaton, who felt very much fatigued.[24]

By 10 p.m. the wind had become violent. However, this subsided somewhat, and the night passed pretty quietly.[25]

The ship's log reads: "During the night, wind and weather much the same,"

---

20. Wirtz account.
21. Livingston.
22. Auchinleck. Fremont tells us that the engineers slept in a state room with 12 berths, situated close to upper steerage.
23. Wirtz account.
24. Eaton.
25. "By 10 p.m. the wind..." Wirtz account.

meaning light breeze from the southwest and clear weather. Aside from one or two worrying moments, it had all been so peaceful since they had pulled out of New York. But things were about to change. Alex Auchinleck says: "At 12 o'clock the first and second engineers were ordered below on duty." This time, as the ship sailed into Christmas Eve, the wind was coming up again, stronger than previously, with something in the air that had not been there before.[26]

---

26. "The ship's log reads..." Mellus account; Auchinleck.

Friday
December 23

Throughout the dark, early hours of her first full morning at sea, the *San Francisco* was assaulted by a heavy wind coming in from the northwest. At daylight, those passengers who happened to be up and around and gazing up into the dull and gloomy sky, could feel that wind breezing up even stronger and hauling to the westward, and so the crew set the fore and aft sails. As Dr. Wirtz delicately put it, the ship was "making such motion that many, who up to that moment had not felt the sickness that usually destroys the landsman's pleasure of a first voyage, were rendered very uncomfortable."[1]

Lucia Eaton describes this morning as quite rough, and so, as she was feeling quite seasick, she felt it best to remain in her berth. She heard the clatter of knives and forks, and presumed that the noise came from breakfasters, "the majority being gentlemen."[2]

Just after breakfast the weather ameliorated, and once again the *San Francisco* seemed to be heading into a balmy, pleasant future. By mid-morning, indeed, the temperature had become milder, certainly when compared to the chilly weather of the day before. As Dr. Buel remembered: "Friday morning, the 23rd, rose brightly on our course. We entered the Gulf Stream. Weather mild and lovely, and the day passed without incident of any kind, and gave no presage of the awful disaster about to follow." Rio-bound passenger Fred Southworth agreed with Dr. Buel: "On the 23rd the weather was as pleasant as could be expected in the Gulf Stream at this season of the year."[3]

At 11 a.m., with the wind southwest, they set the fore topsail, the fore sail, and the fore top gallant sail, and, shifting half a degree to the east, set a southeast course. At noon, as the nautical day ended with a fresh breeze from the westward and passing clouds, they set the square sails, and the crew was employed in bending studding sails for making all sail.[4]

---

1. Fremont; Auchinleck; Gretton; Mellus account; Wickham; Wirtz account.
2. Eaton.
3. Buel, 1854; Buel, 1872; Southworth.
4. Wickham; Gretton; Mellus account.

But there were men on board the *San Francisco* who had been at sea a long time, old salts who could smell danger from afar. Now, as they gazed out onto the limitless ocean, all their senses alert, watching a cloud creep here and there along the sky, and feeling that extra heave of the sea as it worried the hull of the steamer, they knew from experience that something bad was out there. And they were not the only ones. From time immemorial well-seasoned ocean travelers had developed the habit of watching the ship's captain to get an indication of what was coming. It was the women who were remarkably quick in detecting anything of this sort, and for one or two of them aboard the *San Francisco* Commodore Watkins's face was a good barometer. Interpreting the shadow of anxiety that crossed his face as his glance ranged the horizon, they could tell, as early as this Friday afternoon, that there was going to be a storm. But, as people going to sea have to expect rotten weather as a matter of course, everything went on as usual, and no one appeared to pay any attention to the increased motion of the ship and the gradual rising of the wind. Not one of them, sailors or passengers, could possibly have had any idea of the size and malevolence of the monster heading their way.[5]

As the wind increased throughout the afternoon, there was not much gaiety at dinner, where some of the familiar faces were missing, "and many of the viands set before us were eyed suspiciously by both ladies and gentlemen." Still no idea of any impending danger was entertained, and they only looked upon the change of weather as the commencement of the serious part of the voyage. They were determined to enjoy the Christmas holidays, and talked among themselves about Yuletide festivities in which they had participated in the past.[6]

Lucia Eaton, still affected by the change of weather, had remained in her berth all day, and did not attempt to get up. She knew that if she did she would get even sicker. At dinner time one of the waiters came to her room, bringing some soup and crackers, but she hardly touched it. By sundown the wind was blowing very hard.[7]

At tea time, quite a number of passengers, including a few ladies, met around the table. For some, who didn't know they were condemned, this would be their last meal, at least on Earth. Not that they would be worried about that unduly, what with the abundance of ambrosia to come in the next life. Miss Eaton was still in her room, and the waiter brought her some tea and a cracker. Soon after that she fell asleep. Dr. Buel, on the other hand, retired soon after tea to his state room on the spar deck forward, read for two hours as quietly as if he had been on shore, and then undressed and went to bed. There was more roll to the ship than he had experienced previously, and he could hear the wind freshening, but he had been at sea before, and thought nothing more of it. "There was no such thing as sleeping, however."[8]

By four o'clock that afternoon it had come on to rain, and the weather was look-

---

5. Wirtz account.
6. Wirtz account.
7. Eaton; For this last sentence, Miss Eaton was relying upon Lieutenant Fremont's court room testimony of February 1854.
8. Eaton; Buel, 1854; Buel, 1872.

ing bad, so the crew put the studding sails away again, and began to secure everything for the night. For the next hour or so the weather was so changeable that it appeared to be toying with the *San Francisco*, as the great vessel plowed through the Atlantic at 8⅛ knots. At six o'clock, with the air temperature reading 54 degrees, the water registering 57 degrees, and the barometer going down some, the wind suddenly died away to a light baffling breeze. However, the sky looked very threatening, and so they took in the square sails. Almost immediately the wind came up again, the sea got up very fast, and they furled all sail.[9]

"As the hours passed, the storm increased," Miss Eaton says. Her room was separated from her sister's by a little passageway, and as both doors were open, the two ladies could talk. But Sarah was very sick, and her husband, Lieutenant Lucien Loeser, was often there to attend to her, as Lucia remained all the while in her room.[10]

Dr. Buel, who not long before had thought nothing of the weather change, now began to be very alarmed indeed. The ship rolled and pitched to such a degree that it was difficult for him to keep his berth. All books and loose articles upon his table were tossed to the floor; indeed, every article in the room, even though it might have been scotched in, was thrown about in an alarming manner.[11]

As Fred Southworth expresses it: "…as the golden sun set behind the dark clouds along the western sky, indications were given of a coming gale."[12]

The rain showers got heavier as night began to settle in, driving nearly all of the passengers under cover, "but we rather profited by the incarceration, as the social circle within doors was only the cozier for the dreary scene outside. We scarcely noted the hours as they wore on, although once in a while a plunge and roll of the ship and the quick tramp of the crew on deck might have warned us of a stormy night. The vessel was going finely through the water, and everything spoke of confidence and regularity."[13]

Meanwhile, at eight o'clock that evening, not very far away, but completely unknown to those on the *San Francisco*, the brig *Napoleon*, on her way from Cuba, was hit by her third severe gale, which soon turned into a perfect hurricane from the northwest. The brig, with lost sails and a leak, was hove to under a balance reefed mainsail, and fighting for her life. The crew had had to stave 21 casks of molasses to ease the vessel.

The fine clipper *Eagle Wing*, on her way from Boston to San Francisco, under the command of Captain Ebenezer H. Linnell, found herself in the same storm that was threatening the *San Francisco*. At eight o'clock she had to heave to under close-reefed main top-sail and spencer, the ship lying with her lee rail under water, nearly on her beam-ends.[14]

---

9. Gretton; Mellus account; Wickham; Wirtz account.
10. Eaton.
11. Buel, 1854; Winder, 1883.
12. Southworth.
13. Wirtz account.
14. Maury.

December 23, 1853, at 9 p.m., was one of those defining moments that would live forever in the minds of those on the *San Francisco* who survived the wreck. At that very hour the wind came out of the northwest like a moaning wraith, suddenly and with tremendous force. The sea rose up rapidly, churning the ocean with enormous violence. The crew managed to take in the fore and aft sails while the tempest whistled around them and the seas, now white with foam, came ever higher up the side of the steamer, causing her to roll very heavily.[15]

At the moment the gale hit them, the men were all above deck, except the colored head steward, Mr. Charles Sanford. The women and children fled from the ladies' saloons and their berths in great consternation. Catherine Livingston, the stewardess, did her best to calm their fears, which required no slight effort amid the shrieks of the women and the screams of the children. A number of the females were mothers of several children, who were all clinging to them at once, and several had helpless infants at the breast. Anxious to see what was going on above they clustered around the stairway, crowding it almost to suffocation point, and would remain there during the night.[16]

Dr. Wirtz, the Third Artillery's assistant surgeon who, along with several other individuals had, only a little while before, escaped the rain, was still enjoying his enforced incarceration. All of a sudden they heard all hell breaking loose, and with no formal termination of their cozy chat, they all dashed up to the deck, where the sight that met them at the door was "very fine, with just enough of the fearful in to make it rather agreeable than otherwise, as a specimen of the Atlantic in a pet. Some of the old fellows even joked about the matter, and considering all the circumstances, they were excusable. But their coolness was soon ruffled." Those first plunges of a great ship in a heavy gale were enough to convince any but the most seasoned voyager that the ship was going down for good, and before ten o'clock that evening the *San Francisco* had made a dozen such plunges, which tried the nerves of many a passenger.[17]

As vague images of hell danced before their eyes, the passengers and crew of the *San Francisco* were becoming more and more alert to the concept of "defining moments." Ten o'clock was such a moment.

James Lorimer Graham, Jr., was a tall, well-fixed New Yorker, not yet quite 19, heading back to Rio, where he had relocated after an expensive education in France. Like William Wickham, the *San Francisco*'s young storekeeper, Mr. Graham had once been an employee of Howland & Aspinwall, in New York, and now, as that company's new steamer found itself in trouble in the Atlantic Ocean, Graham was sharing a state room with George W. Aspinwall, the ship-owner's brother. Thanks to Lorimer Graham and to the *New York Herald* of January 16, 1854, we cannot pinpoint the position of the *San Francisco* at the time this violent nor'wester sprang upon them; Graham says about 200 miles east of Charleston and the newspaper tells us about

---

15. Mellus account; Mellus testimony; Wickham; Gretton; Marshall, Jan. 16, 1854; Winder, Jan. 6, 1854; Wirtz account; Brown account.
16. Livingston.
17. Wirtz account.

150 miles out from Sandy Hook. These two reckonings cannot physically be reconciled in any way, which shows how off-beam the reporting was.[18]

The *San Francisco*'s oscillating engine had a limit of 22 revolutions per minute. If it were to be coaxed beyond that, the engine would blow. Prior to the departure of the steamer from New York, the Chief Engineer, Mr. J.W. Marshall, had received strict instructions from the owners not to push the engine over eight revolutions per minute for the first four days out. For a day and a half now the engine had been performing admirably, making 7½ revolutions per minute, and then suddenly, two hours short of Christmas Eve, the *San Francisco* broached to, head to northward.[19]

For a ship to broach to is as dangerous a misfortune as it can suffer. Instead of cutting through the ocean prow-first, the out of control vessel spins around, in effect, and presents its broadside to the oncoming waves which in the Atlantic during the night of January 23, 1854, were enormous. This could easily capsize the vessel. "Flying into the wind" was what a lot of sailors called it. Those were the words used by Mr. Gretton, the ship's second officer: "The ship flew into the wind, carrying everything away on the upper deck with the lurch—bales of hay, barrels of vegitables [sic], etc."[20]

Dr. Wirtz explains how and why this happened: "At 10, the ship failed in her onset at a gigantic billow, that, although rolling forward with her, was so vast in its ascent, and so slow in its apparent subsidence, that it almost had the effect of a tremendous sea meeting her in full career." The *San Francisco* pitched downward right into the giant wave, and with a sudden whirl lost steerage-way and broached right to in the trough of the sea, with the angry waves, one after another, crashing into the weather side of the vessel, carrying away parts of the guards, and threatening to crush the ship by sheer force. Nearly all those passengers who were standing at the time were jerked from their feet, some being washed overboard into the roaring ocean, along with boxes and livestock. Planks creaked and strained; loose articles ranging from dishes to pieces of furniture were dashed about on deck and in the cabins; the topmasts seemed to switch from side to side with their heavy cordage, and the whole vessel shuddered with a mighty effort. The water was starting to come into the state-rooms through the port-holes, and from above.[21]

---

18. Graham; *New York Tribune*, Jan. 16, 1854; *New York Herald*, Jan. 16, 1854.
19. Franklin Institute.
20. Marshall, Jan. 16, 1854; Mellus account; Gretton.
21. Wirtz account. The guards were the overhanging portions of the deck, extending out a few feet, and, according to Partridge, were formed by allowing the main deck timbers to project over or through the sides. They were supported by sponsons, or brackets, not very closely spaced on the hull, and were there to protect the ship against collisions. Again, relying on Partridge, the Pacific Mail Steamship Company steamers were rather peculiar in that they had guards at the level of the main deck. Beginning at nothing forward, they gradually widened to the full width of the paddle boxes, which were to be found halfway along the ship on each side of the vessel, on a line with the two black smoke stacks, each of these stacks having a diameter of 4 foot 6 inches and rising to a height of 30 feet off the main deck fore and aft, roughly amidships. Going aft from the paddle boxes, the guards were carried around the stern, but with less width. There was almost no overhang to the rounded stern. The *New York Tribune* of Jan. 23, 1854, pointed out that the *San Francisco* was not the first steamer in which overhanging guards had extended the whole length, having been preceded in this respect by the *John L. Stevens*, at that point in time running successfully between Panama and San Francisco; by the *Senator*; and perhaps by several others designed to navigate the Pacific.

It was now that the indomitable coolness and courage of the ship's officers began to show, and for a while at least, they were successful in bringing the beleaguered vessel under some sort of control. The *San Francisco*'s head was quickly brought around again, and she once more began to ride ahead. Still, from moment to moment the gale increased, and the throbbing of the engine became more noticeable, as the huge ship was tossed from side to side, to and fro like a mere cork. Wirtz, ever the existentialist, was enthusiastic: "During the next hour the scene without was frightfully grand."[22]

The crew set the jib and the fore-spencer, and got the ship back on course. They put preventer braces on the fore yard, and preventer tacks and sheets on the foresail, which they also set, and at that moment Commodore Watkins went into the engineers' room and directed Mr. Marshall to drive the engines with all the power he thought prudent. The chief engineer was caught between a rock and a very hard place. The company had warned him not to exceed eight revolutions per minute for the first four days out, yet here was his ship in an emergency that definitely required more than eight—a lot more. What would happen if he pushed the engine to, say, 12 or 13? Of course, he couldn't say, it was uncharted and potentially perilous territory out there beyond eight. But one thing was for sure, he had to get the steamer out of this immediate danger, and the only way to do it was to face the unknown. They were already facing it anyway. It was his decision. And so he worked the revolutions up to 12½—four and a half per minute beyond his instructions. Now carrying a full head of steam, together with the extra sail which had been rigged up, the vessel paid off and ran in good style at about 10 knots for the next hour or so.[23]

As the night wore on, the storm continued with increasing severity, soon turning into a hurricane. But despite this there was as yet no evidence of fear on board, so firmly did everyone rely upon the strength of the *San Francisco*.[24]

But their troubles were only beginning. Being of such great length, and heavily laden, and therefore so deep in the water, the ship was not responding to the helm and was simply being tossed around like a plaything of the enormous billows. Just before 11 o'clock, in the dead of night, finding it almost impossible to run before the hurricane that was savaging them, the crew had no choice but to begin taking in sail. However, to their dismay, they found that they had run her too long and couldn't get the sails in. As soon as they started a rope and the sail began to shake they could do nothing with it, and so they slacked up and let the fore staysail blow out of the boltropes. One sail after another followed, and finally the furled spanker was blown from the gaskets sails. However, they did finally manage to haul up the foresail. All this time they were trying desperately to keep the head of the ship as near to wind as they could, in order to avoid broaching to again, although the vessel would at times fall off into the trough of the tremendous sea like an immense log, or one of the big trees of the Yosemite, making very bad weather of it.[25]

---

22. Wirtz account; Southworth; Mrs. Gates; Fremont.
23. Mellus account; Wickham; Marshall, Jan. 16, 1854.
24. Marshall, Jan. 14, 1854; Wirtz account; Winder, Jan. 6, 1854; Winder interview, 1854.
25. Gretton; Mellus account; Wickham; Buel, 1872; Partridge.

At that very moment, as the hour hand reached 11, Dr. Buel, the ship's surgeon, was lying wide awake in his room on the upper deck forward. Unable to bear the motion and noise any longer, he got up, dressed hurriedly, and stepped out on deck, where he experienced a wind more terrific than anything his life had ever prepared him for. "The outlook was fearful; the sea covered with foam, boiling and seething like a cauldron." Ducking smartly back inside, he snatched his watch and valuables, and then left his room again, this time never to return to it. All the standee berths had collapsed, and the soldiers had crawled out. On deck Buel found that the lanterns were going out all over the ship, and visibility was close to zero. "[A]n Egyptian darkness prevailed." He stumbled over dead soldiers, and from the knapsack of one of them he cut a leather belt with his penknife and, fastening it to a secure carline, made a safe place for himself to hang onto for about an hour. Then he tried to make his way to a more stable spot, but, being unable to stand erect for even a moment, he seized the iron brace connecting the king bolts, surveyed the scene for a moment, then dropped to his hands and knees, crawling to the nearest hatch, which was over the forward galley. From here he swung himself down by the cabin and found himself on the main deck forward, amid a scene of dire and unutterable confusion. The roar of the sea, the voice of many waters, the groaning and creaking of the timbers, the shouts of the captain through his speaking trumpet, all combined to produce a scene which "may be imagined, but which human language could not adequately describe."[26]

Meanwhile, in the engine room, Mr. Marshall received orders to lessen the speed, but before he had time to execute the order the vessel broached to the second time, this time to northward.[27]

This was just what the engineers and sailors had feared the most, and Dr. Buel was just in time to witness it. There was nothing the ship's crew could do to get the head of the huge steamer around again. As the doctor put it: "It was her final and unconditional surrender before the awful power of the tempest—her motive power whether of wind or steam utterly gone and sails all carried away—engines completely smashed up and crippled. Her immense broadside lay exposed to the winds and waves which thundered against them like guns against the gates of a beleaguered city." He was not quite right about the engines being smashed, not yet anyway; they were merely powerless to do anything meaningful in the face of the inexorable elements. Not all, only some of the sails had gone by the board, but in all other respects Dr. Buel was right.[28]

It was inevitable that confusion and alarm should spread rapidly, but Commodore Watkins and Mr. Mellus, the first mate, went around cheering everyone up, assuring the more nervous of the passengers that all was sound about the ship, and greatly restored the good humor of the whole company, many of whom retired, com-

---

26. This account of Buel's adventure is a melding together of the two quite differing accounts he gave: Buel, 1854 and Buel, 1872. He claims to have been washed overboard shortly after leaving his cabin, but if that is true, which is very doubtful, then a succeeding wave must have brought him back on board.
27. Marshall, Jan. 16, 1854.
28. Buel, 1872; Wirtz account.

paratively satisfied that the morning would find the storm abated, and the vessel on her course.[29]

Commodore Watkins countermanded his previous order to the Chief Engineer, and now directed that a full head of steam should be got on. But again, Mr. Marshall, like everyone else on board, had no actual experience of these new oscillating engines, and so couldn't even guess what their breaking point really was. Already, after less than two days out of port, he had pushed the ship up to over 12 revolutions per minute, four more than his instructions allowed. Commodore Watkins too had no idea how much punishment the engines could take, where the red warning bar—and his ship's luck—truly ran out, but to get back on course he had no choice but to give Mr. Marshall the order. If the engines broke now, then come morning, with the storm abated and many of the sails gone, how would they get back to land? But this was a storm of rare proportions. What if it had not abated by morning? What would happen if it just got worse? But then, they'd probably all be dead, and the *San Francisco* would be thousands of feet below, in Davy Jones's Locker. "Give her more revolutions, Mr. Marshall."[30]

They were now doing at least 10 knots, perhaps a lot more since they were being jockeyed along by the force of the wind and the forward underdrift beneath the ship. Notwithstanding their great velocity, the billows, white as snow with foam, swept seethingly by them, far outstripping the speed of the steamer, which was an additional danger in heavily laden vessels. The noise of the storm was deafening: The creaking and groaning of spars and timbers; the terrible harping of the wind among the cordage and around the smoke stacks, as it caught the ear of the passengers, who were anxiously listening from their state rooms and in the gangways; the hurried tread of the crew and the hoarse commands of the officers; all these combined with the incessant blows of the angry sea upon their quarter, and the wash of the spray over the skylights and hatches, to produce a surreal, all-enveloping roar.[31]

Only Dr. Wirtz has that element of mysticism that can adequately convey the metaphysical aspects of the scene at this moment: "Yet, to those who were gazing out on the storm, a strange kind of silence, which was more appalling than the elemental confusion itself. For instance, when the gale was at its worst, and the noise of the tempest most powerful, those who were standing together, at the cabin doors, clinging to anything that afforded support, could hear each other's lightest whisper. This was peculiarly remarkable, as the ship poised for a second, just as she was about to make one of her dreadful plunges. At such moments, a perfect hush would settle over us, as the huge bows rose up darkly against a billow, and then, as it sank, seemed an instant afterwards hundreds of feet below us, in the black cavity of the sea, apparently yawning to engulf us beyond redemption. The vessel would remain for an instant suspended in that position, and then, while every man held his breath, tremble like

---

29. Wirtz account.
30. Marshall, Jan. 16, 1854.
31. Wirtz account.

a living creature through her whole length and breadth, as if conscious of impending destruction and quivering affright; and then would come the plunge and the billows, closing in on her bows, and hissing up over her topmasts with lightning-like rapidity."[32]

With various sails having been stripped away or blown to atoms, and the ship beating heavily, with no engine power that was of any use against the fantastic storm, this was far from the pleasant cruise of the day before.[33]

Just before midnight the storm was simply terrific, and blew away the forespencer and foresail from the lee yardarm, in rags and splinters. Fred Southworth, standing on deck, watched the waves cascading over the ship and the roaring waters ripping the five-inch thick, edge-bolted planking from its copper fastenings on the after guards, sweeping them and the bulwarks into the ocean, which meant there was no longer any security left outside the saloon and anyone out there could easily get carried overboard. In ordinary weather, an ocean steamer was as safe without guards as with them, but with weather like this going out on the deck became virtually impossible. In fact, according to Fred Southworth and Dr. Wirtz, men were occasionally washed over the side that night. If this is so, then that bears out the army records, which show 27 men being lost that night, the vast majority of them being recruits.[34]

Meanwhile, the officers below were in their places and were joined there by some of the officers from above who had come down on account of the pitching of the vessel.[35]

At midnight, just as Friday the twenty-third was passing into Christmas Eve—land time, anyway; sea time it had been the twenty-fourth for 12 hours already—one of the waiters came to Lucia Eaton's room in order to look at the deadlight, which was a skylight designed not to be opened. When she had first come into the room two nights before she had noticed that it was made very secure by a large rope being fastened to a frame of wood put lengthwise; so it could not possibly be broken away. As soon as the waiter put the candle into the entrance to her room, she asked what was the matter. "Nothing," he said, "I was only looking to see if all was right."[36]

And all was right, for now. In another nine hours, it wouldn't be. What they had just been through was a piece of cake, compared to what would happen to them the following morning.

---

32. Wirtz account.
33. Marshall, Jan. 16, 1854; Southworth; Wirtz account.
34. Mellus account; Wickham; Winder, 1883; Mellus testimony; Gretton; Southworth; Marshall, Jan. 16, 1854; Army enlistment records; Partridge. This from the *Washington Sentinel* of Jan. 18, 1854, taken from the *New York Courier*: "No steamer with guards should ever sail upon the Atlantic." And this: "Every additional strength of the guards of the *San Francisco*, which her builders supposed would insure her safety, was the direct cause of the sad catastrophe." And this: "Just in proportion to the strength with which the guards of a steamer are fastened into her hull, is their power to rend her to pieces in a storm. They become huge levers for the waves, whose every heave racks the vessel to her center."
35. Fremont.
36. Eaton.

Saturday
December 24

The spanker was the fore-and-aft sail set on the after side of the ship's mizzen mast, and the clew was the after lower corner of the spanker. Just after midnight, with the ship laboring heavily, and with some of the planking getting knocked up over the after guards, the crew put a lashing on the head of the spanker to haul out the clew. They ordered the troops forward, except for those who could still lie about the floor of the upper saloon.[1]

Bravely facing the bitter cold, Lieutenant Frank Murray of the U.S. Navy had been venturing out on deck from time to time during the night, and his last walk around was at about one o'clock that morning, at which time the ship was bearing head first into the wind and sea, and, despite laboring heavily, was behaving well.[2]

The *San Francisco* was behaving well because her engine was now running smoothly. Before she left New York she had been supplied with duplicates of all machinery parts, so that if a piece were to go wrong, the engineers could simply replace it. It didn't take much imagination to picture what would happen if an indispensable part broke, one for which, for some unaccountable reason, there was no spare on board. The engine would stop dead, and unless the engineers could fix it, or rig up a makeshift part, then the vessel would have to rely on the sails to make it back to port. On a good day, in fine weather, or even terrible weather, that could be done. After all, that was one of the reasons for the sails—to provide such back-up. But suppose the vital engine part broke while the ship was fighting for its very life in the worst hurricane the Atlantic had ever seen; suppose that hurricane ripped away all the sails and dragged them over the side into the raging ocean. What then? This is why they provided duplicates of all the machinery parts for the *San Francisco*'s maiden voyage; well, all parts, that is, except one—the air-pump piston-rod, a bit of wrought iron three or four inches in diameter, and covered with brass about half an inch thick. Because it was the piece least likely to go wrong, they didn't see the need to send along a spare.

In all the ordinary forms of ships' engines in those days the air-pump was worked by attaching it in some manner to the main engine or engines, in which case it worked

---

1. Mellus account; Wickham.
2. General proceedings at the court of inquiry, Feb. 16, 1854; Murray.

moderately but powerfully, and was so proportioned as to maintain the vacuum on the pistons of the large engine, while making its strokes necessarily in the same time. The oscillating engine, however, afforded no convenient points for attaching this important auxiliary. The *Golden Gate*, for example, running in the Pacific Ocean, and which had two of the largest oscillators in the world, connected both its air-pumps to a crank forged for the purpose in its intermediate shaft. The *Illinois*, plying between New York City and Aspinwall, was arranged in a precisely similar manner, the two engines oscillating directly under the shaft, one on each side, while the two air-pumps stood inclined toward each other on the line of the keel. The ponderous intermediate shaft of the *Illinois*, manufactured at the Franklin Forge in New York City, was probably the heaviest piece of wrought iron ever executed in the world, and weighed in the rough, as left by the hammer, 52,840 pounds, or nearly 24 tons. The single oscillating cylinder of the *Augusta*, running between New York City and Savannah, stood beneath the shaft in the center, the air-pump being worked by a lever suspended above and receiving motion from the crank by a link or short connecting rod. A similar lever was adopted in the steamship *Knoxville*, at that time being completed at the Novelty Iron Works, but this arrangement was considered almost or quite impossible in the *San Francisco*, in consequence of the two engines connecting to the same crank-pin with an addition of guides attached to the cylinders parallel to the piston-rods, the better to control the vibratory movements.

The most convenient remaining method would have been to forge a crank in the paddle-shaft as near as practicable to the engines, and thus to have worked a pair of air-pumps, arranged as in the *Golden Gate*. The single air-pump of the steamer *Edgar*, which contained the first American application of this style of engine to marine purposes, was worked in the manner last indicated. The importance of this portion of the mechanism will be best understood when it is considered that all the steam used in the engines was drawn either in the form of water or vapor through the air-pumps. It was the final means of escape, in fact, for all the steam which passed through the valves of a low-pressure engine. In case it was disabled, the engines could only be worked "high-pressure," or by forcing the steam out against the pressure of the atmosphere, but if that expedient were to be resorted to, the steam pipes had to be in full working order. Without those pipes a sufficient pressure of steam couldn't be maintained. To work one or more air-pumps successfully, independent of the main engines, two engines might be connected to an independent shaft, acting at right angles to each other, or possibly some simple arrangement of levers and links might be applied to a single engine, which, as in the cotton press and printing press, would have given the greatest 'purchase' when it was most needed. But the effect of a steam engine acting directly on an air-pump, without other load, would necessarily have been imperfect. The whole capacity of the pump was not, nor should it have been, completely filled at each stroke with water, a portion being invariably vacant or filled with very thin air and vapor.

The air-pump on the *San Francisco* was 26 inches in diameter, with a solid piston, of five feet stroke, and the steam piston impelling the air-pump was 30 inches in diameter, and necessarily of the same stroke. The air-pump and engine were both laid horizontally and in line with each other, the air-pump rod being merely a continuation of the piston-rod. In this arrangement the greatest force of the steam, which necessarily was at the commencement of the stroke, and the greatest resistance, which was after the air-pump bucket had compressed the gaseous matter and fairly met the resistance of the water, wouldn't, under great stress, correspond with each other in time, and the result would inevitably be a series of kicks, struggles and plunges, subjecting the material to concussions which it would have been almost impossible to estimate in pounds. The difficulty was anticipated and designed to be overcome by the aid of a heavy balance-wheel, or fly-wheel, which could not, however, under the extreme circumstances of a hurricane, be of sufficient size to steady the motion; and to this cause alone, when driving the engines up to pretty nearly their full capacity, the rod would almost certainly fracture and consequently this portion of the machinery would inevitably be crippled.[3]

In spite of the ship still laboring, and the firemen filling the four furnaces with the most combustible material they could find, the crew had just got everything secured and were beginning to think they could ride out the storm when, at precisely 1:15 a.m., while they were running with some speed to get out of the trough of the heavy sea, a fierce wrench of the ocean broke the tapered end of the air-pump piston-rod across the slot, or key-way, just where the rod connected to the piston. The broken end, about three inches wide, was the part that fitted into the bucket, which consequently went adrift. The engines stopped dead. To make matters worse, the two steam pipes were carried away by the raging storm, leaving the engines with no draft. And so, with the sails completely useless in such a violent storm, and thus completely disabled, the *San Francisco* was suddenly rendered a virtually helpless hulk, at the entire mercy of the violent elements, and leaving the crew with no control of the vessel whatsoever.[4]

With the air-pump out of commission they couldn't clean the condenser, which had become choked. The next orders given were to try the engine on high pressure. To do this they had to take the plate off the main exhaust pipe of the large engines. Engineer Auchinleck went on deck, detached a pipe from the donkey-boiler, and he and the other engineers made a joint as well as they could with blankets, inserting the detached pipe into the exhaust pipe so as to create a draft. They raised steam and tried to turn the engines, but success eluded them. The steam rushed through the engine room. The large pipe being gone, however, they could not generate enough steam to get a high pressure.[5]

---

3. *New York Tribune*, Jan. 23, 1854; "Engineer."
4. Marshall, Jan. 16, 1854; Wickham; Mellus account; Mellus testimony; Gretton; Wirtz account; Auchinleck; "Justice;" "Engineer;" Winder, Jan. 6, 1854; Franklin Institute; *New York Tribune*, Jan. 23, 1854; *New York Herald*, July 5, 1853. Auchinleck and Fred Southworth were both under the impression that the air-pump gave out at 4 a.m. James Lorimer Graham and Lieutenant W.A. Winder both thought it was around midnight. "Justice" later wrote that it was between midnight and 2 a.m. But the ship's log was right; it was at 1:15.
5. Auchinleck; "Justice."

The commodore, his officers and engineers decided to keep this disastrous state of things from the passengers for as long as they could. Not even the regimental officers were aware of what had happened. Everyone just assumed the vessel was going on her course. The only persons, except those engaged in the working of the ship, who knew of the breaking of the engine, were Lieutenant Murray, of the Navy, and Mr. Aspinwall, brother of the owner. The ship's problems had to be handled by the crew, and so Commodore Watkins didn't call upon Colonel Gates or any other army officer for help, not at this stage of the game anyway.[6]

Once the engines had stopped, the vessel lost her steerage way, and broached to a third time. If those in the know suspected that they had become mere playthings of the sea gods, then they had occasion not long afterwards to see that suspicion turn into hard fact when the spanker blew away, and the rudder-chain broke. Now they were truly in a desperate position.[7]

Engineer Marshall immediately set to work to rig up an exhaust-pipe by taking the pipe from the small boiler. But it didn't take long to figure out that this wouldn't work, given that the main steam pipes were broken and the blower belts wet by the sea that swept the deck.[8]

Although neither Captain Linnell of the clipper *Eagle Wing* nor Commodore Watkins of the steamer *San Francisco* were aware of it at the time, they were in close proximity to each other in the violent sea, both under dire threat from the same perfect hurricane. As Captain Linnell wrote in his log-book, "In my thirty-one years' experience at sea, I have never seen a typhoon or hurricane so severe."[9]

Shaken and wet through, but determined to get below, Dr. Buel went first into the storage room, but as they began battening down the hatch, with perhaps 100 soldiers in it, he left, and went to the second cabin, occupied by the non-commissioned officers and their families. After waiting here for two hours, and with the gale unabated, he crept into one of the soldiers' berths, pulled a blanket over himself, and after a while fell asleep.[10]

At three o'clock that dark and cold morning, Mrs. Sarah Loeser called to her sister, Lucia Eaton, from the state room in the lower cabin, and in a hopeless voice, said, "One of the masts have been carried away." Lieutenant Loeser told his sister-in-law that it would be better if she remained in her berth, as she would then be quiet. Not long afterwards, he came back to her room and asked her to get up and

---

6. Fremont; Wirtz account.
7. Mellus account; Wickham; Winder, Jan. 6, 1854; Winder, Jan. 13, 1854; Wyse account; Eaton; Brown account. Winder, copying inaccurately from the ship's log, confused nautical terms and has the foremast being carried away at this time. The foremast would not suffer that fate until a few hours later, at 7 a.m. Winder repeated this error in his interview with the *New York Tribune* reporter on Jan. 13, 1854. Major Wyse uses the same expression used by most of the others—regardless of the time they claim for the disaster—"at the mercy of the wind and waves," a turn of phrase first used in this story by Mr. Mellus in the ship's log.
8. Marshall, Jan. 16, 1854.
9. Maury.
10. Buel, 1854; Buel, 1872.

come into his room. Just as Miss Eaton was getting out of her berth, a huge wave swept the side of the ship with such force that a large bible was thrown from a shelf onto her bed, at her feet. She and her servant followed Lieutenant Loeser, but just as Lucia was leaving her room, the servant handed her a dressing gown and a thick, corded skirt. Lucia put them on over her night dress, but she couldn't find her shoes and stockings. The storm was increasing every moment and the ship was rolling freely. She couldn't keep her feet and had to sit on the floor, so Lieutenant Loeser picked her up and carried her into Sarah's room, where she and the servant threw themselves on the floor. "I was then very sick, so much so that I could not support myself." Loeser's pessimism didn't help. Nothing could be done to save the ship now, he told Lucia, and only the Almighty could intercede on their behalf. All this time, over the howling of the wind and the roar of the waves, they could hear droning in the background. It was the preacher, Mr. Cooper, in the cabin, pleading with that very same Almighty to have mercy on them, to spare them from such a fearful death.[11]

After the spanker blew away, the ship labored even more heavily than before, unmanageable in the trough of the sea, and rolling both sides under, with every giant wave sweeping over her, striking tremendous blows under the guards, the rabid ocean ripping up the planking fore and aft on both sides of the ship, and carrying away the houses on both fore guards. Because the deck planks ran over the hull of the ship onto the guards some of them broke off inside, leaving the timber heads bare and letting sea water down in great quantities. At the same time the fantastic volume of water tore away the railing on the upper deck, the hencoops, hay-boxes, barrels, and so forth, all being swept away into the sea in a confused mass.[12]

With such a huge volume of seawater coming into the ship, the crew was ordered to man the hand pumps on deck. The two Worthington steam pumps were fixed to the side bulkhead under the lower deck, and were connected to a small boiler on the spar deck, so that they might be worked when the large boilers were not fired up. Both of these pumps were started and kept running. But under such conditions as these, it was no longer possible for the officers and crew to manage the ship unaided, and, as there were a number of soldiers aft in the cabin, Mr. Sanford, the head steward, turned them out to go forward and help the crew work the pumps. All the other soldiers were organized into three separate bailing gangs, 40 or 50 men working at one time, each gang forming a line to pass the water up through the engine-room in fire buckets, and then hoist it up to the deck using the ash buckets. Major Wyse went to Colonel Gates and asked to be given complete authority to order officers into the engine room, to superintend the bailing parties. Not all the officers wanted to do it, but it had to be done. "Very well, do it," said Gates. But, despite the fact that the steam pumps would keep the ship relatively free of water for the next several hours, still the yawning sea threatened everyone with a watery grave. The whole exercise appeared to be a losing proposition, but in spite of any negative feelings the men

---

11. Eaton; Mrs. Gates.
12. Mellus account; Wickham; Gretton.

might have had, every nerve was stretched in the attempt to get three feet of sloshing water out of the hull, and keep it out. The word was given to lighten ship, and part of the crew was taken from the pumps to handle this new chore. The passengers joined in, and, with a will, they all began to throw overboard everything they could find.[13]

The ship was being lightened, all right, but in ways more sinister than just tossing stuff overboard. Right from the first panic on board, while nearly everyone was going through their first hour in hell, the robbers were at it. Theft was the order of the day, "to an extent almost unparalleled in fiendish atrocity." Crewmen, soldiers, camp women. Tongues lolling between greedy, drooling lips. Dull, plebeian eyes suddenly afire with the glow of jewelry as the lowest form of human scum ripped open trunk after trunk, a smirk and a leer and a wink passing between them now and again as they dimly recognized that for once they had gained the upper hand over their superiors, and that, on their return to New York a veritable host of bent pawnbrokers would be just waiting there to receive them with open arms. The streets would be paved with gold—that is, if they got back. And if they didn't, if they were to sink with the ship out here in the middle of the ocean, then they would die rich. In the meantime, their pockets stuffed full of stolen goods, and their oh, so damaged hands covered with rags to hide the rings on every finger, they acted the hero, contributing to the general welfare by slinging the trunks over the side into the ocean. Good work, boys. keep it up. "Even the dead were set upon and robbed as if by so many wolves."[14]

Bill Winder relieved Lieutenant Chandler at the engine every two hours, and while he wasn't doing that he was supervising the lightening of the ship from the after-hold. "I was on duty about twelve hours out of the twenty-four for the first three or four days; the duty was bailing water from the engine room, lightening the ship, and gathering the men for fresh details for work."[15]

For the next few hours, until daylight arrived, things went along about the same, the ship laboring very heavy and the sea tearing her guards. The water was still coming in to the state rooms through the port-holes and from the upper decks. Those not bailing were employed in clearing the wreck of all stock and provisions. The ship's officers got the crew together, cleared away the standees that had been thrown all over the place, and stowed them forward. This left the enlisted men without shelter, and with many of them crying with the cold. The officer of the day, Colonel Martin Burke of Company I, took into the upper saloon as many of these poor fellows as could find standing room—about 80, as it turned out. As Surgeon Wirtz was to say later, with bitter irony, "This humane act subsequently proved the doom of the whole party."[16]

---

13. Wickham; Mellus account; Gretton; Eaton; Gretton; Marshall, Jan. 14, 1854; Marshall, Jan. 16, 1854; Gardiner; Wyse testimony; Gates testimony; Winder, Jan. 6, 1854; Franklin Institute; *New York Herald*, July 5, 1853.
14. *Presbyterian Magazine*; Mrs. Gates; *New York Tribune*, Jan. 16, 1854, which got the "fiendish atrocity" quote from one of the officers who had been aboard the *San Francisco*.
15. Winder testimony; Winder, 1883.
16. Gretton; Fremont; Southworth; Graham; Mellus account; Wickham; Wirtz account.

The first ray of dawn awoke Dr. Buel in the soldier's berth. Getting up, he went through the store-room and pantry and succeeded in gaining the main saloon.[17]

Bill Winder was officer of the guard that morning, and very sick, as he had been since the day he left New York. At daylight, Major George Taylor came up to him, and said, "You have been up all night; go and turn in; I will keep the balance of the watch." Upon reaching the upper deck, Winder found that water was gushing freely into his state room, and so he and a few others who were quartered there decided they had better leave. They made their way out into the upper saloon, where the first thing they saw was four or five waiters holding the doors to prevent their being burst open by the wind. From there, Winder and his party went down the staircase to the lower cabin, where, on the floor, they found a group of women huddled together on mattresses near the foot of the steps, to keep themselves out of the water, which had driven them out of their rooms and was now washing about the cabin. Winder lay down on one of the mattresses and held onto the bannisters to keep himself from being dashed about the cabin. He soon fell asleep. "How long I remained so I cannot tell; but I think it was not long."[18]

At 7 a.m., with daylight about to arrive, and as they were busy bailing and lightening the ship, four of the lifeboats crashed into the ocean, and the spars were wrecked. At the same time a "tremendous crash awoke the hundreds of fatigued men from their morning sleep." It was the huge wooden foremast snapping off at a height of about six feet from the deck, toppling over like a huge tree onto the hurricane deck and crushing it, splintering to the berth deck, and then thundering over the side of the ship, with everything attached to it, canvas and all, going as well. This all happened almost over Dr. Buel's head. "The longest night must have an end. Daylight dawned again upon the awful scene."[19]

"To those who rushed, at that moment, from their state rooms, the disabled condition of the ship was revealed for the first time, and dismay began to appear in their countenances."[20]

After the foremast had been blown away, they went on clearing the deck forward, which had become completely blocked up with the planks and houses from the guards, as well as barrels of provisions and about 500 boxes and trunks belonging to the troops. To make it worse, the partition dividing the soldiers from the pens housing the pigs, sheep, and cattle was smashed through by the waves, and very soon there

---

17. Buel, 1854.
18. Winder, 1883; Winder interview, 1854; Winder, Jan. 13, 1854; Winder testimony; *New York Tribune*, Jan. 14, 1854.
19. Mellus account; Mellus testimony; Wickham; Gretton; Marshall, Jan. 14, 1854; Partridge; Southworth; Buel, 1854; Buel, 1872; Watkins; Wirtz account. The quotes are from Wirtz and Buel respectively. Southworth has the foremast breaking at midnight, and Buel, in 1854, has it coming down about 1 o'clock. Watkins, writing after he got to Liverpool, has the loss of the boats, spars, and foremast at 5 a.m. All are wrong. It was 7 o'clock that morning. All of the *San Francisco*'s boats had been stowed inside, on the spar deck beneath the hurricane deck (*Daily National Intelligencer*, Jan. 9, 1854).
20. "To those who rushed..." Wirtz account.

was a confused mass of men and animals, so much so that Sergeant Elijah Brown and his men were forced to slaughter some of the livestock.[21]

Lieutenant Murray and several other officers were grouped around the hatches for some time, watching the clearing of the wreck, and speculating upon the inevitable consequences of their mishap if the gale were to hold on. The sea was, at the time, like "a boiling cauldron, and our once superb steamer was in a pitiable plight—battered, dismantled, and helpless." Forward everything was in confusion. "The poor soldiers, bruised, drenched and exhausted, excited our warmest sympathy."[22]

Captain Watkins went down into the engine room, where it was still dark. The engineers asked him why he didn't put up the topsail, only to be told that the foremast was gone, and the wheelhouse too. First Engineer Alex Auchinleck looked at the skipper and said, "And we are gone too, are we not?"

"No," replied Watkins, "No. Cheer up! Cheer up!"

That was typical of James Watkins. He would go around to his crew and his passengers, give them cheer, talk to them of other things to take their mind off it.[23]

Surgeon Wirtz left his own berth above at about 8:30, and went down "into the lower cabin to see how some of my friends were faring there. Everyone was endeavoring to cheer the rest." Some said there was no pressing danger, while others were telling each other that they were in a noble ship, and should live it out, after all.[24]

The upper saloon was crowded, especially with the enlisted men having been moved in there out of the cold. The forward deck cabin and state-rooms were filled with soldiers, accompanied by their wives and families. Now, there were about 150 in the saloon, all told, "despair depicted on the countenance of all."[25]

At about nine o'clock, and in coordinates 39°N, 70° W, the vessel was rolling helplessly in the trough of the sea, surrounded on all sides by mountains of raging green water threatening to engulf her at any moment. Oddly, in spite of all this, and even though it was cold, the sky was brilliantly clear, just as if it were a summer's day. As Surgeon Wirtz put it: "Notwithstanding the forlorn prospect before us, we could not help admiring the splendors of the morning sun, which, disclosing its glorious disc from time to time between the broken masses of cloud overhead, inspired us with fresh hope and courage." Or, as James Lorimer Graham reported: "As we stood there upon the deck in one of the highest seas I have ever witnessed, and the wind howling around us to agitate the waters, the sun arose suddenly in all his glory, throwing its rays of brightness and of hope athwart the vast space around us, and saw itself reflected in each wave which rose foaming and brilliant into sight."[26]

---

21. Gretton; Brown account; Buel, 1854; Buel, 1872. The livestock episode as told by Buel is so like that of Sergeant Brown that it is obvious that he copied it. However, Buel places it on December 22, whereas Brown, almost certainly more correctly, places it on the 23rd.
22. Wirtz account.
23. Auchinleck.
24. Wirtz account.
25. Southworth; Winder, Jan. 6, 1854. The quote is from Winder.
26. Maury; Wirtz account; Graham/Kilby. One reads, in the *New York Times* of Jan. 17, 1854, that the steamer was wrecked in 40° 12' N, 59° 30' W.

With the exception of Mr. Auchinleck, who was in the baker's house trying without success to open a stop valve, the engineer's people were below, getting up an exhaust pipe to try to get the engines started under high pressure. Captain Watkins and his officers and crew were forward on the main deck, busily clearing away the wreck. Lieutenant Van Voast was in the lower after cabin.[27]

Then suddenly the Devil himself came roaring out of the ocean with such dazzling speed and awesome power that, within mere seconds, with no negotiation whatsoever, the game was over for the *San Francisco*.

The wave came in so fast, no one on board could possibly have prepared for it, and it was so big it wouldn't have mattered if they had. It was the most starkly brutal reminder to even the most optimistic shipbuilder that in a fight with a raging sea, man and his artifacts stand as much chance as an Episcopalian clergyman's prayer.[28]

The inundation was so gigantic that it felt like two monstrous seas, and that is really what it was—the culmination of several great waves, one after the other in rapid succession. The first blow hit the steamer's stern and midships at the same time, like a boxer using the old one-two, sweeping everything before it, and then, immediately, came the next fantastic punch, which swept the decks entirely.[29]

The two vast waves smashed in the hurricane deck abaft of the paddle wheels and swept it half over the side of the ship, while the other half crashed onto the cabin floor of the spar deck beneath, staving in about 50 feet of that deck around the upper saloon aft. The saloon was literally ripped off its foundations and its 24 state rooms, 12 per row, were immediately washed overboard, along with all the people in them. The rest of the saloon plunged down through the huge hole that had been created on the spar deck, crashing onto the lower saloon on the main deck below. The guards were broken up and swept off the side of the ship, as was the enlisted men's sleeping place on deck. The starboard wheelhouse with its after kingpost were lost, as were both huge smoke stacks, while the main deck hatch was stove in, as well as half the quarter-deck. The chicken coops were dashed into the sea, parts of the galleys were destroyed, two men being killed in the crash, and books, records, the regimental colors, arms, accouterments, baggage, and the entire personal property of all, disappeared into eternity. And boding tremendously ill for the future was the fact that

---

27. Watkins letter; Wirtz account; Buel, 1854; Mellus testimony; Gretton; Marshall, Jan. 14, 1854; Eaton; Auchinleck; Charles S. Winder; Southworth; Winder, Jan. 6, 1854; Winder interview, 1854; Van Voast; Graham.

28. Buel, 1854; Mellus testimony; Gretton; Marshall, Jan. 14, 1854; Eaton; Charles S. Winder; Southworth; Winder, Jan. 6, 1854; Winder interview, 1854; Watkins letter. There can be no doubt as to the time of morning that this catastrophe occurred, as the flow of the story demands 9 o'clock. Mellus, Wickham, and Gretton all say 9 o'clock, as does Marshall in both his accounts. There was a difference of opinion, however, but that was largely due to bad recollection and some witnesses listening to others. Commodore Watkins and Lt. Charles S. Winder both say 7 o'clock, which is hardly surprising given that the two men spent quite a bit of time together after the wreck. Fred Southworth and James Lorimer Graham believed it to have been 8 o'clock, as did Lieutenant William A. Winder in both his account and interview.

29. Buel, 1854; Brown account; Marshall, Jan. 14, 1854.

those that remained of the steamer's lifeboats, all stacked on the spar deck, were lost soon thereafter to the desperate ocean.[30]

It was not just articles that were carried away; screaming men and women, some walking about on deck, but most of them in the upper saloon when that structure was ripped away, went overboard in a grim admixture of flailing limbs, cattle bellowing with sheer terror as they fell directly on top of the passengers floating for their lives in the foaming sea below.[31]

The number of souls washed overboard could only be computed when a roll call was taken later. However, the figure that emerged when the survivors of the wreck started to get back to civilization, was 150.[32]

Four Artillery officers were in the upper saloon at the time of the cataclysmic wave. Colonel Washington was asleep in his state room. If he ever woke up before he spiraled down the eternal vortex to Davy Jones's Locker, it is not recorded, nor will it ever be known whether Captain Field was awake, asleep, or enjoying the effects of opium. Major George Taylor and his wife were swept out of the saloon to the edge of the ship. Assuming that they were going down anyway, they jumped overboard together, hand in hand, and were last glimpsed in the raging waters, with life preservers around them. He sank first, but she was seen buffeting the waves for a full five minutes before she too went under. Lieutenant Richard Smith's wife had remained at home in delicate health, and it was just as well she did, otherwise she would have suffered her husband's fate. Colonel Gates's first wife, Sarah Reed, had died of heart disease in Savannah 10 years earlier. One of the children from that marriage, Charles Gates, now 21, was in his state room. He was never seen again. In a single, dazzling moment, young Ned Tenney's relationship with Lizzie Andrews was brought to an end. Rebecca Jane Slater Belton, daughter of the late Captain Belton of the British Army, was traveling alone. She would never travel again. Two other citizen passengers who were swept overboard were Howard M. Cole and his new wife, the former Louise

---

30. Buel, 1854; Brown account; Graham; Marshall, Jan. 14, 1854; Gates; Marshall, Jan. 16, 1854; Gretton; Mellus account; Charles S. Winder; Wickham; Winder interview, 1854; Watkins letter; Wirtz account; Eaton. Commodore Watkins, Mr. Wickham and Mr. Gretton all say that the whole of the upper saloon was washed away, but they were only copying what Mr. Mellus had written in the ship's log. James Lorimer Graham says that the wave carried away "the entire main saloon." It was really only the upper saloon aft.

31. Buel, 1854; Brown account; Marshall, Jan. 14, 1854; Marshall, Jan. 16, 1854; Southworth; Watkins letter; Eaton; Brown account.

32. Buel, 1854; Buel, 1872; Gretton; Marshall, Jan. 14, 1854; Marshall, Jan. 16, 1854; Watkins letter; Wirtz account; Winder, Jan. 6, 1854; Mellus account; Wickham. First Officer Mellus simply says "a large number of soldiers," whereas Mr. Wickham, the ship's storekeeper, and Mr. Gretton, the ship's second officer, both say "about 150 privates." Bill Winder says: "about 150 people," and Commodore Watkins has "about 150 souls," but when writing from the ship *Antarctic*, in Liverpool, a few weeks after the wreck, the commodore is more specific, listing 142: The four officers, Mrs. George Taylor, Colonel Gates's son, Ned Tenney, 130 soldiers, four crew, and an unknown gentleman. Dr. Buel estimated that the great wave "carried into eternity, at one fell swoop, one hundred and fifty human beings, officers and soldiers of the Third Artillery, besides two or three ladies," while Lucia Eaton, using Buel's account, claims: "One hundred and forty beings were launched into eternity. Many I fear were unprepared to meet their Maker." According to Mr. Marshall, the chief engineer, "more than one hundred souls" were washed overboard. Matthew Fontaine Maury, in his book *Physical Geography of the Sea*, says, "by one single blow...one hundred and seventy-nine souls, officers and soldiers, were washed overboard and drowned."

Torbert, both of Philadelphia. Mr. Cole had once been a soldier himself, having fought in the Mexican War as a corporal with the First Pennsylvania Infantry. On April 15 of that very year, 1853, the Coles had had a daughter, Nina Barbara, but they had left her behind in Philadelphia, in the care of a relative. She would not become aware of it for some years to come, but just after nine o'clock in the morning of Christmas Eve, 1853, she became an orphan.[33]

Others from different parts of the ship were also swept overboard. Mr. Gretton tells us that two or three soldiers' wives were killed in this way. Three of the crew were killed by the crash of the enormous wave: Brooks, one of the negro waiters; the negro barber; and Franklin Duckett, the white steerage waiter.[34]

Actually, only 83 were washed overboard that morning, not 150 or 142. One thing is reasonably sure—56 soldiers were killed, one from Company D, six from Company G, seven from Company H, 28 from Company K, and 14 from Company B.[35]

And there were those who were not drowned, but killed by falling wreckage. Surgeon Wirtz saw "two or three crushed bodies near me, covered with blood which stained the broken planks and even dripped to the steps and through the seams of the lower cabin." Dr. Buel says: "Two or three dead or dying soldiers, killed by the crash of falling timbers, lay on the deck." And Catherine Livingston, the stewardess, tells us that one of the soldiers had been going up some stairs right in front of her when he was killed outright.[36]

The sky, which only seconds earlier had been so glorious, was now black with clouds, and the rain poured in torrents, and in all directions vision was limited by roaring billows, white with froth and foam.[37]

Of course all the survivors would ultimately have their stories to tell, where they were and what they were doing when the awful wave came, but the modern-day reader has to approach these accounts with some caution. Most of these reminiscences were published by the leading New York City newspapers in January 1854, in the days immediately following the return to civilization, when the memory was fresh. Or rather "relatively fresh." Three weeks had passed since that nightmare morning of Christmas Eve, and in that time, with people incessantly discussing and re-hashing it among themselves, recollections had tended to become intertwined, to form what might be considered, to some extent, a memory in common. This phenomenon was

---

33. Watkins letter; Brown account; Mellus account; Wickham; Winder, Jan. 6, 1854; Mrs. Gates; Eaton; Loeser; Graham; obituary, *New York Herald*, Jan. 21, 1854; Marshall, Jan. 14, 1854. After the horrendous day was over, the only thing Lieutenant Bill Winder managed to save from the wreck was a sword and a case of revolvers. The sword, battered and bruised, had been the companion of Colonel Washington through many years. The sword made it. Colonel Washington didn't. (*New York Tribune*, Jan. 16, 1854).
34. Gretton; Mellus account; Wickham. Wickham calls the waiter Brooks, whereas Mellus, in the log, calls him Brooke. There is probably no way, at this remove, to tell which spelling is correct. As for the barber, we do not know his name.
35. Army enlistment records.
36. Wirtz account; Buel, 1854; Livingston.
37. Marshall, Jan. 14, 1854.

much more in evidence in those who had access to Mr. Mellus's log book. Other individual articles would trickle out, in one form or another, over the years, some by men and women who had written of the adventure previously. Sometimes these latter-day accounts are inconsistent, which is hardly surprising, given the passing of the years, while others, in true nineteenth-century spirit, clearly borrow some of their "facts" from articles previously published by others.

For the two hours before the giant wave hit, Bill Winder had been asleep on a soggy mattress in the cabin of the lower saloon on the main deck, surrounded by women. Suddenly he was awakened by a tremendous crash and the next second a huge "deluge of water," together with the debris of the upper saloon from the spar deck above, came flooding down the companionway and landed right on his head and chest, sweeping him twice across the cabin and back again with terrible force and stunning violence. He had never experienced anything like it. "The dreadful screams of the ladies, drowned in the rush of water." After three desperate attempts, and with great effort, he succeeded in regaining his feet. He supposed that the ship had broken in half, and that they were fast sinking. Sitting within a few feet of Winder on the bottom steps of the cabin was Franklin Duckett, the steerage steward, brother of the ship's carpenter. "The next moment he was a corpse," decapitated and crushed by the falling-in of the upper cabin. Young Duckett was only 17. At the head of the stairs, with one leg hanging over, was a dead soldier, "his head mashed into jelly." Then Winder saw some people climbing up the steps, and so, crawling over one of the two bodies, he followed them up onto the deck.[38]

Surgeon Wirtz, in an account that sounds like a paraphrasing of Bill Winder, says: "There came an awful crash on the upper deck that seemed to bear the whole vessel down bodily into the deep." He then uses Winder's "deluge of water," but adds that it brought with it splinters of broken timber upon them. "We heard a dreadful shriek of many voices, and every soul among us, in that instant, probably, felt the pang of death, since no one could imagine anything else than that the ship was already deep in the ocean." A minute or two, however, restored them sufficiently to enable certain individuals to reach the upper deck, where the horror of the accident burst upon them. "As I crawled to the hatch, I beheld the open sea where a moment before there had been a cabin crowded with human beings. A glance told me all." After he had taken in his surroundings, Wirtz's "eye caught the crests of the billows to leeward, the bleeding heads of my late room-mates dipping and rising through the foam, as they struggled in their last agony."[39]

Dr. Buel was able, for the first time, to reach the main saloon aft, but a moment before he entered it, just as he was passing between the second and after cabin, "a terrible wave broke over the hapless vessel's starboard quarter." Buel was just in time to witness the fearful spectacle, "the sea for a moment all around covered with human bodies, like black specks upon the water. It was but for a moment, when they disap-

---

38. Winder interview, 1854; Winder, 1883; Winder, Jan. 6, 1854. Winder, 1883.
39. Wirtz account.

peared and sank to rise no more till the sea gives up her dead." The saloon in which all the ladies and children were huddled together, all in their night clothes and drenched to the skin, was knee deep with water. "All faces gathered paleness. Some wailed and shrieked. Some sat in mute despair. All supposed their last hour had come, and that in a few minutes they would meet their Maker."[40]

Fred Southworth, the citizen passenger with the inventive mind and the dubious past, was lying in his stateroom in the upper saloon, with a traveling companion, James Stockwell, "when there came a shock and a sudden crash of breaking timber," and he felt himself rolling like a top in the water, with salt brine washing into his mouth and almost blinding him. "When I arose to the surface of the ocean, a harrowing sight was before me." He found himself a half mile from the steamer, and surrounded by about an acre of floating timber. He could make out some 40 people struggling for their lives in the sea, perhaps half of them with blood streaming from head wounds. Fred put his hand to his head to wipe the salt water from his eyes, and found it was not water at all, but blood from a wound on his brow. He was clinging to a floating timber when up came Stockwell from the deep and latched onto the same piece of timber. Fred grabbed a hold of another piece and made his way the best he could toward the ship. "Two or three huge swells soon tossed me near the ship, and I grasped a rope forward of the wheelhouse, to which I clung for refuge, raising and falling with the pitching vessel." It was while he was in this parlous situation that he saw a man standing on the paddle of the wheel. This man was plunged into the ocean at every roll of the steamer, and "probably perished." Losing his strength, Fred dropped from the rope to which he was clinging, and fortunately a friendly wave threw him against the guard of the vessel. He seized hold of the guard, and the next plunge carried him still higher on the guard. At last he was able to crawl onto the upper deck, and there, with his hand, broke open the window of a state room that had managed to remain in place, and crept into it half-drowned. Mr. Stockwell never made it.[41]

Mr. Southworth claims that, among those washed away, he and William G. Rankin were "the only two of this entire company who were successful in regaining the ship. All the rest sunk into the jaws of death." Lucia Eaton appears to confirm Fred Southworth's story, but in actual fact she only learned about it upon reading the newspapers. It was too good an item for her to omit from her narrative, which was written six months after the event: "Mr. Rankin and Southworth were washed back upon deck three times, the last time so far that they succeeded in getting hold of some part of the deck and were saved. Their escape was truly miraculous. Mr. Rankin was put into one of the berths, and for some time he appeared like one dead." Just because Miss Eaton cheated, that doesn't mean to say the incident never happened. Bill Winder mentions it too.[42]

---

40. Buel, 1854; Buel, 1872.
41. Southworth. James Stockwell's name is also given as D.C. Stockwell.
42. Southworth; Eaton; Winder, Jan. 6, 1854.

However, it appears that the sea gods may have spared other mortals besides just the inventor and the regiment's sutler. The women had been hurried down below into the second cabin, and First Sergeant Elijah R. Brown, of Company G, afraid that they might get out and be washed over into the raging seas, had locked their door. Brown was then ordered to cut away the forward hurricane deck, but the gale was so fierce he and his men were forced to lash themselves to the guard lines while hacking away at the debris. It was then that the monstrous wave struck the ship, and the sergeant was thrown over the side of the steamer into the ocean, striking the side of the vessel as he went, but being prevented from drowning by the lashing line. He then went forward and was swept overboard, not once but three times, and on one of these occasions was "as much as twenty feet from the vessel." He later claimed that he "jumped in after a daguerreotype portrait which I had lost out of my pocket." Brown says that there "were several [persons] in the water, and three besides myself were saved by the waves throwing us back."[43]

Mrs. Gates was in her berth on the main deck, with her infant and the nurse. Her husband had only just gone out on deck when suddenly he saw a mountain of water coming at him with tremendous speed. He rushed below and was standing in the state room when the monster struck the ship, "sweeping off the saloon and crushing in the deck over our heads." The Gateses rushed out into the cabin with the children as fast as they could, clambering over chairs and tables, everything in confusion. The Colonel peremptorily ordered everyone in the cabin to come with him aft, and they did; other people seeing this, followed, rats deserting a sinking ship, but with nowhere to go, and no one to lead them except a pied piper who had no idea what to do or where he was going. When they reached the afterpart of the steamer, the hatch was open, and Major Merchant, having brought his family there, fell through the hole into the hold. It was a long drop, and he landed on his chest. When they picked him up, he was "more dead than living." Indeed, he himself thought his time had come, and was calling for his wife and daughters. Soon after this the steward passed by, and Mrs. Gates asked him what they could do. "Nothing," he replied, "We can trust only in God." As Major Merchant was carried off to his cabin, blood oozing from his lungs, and his daughters shrieking that their father was dead, Colonel Gates, having come down below to see to him, was thrown violently against a rocking chair, "which created a severe wound in his eye." Then he was struck in his other eye. Colonel Gates's two black eyes and the bruise on the side of his face would remain a startling feature of his physiognomy for some weeks afterwards.[44]

Aft was now filling up, and everyone was looking for a place where they could lie down. They were all in their night clothing, saturated with water and freezing with cold. Each wave dashed more water upon them. "Oh, God!" was frequently heard as each new wave hit them. Some were praying, the children were screaming lustily, and the camp women were shrieking a great deal. On the other hand, the

---

43. Brown account.
44. Mrs. Gates; Satterlee testimony; Fremont; Eaton. The quotes are from Mrs. Gates.

ladies were almost universally calm, clinging speechless to each other and the little ones. That's why they were called ladies, rather than women. Everyone would remain that way throughout the day, and finally the steward came down with news from the skipper that the hull was sound, and that they would probably all be saved. This quieted them down.[45]

While Miss Eaton and her group were lying in Sarah Loeser's berth in the lower cabin, and pouring out their hearts to their god in prayer, they heard a terrific crash which seemed to have separated the ship. It was that awful, Miss Eaton wrote. "A fearful wave had risen like a huge mountain and swept over the ill-fated steamship and carried everything before it in its wild embrace. That one wave swept the entire upper deck."[46]

Wasting no time, they went running into the main part of the saloon, where families were clinging to each other while water poured in from above. Miss Eaton quickly realized that if her family didn't get out of there very soon they would be trapped in the ever-rising water, and it wouldn't be long before they drowned. The deck was their only hope. They had to get out on to the upper deck. Calling out to anyone nearby to help them grope their way through the three feet of bilge that was swirling madly over the saloon floor, they finally ran into Lieutenant Fremont, who led them to the foot of the staircase. "The water was pouring down in torrents from above, and we were completely drenched in a few moments."[47]

But when they got to the stairs they found they were filled with not only all sorts of rubbish but also masses of wretched-looking beings desperately embarked on the same mission—to get to the freedom of the deck—their faces expressing the greatest agony. They could only reach the top when a roll of the ship threw them off their footing, and then men, women, children, bilge, and garbage would all would collapse in a heap together. They then had to struggle to get on their feet again, as there was great danger of being trodden upon or crushed. It was all panic, everyone trying to save themselves. At last they succeeded in gaining the top stair and the deck. They then went through a doorway and found their way into the galley, where the soldiers immediately gave them some blankets. They seated themselves in a corner of this little place and clasping their arms around each other prepared to meet their sad fate. The water was rushing over them constantly, each wave making a sweep directly into the galley then taking out some article off into the sea. The boards on the upper part of the ship were breaking away very rapidly. "We could hear a fearful crash and soon would learn that another part of the ill-fated steamship had fallen into the yawning abyss."[48]

The first intimation Engineer Auchinleck had of the sea striking them was the "noise of the cracking timbers over my head. The guard was swept away by it, and I saw people floating in the sea who were washed overboard. I had the presence of

---

45. Mrs. Gates.
46. Eaton; Graham.
47. Eaton; Graham.
48. Eaton.

mind to step back under shelter and cling to the posts, which saved me from being swept off also."[49]

The *San Francisco*'s professional stewardess, Mrs. Livingston, was climbing the stairs a foot or two behind "a boy" when the crash came. The boy was killed, right in front of her, and she beat a hasty retreat down the steps. "My first impulse was to relieve the passengers from the ruins of the deck, which held many of them firmly to the floor, amid the most drenching flood of water."[50]

Mrs. Livingston's main mandate was the ladies, women and children, and among them she found many bruises, but no broken limbs. "But the fright and agony of the scene was terrible." As soon as she could, she got help, and collected the women and children aft, in the main saloon, and placed them on the mattresses, wrapped in blankets, so as to make them as comfortable as possible. The children began to manifest great hunger, having eaten nothing since the day before, and so the able stewardess busied herself getting some warm food and drink for them. While so doing, all the passengers, including the soldiers and their wives, rushed aft, and crowded the main saloon to suffocation. "The soldiers' wives I found particularly unmanageable. Many of them were fully conscious of their sudden widowhood, having just seen their husbands swept into the sea with the deck. The excited crowd of men who broke in upon our retreat made the situation of the women and children much less comfortable than I otherwise could have made them. But the poor fellows could not help it, in their consternation."[51]

Only a few months before, in August, two European immigrants in their early twenties, a boatman and a teamster, enlisted at Toledo. Joseph Mit, from Paris, and Anthony Fleck, from Baden, went into Company K together, and now, after four months and two days, the Frenchman lost his friend to the big wave. Private Mit was on the upper deck when the hurricane deck collapsed on him. His head went through a skylight in such a way that he was only slightly injured, except that a splinter of the wood ran into his cheek and they couldn't get it out. The wound healed up in time but Monsieur Mit was still carrying that splinter around three weeks later.[52]

Lieutenant Colonel Martin Burke, was in the lower cabin when, without warning, a heavy brass railing came crashing through the skylight of the upper deck and landed on him, crushing his hand and severely injuring his back. He collapsed to the floor and just lay there, without a murmur, staring up at the hole in the ceiling. He was alive, but he was definitely out of the game. Although it was the last thing on his mind at that moment, his active position as commanding officer of Company I had come to an abrupt end, and would soon be taken up by Brevet Second Lieutenant

---

49. Auchinleck.
50. Livingston.
51. Livingston.
52. Brown account; Southworth. Fred Southworth, talking about Captain Gardiner, mentions that the dragoon officer "at one time found a man by his side, with a splinter thrust through his head, which must have killed him instantaneously." This is Private Mit, of course, but Southworth errs when he supposes the Frenchman died.

J.G. Chandler who, although he could have no way of knowing it, was, just at that very minute, back in Washington, being given an early Christmas present—promotion to substantive second lieutenant.[53]

James Lorimer Graham's friend, Gardiner of the Dragoons, was asleep in his state room in the upper cabin on the spar deck when the great wave hit the steamer. No sooner had his manservant entered the room to tell him that they were in great danger than the hurricane deck fell in on them from above. The captain was hit on the head and then swept out onto the deck. The servant was not so fortunate, and was dashed overboard, never to be seen again. Gardiner, the only man on that deck who survived, was lying there completely covered by the debris from the hurricane deck. Still stunned by the blow he had received, and suffering from rheumatism, he finally made his way to the lower cabin, the only safe place.[54]

"A man was lashed to the helm, as it was impossible to stand on deck, but in one of the rolls of the ship his leg was broken and he was taken down."[55]

Several, in the excitement of the moment, sprang overboard, and among those first to reach the upper deck there was a feeling that the ship was foundering, and that it would be useless to go below again. James Lorimer Graham believed this, and so he and the others remained many hours upon the deck, the sea covering them at every lurch, and the cold nor'wester chilling them all to the bone. About 100 people were clinging for their lives to spars, doors, and other fragments, but then the next huge wave carried some of them overboard.[56]

After the accident everyone was drenched with water. Women and children were taken to the after part of the cabin and rolled up in blankets as well as they could be by their husbands and fathers, servants in some instances having gone forward. And so they would remain for several days. No lady or child could walk in the cabin without the assistance of a gentleman.[57]

Dr. Buel "was one of the many who immediately gained the upper deck, supposing that the vessel was fast foundering; and under this supposition we clung together, some with life preservers, others with chairs, ready to precipitate ourselves at a moment's warning into the angry billows that ranged around us."[58]

On reaching the deck, Bill Winder surveyed a "scene of desolation." The entire upper cabin had been swept off and the main deck crushed in by that one terrible sea. In a desperate struggle to save themselves, men and women were clinging to the pieces of debris which were strewn about all over the deck, and the surface of the ocean looked like an immense mass of boiling water, covered with wreckage and human beings. "These last disappeared in a few moments," and Winder's "blood ran

---

53. Graham; Wyse testimony; Satterlee testimony.
54. Graham; Satterlee; Satterlee testimony; Gardiner; Southworth.
55. Eaton. Although this accident at the wheel did happen to the unfortunate seaman, it took place on this tragic Christmas Eve, rather than on Monday the 26th, the day given by Miss Eaton.
56. Graham.
57. From general court proceedings at the court of inquiry, Feb. 16, 1854.
58. Buel, 1854.

cold at the sight of some poor fellow struggling among the fragments in the sea." Not a sound was heard from the drowning men as they strove, with all the energy of despair, to save themselves. "There they were, 150 human beings, beyond the possibility of human succor, and soon the last one sank to rise no more." The waves were, "to my eyes, frightful—we could render no assistance whatever, and, in fact, expected ourselves that we should go down every minute. With great difficulty we clung to the deck, the sea making a perfect breach over us, and the cold so great that an hour longer must have finished us."[59]

While sitting there, drenched to the skin, and looking around hopelessly, waiting for the end to come, he saw Frank Murray of the United States Navy trying to make his way over toward him, but with the heavy sea washing over the deck, Murray could only get as far as the mizzen mast, which was the only thing left standing up there. It occurred to Winder that if there was any chance left, the naval lieutenant would know it, and so, plucking up nerve, he struggled aft and joined him. He asked Frank why he was standing there holding on to the mast, and Murray told him that sometimes steamers broke in two and one part might float. Winder found this so plausible that he stayed there with Murray, holding on to a rope. They talked over their chances for escape, and came to the conclusion that they couldn't survive 20 minutes, being ducked by each giant wave that breached over them at every roll of the ship. Fortunately, given that they were in the Gulf Stream, the water was quite warm, but when the ship rose and the cold late December wind blew upon their wet mass of clothing, their suffering was quite intense. Two negro stewards came along with life-preservers, but, assuming the vessel would go down any minute, and it being so cold, Winder and Murray figured it would only be prolonging their misery, and so they declined the offer. They remained together at the mizzen mast for perhaps two hours.[60]

At the very minute Dr. Buel and James Lorimer Graham made it up onto the upper deck, Mr. Mellus, the first officer, was bullying his way aft through the elements and the ruin of his ship toward the mizzen mast, axe in hand. Writhing and twisting like a young sapling and so posing a tremendous threat, the mast had to go, and it had to go now, in a controlled way. But Mellus was thwarted in his attempt. With the sea running so high, he couldn't maintain the necessary position, and so had to give up.[61]

The exposure was so benumbing that Winder and Murray began to cast around for shelter. Leaving the mizzen mast they managed to find their way across the deck, holding on to various parts of the wreck, and finally succeeded in getting toward the stern, where they fell in with Dr. Satterlee, Surgeon Wirtz, Lieutenants Chandler and Van Voast, and Major Wyse. Satterlee, the chief medical officer with the troops, who had left his family to go on this trip, was lying on the deck with only his night garment

---

59. Winder, Jan. 6, 1854; Winder interview, 1854; Winder, 1883.
60. Winder, Jan. 6, 1854; Winder interview, 1854; Winder, 1883.
61. Graham/Kilby; Winder, Jan. 6, 1854; Buel, 1854; Mellus account; Wickham.

upon him, and perfectly drenched with water, his limbs having been severely bruised when the main deck fell in. He was carried below. "Close by me was Maj. Wyse, his young wife and babe. It was truly a heart-rendering [sic] sight. The poor child must have been nearly frozen." They all looked out at the harrowing spectacle of what seemed to be a total wreck and were under the impression that the steamer was full of water which had settled down to the level of the deck. "The surface of the water for a large space around was covered with the debris of the upper works, and holding on to these, and struggling with the wreck of matter, were many men, I suppose 150, attempting to save themselves in the raging sea, by catching at the broken timbers." The wind was blowing a perfect hurricane, and it was with the utmost difficulty that they held on and prevented themselves from being blown overboard. Then Commodore Watkins came along, and the group asked him what their chances were. "If she does not sink before we can get some of the cargo over, so as to raise her out of the water, we may be saved."[62]

After the immediate panic was over, at about ten o'clock that morning, the people began to realize that the ship was not going down, and so all hands got to work at once, clearing decks by throwing unwanted stuff overboard. About an hour later, Sergeant Elijah Brown of Company G, fresh from having been washed back on board for the third time, took it upon himself, with no orders from the officers, to assemble a bunch of soldiers who were quartered in the neighborhood of the engine room. He formed two lines of these volunteers and they began bailing from below and up through the engine room, exerting themselves to their utmost, and some of them working until they dropped from sheer fatigue. Another gang of soldiers was set apart to hold blankets around the shafts to prevent the flowing in of water.[63]

At the worst time of all, and when they were shipping the most water, one of the corporals gave the alarm of fire, and all the inmates of the lower cabin who were employed in bailing, rushed simultaneously for the door, and put an end to work for a moment. Sergeant Elijah Brown sprang up onto a table, drew a revolver, and threatened to shoot any man who repeated the alarm. That quieted them and they went on with their work again.[64]

Two passengers remained upon deck for five hours after the accident, in the belief that nothing but the deck itself was left, and that it was floating at the mercy of the waves. One of these persons was brought downstairs with his hands and feet frozen, but owing to the kindness and prompt attention of Lieutenant Frank Murray and Surgeon Wirtz, the torpid circulation of his limbs was restored by stimulating applications.[65]

---

62. Winder, Jan. 6, 1854; Winder interview, 1854; Winder, 1883. Eaton. The quotes are from Winder.
63. Gretton; Brown account; Winder, 1883; Buel testimony; Fremont; Marshall, Jan. 16, 1854; Mellus account; Wickham.
64. Brown account. Lucia Eaton had read Sergeant Brown's account in the newspapers, and in her narrative reproduced the episode thus: "One of the hands attempted to set the ship on fire that Saturday night. He was put in irons."
65. Graham.

Many of the ladies unnecessarily exposed themselves to peril during the whole time, thus putting additional pressure on the men. One of the single ladies, Mariana Noland, while on the main deck in imminent danger of being swept away by the surf, came up to Sergeant Brown and his men while they were bailing, and asked if she could take a turn. Sergeant Brown declined the offer, and told her to go down to her berth. But she refused, and he was forced to carry her down below.[66]

The dying George Aspinwall, who had left New York to try to enjoy whatever health he had left, was in his cabin at the time of the great disaster. Hearing that the ship was leaking, he immediately went below, took off his jacket, and started bailing. For several hours he continued in this work, cheering the people on until finally his strength gave way and he was carried on a litter into the cabin where the ladies were assembled.[67]

Nearly all the sailors showed an unconquerable aversion to going near a dead body. For example, after the crash, young Franklin Duckett just lay there hour after hour, minus his head, and no one came near it. "The females on board evinced the utmost coolness and presence of mind throughout the whole of the time. Some of them would come up to me, and ask me whether we were in danger, and when I replied that there was great danger, but everything depended on our own exertions, they appeared perfectly satisfied, and returned to their quarters."[68]

Things were already happening in the engine room at a feverish pace. When the piston-rod broke, there had been no means of obtaining a vacuum, and so the driving engines stopped. An effort was made by the engineers to exhaust into the open air, by using for the purpose the smoke pipe of the small boiler, and so to continue working while trying to repair the broken rod, but because of the loss of the smoke stacks, and the fact that the blower belts were so low as to be covered by water, steam could not be maintained in the boilers to work the driving engines without condensing. It was also found that the small boiler had to be used for the steam pumps, and so the pipe could not be used for the purpose. Mr. Marshall, the chief engineer, gave orders to disconnect the head from the air-pump, to see what they could do about mending it. But there was another problem. The brass covering of that portion of the rod had cleaved off in the concussion and become irretrievably lost. Under those circumstances, its repair could be effected neither strongly nor snugly.[69]

Lieutenant Bill Winder was sitting with Frank Murray and the other officers up on the deck when they discovered that there were many persons in the lower cabin under them, principally officers' ladies. So he and a couple of other officers decided to go below to see what sort of refuge it would be. On their way they found that the

---

66. Brown account.
67. James Lorimer Graham tells us that while soldiers were grumbling about their rations, Mr. Aspinwall would chow down with the sailors without a murmur, taking whatever was doled out to him. He was that kind of man. Of course, he was also the brother of the *San Francisco*'s owner.
68. Brown account.
69. Auchinleck; *New York Tribune*, Jan. 23, 1854.

ship was not in such a bad condition as they had thought she was. In the after part of the cabin they did, indeed, find a number of ladies collected there, and also several officers and children, all in as dry a place as they could find. On coming back up on deck they induced Major Wyse to join them down there with his wife and child. "We then covered ourselves up with wet blankets, for we were nearly frozen," few of them having on anything but shirts and drawers. Here they would remain the greater part of that day, fully believing that the vessel would sink sometime during the evening.[70]

With great exertions, Commodore Watkins and his officers succeeded in stopping the worst leaks around the guards and at the end of the beam, as well as repairing the decks with old pieces of sails, and otherwise patching them up to try and save the ship. The decks were then temporarily repaired by planking and nailing sail and oil cloths over them. They kept reliefs of three or four men with mattresses at each end of the shaft to prevent the water coming in there, where it came in by the bucketful. They were cheered by the prospect of setting the machinery in working order, so that the vessel might get into port. A temporary steering apparatus was erected, and an attempt was made to get the ship underway, which, up to this time, had been at the mercy of the waves.[71]

Lucia Eaton and her family prepared to die. Huddled together in a corner of the galley, arms clasped around each other for fear that they might get separated, there they sat, up to their waists in freezing water, with faces ghastly pale and hair hanging in wild disorder. Lucia glanced around and saw that there were several soldiers, and two or three of the black waiters. The waiters seemed to be perfectly paralyzed, standing like statues, not even moving their lips. "There were also two or three women near us. They were shaking from fear, and the piercing wind was blowing upon them." There was a kind of cupboard just behind Miss Eaton, and she braced herself against it, feeling it would be a support if the boards were to give way on that side of the ship.[72]

Assuming the ship was about to go down, it "was useless to think of touching a life preserver as we did not wish to prolong our misery." She and her sister Sarah had prayed all their life, of course, but never more ardently than in the last few hours, and now they had resigned themselves to that magic moment when their Lord would take them home.[73]

But it was not their god who appeared, it was Captain Judd and his dyspeptic wife. The couple had managed to make their way into the galley, and Miss Eaton's party gave them one of their blankets. And so, wet through and with water running off them, and with sopping blankets around them, they prayed again. Lieutenant Loeser wrapped a blanket around Lucia's feet to prevent them from freezing. She had cut a huge place on one of her feet, but didn't realize it until two days later.[74]

---

70. Winder, Jan. 6, 1854; Winder interview, 1854.
71. Winder, Jan. 6, 1854; Winder interview, 1854.
72. Eaton.
73. Eaton. Lucia Eaton's quote about the life preservers is almost a direct copy from Bill Winder's Jan. 6, 1854, article published in the newspapers.
74. Eaton.

While they were crouching out their lives in such misery, Colonel Burke dragged himself up to them. But it was too much for the badly injured officer, and he fell back on the floor, deathly pale, blood streaming from his head and ears. "We were afraid he would be taken out by the waves, and had him placed near us." They gave him a blanket but could do nothing more to make him comfortable as, unable even to sit, he just lay there. "He was suffering very much and his groans expressed the greatest agony."[75]

It was only now that Lucia discovered that her servant woman was not with them, in fact hadn't been with them since they left the state room in the lower cabin. With great regret Lucia was forced to the conclusion that she must have perished as they were making their way to the galley.[76]

Lieutenant Loeser had been trying to find a more comfortable place for his ladies, and now one of soldiers came up to him and said he would try to get them down to the second cabin where it was quite dry. "We were perfectly amazed when we heard there was such a place left and were willing to leave the deck." They were taken, one at a time, along by the side of the ship, holding on for their lives, being obliged to take just so many steps between the time of a roll of the ship. Then they were taken through a window, and down a staircase into the second cabin. The place was filled with soldiers and some of the camp women. "They were all very kind to us, giving up their beds and what clothing they had to spare." Lucia sat on the floor. Colonel Burke was brought down, and the Loeser party begged the soldiers to let him lie down and rest. One of the women took charge of him, and placed him in one of the beds, doing everything she could to make him comfortable. Another woman offered some blankets and one or two articles of clothing to Miss Eaton and Mrs. Judd. "All I have to give you is a flannel skirt," she said, putting it on Lucia. As the woman had used all her common pins, she pinned it on with a brooch, an obviously valuable piece of jewelry, set with pearls, but one which she gave without hesitation. She then wrapped a blanket around the shivering Miss Eaton, who looked up into the woman's face and thanked her for her kindness, to which the woman replied: "You need not thank me; your mother was kind to me when I was at Fort Preble, and I would do anything for her daughter."[77]

The Loeser party were taken into the sleeping apartments of the cabin and put into one of the berths. There were six of these berths, or bunks, on each side of this room. A passage lay between which lead up to the dead light "a door but no door," as Miss Eaton puts it. "We were put into the beds with our wet clothing on us, being wrapped up in blankets, others being piled upon us." It was a long time before they could get warm.[78]

At noon the weather was still much the same, with very rough seas coming up

---

75. Eaton.
76. Eaton.
77. Eaton.
78. Eaton.

high against the sides of the ship, and a heavy gale continuing to blow from the northwest. The *San Francisco* was laboring greatly and making much water, but they were just about managing to hold their own with the leaks, with every pump going like mad and all hands frantically engaged in bailing.[79]

That afternoon, as a reward for their sufferings, Lucia Eaton's god bestowed a miracle upon his devotee and her equally faithful sister. Their servant woman, who had drowned the day before, had been raised from the dead and was now brought into the galley. But, of course, it wasn't really a miracle, no matter vociferously it was proclaimed as such. Like most miracles, it turned out to be rather prosaic, but that didn't in any way detract from the joy of their reunion. What had happened was that when the woman had come into the Loesers' state room the morning of the day before, she had found them gone, thought they were dead, and so she just lay down on the bed, wanting to die herself.[80]

The second cabin was a fearful place for the Loesers. It was filled with soldiers, and the little trio could hear everything that was being said and could see all that was going on. The recklessness of the men and their language was "truly horrible." It was difficult to control them. The officers would come into the cabin and try to reason with them, telling them that they, the officers, were doing all they could and if only the men would help then things would be better. If they didn't work the pumps the ship would go down, as the water was rapidly gaining on them. A regular detail was made out, of nine shifts, and at the end of each shift the men could go to bed if they chose to. Most of them would take their fair share in the work and after being relieved would come back to the state room exhausted, get into the berths and have a good sleep for a few hours. But there were some who simply were not affected by the officers' pep talk, and, whenever possible, would disappear when the moment came, and hide under mattresses or any other place where they wouldn't be found. But, despite the fears that had been running through the heads of the Loeser party, the enlisted men proved rather gallant, being very kind to them while they were in the cabin, and constantly bringing them things from the store room—preserves, preserved meats, dried and canned fruits, crackers, and any nice little delicacy they could find. It was then, when the men were at their kindest, that Lucia and Sarah would beg them to work and tell them that they would be rewarded if they did their duty. The ladies asked them if they had wives and children with them, and, because many had, wouldn't it be better to work for them?[81]

But there was another side to the men, of course, and that side would be brought out by the demon booze. After the wreck there were no arms left except a handful of old carbines belonging to the officers of the ship, and Major Wyse had detailed a few men to guard the stores. But a few were not enough, and the store room had been broken into. While looting the room, they got at some brandied peaches. Lucia

---

79. Mellus account; Wickham; Gretton.
80. Eaton.
81. Eaton; Buel, 1872.

Eaton and her sister, after finding out how these enlisted men had obtained the goodies they were so kindly handing to the ladies as presents, would ask for the bottles, and when Captain Judd, or Lieutenants Loeser or Bill Winder came in, they would have them broken on Major Wyse's orders. The men would sit composedly at the table, perfectly unconcerned. They even ferreted out the bay rum and were drinking it, when Loeser took it away, telling them it would poison them. Fortunately Judd and Bill Winder came in in time to prevent them breaking open the actual casks of liquor. Small amounts were doled out instead, to keep the soldiers' spirits up.[82]

That afternoon, Reuben Twist, the old first sergeant belonging to Colonel Burke's company, came into the Loesers' state room and asked if he could get into one of the vacant berths. Lucia Eaton had last seen Sergeant Twist at an assembly in a little town in the state of Maine, where he had been the leader of the band, one of the gayest men assembled in that ball room. Now he had injured his back and looked very ill.[83]

The Eaton/Loeser group would remain in the second cabin until the afternoon of the following day. They had but one candle in this cabin the whole night, and it looked very dismal. Once during the night an old woman took the light away, and from there on Loeser put the candle in charge of one of the soldiers.[84]

As 6 p.m. sounded, they found that the water level in the *San Francisco* had risen two inches, and so they set watches for the night, dividing all the troops as well as the crew into three watches, bailing and pumping. The lady passengers were moved forward into the forward cabin, as the safest place then, and Colonel Gates came forward and used encouraging language to console them.[85]

Being so soon after the disaster, there was as yet no system in place for issuing water and provisions. After sundown, quite dusk, Mr. Sanford, the head steward was strutting up and down the ship, in full view of the officers, barking orders to the other negro stewards to lighten the ship and so forth. Colonel Gates hailed him and asked him to have water brought for his children, but to the colonel's astonishment, Mr. Sanford, instead of complying instantly, as he should have done, replied in a way that, by rights, would have led to his being clapped in irons. Lieutenant Bill Winder heard the exchange and Sanford's insolent reply, and although he didn't catch the actual words used, he thought the steward told Gates to be quiet, that they were doing all they could to save the passengers. Captain Gardiner, the dragoon, considered the man's tone and manner exceeded insolence. And of course he was right, or would have been, if Mr. Sanford had been operating under normal circumstances.[86]

But Mr. Sanford was no longer the polite, subservient negro he had pretended to be all his life. The humiliating façade necessary to get ahead in a white man's world was starting to crack. Bill Winder assumed he was drunk, but, in the light of what

---

82. Fremont; Eaton; Winder testimony; Buel, 1872.
83. Eaton.
84. Eaton.
85. Gretton; Gorham.
86. Winder testimony; Gardiner; McIntyre.

was to happen a few days later, was forced to amend his diagnosis: "He turned out afterwards to be insane."[87]

The steward was not the only one breaking under the pressure. Colonel Gates had just lost his son, Charles, and, at 65 years old, with the awesome responsibility on his shoulders not only of securing the safety of his wife and young children but also of everyone on board, would henceforth behave in a manner completely unbefitting his position as regimental commander. If he couldn't get a steward to get water, he would get it himself.

Dr. Buel and the purser, Mr. Schell, were talking in the engine room that evening while watching the men bailing, and agreed that the men were not working to advantage, because no officer was there to institute a system. Buel went to Wyse to suggest it, and the major went to Commodore Watkins with the idea. Watkins found the officers in the lower cabin and requested them to do bailing, and Sergeant Brown formed the whole regiment into reliefs, with two officers going to the engine room at any one time to supervise. They all worked throughout the night, each man being relieved every hour and each officer every two. Charlie Winder and Lieutenant Van Voast relieved each other at one side of the engine room, and would continue to do so for four days, while Bill Winder and Lieutenant Chandler did the same on the other side. But their pumps failed, the water kept on gaining on them fast, and so it was back to the buckets.[88]

Lieutenant Lucien Loeser was giving directions to the bailing parties to pass into the engine room, when he saw Sergeant Joe McIntyre, his commissary sergeant. Afraid that the provisions would get thrown overboard, he ordered McIntyre to go to the hold and get out the bread, beef, pork, biscuit and pickles, so they could be saved. They opened whatever provisions could be used without cooking and placed them where the men could get at them freely.[89]

In the meantime, Sergeant Elijah Brown made a detail of three men to assist in bailing at the forward pumps and, following his orders, they went out through a door from the second cabin up onto the deck, where they were promptly washed overboard. As soon as Brown heard this, he went aft and spoke to his superior officer, Lieutenant Bill Winder, to request permission from the officers to cut away a particular partition that separated the second cabin from the hospital, so his men could get forward safely. It was Lieutenant Van Voast who finally gave him the necessary permission. At that very moment, Sergeant Brown bumped into Colonel Gates leaving the second cabin to go up the stairs to the door through which the three unfortunate soldiers had passed not more than 15 minutes earlier.[90]

---

87. Winder testimony.
88. Buel testimony; Brown account; Winder interview, 1854; Winder, Jan. 6, 1854.
89. Loeser; McIntyre. Joseph Stuart McIntyre was born in Bristol, England, on May 10, 1816. He arrived in Bangor, Maine, on February 9, 1840, and on June of that year moved to Boston. When he first enlisted, at Bangor, on June 23, 1840, he claimed to be a lawyer. He enlisted again, in 1848, at Portsmouth, New Hampshire, this time claiming to be an apothecary. He went into Co K. He became a U.S. citizen on Oct. 6, 1848, in Boston. On Nov. 1, 1853, at Fort Columbus, he enlisted again, still in Company K.
90. Brown testimony.

With a water-can in his hand, Colonel Gates was on his way up to the spar deck, where there was a fresh-water pump forward of the main cabin. He asked the sergeant how to get there, and Brown showed him the way, the same way the three now-dead men had tried, the only possible way to get out on deck at this moment before the partition was cut—through the steward's pantry on the starboard side of the vessel, from there into a narrow passage, then over the shaft of the machinery and through the door of the engine room on the left hand side, and into a small store room which connected immediately with the forward steerage cabin, where the men and women of the command were. Then through a doorway that the men had now fastened, the same door way the three men had passed through just before they died. Then up the stairs, out onto the main deck, and from there up onto the spar deck.[91]

Sergeant Brown tried to warn the old man of the danger, told him that three men had been washed away trying it, and that if Gates had any orders for forward, he, Brown, would take them. Gates replied lightly: "Never mind," and, using the lit candles below as his guide, off he went into the night.[92]

Not long afterwards, Colonel Gates returned from his dangerous venture. He was carrying water.[93]

But the Devil wasn't finished with them yet. Again, he had been provoked by the prayers of the Reverend Cooper, and later that night the storm recommenced with greater violence. From time to time the high raging seas would crash right over the freely rolling steamer, and every time this happened a great deal of water would come in from the top sides due to a large hole in the main aft deck, and to the fact that a great many of the timber heads were bare. The men couldn't bail it out quick enough. The waves would come against the side of the deadlight with such force that it seemed they would break through. People in their berths would nod off, but then be awoken by another crash, and exclaim: *"We are going. Oh, we are going!"* Many of the passengers were now lying in about three inches of water, and begging the soldiers and sailors for more dry blankets. Commodore Watkins, walking back and forth, to and fro, tried to cheer them all by reminding them yet again that the hull was sound and that the sea would soon have to go down. But, just in case the Commodore was wrong, the Reverend Cooper launched into yet another round of ardent prayer, one that lasted for the rest of the night.[94]

Then, all of a sudden, at midnight, the weather started to moderate, the storm to subside. It was only a slight improvement, but it was noticeable.[95]

---

91. Winder testimony; Brown testimony; McIntyre; Gorham.
92. Brown testimony; McIntyre; Winder testimony; Gorham; Gardiner. Sergeant McIntyre dates this Gates episode as two or three days after the Christmas Eve disaster, i.e., the 26th or the 27th of December. Sergeant Brown did not remember the date, and none of the other witnesses even mention a day. The Army enlistment records do not convincingly mention any man being washed overboard after the 24th, and they almost certainly would have done. Therefore, the best guess is that this happened on December 24.
93. McIntyre; Gates testimony; Winder testimony.
94. Eaton; Mrs. Gates; Graham/Kilby.
95. Gretton; Eaton.

Sunday
December 25

All through the dark hours of the morning and into the daylight, in a different part of the unusually violent Atlantic Ocean, the *Three Bells* was battling for her life against a tremendous gale that carried away much of her sail. It needed two men at the wheel, but even that strength proved inadequate when, with one sudden giant punch, the storm broke the wheel to pieces. The two sailors took the full brunt of the explosion of wood and metal, and were so badly injured that they would be out of commission for several days. With extraordinary thunder and lightning raging for five or six hours, the scene on board was horrendous and very frightening. The second mate, John McLean would later say it was the worst lightning he had ever experienced, and he had been at sea for 14 years.[1]

Above and around the stricken *San Francisco*, the weather continued to moderate a little in the early hours of the morning. However, no provision had been made on board for lights, and for two or three hours many of the passengers remained immersed in total darkness while slopping about in water. A piece of candle was finally found by the steward and put in a bottle.[2]

The passageways in and about the engine room, and those leading from there to the forward cabin, were so narrow and crowded that men couldn't stand abreast in them, and so it was impossible, during this difficult period, to establish any regular order. What made it worse was that by two o'clock that Christmas morning there was an average of two feet four inches of water in the ship. However, with the deck hands heaving provisions and coal overboard—anything they could find to lighten

---

1. Burnside. The only other crewmen on the *Three Bells* for whom we have names are: First Mate James Gibbs; the ship's doctor Philip O'Hanlon; the carpenter Adam Cairns; the steward William Parmer; and the cook Francis McClusky. In addition, there were 21 seamen, including James Taylor, Alexander McBeath, and W.K. Thyne. Much later, Gibbs, McLean, and Thyne would be awarded silver medals for their roles in saving lives of *San Francisco* survivors. There were sixteen passengers altogether as the *Three Bells* left Glasgow. In the cabins were Thomas Burnside, aged 30; William Ewing McDougall, of Glasgow, aged 29, a merchant; William Smith and lady, from Manchester, both 26; and James Muirhead, of New York, aged 21. In steerage were John Bain, aged 22; Joseph Cairns and wife, aged 22 and 24 respectively; Robert Geddes, aged 32; Agnes Leitch, aged 20; Thomas McCabe, aged 20; Alexander McInroy, aged 22; Walter Stewart, Sr., aged 40, Margaret Stewart, aged 27, and Walter Stewart, aged 17, all of Glasgow; and John McGowan, of Antrim, aged 29.
2. Mellus account; Wickham; Mrs. Gates.

the ship—and the bailing crews working constantly, the water finally started to go down, so that the engineers could get down to trying to fix the air-pump. With the loss of the steamer's pipes, they had given up trying to work the engines at high pressure.[3]

Now that things had calmed down a bit after the massive disaster of the day before, Commodore Watkins went around what remained of his ship, assuring the passengers that the hull was still sound, and that the storm would soon be over. There was a general rush for the lower cabin, where the ladies had been placed, and there, upon the floor, several persons gathered together. It was the Reverend Cooper's little flock, with Mr. Aspinwall and others, including, of course, Mr. Cooper himself fervently offering up prayers to celebrate the birthday of their Savior, to thank his deity for having spared them, and to beg for their continued preservation. "As we laid here, it seemed during the long, long days of suspense, more like some horrid dream than like reality. Each hour some new name was spoken of as having gone—and still the passengers kept up their spirits to the last."[4]

Some of the passengers might, upon reflection, have taken it into their heads that it was the Reverend Cooper who was responsible for the complete and utter tragedy that had befallen them. By praying so energetically for deliverance even before the great sea had come upon them, Mr. Cooper's professionally tremulous voice, raised toward the heavens, evidently failed to reach his deity, otherwise the survivors of the wreck would not be in the mess they were in now. Perhaps he didn't pray hard enough, or it might be that his god's attentions were elsewhere. However, if one puts any stock in ancient idols hearing the pleas of mere mortals, then Mr. Cooper's invocation was certainly heard by the Devil, who decided that here was his chance for a bit of sport. And now, in the evening, with the storm abating, the same clergyman was offering up prayers of thanks to the same god, while the Devil looked on, amazed as always by the obstinate refusal of frail sinners to give credit where credit is due. Given that scores of innocent people were dashed to their deaths that day, some degree of skepticism must be forgiven, especially in the light of this from the *New York Tribune* of January 18, 1854, in a lengthy item reporting the services at Grace Church, after it was all over: "Through the prayers of the Minister of God, and the supplications of children, the good God brought them safely through the trials of the deep. One remarkable instance of an answer to prayer occurred on the ship. The minister was praying to God for help and pleading the wants of the sufferers, reminding him of his mercy in stilling the tempest on the sea of Galilee, when suddenly the heavens opened, the rain poured down, and the waves were calmed. After many weeks of confinement on that ship, protected by the mercy of God, they are at length brought safely here to thank him for his goodness."

As daylight slowly began to replace the misery of the late December darkness, those up and about the *San Francisco* could think back to those hopeful moments only 72 hours before, when, on this same deck, as they were standing down New

---

3. Winder testimony; Mellus account; Wickham; Gretton.
4. Buel, 1854; Graham. The quote is from Buel.

York Harbor, they had been discussing with one another how stentorian their first "Merry Christmas" greeting was going to be, and whether it should be in English or some other language—"Joyeux Noël," for example—the only occasion on which such pretentiousness might be mistaken for bonhomie. Now, after what had just happened, no such happy salutations were passing anyone's lips. But then, like a lightning bolt, the sun came out.[5] Their Savior had not forsaken them after all. Well, not all of them, anyway. Those who survived had been forgiven of their sins, purged of evil through the unspeakable sufferings of those Christian martyrs who had died for them the day before. Feliz navidad.

As the Loeser party lay in their berths rejoicing at the first ray of bright morning sunshine coming through the deadlight, they heard a terrific crash above them, and assumed this was the end. Lucien Loeser and Captain Judd rushed up on deck, followed by a number of soldiers, and found that the two iron safes had broken loose and were careening about the ship, dangerously rogue. The men attached large ropes to them and, waiting until a suitable roll of the ship favored their plan, threw them into the sea.[6]

On the *San Francisco* there was always an officer of the day and two officers of the guard. Early in the morning of the twenty-fifth, Lieutenant Fremont, disabled by a severe attack of pleurisy brought on by his exertions of the day before, detailed Lucien Loeser as officer of the day. Lieutenant Loeser would remain in that role until the evening of the twenty-sixth, and would receive no order during that time. He was on his own, as far as decisions went. As for Lieutenant Fremont, it would be another day before he was up and around and could relieve Loeser.[7]

Then, all of a sudden, and much more to the point, in the first gleaming of morning they saw a light far off in the distance. Was it an illusion, like the day before, when in the surreal aftermath of the wreck people's ability to distinguish between fact and phantasm had whipped up such hopes, only to have them dashed to pieces with the breaking of the ship? Was it lightning? No, it was a steady light. It was a ship. This was to be expected, either because they were in the shipping lanes or because the Reverend Cooper's prayers had finally been answered. It didn't really matter. But would this ship see them? The couple of sails they had spotted the day before had just gone right on by, but it might be different this time. Unlike yesterday, when they were in such extremis, now they could signal a distant vessel. And they did. But within minutes the light had gone, and it didn't come back. Perhaps the Reverend Cooper's deity was playing with them again. Perhaps it was bad luck. Either way, for most on board at that moment, it was God's will. For the others it was just a cruel disappointment.[8]

At 7 a.m., with a dreadful sea running all the time, the brig *Napoleon* was still hove to, trying to sit out what was left of yesterday's hurricane. Captain Strout and the wheel man were on deck just as a most welcome sun came squeezing itself out

---

5. Eaton.
6. Mrs. Gates; Eaton.
7. Fremont; Loeser.
8. Winder, Jan. 6, 1854; Graham; Graham/Kilby; Eaton.

of the eastern horizon, signaling a new day and new hope for all. With the coming light, Strout circled the ocean with his eyes, and then he saw it, on his weather quarter, seven or eight miles away, bobbing about in the ocean.

"We are not alone," he muttered to the helmsman.

Putting the spyglass to his eye, he took a better look. The *Napoleon*'s crew were all out on deck now, craning their vision in the direction of the skipper's telescope. They could see a dismasted vessel they took to be a bark, bearing southwest, and they could make out that only her mizzen mast and mizzen topmast were standing.[9]

By 7:30, now from only six miles away, Captain Strout could see that the distant vessel was in desperate trouble; her ensign was union down, with the union or canton at the bottom of the flag instead of at the top, the universally understood distress signal. However, they couldn't quite make out the flag in sufficient detail to see the ship's country of origin. But the *Napoleon* was not doing too well either. Almost in mockery of the promise held by the sky, the brig was rolling very deep, and seas were breaking over her. Captain Strout set her under three reefed mainsail, reefed main staysail and foretopmast staysail, and now, making headway, and with her head up to the sea, the *Napoleon* ran for the distant vessel.[10]

It was just then that Lieutenant Murray, who was up and about on the deck of the *San Francisco*, saw the brig's sails off the port quarter. Again, the steamer's crew lost no time in signaling the distant vessel. Could it be, finally, that after all they had been through, their troubles were about to end, and that, very soon, they would be taken off the wreck and carried back to land? Had the distant vessel seen them?[11]

At 8 a.m., Captain Strout set the colors in the main rigging, to let those on the other ship know that he had seen them, and 30 minutes later the *Napoleon* wore ship, although it wasn't safe for Strout to turn his vessel away from the wind like that.[12]

By the time the engineer succeeded in finishing the repairs to the *San Francisco*'s air-pump, it was nine o'clock in the morning, and the engine was duly set in motion. Unfortunately, after working some 10 minutes, the bucket again gave out, and they were obliged to abandon the main engines entirely. At that point, Engineer Marshall decided to try something new with the air-pump.[13]

During the latter part of the morning the weather was more moderate and quite clear. The wind, although still blowing violently from the northwest, had lulled somewhat, but the sea was still running dreadfully high. By 11:30 the disabled steamer had drifted to the leeward of the *Napoleon*, in a south-southwest direction, and was now distant some four miles. Captain Strout could see through the glass that the *San Francisco* was manageable but lying in the trough of the sea, rolling to and fro, and now drifting southeast at a rate of one and five-eighths knots. What he couldn't see from that distance was that Mr. Marshall and the other engineers were hard at work

---

9. McCarty; Strout.
10. McCarty; Strout.
11. Gretton; Graham.
12. McCarty; Strout.
13. Marshall, Jan. 16, 1854.

at the air-pump. Nor could he make out the soldiers bailing and pumping the water anew, and throwing provisions overboard to lighten the ship. At noon, with the *Napoleon* in 38° 04' N, 69° 30' W, Captain Strout set a reefed main staysail and fore topmast staysail, and, with the weather moderating even more, continued on course for the wreck.[14]

A half hour after noon, as the *Napoleon* was fast approaching the *San Francisco*, her crew could now see quite clearly that the vessel was a side-wheel steamer. Although her wheelhouses were gone, the wheels were entire, both guards were in good order, and her black-painted hull and the rudder appeared to be sound. All above decks had been swept, including the foremast. The only thing left standing, as they had previously descried from afar, was, indeed, the mizzen mast. As they worked up under the steamer's quarter, they could make out her sharp, plain clipper bow, and her very short bowsprit, also painted black but with no figurehead. Just as they passed to leeward abreast of her and came within hailing distance, they could now see quite clearly men throwing overboard all the heavy articles they could get at, in order to lighten the ship. And because they could see no one at the pumps, they assumed the steam pumps were working.[15]

Captain Strout hailed the *San Francisco* twice before receiving an answer. "The third time I was answered by the Commander, who, I should judge from his appearance, had been asleep, for he came up rubbing his eyes, and had no hat on. Don't know as I should have been noticed at all, if it had not been for the soldiers cheering."

It was indeed the stout figure of Commodore Watkins, dressed in a dark coat, either of cloth or of leather, and, speaking the *Napoleon* through his trumpet he yelled, "Brig ahoy!"

Captain Strout answered.

Watkins shouted, "I want you to send a boat."

Strout told the Commodore he couldn't do that. No "boat could live in so fearful a sea." He then asked, "Where are you from?"

"From New York, bound to California."

"When were you disabled?"

"On the night of the 23rd—my vessel is making water fast." But Watkins didn't say how much water. Strout wasn't surprised that the *San Francisco* was leaking, for she was lying broadside to the sea, and the ocean spray was making a complete breach over her.

Strout then said, "I am in distress too, and short of provisions."

"I have plenty of provisions," said the man on the *San Francisco*, upon which he ordered spares thrown overboard in the direction of the brig.

---

14. Mellus account; Gretton; McCarty.
15. Strout; McCarty; Winder, Jan. 6, 1854; Gretton; Mellus account; Wickham; Partridge. Mellus, in the ship's log, says that the two ships spoke about noon. He was off by an hour. Wickham, copying from the log, is also off. Lucia Eaton says, "At three o'clock in the afternoon we heard that a ship or brig was in sight. Afterwards she came quite near. I found out later it was the brig *Napoleon*. We heard Captain Watkins speak but could not hear the reply."

Watkins asked that the brig lie with her, to which Strout replied, "Put up a light at night."[16]

They then passed out of voice range. As the *Napoleon* came under the stern of the *San Francisco*, they saw some 20 persons come from the remains of the steamer's upper after cabin onto the deck, wearing dark clothes and caps. The *Napoleon*'s crew could now also get a better look at conditions aboard the wreck. The damage was mainly in the upper works amidships, it seemed to them. Part of the hurricane deck forward of the wheels was still standing and the crew was busily engaged in cutting it away and throwing it overboard. Although the smoke stacks were gone, the *Napoleon*'s chief mate saw smoke, or steam, issuing from a small pipe amidships, and guessed this to be coming from the *San Francisco*'s galley, which he guessed, rightly, had not been washed away. The galley, or at least most of it, may have been saved, but, at the moment it was of little use, because with the ship rolling so much, whatever was in the pots would have fallen out, and lighted fires would have been too great a danger. The mate also saw, on the *San Francisco*'s forward deck, some 100 or 150 men in caps and blue coats, and he took them for soldiers. As they passed, the large crowd gave three hearty cheers.[17]

For the next half hour the brig was under the steamer's stern, at a distance of a mere 50 or 60 yards. The crew on the *Napoleon* could distinctly read the words "San Francisco New York." Unfortunately, with the vessel in distress being to windward, and with the wind blowing so fiercely and the sea running so high that there was no way to get a boat across, it was impossible for Captain Strout to render the steamer any assistance but moral. Ironically, given the condition of the *Napoleon*, the people on the *San Francisco* were safer where they were.[18]

As the wrecked *San Francisco* was drifting faster than the brig, Captain Strout did not wish to be on her lee at that point in time, so, a little after one o'clock, and now with only about 30 yards separating the two vessels, the *Napoleon* came out from the shadow of the enormous floating hulk and ranged ahead of her.[19]

By 2 p.m., there were only six inches of water in the *San Francisco*, and the seas were no longer going over her decks. All hands were at work covering the timber heads and main deck. During the afternoon those who were on the steamer's deck could see the crew of the *Napoleon* plucking the floating provisions from the sea.[20]

Lieutenants John Chandler and Bill Winder came in to see the Loeser party, and to Lucia Eaton they appeared so changed by the disaster that she was shocked. Winder had just come from working in the engine room, where a fireman had given him a drink of water, his first in over 24 hours. The two lieutenants had pieces of blanket tied around their heads, since their caps had disappeared during the great nightmare

---

16. Strout; McCarty; Wickham; Winder, Jan. 6, 1854; Winder interview, 1854. For the interchange between the two captains we rely exclusively on the reports given by Strout and McCarty.
17. McCarty; Fremont.
18. McCarty.
19. Strout; McCarty; Partridge.
20. Gretton; Wickham; Winder interview, 1854.

of the day before, and, as they had also lost their uniforms, they were now dressed in any clothing they could find.[21]

Then Lieutenant Frank Murray came in to see Miss Eaton and her group, and advised them to join the other ladies in the saloon, where they would be away from the soldiers and much happier in the company of their fellow passengers. As they were wrapping blankets around themselves, one of the women kindly gave Lucia a pair of shoes, and then they left that fearful cabin, threading their way along the narrow passage past the engine room, where the men were still at work. Soon after they passed by, the small engine was put in order, and that kept the engine room free from water. Miss Eaton's party were then taken through all the passageways and at last found themselves in the once elegant saloon, whose passageway was now filled with all sorts of rubbish. The once beautiful and useful furniture, the velvet cushions and the satin damask curtains, were all a thing of the past. The deck on one side was broken in and was now patched with boards and anything that would fill up the opening, the whole being supported by rough stanchions. The floor was extremely wet, and the tables from which they had taken their last tea the previous Thursday evening were now covered with trunks, chairs, mattresses and all kinds of truck. The state rooms, which had been elegantly gilded and hung with chintz, were now soiled, and the hangings were torn away in some places. The whole stern of the ship was filled with human beings, most on mattresses, some sitting up, and others, the weaker ones and the injured, lying down. Everyone was happy to see the Loeser party. "The lost are found." The passengers made room for the new arrivals, who then sat down on a mattress. James Lorimer Graham was sitting a short distance from Lucia, and looked very ill. Lucia heard that Graham and a colored servant had lashed themselves to a remaining mast the morning of the wreck, supposing that they were the only ones alive. Some friends had seen them and come in time to save them as they were quite exhausted. Major Merchant was there, among the injured, but the good news was that he had by now made a fair recovery. It was not long before stewards came and arranged their beds for the night, and, after taking a cup of tea and eating a cracker, Lucia fell asleep. That was the end of Christmas Day for her.[22]

Captain Henry Bethel Judd was only 34, but he was a sick man. However, coming as he did from a good family in New London, Connecticut, and being an old Indian fighter and a veteran of the Mexican War, he was too much the officer and gentleman to show it. "For a long time previously to the departure of the *San Francisco*, I had been an invalid; I was in a feeble state of health on the day of the wreck; I was not reported sick." His reason was simple—"I did not report sick, thinking it necessary that every man should exert himself as far as possible."[23]

And exert himself he did. For the 15 hours or so of Christmas Eve that remained after the wreck, and for all of Christmas Day, Judd had been in the forward cabin,

---

21. Eaton; Winder, 1883.
22. Eaton.
23. Judd.

without rest amid the noise and confusion, engaged in forming details of soldiers for the pumping in the engine room, and constantly trying to keep order among the men, many of whom, being recruits, were unused to taking orders. "Undisciplined rabble," Lieutenant Fremont called them, although he was the first to admit that there were honorable exceptions. Although they obeyed the officers' commands, they were reluctant to do so, and so Fremont appealed to their better instincts, tried to jolly them along with the line that they would be saving their lives and those of others. What made it worse was that the negro waiters and colored firemen coming up from their watch below had broken into the steward's room, and the rank and file among the soldiery wanted at its contents, an abundance of liquors, ales, preserved meats, and a variety of choice articles of food. *"Had there not been some discipline, they would have made a rush at it, filled the cabin, and taken it."* But, helped by Commodore Watkins, and with the assistance of Lieutenant Loeser, a few sergeants, and some old soldiers, Judd was able to keep control, and few cases of decided insubordination occurred, the men obeying the orders, albeit slowly, even down to the hardest thing a soldier can do—destroy liquor. Expending energy he no longer really had, Judd, with the aid of his men, passed the alcohol, including two barrels of rum, up through the companionway, and threw it over the side into the sea.[24]

Remarkably, there were virtually no instances of drunkenness. In fact, there seems to have been only one such case, and that was Private Hyland of Company A, who was immediately placed under guard.[25]

Captain Judd had other problems. Aside from commanding all the recruits of Companies B and L, he suddenly found himself in the impossible position of having inherited most of the rest of the command. Companies A and I were quartered further forward than the forward cabin where Judd was concentrating his activities. The officers of Company A had perished in the big wave, and the commanding officer of Company I was disabled, which meant that those two companies had no officers looking after them.[26]

For 48 hours or so after the wreck, night and day, there had been a number of men, women and children lying between Colonel Gates and the invalided Captain Gardiner. Gates estimated the number at between 15 and 20, but the dragoon captain felt the colonel's estimate was nowhere close—more like five to ten. Regardless of who was right, on the night of December 25, Gardiner was moved into a small wash-

---

24. Judd; Fremont; Wyse testimony.
25. Judd; Fremont; Wyse testimony; Army enlistment records. The story of Private Hyland is fairly typical of soldiers in the regular U.S. Army of the 19th century: On January 21, 1852, one Patrick O'Brien enlisted in New York, claiming to be a cabinet maker, aged 21, originally from Dublin. He was put into Company A of the Rifles, but deserted on October 14 of that year. On September 6, 1853, at Buffalo, a laborer named John Hyland, aged 23, claiming to have been born in Limerick, enlisted, and was put into Company A of the Third Artillery, in time to go on the *San Francisco*. On January 29, 1854, two weeks after the *Three Bells* got back to New York, he surrendered himself as Patrick O'Brien, the deserter from the Rifles. He was discharged from the Artillery on February 3, and transferred back to the Rifles. He deserted again, on July 3, 1856, but was apprehended on August 6. But they forgave him, and he finished out his term, with time added for bad behavior, on May 15, 1858, at Fort Staunton, N.M.
26. Judd.

room without a door, about 20 feet from that portion occupied by Colonel Gates. Gardiner would remain in the washroom two nights and one day, unable to move.[27]

This evening, Lieutenant Bill Winder heard a voice say, "*"Young gentlemen, go forward and assist in bailing."* It was Colonel Gates, giving the only order Winder had heard him issue since the wreck. The officers were doing all they could to regulate the men, and keep them at bailing, so Gates's order was entirely superfluous.[28]

Captain Strout kept the *Napoleon* merely under steerage-way, and with the steamer about three miles to his eastward, continued to keep her in sight until dark.

At sunset it began to breeze up again from the northeast, and after dark the weather was much the same. The *San Francisco* was by now on the southeast edge of the Gulf Stream, fast drifting eastward out of it. Despite the later false testimony of three of the crew of the *Napoleon* that by eight o'clock the storm had abated enough for Captain Strout to take off some passengers but that he simply cut out instead, the brig tried hard to keep up with her doomed companion, but, with the steamer being so low in the water and her lights visible one minute and gone the next, there came that moment, as midnight approached, when the *Napoleon* lost sight of her forever.[29]

---

27. Gates testimony; Gardiner.
28. Winder testimony.
29. Mellus account; Wickham; Gretton; Strout; McCarty.

Monday
December 26

A fresh and very heavy gale blew from the northwest during the night, and with the seas continually breaking over the *San Francisco*'s deck there was more work to be done, serious work, and it had to be done fast. Sergeant Joe McIntyre had reported to Colonel Gates that every time a big swell came over the ship a huge volume of water went down the forward hatchway right into the companionway of the second cabin, creating tremendous flooding. They were in danger of swamping. The hatchway had to be battened up, or the ship might go down. The colonel took control, gave the sergeant directions, and assisted him in cutting away the bannisters so they could make boards to cover the hole. Gates personally carried the boards to the hatch, and then he hurried to the main deck aft and, with the assistance of some of the crew, broke open the oilcloth and brought it forward. They shored up the oilcloth by putting about a dozen stanchions under it, while on top of it they secured a mass of canvas and painted carpeting. Finally, with Sergeant Gorham personally passing the freshly cut boards up to Colonel Gates, they nailed the wood, piece by piece, firmly down over the whole lot, and secured the hatchway. They went on to repeat this heavy, laborious process at various hatchways throughout the ship. Other crewmen cut a new hole in the rudder head for the tiller, shifted it down, got the wheel from forward, bolted that down, put in bolts for blocks, rove the wheel ropes, and got everything ready for steering the ship, as Mr. Marshall, the chief engineer, felt that they would have the piston-rod repaired sufficiently for working the engine by morning.[1]

Indeed, Colonel Gates was everywhere. When he wasn't working on the battening he was assisting others in putting up mattresses at the door of the upper companionway that led into the second cabin, or wielding an axe to help cut away the huge, unmovable part of the hurricane deck that had fallen on the deck. And he wasn't finished yet. He went about securing life-lines around the decks and giving directions to others engaged in the same work. All in all, given his age and his state of mind after losing his son, it was quite a tour de force.[2]

At four o'clock that morning the engineers announced some good news. They

---

1. McIntyre; Gretton; Brown testimony; Watkins testimony; Gorham.
2. Brown testimony; Watkins testimony; McIntyre; Gorham; Smith.

had been at work unremittingly for almost 48 hours, attempting to fix the air-pump. The first thing they had done, just after the wreck on the twenty-third, was to disconnect the head from the pump. Then they had drilled a hole one inch in diameter, 20 inches from the end of the rod, and put a bolt through it. After that they took two large water-wheel hoop bolts, put the hoops to the rod, and screwed it on the outside of the pump. But all that work had come to naught on Christmas morning, when the engine failed again. They had been forced to take a different approach, to see if they could rig it up as a bilge pump, to pump water out of the ship. Finally, in the dark hours of this morning, the day after Christmas, they had taken a cylinder bolt and drilled a hole seven inches deep and an inch and a quarter in diameter into the end of the air-pump piston road. Now the air-pump was partially repaired and, although there was never going to be a way the pump could contribute to the running of the engines, it could now be used by the crew to get the sea-water out of the ship. By six o'clock that morning the water was almost all gone, the deck-pumps and two steam donkeys were pounding away, the bailing gangs were reduced to one only, and the officers could be detailed for other duty. This now left the engineers free to work again on trying to fix the air-pump piston-rod, so that the ship could get moving again.[3]

At daylight the wind was blowing very heavy, and the ship was making bad weather in the high waves. Now that better light had come, they stared out to sea, but there was nothing in sight. The *Napoleon* was gone. She had either drifted away or, as some on the *San Francisco* feared, deliberately run away from them.[4]

But Captain Strout hadn't deserted them. The *San Francisco* had drifted a distance of probably 23 miles during the night and, come daylight, as hard as the crew of the *Napoleon* stared into the horizon, they couldn't make out a thing.[5]

Lucia Eaton, when she awoke, could keenly hear the wind and feel the roll of the waves, and she and several of her fellow passengers passed the day on mattresses, being too weak to sit up.[6]

The disappearance of the *Napoleon* weighed heavy upon the people on the *San Francisco*. Suddenly there had been hope—the hope that only a Christmas day can bring—and then that hope was gone. To try to cheer them up, Commodore Watkins sent word to the passengers that the hull was still sound and that the *San Francisco* would not go to pieces.[7]

The despondency didn't last long. Within minutes they spotted, off their lee quarter, another vessel in the distance, with her foresail and mainsail set. Again, those most welcome of words, "A sail in sight," were passed from mouth to mouth.[8]

By late morning, with this new ship steadily approaching them, the wind had

---

3. Marshall, Jan. 16, 1854; Auchinleck.
4. Gretton; Mellus account; Wickham; Eaton; Strout; McCarty; Winder interview, 1854.
5. Strout; McCarty. As will be seen a couple of days later, the *Kilby* also lost sight of the *San Francisco* for a while, for the same reason.
6. Eaton.
7. Eaton.
8. Gretton; Graham. Gretton says they spotted this vessel at 7 a.m., which seems a little early, perhaps by an hour or so. Graham is way out when he says "towards evening."

moderated and was nearly calm, and the men on the *San Francisco* settled down to clearing the wreckage off the quarterdeck, and lightening the ship by throwing overboard all the heavy articles they could get at.[9]

At noon they were in 38° 20' N, 69° W, in other words 300 miles east of Cape Henlopen or the Capes of Delaware, and 260 miles ESE of Sandy Hook. It was still blowing heavy from the northeast, and, although the weather was clear, the sea was rough. As the very welcome vessel came close enough her crew could gauge immediately the disabled state of the *San Francisco*. They could see that her drag was out forward and that her head was to the wind, that her engines were not working, that her smoke-stacks were gone, that she had lost her boats, and that her decks were swept of everything. The skipper could make out at least 150 persons on board. But, all in all, things didn't look as bad as they could have.[10]

Then, at one o'clock that afternoon, the captain spoke to Commodore Watkins through his voice trumpet.[11]

The *Maria*, an hermaphrodite brig of 130 tons, was out of Augusta, Maine, built in late 1846 for merchant Thomas H. Haskell. Her first and only skipper was William T. Freeman, a family man from York, Maine, who, by December 1853, was in his forties and a captain much experienced in the Atlantic sea trade.[12]

Commodore Watkins informed Captain Freeman of the situation, and asked him if he would lay by for a day or two. Freeman promised to try, but he was doubtful if they would be able to as his tiny vessel had experienced very heavy weather and had lost most of her sails.[13]

While they waited on the *San Francisco* for something to happen—anything good—they made themselves as comfortable as possible, got something to eat, and began to get some dry clothes, as they had been wet for three solid days now.[14]

The afternoon continued with a heavy sea stirred up by a strong gale from the northwest, but despite this, the men were employed in clearing the wreck and lightening the ship, as well as in pumping and bailing. They cut away the officers' rooms and the upper deck, and shifted the steering wheel aft on the quarter deck. All this continued into the evening and the night.[15]

The passengers in the saloon took some refreshments in the afternoon, after which, with the assistance of several officers, Lucia Eaton succeeded in getting to her state room. There she found a dress that her sister Sarah had taken out of her trunk for her. She put it on, thankful for an opportunity to shed the blanket. She told the other ladies that they were perfectly welcome to the clothing in her own trunk, if they could get to it, but unfortunately that was impossible at the moment, as there were several others piled on top of it, the whole stack having been placed so that they

---

9. Mellus account; Wickham; Gretton; Winder, Jan. 6, 1854.
10. Freeman.
11. Gretton; Freeman.
12. Mellus account; Wickham.
13. Gretton.
14. Winder, Jan. 6, 1854.
15. Mellus account; Wickham.

wouldn't roll about. Lucia was starting to get weak, and so she hurried back to her mattress to save herself from fainting.[16]

In the evening the steward made the two sisters a bed on the seats between the table and an old state room. But they couldn't rest quietly there, and so they went back to their friends and slept on the floor. However, the steamer seemed to be rolling more than it had during the day, and, from time to time, would go down so far into the trough of the sea that it seemed as if it were lying on its side. Then the huge waves would break directly over the entire vessel. The mast up on deck could only take so much of this bombardment before it became loose, at which point the water started to gush down around the newly created gaps into Miss Eaton's quarters, flooding the floor and soaking the mattresses. The men couldn't walk through the saloon without taking hold of the tables which were fairly secured to the floor. Sometimes they would take hold of the stanchions which had supported the deck, but as those stanchions were now very frail, no one was allowed to touch them. Every few minutes Lucia and her crowd would hear the officer call out, "Let go of the stanchions!" The opening above, which had been made for the purpose of admitting light and air to the lower saloon, found itself entirely open when the upper deck was carried away, and so they had taken up the oil cloth from the floor and nailed it over the opening so as to prevent the water from coming down. "We had but little air and it was quite dark when this was closed up."[17]

Things looked rather desperate, so Lucia Eaton's group had prayers, with Mr. Cooper again beseeching his capricious god to spare them. As the sound of the last of Mr. Cooper's heartfelt amens died away, several of the ladies sang, and then they all tried to sleep, but at every roll of the ship they would start up in horror, their first thought being that they were sinking. The steamship had received such a severe wrenching that the boards of the state room just behind them were quite loose, and they couldn't lean against them.[18]

During that whole Monday afternoon and night the engineers were still working like devils down in the pit of hell trying to put the engine in order. They had been at it for what seemed like their whole life, and had already had one failure to discourage them. Now they were just about dead on their feet. But still they kept going. They had to. Short of a miracle, they were the only hope left. Encouraging word would be brought in to the passengers that the work was progressing very rapidly and that the ship would soon get up steam and be able to steer for the nearest port. But there was drama behind the scenes. Mr. Marshall, the Chief Engineer, hadn't left his post in the engine room during the whole of this trying scene, and for the two and half days since the first sea was shipped, he hadn't even gone on deck. Alex Auchinleck, one of his first engineers, saw him up for 50 hours consecutively. He would sometimes get a nap of 20 minutes by sleeping on the gratings, and finally

---

16. Eaton.
17. Eaton.
18. Eaton.

became so exhausted that he was unable to walk, and was reduced to crawling about on his hands and knees. Finally the crew had to carry him from position to position, wherever his services were required, to superintend the work going on about the machinery. As if that wasn't bad enough, two of the firemen were lost. And Auchinleck himself, that night, exhausted from being in the water, fainted for the first time in his life.[19]

A new and potentially menacing problem presented itself this night. Many of the raw recruits had been so overtaken with despair that they had became insubordinate, and now they came down en masse into the cabin where the women were. After a tricky moment or two they were finally persuaded upstairs and back to work by the officers.[20]

That night the gale was still blowing from the northwest, but there was less sea running. But then it turned into a hurricane, and the *Maria* was forced to lie to. It was while she was in this immobile position that the *San Francisco*, having no power of her own, and being completely at the mercy of the wind and waves, floated away from her. There was nothing anyone could do about it. It was the last time the *Maria* saw her.[21]

---

19. Eaton; Marshall, Jan. 16, 1854; Auchinleck.
20. Mrs. Gates. Fremont tells us that there were about 50 or 55 women in the cabin. These were not laundresses, but the wives of enlisted men.
21. Graham; Gretton; Freeman.

Tuesday
December 27

Come daylight, from the *San Francisco* nothing was to be seen of the *Maria*, the two vessels having drifted so far away from each other during the night that the only thing the men could see from their respective decks was empty ocean and sky. Captain Freeman, the brig's skipper, having cruised around as well as he could, looking in vain for the wreck, felt that the *San Francisco* must have foundered during the gale of that night. However, the *San Francisco* had not foundered.[1]

After the tremendous blow of losing contact with the *Maria* so soon after the *Napoleon*, the survivors aboard the wrecked steamer needed some good news. Some very good news. Perhaps a miracle. And they were about to get one. It was not a miracle exactly. It was the result of more than 60 hours of intense grind in the *San Francisco*'s engine room. But the news was received as a miracle by the passengers later that morning when Mr. Schell, the purser, came into the saloon in the highest of spirits. "The engine will be put in motion very soon and we will steer for the nearest port."[2]

And indeed, at 10 a.m., the engineers succeeded in closing the head of the air-pump, and, holding their breath and crossing their fingers, they made a second attempt to start the engine for a few turns. They got up steam and succeeded in getting the ship's head to the sea. Everyone aboard became acutely conscious of the throbbing coming from the engine room, and the change of direction of their vessel. It was working beautifully, and the commodore was delighted. Hundreds of hearts pounded hopefully in rhythm with the engine that had come back from the dead. It was new life for them all, their rescue from the brink of hell. But then what they had feared most happened. After a few revolutions, they found that the pressure of water against the pump had bent the bolts, and deranged the whole apparatus, rendering the piston unable to stand the pressure of working the engines. The crucial bucket of the air-pump had failed again and they began to lose steam. After 10 minutes it was all over. The paddle-wheels of the ill-fated vessel had made their last revolutions. With the engine and sails gone, the wrecked steamer *San Francisco* now had no

---

1. Mellus account; Wickham; Gretton; Freeman.
2. Eaton; Auchinleck; Gretton; Mellus account; Wickham.

motive power of its own, and no hope of getting any. She was entirely at the mercy of the wind and waves. And so were the passengers.[3]

Although steam was not forthcoming for the engines, there was certainly plenty of it escaping into the saloon since the partition separating the saloon from the engine room had fallen away. Given that the ship's two steam pipes had been wrecked three days earlier, and that there were no windows or openings for ventilation in the saloon, Lucia Eaton's group lay gasping in horror on their mattresses, perfectly exhausted, trying to catch a breath of air by fanning themselves with handkerchiefs, bits of paper, or anything they could find the strength to handle. The badly injured Dr. Satterlee, lying near Miss Eaton's group, was begging to be taken to where he could get some air into his lungs, protesting that he would die if he remained in this place. Two of the officers led him out and he soon revived. Then word came that the engines had failed, that they were totally useless. But the silver lining to that cloud was that the steam ceased in the saloon, and no one muttered a word of complaint about the engineering failure. The soldiers were still kept bailing, but, having had little rest, they were worn out.[4]

It was not just the troops who were worn out, but the officers too. Lieutenants such as Van Voast, Chandler, and Bill Winder, when having nothing to do, would come into the saloon, throw themselves upon a mattress, and try to get a little sleep. But as soon as Commodore Watkins called for help, they were up and running. There was cooking done twice during the four days after the wreck, and Lieutenant Lucien Loeser issued those provisions at the galley to the men. As for the commodore, he took a roasted potato when he could get one, and more often than not would divide it with someone even more needy. On one occasion, the purser was invited to partake of a sumptuous repast in the coal bunker. The dinner consisted of roasted potatoes and a slice of bacon. Sergeant Richard Hopley of Company H, aged 23, did not make that dinner.[5]

The idea occurred to Engineer Auchinleck that by working the large engines they might possibly break down the air-pump, so that, instead of serving in its normal role as a vital part of the motive power of the ship, it could be used, in conjunction with the donkey pumps and the 30-inch pump, to pump out the bilge water from the ship instead. As for the donkey pumps, the engineers took them to pieces and found them to be full of felting from the boilers, which had come up and choked the valves. They were of no use until they were overhauled, and so the engineers got to work on them immediately, and by late morning, with the wind blowing heavily from the northwest, the donkeys and the 30-incher were running fine and proved sufficient to keep the ship free of bilge without the labor of bailing. But this was far from sufficient to restore the navigation of the ship even after the wind had declined and the sea was favorable.[6]

---

3. Eaton; Auchinleck; Gretton; Mellus account; Wickham; Winder, Jan. 6, 1854. Gretton puts the time at 6 a.m., but he was four hours out.
4. Eaton.
5. Eaton; Loeser; Auchinleck; Army enlistment records.
6. Gretton; Auchinleck; "Justice;" *New York Tribune*, Jan. 23, 1854.

It was all a grave disappointment, but there was also a tragedy while the crew were bending a storm mizzen sail. Alexander, one of the seamen, was on the spanker boom clearing away the spanker sheets when the sea struck the ship with such force that it threw him from the boom into the water. He was never seen again.[7]

While walking along through the fast-disappearing bilge, Alex Auchinleck, the engineer, stumbled over a man whom he supposed to be a dead soldier, but who proved to be his chief engineer, Mr. Marshall, busily engaged about the engine. The ever valiant Marshall, whose vocabulary simply did not admit of the word "despair," sang out that he would be through in a moment, and assured Auchinleck and the boys that they would all be saved if they would trust to their own exertions and look to a higher power. His attitude was infectious, from his engineers down to his firemen, who were generally very attentive to their duties, and seemed to want to do all in their power.[8]

Although they kept the pumps at work constantly from that time out, they tried fixing the air-pump again, but with as little success as before. This time they couldn't even get the big engine underway. The difficulty was that they couldn't get steam, since the pipes were gone. Their wheels kept good, but the hog braces were out away by the sea.[9]

James Lorimer Graham was as taken as anyone by that paragon of virtue, the Admirable Murray. "There was one there, one of those noblemen with which nature loves to adorn itself—who went far to cheer, to comfort, and to assist those of us who were weak and downhearted. I speak of Lieut. F.K. Murray, of the United States Navy, whose name will remain dear to every soul on board, until they themselves have passed away and are numbered with the things that were." And this: "A strange fate seemed to be hanging over us and despair was more clearly depicted upon every countenance. All hopes seemed now to have vanished, and had it not been for Lt. Murray—the good Samaritan of our little flock—many, I fear would have lost their reason."[10]

Most of the ladies were nearly dead from want of food and clothing, having lost all their baggage and every article of dress except basically what they were wearing, and those on board who had managed to save extra clothing shared it generously with the others. Engineer Donaghan, for one, gave them all his linen. Several hours each day would be spent trying to substitute dry for wet clothing, and Engineer Auchinleck acted as a sort of hospital nurse.[11]

"The sea, which had been continually breaking over the vessel, came rushing in at intervals from the port-holes and skylights above, so that the floor of the cabin was always wet, and the mattresses upon which we laid were perfectly saturated."[12]

At noon and throughout the afternoon the gale blew heavy from the northwest, with the sea getting up again. Everybody got to work lightening the ship. They set

---

7. Mellus; Wickham; Gretton.
8. Auchinleck.
9. Auchinleck.
10. Graham; Graham/Kilby.
11. Graham; Auchinleck.
12. Graham; Auchinleck. The quote is from Graham.

four gangs to get up the coal, two hoisting it up with the ash buckets and two passing it with bags, baskets, and fire buckets through holes cut in the deck over the wing bunkers. Part of the crew went to work hoisting provisions up the fore hatch, while others were employed with fire axes cutting away the guard beams. It was slow work, the ship rolling as it was. A man had to be lashed amidships with a line made fast to the man with the axe, who waited till the ship got a little steady before running to the beams. In that brief moment while he had time, he would cut away until the ship rolled down, at which point the man amidships would haul him up. Then they would wait for another chance.[13]

Then, at 2 p.m., to windward on their weather bow, they saw, in the distance, a bark hove to. Commodore Watkins went into Colonel Gates's cabin to let him know the good news, and soon everyone on the *San Francisco* was out on deck. It was obvious to the crew on the bark that the steamer was in distress, and so they set a course toward her. At 4 p.m., with the bark now within hailing distance and coming in as close as she dared, Commodore Watkins spoke her. She proved to be the *Kilby* of Boston, under the command of Captain Edwin T. Low, an Irishman who had been raised in Baltimore. The *Kilby* was 48 days out of New Orleans and bound home, laden with cotton. She was under courses, her jib and spanker having experienced very bad weather, and she had lost most of her sails. She was also short of provisions, and had only one cask of water aboard. Watkins informed Captain Low of the *San Francisco*'s situation, and Low promised to lay by them and try to get the survivors off if possible. But it was not to be that day, as the sea was running very high, and so Captain Low promised to remain by them overnight.[14]

So, deliverance was now just a matter of time, that is if the weather ameliorated, and, of course, providing the *Kilby* didn't drift off during the night as the *Napoleon* and the *Maria* had done. Despite these fears, the men on the *San Francisco* were energized by the hope of rescue, and began to plan with a will for the transshipment of souls on the morrow. Colonel Gates gave orders that everything should be done quietly and in order, without confusion, as there would be time for everyone to disembark without hurrying. He then gave the order for all to get themselves in readiness for their departure from the wreck the following day.[15]

Major Wyse had, only the year before, married Mary Eliza, the beautiful 18-year-old daughter of Commodore John Pope, U.S. Navy. Their first child had been born the following April, and, now, at nine months old, this baby was one of the

---

13. Gretton; Mellus account; Wickham.
14. Buel, 1854; Gretton; Mellus account; Wickham; Eaton; Wyse testimony. There can be little doubt that 2 o'clock was the time they sighted the Kilby, just as Gretton says. However, the ship's log, written by Mr. Mellus, has, "As night closed in." Mr. Wickham, who normally copied from the log, has the sighting as his last entry before noon of that day. Lucia Eaton says: "On Tuesday afternoon we heard the joyful news that a bark was in sight." Gretton says the *Kilby* was 48 days out of New Orleans; Miss Eaton says 30 days, and in another place 60. The only crewmen on the *Kilby* whose names we have, aside from the skipper, are Frederick Lincoln, the cook, whose name may, in fact, really have been Frederick Lucien; John F. Crowell, a seaman who would, when the time came, display great courage in saving human life, and be awarded a silver medal; and Robert Gibson Garthley.
15. Eaton.

youngest passengers on board the *San Francisco*. For these reasons, and perhaps others, the major was anxious to get off the steamer early the following day, in case things should go wrong with the transfer. But he was the commanding officer of Company D, and would have to supervise the transfer of his men. This might well mean he would be one of the very last off the ship, whereas his wife and child would be among the first group off. Indeed, the major might not even get off at all. He and his wife and Lieutenant Van Voast were in the cabin talking about that very issue, the order in which the officers should leave the *San Francisco* on the morrow, when Wyse declared, rather hollowly, that each company commander, himself included, should remain aboard until every single one of his men had been transferred to the *Kilby*. Mrs. Wyse objected to this, and so the obliging Van Voast offered to substitute for the major. Wyse saw his opportunity immediately, of course, but his grave expression never changed for an instant. He wasn't sure. He didn't know for certain whether that was a good idea or not. Well, perhaps it was. Yes, that should be all right. No, it would probably not be necessary for him to stay.[16]

As if on cue, during the night the wind hauled around to the southward, and began to moderate. Just as good news was that the steam pumps were now able to keep the water out of the steamer. Tremendous elation roamed the *San Francisco* that night, even though, with no lamps, they could hardly see a thing. As Lieutenant W.A. Winder later remembered: "The long dark cabin was lighted by two candles just enough to make a dark moonlight; the forms of the men moving quickly about, uttering no sound..."[17]

At seven o'clock that evening, Lieutenant Fremont came on for his 24-hour stint as officer of the day.[18]

---

16. Van Voast.
17. Winder, 1883.
18. From general court proceedings at the court of inquiry, Feb. 16, 1854.

Wednesday
December 28

On the *San Francisco* that morning Lucia Eaton's party awoke to the joyful news that the bark *Kilby* was still in sight. But it was a long way to the windward of them. By complete daylight, with the weather quite moderate now, the distance between the two vessels had been reduced to about five miles, with the *Kilby* off the steamer's weather bow, and as soon as the crew on the bark spotted the *San Francisco*, they headed in her direction. However, the wind was dying away, and the *Kilby* had very little sail on, and came down with frustrating slowness.[1]

Unknown to anyone on board the *San Francisco*, for the last few days a fearful specter had been lurking in one of the dark recesses of the wrecked steamer. Late in the morning it finally emerged in the fore cabin to deal its first death blow. After hours of writhing in agony, Johnson, one of the negro head waiters, could take no more.[2]

Dr. Buel put Johnson's death down to a case of severe congestive diarrhea, but then others started to die in the same terrible way, and it wasn't long before bodies were being thrown overboard. For the survivors who thought they had lived through every horror imaginable in the last 100 hours, this was all they needed. And it wasn't just a few isolated cases now. It had rapidly become an epidemic.[3]

Prior to this, Dr. Buel had seen no disease on board the *San Francisco* that even approached epidemic proportions, and that may have been due to the fact that the recruits from Governors Island were picked as having the best physique and possibly the best morale, at least according to Buel. Of course the Gates children had measles, or were getting over it. And there was only one case of varioloid and one of smallpox, both among the soldiers. And, soldiers being soldiers, there were some slight cases of venereal infection. But this new disease was something else.[4]

Now, with more experience of the phenomenon, the doctor was forced to re-evaluate his original diagnosis. It wasn't just diarrhea, as he had first thought. He

---

1. Eaton; Mellus account; Wickham; Gretton; Buel, 1854.
2. Mellus account; Wickham; Graham; Winder, Jan. 6, 1854; Wyse testimony; Buel testimony; Buel, *American Journal*; Partridge.
3. Buel testimony; Mellus account; Buel, *American Journal*.
4. Varioloid is a mild case of smallpox, usually afflicting only those who have had the actual pox before or have been inoculated against it. As Buel tells us, this disease was transmitted to only one other person while on board.

sought out Commodore Watkins for a private audience, and revealed his findings to the skipper. The symptoms of this new disease—its malignity, fatality, and rapidity of termination—differed in no respect from those of one of the greatest scourges of mankind. There was no other way Buel could say it. The *San Francisco* had become a plague ship. The dreaded menace of cholera was among them.[5]

The two men agreed that it was best not to mention the word "cholera," for fear a panic would be produced, and so they decided to stick with "diarrhea."[6]

After some investigation Dr. Buel came up with what he considered to be the causes of this new disaster. One was alimentary and the other sanitary. The first was brought about by the imprudence of some of the troops and waiters in eating some pickled cabbage, potted and canned meats, and such articles as they could procure, and by the drinking of molasses with water when the men came out of bailing in the incredibly hot engine room. It might have been different if they had been able to cook the foods, but with the galley out of commission since the storm began, this was out of the question. Then Buel looked into the conditions prevailing in the part of the steamer where the sickness first occurred—in the second, or forward, cabin. There was an upper and lower forward cabin, and the outbreak occurred in the lower of the two, a part of the ship occupied by the families of the non-commissioned officers. Two other parts of the forward cabin, forward steerage and the portion that had been used as a females' hospital, had been, to some extent, made into one by the knocking down of the bulkheads between them. The arrangement of the berths in both parts was identical, a fact that was important when studying this cause of the disease. They were placed not by the side of the ship but running athwart ships. They were not exactly state rooms, because they had no doors, but formed a sort of alcove. In each alcove there were 12 berths, six upon each side, and three feet deep, one above another, and the consequence was that at the end of these places the atmosphere was necessarily very bad. They had in each alcove an air port, which, because of the heavy sea, could never be opened. Thus there was no chance of proper ventilation, and a great amount of the disease occurred in these two rooms. Buel says that by later in the day of the twenty-fourth, the total number of persons left aboard the *San Francisco* was 620. After the wreck, those surviving soldiers who had been quartered on the main deck all went below, and so now there were about 500 men, women and children crowded together in a space that was never designed for more than 200 or 250, and barely that.[7]

Not everyone believed the "diarrhea" story. On January 14, 1854, the day after the first of the *San Francisco* survivors got back to New York on the *Three Bells*, the *New York Times* ran an article in which the culprit was declared to be cholera, "occa-

---

5. Buel testimony; Buel, *American Journal*.
6. Buel testimony; Buel, *American Journal*.
7. Mellus account; Wickham; Graham; Gretton; Winder, Jan. 6, 1854; Wyse testimony; Buel testimony; Buel, *American Journal*; Partridge. Today we would call an air port a port hole. The *San Francisco* had numerous ports, and like her skylights, they were large—in the case of the air ports two feet square with a circle of glass in the center, affording, under normal circumstances, an unusual amount of light and ventilation (*New York Herald*, July 5, 1853).

sioned by the dissipation of a portion of the troops, and of the white and colored waiters." On Christmas Eve, while the ship had been at the mercy of the ocean following the giant wave, many of these individuals, "as is too often the case at such seasons, determined since they had given up the idea of escaping, to enjoy themselves before the ship went down." In the confusion that prevailed, continued the article, the store-room had been left unfastened, and the contents were "too tempting to be withstood. They accordingly indulged their appetites without restraint. They partook of preserves, cakes, sweetmeats, dainties of all kinds ad libitum, and then repaired to the spirit room, where they washed down their repasts with copious and undiluted draughts." The effects of this conduct unexpectedly manifested themselves in violent attacks of cramp and diarrhea. Some of the debauchees died in less than 10 hours from the time of seizure; "others laid a day or two," while some recovered altogether. "We are informed by an officer that nearly sixty individuals perished in this manner, some dying on board the *Three Bells*, while on her way to New York. Others were put on board the *Antarctic*, so much reduced by diarrhea as to give but little prospect of recovery."[8]

Not everyone believed the "cholera" story either. One of the stewardesses, Catherine Livingston, who would be taken off on the *Three Bells*, differed with Dr. Buel as to the nature of the sickness, the same cholera, of course, that would be transferred onto that vessel from the *San Francisco*. "A word about the sickness on board the *Three Bells*. This was very destructive, some thirty one grown persons and six children dying." And that was just on the *Three Bells*, and did not include those who died or would die of this disease on the *San Francisco* itself, or on the *Antarctic*. "Various statements about it have been published," she says, and "one of these represent it as cholera. I have seen patients die of this disease frequently, and the symptoms were altogether different. The more apparent causes, viz: cold, fatigue, loss of sleep, proper food, fright, etc., were quite sufficient to account for the mortality, without any such theory as the prevalence of cholera, or indeed any other epidemic disease."[9]

That morning Lucia Eaton was not feeling well. In spite of that, she managed to swing into action. Although she "could as soon have gone without" a hat, "for I cared but little for appearance at those times," she still had to make herself look presentable for her debut on the *Kilby*, and that meant, among other things, dry clothing. Colonel Gates had decreed that each person could take one trunk onto the *Kilby*, but many passengers had lost theirs on the morning of the wreck. Of those trunks still aboard, only three ladies had dry ones: Miss Eaton, her sister, Sarah Loeser, and their servant. All the rest had been wet through and through. Lucia and Sarah could only wear one dry outfit apiece, of course, but they could still take their own trunks. Their main concerns were not for themselves, obviously, it was just that they would be able

---

8. *New York Times*, Jan. 14, 1854. At the later court of inquiry, Dr. Buel estimated 70 deaths from this disease: 50 soldiers, ten women, five children, and five crew. However, not all of these deaths took place on the *San Francisco*. Fifteen were of people who would be taken off in a dying condition onto the *Three Bells* on January 4. Dr. Buel does not include those who died on the *Antarctic*.
9. Livingston. No one died of cholera aboard the *Kilby*.

to share with the needy. But the two ladies couldn't immediately get to their trunks, as they were still hemmed in by scores of others. Fortunately the servant woman, the one with the big trunk, was able to get to hers, so the good woman gave Lucia some of her clothes, while Sarah gave her sister half a shawl and a summer hat she had saved for her. Sarah kept the other half of the shawl, and gave a hood she had been wearing to a poor hatless lady. Lucia gave a saque she had been wearing to a needy lady who had lost all her clothing, and the servant gave her other articles of dress.[10]

After completing her toilet, Miss Eaton took her place upon one of the highest seats in the saloon, and in casting her eye around, she took in the whole scene at a glance. The floor was covered with mattresses on which people were sitting, while around them on all sides articles of clothing were strewn about, "in not elegant confusion," hats wet and bent up into all imaginable shapes; clothing of all kinds: cloaks, dresses and shawls, some of them having changed their color entirely as a result of the corroding influence of sea water. The ladies would take up an article of dress to see if it could be used but, finding it too wet or not clean, it would be cast aside. All who had clothing shared it with the needy. Those who had children found it very difficult to find clothing enough to make them comfortable. One or two of the ladies, in getting ready, had worked themselves too much and fainted away. One was lying at Lucia Eaton's feet, and she gave her a bottle of smelling salts and exerted herself as much as possible in fanning her so as to restore her to consciousness. There were but three or four of them who had hats. Mrs. Wyse wore one that Miss Eaton had taken out for spring wear. "While I was sitting quietly, and sometimes lying down, still watching those wretched-looking beings, someone came up to me and placed my Bible in my hand. I had left it in my room the night before we were wrecked, and since that time I had not thought of it. It was wet through and through, and the cover was loose, but I prized it more highly for all it had passed through." It had been a present from Lucia's father, and she was delighted to see it again. Mr. Cooper told her, "It is far more valuable now than ever." Lieutenant Loeser put it in a little carpetbag, which he intended to carry over to the *Kilby* in his hand, and in that way it was taken from the wreck. Mr. Cooper was praying again, to thank his god for delivering the survivors up, and to beseech the same god for a successful transfer to the *Kilby*.[11]

As she sat patiently waiting to be called upon deck, Lucia looked around the saloon. Furniture broken, bedding strewn about, trunks opened and the wet clothing lying on the floor. She saw the drawn, pale faces of the survivors. Everything that had happened Lucia attributed to her god, who was presumably the same god as Mr. Cooper's. This god of hers, whom she calls the Almighty, was, according to her, so whimsically wrathful that, just because he could, he "saw fit to stretch forth his hand in wrath and command those fearful waves to sweep the deck in their fury. We poor helpless creatures and that steamship were as nothing before him. And yet the

---

10. Eaton.
11. Eaton.

Almighty was merciful to us, unworthy and sinful as we were." Miss Eaton then says: "Did He not say to the angry sea?: 'Thus far shalt thou go and no further and here shall thy proud waves be staid'?" One minute she is attributing the storm entirely to her wrathful god, the next minute that very same god is stepping in to stop the storm which he had created in the first place. It was not just Miss Eaton. This was the general state of occult belief in the United States at the time.[12]

The latter part of the morning remained quite moderate, as the crew of the *San Francisco* made ready to transfer passengers. The afternoon started with light southerly wind and clear, pleasant weather, the sea going down quite fast, and by 1 p.m. the *Kilby* came alongside the weather side of the *San Francisco*, near enough to board. They sent a boat over to the steamer, the *San Francisco* having lost all eight of her own lifeboats during the massive wave of Christmas Eve. Two men prepared to be swung down the side of the steamer into the boat. Their mission was one of critical importance to the survivors of the wreck of the *San Francisco*.[13]

Colonel Gates, a desperate man in charge of a desperate contingent of souls, had given Lieutenant Fremont explicit instructions for this mission; in the name of the U.S. Government—always a powerful reference—to attempt to negotiate a charter with Captain Low of the *Kilby*, to convey the surviving troops to the nearest accessible port. He was to offer $15,000 for taking off as many passengers from the wreck as possible. Commodore Watkins, as skipper of the doomed Pacific Mail Steamship Company vessel, was to go over with Fremont, to represent his employers. His offer to Captain Low was $200 a day if the *Kilby* would stand by him until he and his crew were ready to leave the steamer.[14]

And so, fully primed, the lieutenant and the commodore walked to the ship's stern, where the crew had rigged up a whip, a huge, strong rope tied securely to the end of the spanker boom, and fashioned in the form of a swing, with a knot being tied just above where the passenger's head would be. Watkins went first, taking his seat in the swing. Told to take hold of the ropes above him, he began his descent over the edge of his ship, but the seas were still quite high, and, with the little boat rising and falling on top of the waves beneath him, it was only with enormous difficulty, and after an agonizingly long time, that the commodore was finally lowered into the little wooden vessel. Colonel Gates quickly realized that if Fremont were to follow suit, they would never get to the *Kilby*, and so he ordered his lieutenant to make sure that Watkins, then sitting in the boat, fully understood the army's part in this drama. Then the boat pushed off, and soon afterwards Commodore Watkins boarded the *Kilby*.[15]

The commodore asked Low what he would charge for taking the people on

---

12. Eaton.
13. Gretton; Fremont; Mellus account; Wickham; Buel 1854. Mr. Gretton says it was Thursday, the 29th, at about 1 p.m. when the *Kilby* sent over the first boat. He was right, of course; it was the 29th, using sea time.
14. Mellus account; Wickham; Murray; Eaton; Gretton; Buel, 1854; Graham.
15. Fremont; Gretton.

board, to which the bark's skipper replied, "I am a very young man, and as you are an older and more experienced seaman, I throw myself entirely on your better judgment for advice, as one sailor will do to another."[16]

It wasn't long before Watkins returned to the *San Francisco*, mission accomplished.[17]

Lieutenant Frank Murray, of the U.S. Navy, approached Commodore Watkins upon his return to the *San Francisco*, and offered his services in any capacity that Watkins though fit, as he had done on several occasions before. Watkins instructed him to go aboard the *Kilby* with an officer of the regiment and a working party of soldiers, to "break out her cargo and prepare her to receive the passengers." Murray, being Murray, told Watkins that unless everyone, including the crew and captain, were to go on to the *Kilby*, then—why—he, Murray, would not leave them on the *San Francisco*, but would remain on the steamer to the last. Watkins assured him that everyone would be transferred, that he had made a contract with the skipper of the *Kilby*. At this point, Murray realized that it was Watkins's intention to stay aboard the *San Francisco*, or rather what was left of her, until the engineer decided one way or the other whether the engine could be made to work again.[18]

Indeed, that was Watkins's plan. He was struggling desperately to come up with a reasonable way in which a last-ditch effort might enable him to bring the *San Francisco* back to land. He asked Colonel Gates if he could call for 20 volunteers to stay by him, and in 10 minutes he had 40.[19]

Colonel Gates, through his adjutant, Lieutenant Fremont, ordered Second Lieutenant Van Voast to form a detail of 20 men to go over immediately to clear the *Kilby*'s hold of its cotton cargo in order to allow for the influx of hundreds of persons. Soon afterwards, Captain Judd, who was still an invalid, was added to this detail. Van Voast instructed Sergeant Gorham to pick out only men who were fit for the job.[20]

Lucia Eaton writes: "After waiting for a short time one of the officers came up to my sister and myself and asked us to go up on deck." They were taken up on a ladder and through an opening above. This was the first time since the wreck that Miss Eaton had been on the spar deck, a place she hardly recognized now, it had changed so much. Standing there, she and Sarah noticed that the hurricane deck, all the state rooms, and the smoke stacks had gone, and that the wheel houses were badly broken or gone entirely. "There was but one mast left, which was useless, as all the sail had been carried away." They were led to seats on the side of the steamer and, upon sitting, were obliged to hold on to the railing, so as to prevent themselves

---

16. *Boston Daily Atlas*, Jan. 21, 1854.
17. Mellus account; Wickham; Murray; Eaton; Gretton; Buel, 1854; Graham. Murray, in his Feb. 10, 1854, testimony, says Watkins returned within half an hour. Gretton says "in about 40 minutes he came on board again," and gave orders to prepare to send the passengers to the *Kilby*.
18. Murray; Eaton; Winder, Jan. 6, 1854; Winder interview, 1854; Eaton; Watkins testimony.
19. Winder, Jan. 6, 1854; Winder interview, 1854; Eaton; Watkins testimony; Fremont.
20. Fremont; Eaton; Van Voast; Gorham.

from falling off. "The steamship was still in the trough of the seas. She had been lightened very much by having the freight taken out of the hold and thrown into the water. She rolled fearfully as the sea was running very high. One moment the deck would touch the water and then going down on the other side we would be mounted high in the air." They held their breath in horror, and grasped the railing even tighter.[21]

Major Merchant had been confined in his cabin since the morning of the wreck, four days before, and was now taken on deck to be transferred to the *Kilby*. Here he was joined by the injured and rheumatic dragoon Captain Gardiner, who, all that day, had remained in the lower cabin until he was told that a boat was ready to take him to the *Kilby*. Lieutenant Loeser was there too, waiting. Major Wyse had given him permission to take supplies over. That way Loeser could see that his female charges were safely ensconced aboard the *Kilby*. But he had to return. That was an order.[22]

At about 2:30 in the afternoon, with the sea now becoming quiet, the crew of the *San Francisco* again set up the whip on the spanker boom in order to let passengers down over the side of the stern, one at a time, into the small craft that would soon arrive and be waiting below the steamer's stern. Although both *Kilby* boats had been assigned to the mission, only one of them was used for this first crossing, to test the water.[23]

With the steamer's stern rising and falling a good deal with the sea, they had to move as fast as possible commensurate with safety because it would soon be dark, and then they wouldn't be able to see to lower the people down with any accuracy. The passengers were told to wrap themselves in a blanket—two, if they had them— and not to exert themselves until they had been let down to a point immediately over the boat, at which point they would be given precise instructions by Lieutenant Frank Murray, who would be waiting there to catch each person as soon as they were lowered.[24]

As soon as the *Kilby*'s boat appeared under the ship's stern, there was a mad rush for the whip, and more responsible persons were afraid that if the panicked throng succeeded in getting down into the boat it would be swamped. Several officers armed themselves with what few weapons remained on board in order to hold back the madding crowd, and Colonel Gates stood up and made a speech: "I shall be the last man to leave the ship." He hoped the other officers and men would follow his example, and wait for their names to be called.[25]

---

21. Eaton.
22. Eaton; Merchant; Gardiner.
23. Mellus account; Wickham; Gretton; Eaton; Buel, 1854; Murray; Fremont; Eaton. Murray says they started sending passengers over to the *Kilby* at about ten in the morning. That is quite a way from 2:30 in the afternoon, as is the time given by Dr. Buel: "Toward evening the sea became quiet, and the disembarkation commenced." Lucia Eaton says: "I think it must have been at three o'clock on Wednesday afternoon when the disembarkation commenced." Bill Winder, in his Jan. 6, 1854, report, says "about 2 o'clock." 2:30 is much more likely.
24. Mellus account; Wickham; Gretton; Eaton; Buel, 1854; Murray; Fremont; Eaton.
25. Graham; Mellus account; Wickham; Gardiner.

Charlie Winder went up to Fremont and said, in what seems like an echo of Colonel Gates's pronunciamento, "I will remain with my company until the last." The difference was, Charlie meant it and Colonel Gates didn't.[26]

It had been understood that the officers' wives should go first, with their small children, in order of their husbands' rank, but it didn't quite turn out that way, even though Mrs. Gates and her brood went over the side first, followed by Major Merchant's family. As one of the little Merchant girls was coming down in the swing, she started to fall out, and if Lieutenant Murray hadn't caught her just as she slipped out, she would have wound up in the sea. After that came Major Wyse's young wife and her infant.[27]

After a while, Lucia Eaton was called to be lowered down in the whip. Despite the fact that it looked very dangerous, she faced the ordeal with pluck, as everyone else did. Although Miss Eaton herself says, "On getting into the swing, I was lowered without the least trouble," she would later be told, by Lieutenant Murray himself, that she and her sister were in more danger at this moment than they had ever been during the wreck.[28]

Miss Eaton took her place in the bow of the boat beside a large lady. "She had quite a fight in getting down, as she was very fleshy and of course it was more dangerous for her than for those who were slight in figure. As the boat was full her husband could not go with her, and she clasped her hands in the greatest agony, saying: 'My husband! Oh, my husband! I shall never see him again!'" Lucia tried to calm her, telling her that her husband would come over in the next boat, and he would soon be with her. The fat lady wailed, "My poor mother begged me not to go out in that steamship, she told me that I would never get to land. Oh, why did I come, why did I come?" Miss Eaton tried in every possible way to divert her attention, and after a while the fat lady became more composed.[29]

Finally came Lieutenant Loeser with his provisions, and Captain Judd, Lieutenant Van Voast, and their cotton detail. For some reason Sergeant Gorham had been able to find only 10 men, not the 20 as originally ordered. One of those now in the boat was Corporal Taylor, of whom Van Voast did not have a good opinion, judging from his earlier work at the pumps.[30]

The little craft was leaking bad and was almost full of water as it set out for the *Kilby*. Just in order to keep afloat two men had to bail throughout the entire crossing, but even that wasn't enough. The ladies, who were at times completely submerged by water, were called in to help.[31]

Then they were at the side of the *Kilby*, with the sea running very high and the

---

26. Fremont letter.
27. Fremont; Fremont letter; Graham; Eaton; Mrs. Gates; Murray.
28. Eaton.
29. Eaton; Southworth. The quotes are from Eaton. Miss Eaton does not name the fat lady, but it really has to be Senhora Abrio.
30. Fremont; Van Voast; Fremont letter; Winder, Jan. 6, 1854; Van Voast; Gorham.
31. Fremont; Eaton; Mrs. Gates; Southworth.

bark itself tossing about fearfully. Holding on for their lives, each person went up the ladder, Lieutenant Van Voast just behind them to prevent them from falling, a service he was to continue to perform throughout the rest of the day. He had a problem with the fat lady, and she almost lost her life, but she finally made it.[32]

Having delivered that first consignment safely, the boat, along with the *Kilby*'s second one, returned to the side of the *San Francisco*, ready for more passengers.[33]

Upon her arrival on the bark, Lucia Eaton went into her cabin, wishing to see how it looked, and also wanting to put away the blanket she had brought over with her. The *Kilby*'s cabin was very small, about 10 feet by 12 of open floor, with "a kind of locker or lounge, or sofa, I do not know what it was called" filling up one entire side of the room. "It was covered with crash, and very much soiled." A table occupied the center of the cabin, but it would later be taken away to make room for all the passengers in this incredibly tight space. The only other furniture and furnishings in this little space were two trunks, a barrel of hard bread, and a box of crackers. On each side of the cabin was a little place intended for a state room, in which one could barely even turn around, dominated as it was by a kind of bunk or berth, with no sheets or blankets to lie on. Two of these tiny state rooms were occupied by the Colonel Gates group, the first by the old man himself, his wife and three young children, and the second, which had two bunks, by the children's nurse and Mrs. Gates's sister, Miss Carter, who was not strong in health. For his own room the colonel found an old mattress and spread it on the floor of his room to ease the sleeping arrangements. Major Merchant and his wife, Sarah, who was then 50, took another state room, the major sleeping on the floor with a blanket under him. Senhor and Madame Abrio occupied the fourth, but they would later give it up to Lieutenant Loeser's wife, Sarah. After taking a look at the cabin and the tiny staterooms within it, Miss Eaton threw her blanket upon the floor in a corner of one of the staterooms, and went out on deck.[34]

People were constantly arriving aboard the *Kilby*. When Major Merchant's adult daughter, Valeria—known as Vallie—succeeded in getting up to the rail of the bark, she happened to cast her eye back over the route she had just taken, and, and with this new perspective of distance, was able to grasp, for the first time, what a fearful wreck the *San Francisco* was. Despite that, the officers and soldiers left on the steamer's deck looked cheerful and happy, at least from that distance. Miss Merchant and Lucia Eaton stood looking across the water at the doomed vessel until after sundown. It was the last time they ever laid eyes upon the ill-fated *San Francisco*. Some persons told them they could get a cup of tea if they would go over to the galley, so they headed in that direction, being obliged to pass by the hold, where the soldiers and sailors, in order to make room for the passengers, were busily engaged in hauling

---

32. Eaton; Van Voast. As Miss Eaton tells us, the fat lady's husband did indeed come over on the next boat, and she was finally able to sing a happier tune.
33. Fremont.
34. Eaton; Graham. As for Miss Carter, it is not clear which of Louise Gates's two unmarried sisters this was. It was either Frances Lincoln Carter (1819–1907) or Martha Ann Carter (1824–1915).

cotton bales and throwing into the sea. When they got to the galley, the cook did indeed hand them a cup of tea, which they found quite refreshing.[35]

At that moment, in the *San Francisco*'s cabin, Lieutenant Fremont was standing near the dinner table. He was just now beginning to recover from that inconvenient attack of pleurisy that had beleaguered him since the day of the wreck. With him were Colonel Gates and Major Wyse. The three Artillery officers were on the point of playing roles in what can only be described as a farce. Now that Gates had ordered Van Voast over to the *Kilby*, Major Wyse's hopes of an early exit had been dashed. He was not the only one to be shocked in that cabin. Fremont, like all the officers aboard, had assumed that Gates, as colonel of the regiment, would be supervising the entire disembarkation. Then he noticed the colonel heading for the transfer boat. As regimental adjutant, Fremont asked Gates, "Shall I detail Major Wyse to superintend the disembarkation of the troops?," to which the reply was, "Yes, certainly." Fremont then turned to Major Wyse and immediately made the detail. However, it seems that Colonel Gates had already given Captain Judd instructions to supervise the "re-embarcation," as Judd called it. Whether Gates thought Fremont's suggestion was a better one or he simply forgot that he had given the previous order to Judd is not known, but it didn't really matter now—Judd had left the ship. The upshot was that as Colonel Gates walked out of the room to catch the next boat over, Major F.O. Wyse, being the only senior officer not disabled, found himself in command of all that remained of the Third Artillery aboard the *San Francisco*.[36]

Major Wyse did not actually see Colonel Gates make a bolt for it over the stern of the *San Francisco* but when he finally looked overboard, there was the regimental commander in one of the two boats, heading over to the *Kilby*. Regarding Colonel Gates's behavior, Lieutenant Fremont would later write: "As to the principle that the commanding officer should remain until all the men embarked, I have nothing to say; but if the object was to remove the troops as rapidly as possible, nothing was lost by the form that was adopted."[37]

The two *Kilby* boats now at the stern of the wreck were busy taking off all the disabled officers, including the white-haired Dr. Satterlee and the Dragoon Captain Gardiner. Colonel Burke and Major Merchant, being too weak to take hold of the rail, were not let down in the whip but in a tub. It wasn't only disabled officers who went off on this trip. Colonel Gates was aboard too, as were Lucien Loeser and his group of women, the lieutenant, in his role of commissary officer carrying two bottles of champagne over in his pocket, for himself and Dr. Satterlee.[38]

At 3 p.m., a hawser, some 200 to 300 feet long, was run between the stern of the

---

35. Eaton.
36. Fremont; Eaton; Judd; Satterlee testimony. Lieutenant Fremont, in his letter (Fremont letter) tells us that it was at his suggestion that Major Wyse was ordered to superintend the transfer of the troops, it being a well-known principle that the second officer in rank is usually considered the executive officer, and, as such, it was legitimate for Wyse to perform this duty. "I thought it was his right, as I hoped it was his desire."
37. Wyse testimony; Fremont; Fremont letter.
38. Loeser; Gardiner; Eaton; Merchant; Murray; Fremont letter; Graham. These two bottles of champagne were later used by Loeser, the doctor, and several families in the cabin.

San Francisco and the quarter of the *Kilby*, and so, with the two vessels now being kept together, the small boats would not have so far to travel during the transfer.[39]

Below decks on the *San Francisco*, Private Edward P. Ballard, of Company H, was suffering greatly from cholera. Originally from Lincoln, Maine, Ballard had been a harness maker when Major Wyse enlisted him in Boston on September 12, just three and a half months earlier. Now he was dying, and he knew it; twenty-seven years old. They brought him up on deck, and prepared to transfer him to the *Kilby*. But before they could get him into the whip he gave out with a groan and died.[40]

Miss Mariana Noland, who on the day of the wreck had volunteered her services on the bailing gang, was attacked by a sudden indisposition resembling cholera, and died. *"Her death was very affecting,"* wrote Sergeant Brown wistfully, about this woman who may very well have been his "laundress."[41]

As soon as Gates arrived on the *Kilby* that afternoon, he gave orders to Corporal Taylor to throw open the bark's hatches and put the men to work throwing out the cotton while Captain Judd, Lieutenant Fremont and Colonel Gates himself superintended. Not long afterwards bales of cotton were to be seen in ever increasing numbers floating and bobbing around in the ocean.[42]

Soon after getting aboard the *Kilby*, the surgeon assisted Captain Gardiner in getting to the galley, as that was the most comfortable place he could be put at that time. He remained there until after dark, when he went below into the hold.[43]

The *Kilby* was already low on provisions, and the huge influx of strangers made it imperative that supplies be brought over from the wreck. Lieutenant Loeser, the commissary officer, went to Colonel Gates—they were both aboard the *Kilby* at the time—and asked him what to do. Gates ordered him to cross back to the *San Francisco* in one of the lifeboats and get as many stores over as he could.[44]

At that moment, the boats were about to make their third trip over from the *Kilby*, and Loeser missed the ride. However, just in time Gates was able to slip a message to the *Kilby*'s coxswain to hand to Major Wyse, who was still aboard the *San Francisco*. Gates had forgotten to bring with him a pot of preserves for his children. Lieutenant Loeser was coming back over on the fourth trip, and would Wyse be good enough to send it over with him?[45]

Loeser did indeed make it over on the fourth trip, at about seven o'clock that evening, and as soon as he got aboard the wreck set about the long task of getting as many stores as he could. While he was thus engaged, the boats continued to ply back and forth between the two ships, carrying as many passengers to the *Kilby* as they could. On the *San Francisco*, Lieutenant Fremont advised Major Wyse that they

---

39. Mellus account; Wickham; Gretton; Graham; Eaton; Fremont letter.
40. Army enlistment records; Buel testimony.
41. Brown account. Mariana Noland is mentioned only by Sergeant Brown.
42. Taylor; Winder testimony.
43. Gardiner.
44. Loeser; Fremont.
45. Wyse testimony; Loeser.

should just keep running the boats until everyone was off the wreck, and Wyse partly agreed. He felt that they could keep running for a portion of the night, but it might get too dark to continue after that.[46]

It was about dark when Captain Low decided that there should be no more boat trips that night. With his first mate, he sent word over to those aboard the *San Francisco* that the other boat was being hauled up onto the *Kilby*, and that the transfer would resume in the morning. However, Lieutenant Fremont, who was supervising the disembarkation from the steamer, felt that, since the sea was smooth, the boats shouldn't stop now. Major Wyse, the senior officer left aboard, had just dropped down to the cabin for a short while, and Fremont called to him that he, Fremont, should return to the *Kilby* on this last boat in an attempt to hire men at all costs to keep running both boats until all were off the *San Francisco*. Wyse hemmed and hawed, but finally said, "Go on board and return." "Certainly I will return," replied Fremont. Just as he was getting into the boat, Wyse came back on deck and again told Fremont to make sure he returned. "Most assuredly I will, Major," returned Fremont. It would be nice to see his wife and children on the *Kilby*. Fremont was let down into the boat, fully expecting to return to the steamer within a few minutes. Once on the bark he reported his mission to Colonel Gates, and then went to the captain of the *Kilby* and offered $20, $50, or even $100 per man if they would man the boats all night until everyone was taken off the *San Francisco*. Finally a number of the *Kilby*'s sailors agreed to do so and the boats started running again. With his mission accomplished, Fremont should have returned immediately to the *San Francisco*, but something came up.[47]

There was a problem with loosening the bales of cotton. The bales had been put in with screws so hard that only about 10 had been thrown overboard during the whole of the afternoon. Now it was dark, Colonel Gates asked Fremont to come below and study this problem. Unfortunately for Lieutenant Fremont, while he was engaged in cotton bailing, a violent nor'wester sprang up, and, since the steamer was lying in the trough of the sea, the boats could not come alongside her in the suddenly rolling sea except with the greatest difficulty. Indeed, one of the two boats was stove in the attempt. So he couldn't get back to the wreck. He offered the men $100 to rescue the stoved boat, but they wouldn't try even if they offered him $1,000.[48]

There can be little doubt that Colonel Gates fled the wreck, but the case of Assistant Surgeon Horace Raguet Wirtz requires more examination. He did make the crossing from the *San Francisco* to the *Kilby* in one of the last boats. But then, Surgeon Satterlee had transferred in one of the first. However, whereas Satterlee was unfit for duty and unable to walk without assistance, Wirtz was not disabled in any serious way. Wirtz's going left the hundreds of people still aboard the wreck with only one doctor to look after them—William Buel, the ship's civilian surgeon.[49]

---

46. Loeser; Wickham; Gretton; Wyse testimony; Eaton; Buel, 1854; Fremont.
47. Fremont; Fremont letter; Murray; Eaton.
48. Fremont; Fremont letter; Gretton; Mellus account; Wickham.
49. Wirtz testimony.

It is true that nearly all the sick and the worst of the disabled were now aboard the *Kilby*, including Dr. Satterlee. Satterlee was later to testify that when Martin Burke was transferring on the second boat out, he, Satterlee, asked Wirtz to accompany the disabled lieutenant colonel, but it was subsequently decided that the injured Satterlee should go instead.[50]

It is also true that, at the time people were transferring to the *Kilby*, it was assumed that everyone would be taken off the *San Francisco* either that day or on the morrow. There was no way anyone could know what was going to happen at ten o'clock that night that would so drastically change the picture. Defection therefore was not an issue. In fact, Dr. Satterlee, before transferring to the bark, had asked Wirtz to supervise the transfer of some medical stores to the *Kilby*. These would amount to four boxes, two of which Wirtz would ultimately send off with Lieutenant Loeser.[51]

Wirtz had been given no instructions one way or another by Colonel Gates as to whether to remain on board the *San Francisco* or to transfer to the *Kilby*, and so, after the colonel left the ship, he, Wirtz, went up to Major Wyse, now the senior officer on board, and asked permission to go over to the *Kilby*. Wyse replied that if he did there wouldn't be an army surgeon left on the *San Francisco*. Wirtz said that all the sick were or would be on the *Kilby*, and that there was nothing he could do anyway on the *San Francisco* that night. Wyse told him that he had no authority to order him to stay or go. It was up to Wirtz. Wyse never even saw him go over the side. The next thing he knew was that Wirtz was heading toward the *Kilby* in one of the small boats, holding steady the remaining boxes of medical supplies that had been passed down to him minutes before. "The sea was rough, and the boat heavy, and I think they only let down two boxes to me."[52]

Within 20 or 25 minutes after arriving on the *Kilby*, Wirtz sought out Colonel Gates to let him know he was now on board. And on the *Kilby* he remained.[53]

This all seems fairly straightforward, but then Wirtz's testimony begins to look a little shaky. That's because he was trying to shield Lieutenant Bill Winder from a rather embarrassing revelation. At the subsequent inquiry, when asked if any boat trip was made from the *Kilby* back to the *San Francisco* after he had reported to Colonel Gates, Wirtz answered that there wasn't. There was a boat manned to go, he said, and Wirtz gave a letter to the coxswain of the boat to give to Lieutenant Winder, who was still aboard the *San Francisco*. But the boat didn't go. "I think it was stopped; the reason I am not clear about; either the boat was injured, or Colonel Gates thought it not practicable to continue the embarcation [sic] longer; I remember some discussion about it." However, Wirtz was to add that, on re-thinking, he gave the Winder letter to Lieutenant Loeser, not to the coxswain.[54]

---

50. Wirtz testimony; Satterlee testimony.
51. Wirtz testimony; Fremont letter.
52. Wirtz testimony; Wyse testimony. The quote is, of course, from Wirtz.
53. Wirtz testimony.
54. Wirtz testimony.

What was this letter to Bill Winder? The answer lies in the basic premise that Winder wanted to get off the *San Francisco*. It had been the worst trip he'd ever been on, and he'd had enough. As for Winder himself applying to leave the wreck, he didn't do that, as he was quick to point out at the inquiry. But Lieutenant Winder was prevaricating. He made two attempts. Both failed, and for each one he used the his friend Dr. Wirtz as a go-between. The first was about the time the sick were being transferred to the *Kilby* that afternoon. Wirtz asked Major Wyse if Winder could go over to the *Kilby* with medicine and then, of course, return to the *San Francisco*. Although it didn't come out in the inquiry, the answer must have been "No!" Something odd in connection with all this emerged during the inquiry. During that day of the transfer, Winder's Company G was being made ready to be taken over to the *Kilby* that evening, at least that's what Sergeant Elijah Brown told him. Winder had known nothing of that and so he went to Major Wyse and asked him if it was true. Wyse said it wasn't. That's where the story ends. It seems strange that Winder didn't know that his company was being readied for transfer. His second try to get off the steamer came that evening. When Wirtz arrived aboard the *Kilby*, and reported to Colonel Gates, one of the things he asked him was, could Bill Winder transfer that evening? Winder was on the sick report, there was nothing else to do on the *San Francisco* anyway, and he had worked through, even though sick, up to now. He felt he should go. We don't know the wording of Wirtz's letter, or even if it got to its addressee. One thing's for sure. Bill Winder stayed on the *San Francisco*.[55]

And so, after a total of about ten trips, Captain Low called a halt for the night, and his crew drew up one of their two lifeboats onto the *Kilby*'s deck for safe-keeping, so that the transfer could continue the following morning. That left their other boat still at the side of the *San Francisco*, with supplies on it, and now only waiting for Lieutenant Loeser. In the steamer's cabin a group of men were having supper—Commodore Watkins, Major Wyse, Lieutenant Charlie Winder, Lieutenant Chandler, and Mr. Mellus. Lieutenant Loeser came in, having finished his commissary tasks, told the assembled diners that he was heading back to the *Kilby* with the provisions, and asked the first officer if he could come outside and lower him down in the whip. Mellus, who was slightly deaf, wasn't quite sure he had heard right, but he had, and so had everyone at the table, including Major Wyse, who later, at the inquiry, was to testify that he didn't remember this interchange. Mellus told Loeser that there were several people on deck who could lower him into the boat, but Loeser insisted on Mellus. Loeser then turned to Major Wyse. He had brought him a message from Mrs. Wyse, who was over on the *Kilby*. She had sent her love to her husband, of course. Would Major Wyse care to reciprocate? Yes, replied the major. And that was that. Loeser, naturally took Wyse's reply as permission to go back to the *Kilby*, so he boarded the boat and was rowed away. Later, in court, Wyse stated that he didn't consider his "yes" to be permission for Loeser to return to the *Kilby*, that there was

---

55. Winder testimony.

no need for Loeser to accompany the provisions across, that the boat's coxswain could have easily taken care of that chore.[56]

All the passengers from this last trip having come up onto the *Kilby*, and with all the provisions now aboard, the sailors were drawing the boat up with ropes, when all of a sudden a large wave threw it against the side of the bark, and in an instant it was broken to pieces. It was a very old boat, and had looked bad during the day, and so didn't stand much of a chance in this encounter with nature. They now had only one little boat left, and that too was old and leaky.[57]

Lieutenant Loeser had done well in his mission, bringing with him, among other things, a box of candles, a barrel of hard bread, a box of tea, a small box of sugar, a barrel and a half of sea biscuit, three boxes of sardines, and several shoulders of bacon. With the *Kilby* down to about 400 gallons of water, Loeser also brought over three or four barrelsful. He had also located the pot of preserves for Colonel Gates, but much to his surprise, and the ire of the regimental commander, it turned out to be a box of lucifer matches.[58]

It was up to Lieutenant Fremont as quartermaster, to negotiate the contract with Captain Low. Once Fremont got aboard the bark, he and Colonel Gates wrote out a contract in pencil, between the master of the *Kilby*, "on behalf of the owners," and the regimental quartermaster, in the name of the United States, for the rescue of the troops, and their transportation to the nearest accessible point in the United States. The second article of this contract reads: "The party of the Second part (that is the Government) agrees to pay, for the services above stated, to the said party of the first part (that is, the owners), the sum of fifteen thousand dollars ($15,000) in full compensation for the services, also to guarantee the owners any loss they may sustain from loss of insurance in deviating from their original destination." There would be an addendum to this contract, and also, therefore, to the story.[59]

Lucia Eaton encountered Colonel Martin Burke at the *Kilby*'s galley. It was the first time she had seen him since the morning of the wreck, and she was really delighted to run into him once more. He made room for her beside him on the bench. The galley was a very small place, and there were several ladies there, some drying their feet which had gotten wet while crossing to the bark. More people were coming in all the time to get some tea and to warm themselves, and so Miss Eaton left to make room for them, and went back to the cabin.[60]

On the *San Francisco*, they tried making a fire to roast some potatoes, but at about eight o'clock someone yelled out "Fire!" Everyone rushed into the cook's galley and extinguished the fire—and the potatoes—with wet blankets.[61]

Just about the time of the fire, with the two ships still attached by hawser, the

---

56. Mellus testimony; Loeser; Wickham; Gretton; Wyse testimony; Eaton; Buel, 1854; Fremont.
57. Eaton; Buel, 1854; Fremont; Murray; Graham. Mr. Graham reports that the boat was swamped alongside the *Kilby*, but it was actually stove in.
58. Eaton; Loeser; Wyse testimony; Mrs. Gates.
59. Fremont.
60. Eaton.
61. Gretton; Winder, Jan. 6, 1854; Winder, 1883; Auchinleck.

wind hauled more to the northeastward, and a little later, with heavy rain starting to come down and the breeze increasing every moment, strong squalls came up, and soon the wind was blowing very hard. Misses Eaton and Merchant went out on the deck of the *Kilby* to see what was going on. They could see very distinctly the lights from the *San Francisco*, and they asked one or two of the gentlemen who were standing talking with them if there was any danger of another storm coming up. Not being meteorologists, or even experienced seamen, they didn't know, but the two ladies, soon after they returned to the cabin, happened to catch Captain Low looking a little anxious. Given the increasing motion in the bark, Low knew as well as everyone aboard that the sea was getting very rough. But, out here in the unpredictable Atlantic Ocean, any prediction beyond that could only be a guess, but things certainly didn't look good.[62]

The new storm meant that the *San Francisco* had begun to leak badly again, and so those on the wreck had to go to work again bailing, the pumps having given out again. The men had been bailing with the buckets almost incessantly for five days and nights, during which they had had nothing to eat but biscuits and nothing to drink except cold water, and were now so exhausted that it required great exertions to keep them steadily at work.[63]

Lieutenant Murray came into the *Kilby*'s cabin, looking a little troubled, but he assured the ladies that everything was safe, that the bark, being so lightly freighted, would ride the waves, and that they were in much less danger than when they had been on the *San Francisco*.[64]

Thirty-one survivors from the wreck of the *San Francisco* were now filling this rather confined space to suffocation point; the floor was covered with passengers, some sitting up, and those who were weak lying down on the hard boards wherever they could find a space. Colonel Burke was in a bad way, and had to be treated with the utmost priority, but the others were relatively fit. Captain Judd and his dyspeptic wife; Lieutenant and Mrs. Fremont with their three children; Mrs. Wyse and her infant; the Rev. Mr. Cooper, his wife and six children; Senhor Falcão, the Brazilian consul; Madame Besse and her female servant; Mr. Aspinwall; James Lorimer Graham; Mrs. Sarah Elizabeth Chase—known as Sallie—the young widow of Captain Leslie Chase, and her 11-year-old boy, also named Leslie, who were sitting on a trunk; and Lieutenant Lucien Loeser, his wife Sarah, and—sitting on an old box—Miss Eaton. A tea chest acted as a seat for Sallie Chase's sister, Vallie Merchant, and their two younger half-sisters, Virginia, aged 13, and Lydia, who was 11. Doctors Satterlee and Wirtz and Lieutenants Murray and Van Voast could not find room in the cabin, and had to sit in the doorway.[65]

---

62. Murray; Gretton; Wickham; Eaton.
63. Winder, Jan. 6, 1854.
64. Eaton.
65. Eaton; Graham. Lieutenant Bill Winder's wife, Abby, was the daughter of the future governor of New Hampshire, Ichabod Goodwin. Choosing not to go out to California with her husband at this stage of the game, Abby, with her young son Willy, had remained at home in Portsmouth. However, Abby's fifth cousin, Hannah Springer Goodwin, did go on the *San Francisco*. Hannah, 32 years old, had been married for 11 years when she sailed out of New York Harbor on December 22, 1853, bound for Rio to meet up with her husband, Alexander H. Besse.

Vallie Merchant, sitting near Lucia Eaton, could see that she was very much exhausted. She kindly asked her to lean on her and try to get a little sleep, which Miss Eaton did and was soon asleep. However, she was soon woken up by Miss Merchant, who thought the bark was sinking. The wind was blowing very strong, and it was evident that they had encountered another terrific storm, their frail vessel being tossed about on those fearful waves, created, one had no doubt, by Miss Eaton's capricious god, to teach the sinners yet another lesson. The waves would come against the side of the *Kilby* and often sweep over the deck. The hatches were closed down and everything on deck secured. Mr. Cooper offered up prayers to the Almighty God for mercy. All joined in most fervently. What they were actually praying for was for God to give them the strength to meet their fate calmly.[66]

After Mr. Cooper had finished praying, he handed Lucia Eaton a little testament which had been brought on board by Mrs. Wyse, and asked her to read a chapter he was pointing out. It was John, Chapter 14: "Let not your heart be troubled; ye believe in God, believe also in me. In my father's house are many mansions." Lucia read these comforting words to those assembled in the bark, every voice being hushed to create a silence "as if being present our Saviour was speaking to us in those words."[67]

One or two of the ladies sung the hymn "I would not live always," which gave them just the right amount of expected cheer. A young lady sitting beside Lucia Eaton was very distressed, not so much by the singing, perhaps, but certainly by the general misfortune felt by everyone aboard. Mr. Cooper pointed out a chapter for her to read. The tears streamed down her face as she read each line, and her burden was lightened. It could never be said that the Reverend Cooper did not do some practical good at times.[68]

A barrel of hard bread was standing just in front of Lucia Eaton, simply because there was nowhere else it could have been put. Lieutenant Loeser had brought away two candlesticks from the wreck, and a box of candles. Had he not brought them, they would not have had a light for the binnacle, the cabin and the galley. The all-important candle allocated to the cabin was placed on the top of the barrel. But whenever the bark rolled, the candle would slide toward Miss Eaton, and she lived with the constant worry that it might fall on her. Each time the candle headed her way, she would brace herself against the partition of one of the state rooms and push the barrel away. It was under these conditions that they passed their first night aboard the vessel that had saved them from the wreck of the *San Francisco*.[69]

Despite the ever increasing wind and waves, Commodore Watkins had studied the barometer that afternoon and found that it was rising. He felt that, as they had every indication of fair weather for several days to come, and as it would take two days at least for everyone to be transferred from the *San Francisco* to the *Kilby*, there

---

66. Eaton.
67. Eaton.
68. Eaton.
69. Eaton.

would be no problem with the two vessels remaining joined for the night. But anyone can make a mistake, even an old salt like Watkins. At about 10 p.m., with the rain blowing very hard and the sea getting up fast, both ships were laboring so much that the *Kilby* was obliged to let go of the hawser connecting her with the *San Francisco*. She endeavored to keep by the wrecked steamer, but with the wind becoming a gale and the and sea continuing to rise, it wasn't long before the two ships separated into the night.[70]

The news of the separation was brought to Miss Eaton and her group while they were praying and reflecting in the *Kilby*'s cabin. Someone came in and said, "The hawser is broken and we are separated from the steamship." It was evidently the answer to their prayers, although certainly not the answer they had expected. But then it was universally understood that their deity moved in mysterious ways.[71]

Watkins's meteorological misjudgment was to cause a problem that would eventually become a matter of life and death for those on the *Kilby*. Lieutenant Loeser, being the commissary, had given Sergeant Joe McIntyre orders for transferring provisions from the *San Francisco* to the *Kilby*, but, confident that he had all the time in the world, McIntyre had not yet carried out the order by the time the two vessels drifted apart that night, and so, with the huge new intake of passengers on a bark already low on provisions, this would prove a tremendous strain for those on the *Kilby* for their next two weeks at sea.[72]

Corporal James Smith had started life in Queens County, Ireland, 36 years before, and was now, four years into his latest enlistment, an old and trusted Artilleryman, a mainstay of Company G. Only a couple of days before, as he, his wife and two children boarded the *San Francisco* for a four-month ocean cruise to a new life out west, things couldn't have been rosier. But now, not long after the fire scare in the steamer's galley, Smith paid a visit to his commander, Lieutenant Bill Winder. One of Smith's children was sick, about to die. Winder asked him why he hadn't sent his family off to the *Kilby*, but Smith's wife wouldn't leave him, feeling certain that he would be lost.[73]

Before night, the *Kilby* had taken off 108 passengers: 11 army officers and 47 enlisted men; four *San Francisco* crew members; nine male citizen passengers; 18 women, and 19 children. The army officers were: Colonel Gates; the severely disabled Lieutenant Colonel Martin Burke, who got the best accommodations; the disabled Major Merchant; the wounded Captain Gardiner, the dragoon, who was also suffering from rheumatism; Lieutenants Fremont, Loeser, and Van Voast; Lieutenant Francis Key Murray of the U.S. Navy; the badly wounded Dr. Satterlee; and Surgeon Wirtz. The crew members were James Farnsworth, one of the *San Francisco*'s two first engineers; Frederick the Portuguese cook; and two disabled seamen, Anderson and Kelly.

---

70. Watkins testimony; Mellus account; Wickham; Graham; Gretton; Fremont; Murray.
71. Eaton.
72. McIntyre.
73. Winder, Jan. 6, 1854; Winder, 1883.

The male citizen passengers were: Mr. Baker, of whom we know nothing; the Rev. Mr. Cooper; Fred Southworth; George Woolsey Aspinwall, who was quite, quite sick; Mr. Aspinwall's colored servant; James Lorimer Graham, Jr.; Senhor Falcão and his servant; and Senhor Abrio. The women were: Mrs. Gates and nurse, Miss Carter (Mrs. Gates's sister), Mrs. Wyse, Mrs. Merchant and her grown daughters Vallie and Sallie, the dyspeptic Mrs. Judd, Mrs. Fremont, Mrs. Sarah Loeser and her sister Lucia Eaton, the Loesers' servant, Madame Besse and servant, Mrs. Cooper, Senhora Abrio, Marianne Sauer (the bandmaster's wife, the bandmaster himself having remained on the *San Francisco*), and Corporal Taylor's wife. The 19 children were the three Gateses; Mrs. Wyse's infant; the two young Merchants; Leslie Chase; the three Fremonts; the three young Sauers—Anna, Margaret, and Joseph; and the six offspring of the Reverend Cooper.[74]

Thus, after the *Kilby* left, the only officers left on board the *San Francisco* were Major Wyse, Lieutenant J.G. Chandler, and the Winder cousins, with Bill Winder being a sick man. This was not nearly enough, there also being about 325 rank and file and quite a number of camp followers, soldiers' wives and children, as well as most of the crew. As Catherine Livingston, the stewardess, was to write: "The anguish of the wives separated from their husbands, and of even little children from their mothers, may well be imagined." Another way to look at it was that there were five Artillery companies left on board the wreck without a commander. So, given the sheer paucity of officers remaining on the doomed steamer, what with the great number of enlisted men and recruits, and the hard work that faced everyone once the *Kilby* had gone, there was no way the officers could give proper attention to the men. And that was asking for trouble.[75]

"Whatever may be the appearance, there was nothing further from the mind of every officer of the command than the idea of abandoning the men, and I doubt if there was scarcely an officer that would not as soon have remained on the steamer as on the bark that night."[76]

---

74. Graham; Winder interview, 1854; Eaton; Mrs. Gates; Southworth; Gretton; Wyse testimony; Buel, 1854; Mellus account; Wickham; Winder, Jan. 6, 1854. Bill Winder says that about 50 men of Company I were taken off by the *Kilby*. There were, in fact, only 29. There were 47 enlisted men taken off altogether during this transfer to the *Kilby*, from all companies. Mr. Graham refers to Senhor Falcão as Antonio Fales, the Belgian Consul, and to Senhor Abrio as Alrio. One of the two disabled crewmen—Anderson or Kelly, we don't know which—was the man who had had his leg broken at the wheel on the morning of the 24th. Both men were transferred to the *Kilby* on the evening of the 28th. Mrs. Wyse and Mrs. Sauer were not the only ones separated from their spouses. Several of the camp women got off on the *Kilby*, their husbands not yet having made the crossing, and even Joe McIntyre, the commissary sergeant, had been obliged to leave his wife and two little boys behind.

75. Graham; Winder interview, Jan. 13, 1854. Wyse testimony; Livingston.

76. Fremont letter.

Thursday
December 29

Before dawn, as a strong breeze amounting almost to a gale was blowing in from the southwest, Lieutenant Bill Winder received further news from Corporal James Smith. He was dying too, and would like to see his company commander. "On going to him he was found to be in the agony of death, from that dread disease, Asiatic cholera."[1]

Cloud greeted those who were up and about on the *San Francisco* as daylight came. "This morning things looked gloomier than ever, having nothing to eat and being cold and half naked."[2]

Soon afterwards, Mrs. Smith came to Winder to tell him that the corporal and the child had died. Winder put the wife into a state room, but, later that morning she was found dead in bed, her surviving child lying asleep beside her. But that last child didn't last long either. In "less than twelve hours, he and all his family were dead."[3]

One of the colored waiters, Louis Testador, joined the slowly growing roster of soulless bodies who had been littering the wreck since the day before, and a little later that morning, Bill Winder, as officer of the day, was faced with the melancholy chore of overseeing the mass burial. The cadavers, in various stages of decomposition, were sewn up in blankets, a weight was attached to each grisly package, and they were all committed to the deep.[4]

Sergeant Brown found a handsomely bound children's book with an inscription on the fly leaf: "Miss Lydia Merchant, from her friend, Mrs Caroline Phillips, Newburyport, Mass., 1852." The sergeant couldn't give it to Miss Lydia, as she had already been taken off on the *Kilby*, but he intended to send it to her, if he ever got back to the U.S.A. alive.[5]

The *San Francisco*'s pumps had broken down the previous day, so there was still

---

1. Mellus account; Wickham; Winder, Jan. 6, 1854. The quote is from Winder.
2. Mellus account; Wickham; Winder, Jan. 6, 1854. The quote is from Winder.
3. Winder, Jan. 6, 1854; Winder, 1883.
4. Wickham; Winder testimony; Winder, 1883; Mellus account; Wickham. Bill Winder had been detailed as officer of the day the previous night. In his testimony before the court of inquiry, he would claim that this was the only order of importance given him by Major Wyse after they became separated from the *Kilby*.
5. Brown account.

bailing going on all morning, by men who were dropping from exhaustion. Those who weren't bailing were cutting holes through the deck for the purpose of throwing coal, provisions, and other heavy materials overboard, in order to lighten the ship.[6]

Aboard the *Kilby*, the Rev. Mr. Cooper spent the night doing what he did best, leading his flock in prayer for help and for the salvation of those who had been left on the *San Francisco*. "We dared not close our eyes, although we were perfectly exhausted."[7]

The two ships had lost contact during the dark hours, but just as dawn was breaking one of the soldiers climbed to the masthead of the *Kilby*, and let out a "*San Francisco* Ahoy." Alas, it was a false report. Come actual daylight, when they could see everything quite clearly, the "waves were rolling mountains high and nothing but the vast ocean to be seen; not even a speck could be observed by those who were kept upon the watch."[8]

The general feeling on the *San Francisco* that morning was that the *Kilby* had cut out. "We supposed that she had made for the nearest port, being short of water and provisions, and it being unsafe for her to remain any longer by us, as the sea was running very high."[9]

Always jumping to the worst conclusions; a human trait, especially evident under stress. If Bill Winder and the others on the *San Francisco* had been able to look through a magic telescope they would have seen a very different scenario developing on the *Kilby*. With the wind blowing so hard, and the *San Francisco* being somewhere to the *Kilby*'s windward, any hope of contact had become virtually impossible, and so, after hours of fruitless sailing around and around, and with the deck being very difficult to stand on without support, a conference was held that morning in the cabin of the wildly rolling *Kilby*. The debate among the gentlemen was, should they or should they not abandon the search?[10]

There were two key factors looming constantly in everyone's mind. One was that, at this point in the search, the *Kilby* had only two sails of any account left, so that to try to do anything but run before the wind was, as they had been learning all morning, out of the question. The second issue was the shortage of provisions. During the transfer the day before, they had brought over from the doomed steamer only one and a half barrels of hard bread besides what Lieutenant Loeser had carried over. That wasn't enough to sustain the additional 108 people suddenly aboard the bark, which itself had already been short before it even ran into the *San Francisco*. To hang around much longer, therefore, even in relatively placid waters, posed a grave danger. Given that they were so crippled in sails, if a storm should blow up, they would be in desperate trouble. It must be remembered that the *Kilby* was not a steamship, and

---

6. Winder, Jan. 6, 1854; Gretton.
7. Eaton.
8. Mellus account; Wickham; Winder, Jan. 6, 1854; Eaton.
9. Winder, Jan. 6, 1854.
10. Fremont; Eaton; Murray.

relied for its motive power purely on wind and sails. Another thing they had to bear in mind was, even if they found the *San Francisco*, could they do any good? They had only one boat left on the *Kilby* since the other one had been stove in the evening before, and it was very small and very old, and would probably go to pieces after a few trips back between the two vessels.[11]

Most of the officers, including Lieutenant Fremont of the Third Artillery and Lieutenant Frank Murray of the U.S. Navy, were of the opinion that they should continue the search, even if it meant dying of hunger or thirst, or being wrecked themselves. Since, by their estimation, they were about 300 miles from New York, and the wind would be greatly in their favor, Captain Low was all for running for port and sending out assistance from there, the choice Lieutenant Fremont himself would freely admit later at the court of inquiry, was probably the right one. Captain Low did not have to talk Colonel Gates into this as the colonel had already voiced that opinion to Lieutenant Murray earlier that morning. At the inquiry, Fremont wished to stress that to run for port was only Colonel Gates's opinion, in other words he did not try to enforce it on his officers.[12]

There were other things in play to influence the decision. The troops had been perfectly exhausted when they had come off the *San Francisco* the day before, and had had no time in which to recover their strength. Their usefulness as workers was just about spent. In addition to this, one of the *San Francisco*'s engineers was saying that the wrecked steamship couldn't last longer than a day or two, as she was leaking very badly when they left her.[13]

When the discussion was thrown open to the ladies, most of them voted to continue the search. "Oh, do not leave them! Let us stay by them till we know for certain that nothing can be done to render them assistance." Outweighed, Colonel Gates gave the necessary orders, and Fremont passed them on to Captain Low.[14]

After that question had been settled, Lucia Eaton and her group were quietly seated aboard the *Kilby*, and tea was brought to them in a kettle. Each person was obliged to take their allowance then pass the cup, tumbler, or bowl, whichever it might be, to their neighbor. An officer of the day was selected from the newcomers on a rotating basis, his principal duties being the allocation of water and food, and once or twice to throw cotton overboard. The persons on board were permitted two meals a day, breakfast and tea, but had to dispense with dinner as the officer of the day feared their provisions would not last if used too freely.[15]

That morning Lieutenant Fremont, much to his surprise, ran into Surgeon Wirtz on board the *Kilby*. "Doctor, how come you on board? I did not know you were here!" Wirtz gave a reply, but as everyone fully anticipated finding the *San Francisco* again

---

11. Fremont; Eaton; Murray.
12. Fremont; Murray; Graham; Eaton.
13. Eaton.
14. Fremont; Eaton; Murray; Graham.
15. Eaton; Fremont.

soon, Fremont didn't really pay much attention to Wirtz's answer. It was just one of those conversations.[16]

Captain Gardiner, the dragoon, was officer of the day on the *Kilby* about four or five times during the time he was aboard, and during those spells, as part of his job, he supervised the issuing of food and water. Since he had had no instructions from anyone, including any orders about water rationing, he had to judge how much to give out to each person. The normal amount given to the officers and men alike was a tumbler full per four men in the mornings and the same in the evening. However, Colonel Gates felt that these rules did not apply to him or his family, and each time Gardiner was on duty, the colonel of the regiment received an extra quantity of water. Sometimes he ordered it himself, but on occasion he would send his orderly with bottles to be filled up. The first time this happened, on the twenty-ninth or thirtieth, before any regular issues of food and water had been made to the soldiers, Gardiner remonstrated with him on deck, near the entrance to the cabin, telling him that it would have a bad effect on the men, several of whom were suffering from want of water. Gates replied, "I don't give a damn for the men—I would rather twenty of them should die than that my child should suffer." Gardiner then gave him the water, a bottleful. Aside from the orders to furnish him with food and water, Gardiner received no orders from Gates while aboard the *Kilby*.[17]

For the whole day, the officers, soldiers and sailors were on constant lookout for the *San Francisco*, of course. The bark was rolling fearfully, and, if they hadn't been on their guard, the passengers would have been thrown off their seats. They were able to look through the doorway just opposite them, and out upon the water they could see the awful waves which the *Kilby*, being very light, was able to ride most beautifully. Sometimes the bow would seem to touch the water and in an instant mount to the clouds, then a mountain wave would sweep past the vessel. That was how they passed their second day on the *Kilby*.[18]

The pumps were working again on the *San Francisco*, and the water level started to go down. Desperately tired men could finally stop bailing. Sergeant Elijah Brown never left his station, until at last "my ancles [sic] became so weak that I could not stand, and then I stood upon my knees until the Commodore came and pulled me away."[19]

At noon the heavy southwesterly wind was still blowing, the cloud cover was thicker, and it was now showering occasionally, a meteorological situation that was to continue for the next 24 hours. The men on the *San Francisco* carried on throwing coal and provisions overboard. On one occasion, while the ship was rolling violently

---

16. Fremont. Later, when it came time for Fremont to testify before the court of inquiry, he could not recollect what Wirtz's reply had been, but he did offer a possible reason why Wirtz had been on the *Kilby* that morning and not still back on the *San Francisco*. Some time before, while they had all still been aboard the wreck, Fremont had run into the surgeon, whose face was tied up. Wirtz had told him it was neuralgia. At the inquiry, Fremont more than hinted that Wirtz might have made the crossing without the permission of Major Wyse. 17. Gardiner; Merchant; Graham. The quote is from Gardiner, and is uncorroborated.
18. Eaton; Mellus account; Wickham.
19. Brown account; Winder, Jan. 6, 1854.

in the very heavy sea, they were trying to get a barrel up through a hatch onto the deck. It took four of them to steady the barrel, for if it managed to get away from them it would have knocked both heads out before they could hoist it out.[20]

The *San Francisco* labored heavily that afternoon, with the waves striking hard under her guards and beams, so much so that the port afterguard was carried away. The men who weren't throwing stuff overboard were employed in stopping leaks and tossing canvassing over the quarterdeck.[21]

Doctors Satterlee and Wirtz, who should have been attending to the soldiers, had left on the *Kilby*, and now the only medical man left on board the wrecked steamer was Dr. Buel, the *San Francisco*'s surgeon. Even though, under ordinary circumstances, Buel, being a civilian, would have had no authority over the military passengers, these were times that required a departure from protocol, and so Major Wyse called upon him to attend to the sick. There were a lot of them.[22]

During the night the *San Francisco* experienced "heavy squalls, the wind shifting all around the compass and blowing harder, it seemed, from each point of it."[23]

Meanwhile, since Christmas morning, the *Three Bells* had been experiencing bad weather, and the ship was more or less leaky. As for the *Kilby*, in the evening Captain Low gave the order to put up all sail, or what was left of it. A fine breeze having sprung up, they started on their home course, but soon the wind had become too strong for the old and torn sails and so they were taken down, and the *Kilby* was obliged to lie to for the night.[24]

---

20. Gretton; Mellus account; Wickham.
21. Wickham; Mellus account.
22. Buel testimony; Mellus account.
23. Gretton.
24. Burnside; Eaton.

Friday
December 30

The *San Francisco* wasn't the only vessel in trouble out there in the Atlantic that morning. The *Three Bells* was too. At eleven o'clock a sounding taken revealed 22 inches of water sloshing about her, and so the pumps were kept going all through the day and into the evening, the passengers and crew keeping alternate watch. Night for the Scottish bark began with a clear sky, but with high wind and heavy seas.[1]

Come daylight on the wrecked steamer, there was a very heavy sea on and, as nearly every giant wave swept right over the decks, the men weren't able to do anything toward lightening the ship further. They had all the pumps going—two steam-donkeys, two deck pumps, and the large specially-rigged air-pump, by which means they were able to keep the water down to from two to three feet. And they were finding quite a number of the troops newly stricken with cholera.[2]

It was the end of a long road for John T. Salmon, of Company D, at 56 one of the oldest privates still on board the *San Francisco*. Salmon had been in the army, one way or another, on and off, since he was 15, that day in Dutchess County in January 1813 when he enlisted in the New York State Militia to fight the British. He had been re-enlisted in Boston on December 3, 1852, by Major Wyse, for his fifth roll of the dice—one too many, perhaps. But then again, perhaps not. What else was he going to do but die like a man when his time came?[3]

At noon, with the weather beginning to moderate and clear up, all the crew were at work, cutting away the guard beams, covering over the timber heads afresh, and in every other way they could think of trying to make the ship sound enough so they could relieve themselves of the fear that she would go down under them before some vessel could take them off. By that stage most of those aboard had given up hopes of ever getting her into any port again.[4]

The soldiers were still heaving coal overboard and all hands were employed in stopping water out of the ship as the afternoon wore on with cloudy weather and a

---

1. Burnside.
2. Gretton.
3. Army enlistment records.
4. Gretton.

moderate gale from the south and west. Because the steamer was rolling so heavily it was impossible to get from aft forward or from forward aft on deck without holding onto something all the time. There was not even a stanchion left on the outer edge of the deck except the paddle boxes, and so they had lifelines stretched fore and aft. During the night, the weather was still clear, with the wind and sea going down fast.[5]

On the *Kilby*, that morning proved to be very cloudy, and Captain Low, not being able to take an observation, couldn't tell where they were. Wherever it was, they remained there for the best part of a week. Frustratingly, everything they gained during the day when the weather was fair was lost at night when they were obliged to lie to. Sarah Loeser had been very badly bruised, and, suffering considerably, very much wished to lie down. Her husband succeeded in getting an old bed tick and had it filled with cotton, a ponch laid over it, and some cotton rolled up in a paper from a pillow and a blanket to cover her. It was very hard but she felt thankful for it, which was just as well, because, as it turned out, this would be her bed for as long she remained aboard the *Kilby*. Mrs. Fremont and her three little children slept on the floor under Sarah's bed. "She had an old quilt to sleep on, a blanket to cover her."[6]

That night nine gentlemen, nine ladies, and ten children under six years of age—including Lucia Eaton's party—slept in the *Kilby*'s little cabin. Mr. Aspinwall, who was ill with consumption, had the sofa. Colonel Burke was stretched out on the floor, and, as he was still very weak from his injuries, everyone had to be very careful not to touch him. He was very patient and tried to make as little trouble as possible. Some few of the passengers threw themselves upon the floor and slept, being worn out with fatigue. That night Miss Eaton sat on a trunk, unable to sleep. Vallie Merchant sat on a trunk too, but she soon fell asleep. Soon a roll of the bark threw her to the floor, on top of persons who were sleeping. They woke up in alarm, but Vallie stayed asleep, despite her fall. Lucia woke her, and she took her seat on the trunk again.[7]

---

5. Mellus account; Wickham; Gretton.
6. Eaton. "Ponch" is the word that appears in Stackpole's rendering of Lucia Eaton's Narrative. But what is a ponch? We don't know.
7. Eaton.

Saturday
December 31

For those survivors on the *San Francisco* who were up and about at two o'clock that morning of the last day of 1853, it was a long, very dark night, with little to look forward to except a lingering death in the first days of the new year. Then, all of a sudden, the spell of gloom was broken. Way in the distance, the sharp-eyed John Mason, saw a brief flicker of light off their starboard quarter. Alex Auchinleck, one of the engineers, happened to be on deck at the time, but couldn't see what the young fourth officer was pointing at so excitedly.[1]

Was it Mason's imagination, a hope become an illusion? Then Auchinleck finally saw it, more steady this time. It was indeed a long way off, standing to windward, but it was a light. It had to be a ship. They were too far from land for it to be a lighthouse or a coastal steamer. It had to be an ocean-going vessel. Of that there could be no doubt. The effect on the men was galvanizing and within 20 minutes or so the crew had begun firing their guns and rockets, and flashing their blue lights, in order to attract the stranger's attention. But could the men on that faraway vessel see them, or hear the cannon fire? Why not? If the men on the *San Francisco* could see that distant light, then they could be seen in turn. But was anyone on deck to see them? That was the question. For a very long hour and a half the desperate men on the wrecked steamer were kept in suspense as they fired round after round, and flashed their lights frantically into the black night. Was Lady Luck about to bestow her favors on these humans who sorely needed her, or would the distant ship just pass them by like the others had done?[2]

Although the crew and passengers on the *San Francisco* could not possibly have known it at that point in time, the other vessel was the Glasgow ship *Three Bells*, on her way from Liverpool to Nova Scotia under the command of Captain Robert Crighton. And, as it turned out, at the very same moment that John Mason had seen the faraway speck of light, Crighton had spotted the *San Francisco* bearing west-southwest, and he went below, telling everyone what he had seen. Mr. McDougall, one of the passengers, was lying in bed half awake, unable to get to sleep, when the

---

1. Mellus account; Wickham; Buel, 1872; Gretton; Auchinleck; Winder, Jan. 6, 1854.
2. Mellus account; Wickham; Buel, 1872; Gretton.

skipper brought him the news, and by 2:30 he was up and on deck to see for himself. Along with Crighton, Thomas Burnside, and several other crewmen and passengers all staring out to sea, McDougall could make out the twinkling blue lights a long way away, the flash and report of a gun, and rockets being fired. This was obviously a distress signal, so the skipper immediately set his course for a new adventure, at the end of which, for him, would lie fame and fortune and immortality.[3]

Then, finally, at 3:30, with their attention riveted to the general area of inky blackness in which they had last seen the tiny glimmer of hope, those on the steamer began to make out blue lights coming slowly toward them. They had been seen. But the *San Francisco* was drifting fast and several times they lost sight of the approaching vessel. It being far from certain that the unknown ship would get to them before they drifted out of range forever, the hour or two that followed was one of fearful suspense for the people on the wreck. Had they again lost their chance? Throughout the remainder of the night their guns roared into the void every half hour.[4]

It was a few hours later, at seven o'clock, with the winds still running south-southeastwards and heavy seas rolling, that they finally saw, to their leeward, a large ship being carried by the waves. The *Three Bells* was still some way off, but daylight was coming, and the first thing the observers on board noticed was that the *San Francisco*'s smoke stacks and foremast were gone. All they could see was the hull, the paddle-boxes, and the wheels. The *Three Bells* lay to under foresail, mainsail and fore staysail, hoisted the British ensign, and kept away for the stricken steamer.[5]

About nine o'clock the *Three Bells* passed as close as she could with safety to the *San Francisco*, and they tried speaking her. But, despite the closeness of the two vessels—Engineer Auchinleck later said he could have thrown a biscuit on board—no one could hear a thing except the noise of the seas.[6]

Although verbal communication was out of the question, Mr. McDougall and the others aboard the *Three Bells* were now able to get a much closer look at the wreck. "The scene on board was pitiful in the extreme; there was a splendid hull of a very large new steamship, unmanageable and buffeted amid the huge waves." There was nothing standing on her deck but the mizzen mast, with the American ensign turned upside down. Hundreds of men, most of them soldiers, were gazing intently at the *Three Bells* as she passed.[7]

Looking the other way, from the steamer toward the *Three Bells*, those on deck could see men working the pumps. Those pumps had being going ceaselessly and remorselessly on the *Three Bells* since the morning of the day before. They just could

---

3. *Three Bells log*; McDougall; Burnside.
4. Gretton; Winder, Jan. 6, 1854.
5. McDougall; Gretton; Burnside; Winder, Jan. 6, 1854.
6. McDougall; Gretton; Burnside; Wickham; Mellus account; Winder, Jan. 6, 1854; Auchinleck. The *San Francisco*'s log says that the two ships spoke at 9 a.m. Mr. Mellus, the first mate, wrote that, and Mr. Gretton, the second mate, copied Mr. Mellus, as did Dr. Buel, writing in 1872. However, Mr. Wickham writes 9:30, and he was using Mr. Mellus's log as well.
7. McDougall; Auchinleck. The quote is from McDougall.

not keep the water down. The steerage passengers, eight in number, had volunteered to take their turn at the pumps, each watch divided into two parties. There seemed no end to it. There was evidently something wrong with the pumps.[8]

The *Three Bells* danced in the presence of the *San Francisco* for half an hour, but it was a wild, uncontrolled jig dictated by the wind and waves. Finally, at 9:30, she passed behind the steamer to leeward and Captain Crighton was able to see the lettering "San Francisco, New York" on her stern.[9]

There were three ways one ship could speak another in those days a half century before the advent of radio. One was actually to talk, or more often shout, through a megaphone called a ship's trumpet. Another means of communication was to write large and succinct messages on a chalk board and to display the board prominently at a critical moment, at which point the men on the other ship would be able to read the message through their spyglasses. The third way was to write a note, put it into some sort of container, and then hurl it from one ship to the other when the two vessels came close enough. In this case, during the *Three Bells*'s first tack by the wrecked steamer, the weather prohibited any effective use of the trumpet, and it is unlikely, given the evidence, that the chalk board was used. This was one of those occasions when the third method was used.[10]

Alex Auchinleck, one of the *San Francisco*'s engineers, went below, got one of the firemen to come up on deck, and together they wrote a message, dictated to them by Major Wyse speaking on behalf of the U.S. Government, tied it to a wheel-bolt nut, and threw it toward the *Three Bells*. Unfortunately it hit the side of Captain Crighton's ship and fell into the sea. So they had to go through the whole process again. Their second throw struck amidships. Auchinleck watched as a man eagerly picked it up and ran aft to give it to the skipper. As one of the passengers on the *Three Bells*—Mrs. Smith—later told Auchinleck, Captain Crighton read the message out loud to all assembled: "Will you charter your ship? We are loaded with men, women and children. Name your price." It was signed "F.O. Wyse, U.S. Artillery." Whereupon Crighton remarked, "What does this man mean? It's not money that I'm after—I'm stopping for humanity's sake." He sent no reply back.[11]

It wasn't until the *Three Bells* passed the *San Francisco* again on the return tack that Captain Crighton was able to communicate in any meaningful way with the men on the wreck. The actual words written on the *Three Bells*'s chalk board seem to have been: "What wanted?"[12]

---

8. Auchinleck; McDougall. The pumps were of a new design, created by the builders of the *Three Bells*. They were made by Messrs. Smith & Tulloch, engineers of Greenock, and were double-acting, communicating with the several compartments, and also with the sea, for the purpose of washing decks, extinguishing fires, etc. They were situated between the main hatch and the main mast (*Artizan*).

9. McDougall; Gretton; Burnside; *Three Bells* log.

10. Gretton.

11. Auchinleck. This version of the message, as relayed to us by Auchinleck, is much less peremptory than the one as given by Mr. McDougall, a passenger on the *Three Bells*, who offers: "I will charter your vessel for the United States Government. Name your terms."

12. Burnside. Mr. McDougall reports that the message said, "What is wanted?" Given that terseness is everything in those circumstances, one must favor Burnside.

There was no time during this tack for Commodore Watkins to reply, but as the *Three Bells* passed by again he had his own chalk board ready: "We cannot live long! Do not leave us!"[13]

As Crighton wrote in his log of that day, "Hailing her, she invited us to remain with her until the weather moderated; it was then blowing strong from south southeast."[14]

But what gave the survivors of the wreck the most heart was that the men aboard the *Three Bells* gave them three rousing cheers. A similar salutation was given in return.[15]

During the third tack, Crighton told the men on the suffering ship to keep their hearts up, that he would remain with them until the weather moderated.[16]

Lieutenant Chandler celebrated his twenty-third birthday, but there was something worrying him, as there was everyone aboard the *San Francisco*. They were afraid of what Captain Crighton might say when he found that the *San Francisco* was a plague ship. Mr. Gretton, the second officer, says: "Found the sickness was increasing in the ship very much, there being about 20 persons down, four having died and been buried already. Got a fire in the galley; made coffee and advised them to stop eating can meat and vegitables [*sic*], and live on bread and water." The dying continued that day, men, women and children, including William Wilson, the colored waiter. With the men on the *Three Bells* able to see onto the deck of the *San Francisco* as the two ships frequently passed, the powers-that-be on the wrecked steamer decided it would be better to stop throwing the bodies overboard until darkness was able to shroud their actions.[17]

At noon, although the skies were clear, the wind was blowing hard from the southwest. That afternoon, as a strong gale blew up, now coming from the north and northwest, and with the wrecked steamer laboring very heavily, all hands aboard her were employed in collecting up coal and provisions and heaving them overboard. All this time the *Three Bells* was lying well up under the steamer's lee, but because the seas were too rough for Captain Crighton to launch a small boat, no matter how many times they tacked by the *San Francisco* that day, the closest together the two vessels came was 40 yards.[18]

By sundown the wind had increased greatly and was now hauling more to the

---

13. Burnside. McDougall. McDougall says the board read, "Lay by me! My ship can't live".
14. *Three Bells* log.
15. Winder, Jan. 6, 1854.
16. *Three Bells* log; Burnside; Mellus account; Wickham; Mellus; Winder, Jan. 6, 1854. The message most often quoted in the history books is "Be of good cheer, we will stand by you." The first time anything like this is mentioned is in the January 14, 1854, editions of the *New York Herald* and *New York Times*, which published extracts of the *San Francisco*'s log, as written by First Officer Mellus, who says, in his entry for December 31, 1853, that Crighton told the survivors "to be of good cheer, for he would lay by us." Mr. Wickham, who copied from this log, merely says that Crighton "promised to lie by us." Then we come to the January 3, 1854, entry in the log, which discusses the first speaking between the *San Francisco* and the *Antarctic*. Mellus says of this meeting: "The captain of the *Antarctic* then told us to be of good cheer, as he would take us all off." Mr. Wickham says: "...told us to be of good cheer, that he would have us all off."
17. Winder, 1883; Gretton; Mellus account; Wickham.
18. Gretton; Mellus account; Wickham; McDougall.

westward, accompanied by heavy rain. At eight p.m., with night coming on fast, the *Three Bells* tacked around, making way to pass as near as possible to leeward. As she did, Captain Crighton yelled through his trumpet to the men on the steamer: "Show lights during the night and I will lay by you." This was received with tremendous cheering by the poor fellows on the *San Francisco*.[19]

At 9:30 p.m. the *Three Bells* again passed near the *San Francisco*, and saw many lights on below decks. The moon was only a day or two old, and when it made its appearance in the cloudless sky the heavens looked beautiful. At about ten o'clock that night, just as the wind was moderating, an old tar on the *Three Bells* remarked to Mr. McDougall that it was likely to continue so.[20]

On the *Three Bells*, the last several hours of 1853 were spent by the passengers at the pumps, as the ship struggled to the *San Francisco*'s windward, to lie to in order to keep in sight of her for the rest of the night. At about midnight, with the weather now quite mild, Captain Crighton ordered his crew to approach the *San Francisco* again. This time he had something else in mind, something to cheer them up.[21]

Meanwhile, the *Kilby* was in a different part of the Atlantic. At the dawn of her day, everyone awoke. Miss Merchant, seeing Lucia Eaton still sitting on the trunk, insisted that she lean on her to try to get a little sleep. The trick soon worked. The steward brought in tea and crackers at nine o'clock that morning. Because it had been boiled, the rather unappetizing liquid looked like lye, but the compensation was that for breakfast the survivors, soldiers included, had bacon for the first time since the wreck a week before. It had been cut up into small slices with a large pocket knife Lieutenant Loeser always carried about with him. The bacon was then fried and, along with the ration of one cracker per person, brought to the passengers in an old tin pan and one slice handed to each person assembled, their cutlery consisting of fingers for the simple reason that such items as knives and forks were not to be found on the bark. The officers were regularly detailed as officer of the day, and all went smoothly. Lieutenant Murray, of the U.S. Navy, was always close by to give them hope. He always tried to look cheerful.[22]

For the first two full days on the *Kilby*, the twenty-ninth and thirtieth, with everyone settling in, the issue of food was not equitable, by far the largest portions of bacon and bread being given to the ship's crew. And there was no actual restriction on the water. Captain Low, the captain of the bark, was in charge of the distribution, and would bring it around to the cabins in pails, along with crackers that he would leave in the rooms. No demand for water was refused, except occasionally one made by the children, who were always asking for it. Women and invalids were always able to get it whenever necessary. But with the circumstances the *Kilby* had suddenly and unexpectedly found herself in—108 additional passengers, many of whom were now

---

19. Wickham; McDougall; Burnside.
20. McDougall.
21. McDougall; Winder, Jan. 6, 1854.
22. Eaton.

beginning to suffer from violent diarrhea, and no one knowing how long it might take them to get back to land—things had to change. Someone suggested they had better be careful about the issue of water and provisions, and so enforced regulation was imposed by the Artillery officers. Captain Judd, on his own initiative, insisted that the pump of the water cask be kept by the officer of the day and so out of the hands of the crewmen, none of whom, especially the steward, could be trusted. Joe McIntyre it was, as commissary sergeant of the battalion, under the orders of Lieutenant Loeser as commissary, who now issued all the water on the *Kilby*, under the supervision of the officer of the day, whose job it was to be there at those times. Sergeant McIntyre would draw the rations from the cask, and call the roll of the men so as to give to them in turn. As from now, Colonel Gates, for example, got no more water than any other man, woman, or child, although, as Lieutenant Loeser was later to admit, there was occasionally some extracurricular water issued, or even taken by him to various cabins, for example to the ladies. The officers got their water in bottles, sometimes filled, sometimes half-filled, as the officer of the day directed.[23]

The *Kilby* cruised around for two and a half days, hoping to catch sight of the *San Francisco* again, but, with the wind changing once or twice, leaving them in doubt as to the actual direction in which to look, there was no way their mission could be successful. Finally, on the third day of the search, it was decided by the gentlemen that they would continue to sail about during the day, but if they didn't find the steamer before dark, then all sail must be set so that they could get to the nearest port and send out assistance. Even Lieutenant Frank Murray came to the conclusion that it was hopeless, and was now advising a run to New York. The army officers agreed, and Captain Low gave the order for the bark to head for port.[24]

Several hundred miles away, in New York City, a first-class packet ship steamed down the harbor, heading for the open sea. It was the 2,250-ton *Antarctic*, bound for Liverpool on her regular run under the command of skipper George Close Stouffer. Because emigrants came only from Europe to America, and not the other way around, the *Antarctic* was carrying no passengers, and all her necessary berths were already made up, ready to be slept in. Captain Stouffer, originally from Baltimore, was 31, and had been the *Antarctic*'s only master since she had been built a couple of years before by Donald McKay of Boston for Zerega & Co., of New York. Stouffer and his ship had been stuck in New York since November 17—almost six weeks—having arrived at New York after a passage of 34 days. Out of the 519 passengers she had brought in from England, 65 had died on board. That was not unusual, by any means, Asiatic cholera being the big killer on these emigrant ships. The *Empire*, which arrived the same day, had lost 73.[25]

---

23. Merchant; Loeser; McIntyre; Judd; Loeser; Graham.
24. Graham/Kilby; Fremont; Eaton; Murray.
25. Stouffer. The packet ship *Continent*, after a boisterous passage from Liverpool, arrived in New York with 54 of her steerage passengers dead from cholera (*New York Times*, Jan. 18, 1854).

Sunday
January 1, 1854

"A Happy New Year to us." An extra ring of the *Three Bells*'s bell gave all on board, and those on the *San Francisco* who could hear it, notice of the old year going out and the new year having commenced. It was Captain Crighton's little gift to all in those waters. More, it signified a celebratory acknowledgment of life itself, it brought home to all who thought about it that no matter what they had been through—the perils, the strain, the fear, the always impending doom—they were still here, still alive, as yet another new year dawned.[1]

Although the weather was mild and the wind moderate during the dark hours of the late night and early morning, the sea was rather heavy, and the *San Francisco* was laboring greatly. Still, the *Three Bells* stayed in company with the stricken vessel, occasionally passing close under the her lee. At 4 a.m. the *Three Bells* tacked by the *San Francisco* again. Since no information could be passed between the two ships during this tack, or the return, the crew of the *Three Bells* remained unaware that many of the people aboard the wreck were dying fast.[2]

Disconcertingly, from the deck of the *San Francisco*, come daylight, there was no ship in sight. The *Three Bells* had gone. All hands went to work again, heaving over coal and provisions, stopping leaks, and generally trying to ease the dying pains of their steamer. A soldier, two soldiers' wives, and a child had all died during the night, and now they were sewn up in canvas and, after a brief service, thrown overboard.[3]

At 8 a.m., much to their relief, the crew of the *San Francisco* spotted the *Three Bells*, this time off the lee bow. Captain Crighton was putting about again, but at that very moment the wind freshened, and an angry sea showed its crested head. The waves were still running heavy as the *Three Bells* came near. Mr. Gibbs, her first mate, and four of his men, volunteered to man one of their two small boats, but the idea

---

1. Buel, 1872; McDougall. "*A Happy New Year to us*" is from Buel, in what he claims to be a quote from the *San Francisco*'s log. If this quote was truly from the log, then it doesn't appear in either Mr. Mellus's account, or that of Mr. Wickham, both of which were published in the *New York Herald* of Jan. 14, 1854, as reproductions of parts of that very same ship's log. Buel must be quoting from either the original log, or a copy thereof—or he made it up.
2. McDougall; Mellus account; Wickham; Gretton; Winder, 1883; Buel, 1872. Dr. Buel, claiming to be quoting from the *San Francisco*'s log, says: "Gale continues with a heavy sea."
3. Gretton.

had to be given up owing to the violence of the ocean. So Captain Crighton chalked up a new message and displayed it to the men on the steamer. "Make rafts," he suggested, lower them into the sea, fill them with people, and the *Three Bells* would try to pick them up. Commodore Watkins replied that it was useless to try that, as a raft couldn't live in that sea. However, realizing that the waves might abate at any time, he changed his mind, and ordered rafts built. The *San Francisco*'s topmast had been housed, but now the men got it down, cut it into pieces, hacked off the ship's guards and other portions of the forward upper deck, and duly started building a pair of rafts.[4]

The *Three Bells* managed to tack by the steamer again, during which time there was another exchange between the two vessels. On a chalk board Captain Crighton had written: "We are leaky and disabled! Do you mean to leave your ship?"

To which Commodore Watkins, the captain of the *San Francisco*, replied on his own board: "We are ready," and "Lay by me! We are making rafts!"

On the return tack the crew of the *Three Bells* were informed by the *San Francisco*'s chalk boards: "We had 180 swept overboard—lay by me—we have women and children who cannot raft—wait till the weather moderates."[5]

At eleven o'clock, the *Three Bells* was less than half a mile away, and an hour later, with the sky clearing up, one of the *San Francisco*'s rafts was put over the side to prepare for transshipment of souls whenever the moment looked right. They made the raft fast to the steamer's weather bow, but by the time they had finished, much to their dismay, a fresh gale had come up, only slightly more moderate than the one before, this time from the northwest, and the sea, still running high, was sweeping over the raft, making it impossible to put anyone on it. All they could do now was wait.[6]

They prayed over three more corpses on the *San Francisco* that afternoon, two men and a child, and then cast them into the deep. A good many of the still living were lying around sick without anyone to take care of them, the troops being completely demoralized and entirely overcome with fear, the steamer's officers and crew having enough to do on deck without acting as nurses, while the ship's surgeon was doing all he could but getting very little assistance, what with the principal officers of the command having left on the *Kilby*.[7]

When the *Three Bells* tacked by again, Captain Crighton wrote on his chalk board: "Do you intend to come?"

To which he got an answer from the *San Francisco*'s speaking trumpet: "The rafts are ready."[8]

---

4. McDougall; Gretton; Winder, Jan. 6, 1854; Wickham.
"The *Three Bells* managed to tack..." Burnside; Winder, Jan. 6, 1854. Winder reports the message thus: "*My ship is leaky and long. What shall I do?*"
5. McDougall.
6. Gretton; Wickham; Mellus account; Gretton; Winder, Jan. 6, 1854; Buel, 1872. Dr. Buel, who claimed to be quoting from the ship's log, has both rafts being launched, yet Mr. Mellus, who wrote the log, has only one being launched, as does Mr. Wickham, who also copied from the log.
7. Gretton.
8. McDougall.

Commodore Watkins threw another letter over to the *Three Bells*: "We are in great distress—do not leave us, we have already lost overboard about 180. We have U.S. troops on board, and the commanding officer will charter your ship. We have plenty of water and provisions on board. We have now about 420 all told. I find it too rough to do anything with our rafts; they are made and are awaiting a calm."[9]

Captain Crighton had several copies of a letter of his own ready for the next tack, the letter reading: "My ship is making four inches of water per hour; my water is also getting short, so that you will see the necessity on your part of bringing provisions and water with you, as I have none."[10]

The last tack made by the *Three Bells* that day placed her at a distance from the wreck, owing to the wind, but by 8 p.m., with the two vessels now quite close together, the wind abated. However, rain had come on heavy.[11]

By the evening, the engineers on the *Three Bells* had finally discovered the reason why the pumps weren't working right. Two pieces of wood had somehow become lodged in them. As soon as these obstructions were removed the crew were much better able to keep the water level down. However, it was not the end of the leaks.[12]

About midnight the wind hauled round to the southwest, and it began to rain even more heavily than before.[13]

As for that day's events on the *Kilby*, we rely on Lucia Eaton: "It was a very pleasant day and all felt cheerful. Mr. Cooper, the clergyman, read the service for the day. The prayer book he used was one which had been saved from the wreck. It had been the property of poor Captain Field, a present from his wife. It was all we had to take back to her. One of the soldiers found it on deck the morning of the wreck, and brought it to my brother [she means, of course, Lieutenant Loeser]. The day passed very quietly, as we were lying to, the wind being too high for us to put up our poor old sails."[14]

---

9. McDougall.
10. McDougall.
11. McDougall.
12. McDougall.
13. Gretton.
14. Eaton.

Monday
January 2

Just after midnight the lights of the *Three Bells* disappeared from view, and Commodore Watkins ordered the *San Francisco*'s guns to be fired every half hour. By the second salvo no lights had been seen, and people began to worry. Then to make matters more miserable, at one o'clock the raft broke adrift and was lost. Watkins and his crew kept firing the guns every 30 minutes, but still no sign of the *Three Bells*. It wasn't until 4:30 that morning that the men on the *Three Bells* heard the gunfire. Mr. McDougall, the passenger on the *Three Bells*, missed this excitement, having been sound asleep, and at 5 a.m., as his ship was making its way back toward the *San Francisco*, he woke up, refreshed, and got back to the pumps.[1]

"At daylight the *Three Bells* on our weather beam, about 2 miles dist. All the crew at work getting up coal & provisions; the pumps just able to keep the water down to 2½ and 3 feet; buried 4 soldiers and one soldier's wife."[2]

The latter part of the morning the weather was much the same, and by noon was starting to clear up, with the wind moderating down, even though the seas remained quite high. The *Three Bells* put about the ship and neared the steamer close to midday, but not close enough to speak her. However by using the chalk boards Captain Crighton was able to impart news to those on the wreck. It was not good news. The *Three Bells* would have to leave them as her leak was so bad, and because she was short of provisions and sails. Commodore Watkins messaged that if they would send a boat, he would send someone over to the bark to confer with them. On the return tack, half an hour later, the *Three Bells* stood down within a very short distance, under the *San Francisco*'s lee, close under the stern. Captain Crighton informed the men on the wreck that by next tack he would endeavor to send a small boat and get a hawser attached.[3]

---

1. Gretton; Mellus account; Wickham; Buel, 1872; McDougall. Mr. Gretton it is who tells us that both rafts were lost at 1 a.m. The *San Francisco*'s log, on the other hand, written by Mr. Mellus, refers to the loss of only one raft, the one that had been slung over the side of the ship the day before: "At daylight it was gone." Mr. Wickham, copying from the log, says: "At daylight the raft gone." Dr. Buel, also claiming to be quoting from the log, says: "But at daylight they were gone." Mr. McDougall says: "The rafts we saw floating yesterday went loose from their fastening, and were lost during last night."
2. Gretton.
3. Gretton; Mellus account; Wickham; McDougall; Burnside.

It was not until about 1:30 p.m. that Captain Crighton felt it was safe enough to lower the *Three Bells*'s jolly boat. With five men in it, the little craft fought its way over to the *San Francisco*, pulling alongside the wreck just before two o'clock.[4]

Aboard the *San Francisco*, Commodore Watkins was giving his second officer, Mr. Gretton, orders for the crossing. Gretton's mission was to try to induce the skipper of the *Three Bells* to stay by the wrecked steamer until they could get the survivors off. Watkins and Major Wyse, the senior army officer on board, handed Gretton a written agreement chartering the *Three Bells*, signed by the commodore in behalf of the Pacific Mail Steamship Company, and by Major Wyse for the United States Government, pledging both parties to indemnify Captain Crighton or his owners for any loss to ship and cargo.[5]

The crew rigged a whip on the bowsprit, got Gretton into it, and as the quarter-boat pulled in underneath, they lowered him into it. When Gretton stepped onto the deck of the *Three Bells* it was noticed that "he looked exceedingly careworn. He informed us how matters really stood in the steamer, and showed great anxiety about his fellow sufferers." However, Gretton still had his wits about him and succeeded in his mission.[6]

The afternoon continued with a moderate gale from the northwest and cloudy weather, and on the *San Francisco* there were still a great many sick and dying among the troops and firemen.[7]

As evening approached, the *Three Bells* tacked again, but the wind had increased, and the two ships couldn't get to within a quarter of a mile of each other, so Mr. Gretton had to remain aboard the Scottish ship. However, at sundown the wind was out from the southward and moderating fast, with the sea going down. By 9:30 p.m., the weather was still blowy, with occasional showers, and during the cloudy night, with a fresh gale coming up from the northwest, the *San Francisco* almost lost the *Three Bells* again, but, once more, by firing their guns continually, they managed to keep in touch.[8]

---

4. Mellus account; Wickham; Burnside; *Three Bells* log. Oddly, Mr. Gretton says that the *Three Bells* lowered their boat at 4 p.m. This time is so much at variance with everyone else's testimony that it has to be wrong.

5. Gretton.

6. Mellus account; Wickham; Gretton; Burnside; McDougall; *Three Bells* log. The quote is from McDougall.

7. Mellus account; Wickham.

8. McDougall; Gretton; Mellus account; Wickham; Winder, Jan. 6, 1854.

Tuesday
January 3

With the *Three Bells* holding on to the windward, the weather started to moderate during the dark hours of the morning. For four days and three long nights Captain Crighton had stood by, with water pouring into his ship, and with no one—himself, crew, or passengers—objecting in the slightest. They just worked the pumps, and worked them, and worked them. John McGowan, one of the passengers, had been steadily at it from midnight until 4 a.m. on this fourth day, and yet even by the end of his shift there was still two feet of water in the main hold compartment. Exhausted, McGowan woke a reluctant Mr. McDougall to take his place. As McDougall was reaching valiantly for full consciousness, McGowan asked him if he had ever heard of the Storm Fiend. McDougall had never heard of such a being, real or mythical, but it reminded him of a dream he had had only a few minutes before, one that had brought him out of his sleep even as McGowan was shaking him. He was on the deck of a vessel, there were people around, and from under the deck came a hideous sound, as if from a spirit. The noise went around and around in a circle, and then came to rest immediately under his feet. He felt as if the spirit was going to thump right up through the deck and destroy him. But then it vanished, and there was McGowan. McDougall got dressed and went to work for two or three hours on the pumps.[1]

Come daylight, with the *Three Bells* about five miles off the *San Francisco*'s weather bow, the sky was fine and the wind and sea were still going down. They buried six men who had died on the wrecked steamer during the previous afternoon and night, while at least half of the troops were down with cholera.[2]

George Gretton, the *San Francisco*'s second officer, who was still aboard the *Three Bells*, was on deck with Mr. Burnside not long after 7:30 that morning, and a few minutes later they saw a distant vessel on their weather quarter, running full sail down before the fresh northwest wind. Captain Crighton was called and immediately came on deck. Within half an hour, and with a very moderate sea running, others now up and about on deck could make out the ship to windward. At about 9:15 the *Three Bells* set its Union Jack ensign upside down, to attract attention and to indicate

---

1. Mellus account; Wickham; McDougall.
2. Gretton.

distress. The ship was coming in their rough direction, flying the Stars and Stripes, and now headed directly for them. This then was the dramatic appearance of the *Antarctic*, three days out of New York, bound for Liverpool under Captain George Close Stouffer.[3]

The crew aboard the approaching *Antarctic* had no idea, as yet, that a third vessel was in the vicinity, the *San Francisco* being low in the water with nothing but the mizzen mast standing, but as soon as they came close enough to make out with clarity what was going on aboard the *Three Bells*, Mr. Gretton shinnied up to the foretop and, with his hat in his hand, pointed their attention toward the wreck. Captain Stouffer looked through his spy-glass in the indicated direction and, spotting the wreck, set out in her direction. The *Three Bells* made sail, and the two vessels rode the waves side by side toward the steamer, the *Three Bells* soon taking the lead and arriving first. Their position at this moment was 39° 41' N, 62° 00' W.[4]

On the *San Francisco*, it was Little Jack, the sailor boy, who first identified the newcomer as the *Antarctic*. How could he possibly know that?, asked Commodore Watkins. Because the ship was one of the Red Zed line, Jack could tell that by the way she was painted, the red "Z" in the middle of her flag signifying Zerega, the owner. No one else could even see the flag, but as the vessel came closer, and everyone could now make out her name, Jack yelled out to the commodore, "I told you it was the *Antarctic*."[5]

At first the *Antarctic* was just a little too far away from the *San Francisco* to speak her, but then she shortened sail and passed close under her bows and stern, the men on the giant hulk giving her several hearty cheers. Using chalk boards, Captain Stouffer asked them if they wished to leave the steamer, and Commodore Watkins replied in the affirmative. Stouffer then told them to be of good cheer, that he would stick by them, and that he would have them all off. He then filled his main topsail, and shot ahead some three miles.[6]

At noon the wind was west northwest, and despite the fact that it was moderating all the time, with the weather clear and the sea still going down some, it was yet too heavy for a long-boat to lie alongside the steamer. But at about 1 p.m., with the wind and waves moderating, the *Antarctic* wore ship and, getting nearer, was able to lower away two of her six good boats, while the *Three Bells* launched her large quarter-boat. At about two o'clock the transfer began.[7]

Using the same technique as they had during the transfer to the *Kilby* some days before, the men lowered the passengers from the spanker boom in a whip. This was slow work because they had to hold them in the whip sometimes five minutes or longer waiting for a boat to get under them in the still rough sea.[8]

---

3. Gretton; McDougall; Burnside; Winder, Jan. 6, 1854; Buel, 1872.
4. Gretton; McDougall; Mellus account; Wickham.
5. Auchinleck; Gretton. It is Auchinleck who calls him Little Jack the sailor boy, and he was probably just that, a sailor boy. But it might have been John Mason, the young fourth officer of the *San Francisco*.
6. Mellus account; Wickham; Watkins dinner; Buel, 1872; McDougall.
7. Gretton; Wickham; Mellus account; McDougall; Buel, 1872; *Three Bells* log.
8. Gretton; McDougall.

Relatively few of the *San Francisco*'s crew would wind up going onto the *Antarctic*; most of them were transferred to the *Three Bells*. After they had come aboard, Captain Crighton sent a request over that an Artillery officer be brought to the *Three Bells* in the next boat, as there were large quantities of liquor on board, and he was concerned about maintaining law and order. Major Wyse sent over Lieutenant William A. Winder.[9]

"In order to give the seamen a chance to work the oars in the heavy sea, the passengers were required to lie down in the bottom of the boat. So I found myself lying side-by-side with a poor man who died next day of the small-pox."[10]

The *Three Bells* was still leaking badly, and Captain Crighton asked the survivors to go between decks. On reaching the bark, Bill Winder's first mission was have a portion of the cargo thrown over, in order to accommodate the influx of passengers. As this work was going on they discovered the source of the leak. A three-inch pipe of cast iron ran up from the ship's bottom and through the side of the ship, to supply the pump and to wash the decks. This pipe had been broken off by the rolling of the cargo, and water was pouring into the ship. Mr. Dunham, the boiler maker, although much fatigued and worn out by exposure on the *San Francisco*, was persuaded by Captain Crighton to try to rectify the problem. He cut through the outside plate, got the pipe rolled up in canvas and white lead, and in half an hour the water had stopped coming in.[11]

The afternoon continued moderate and pleasant, at least as far as the weather was concerned. The ocean, though, was still playing up. The *Antarctic* and the *Three Bells* lay head to sea so that their boats could lie very easily alongside them on the lee side of their respective ships and take the people up a side ladder without any trouble. And so the trans-shipment of troops and provisions proceeded smoothly, despite the steamer pitching and rolling terribly in the trough of the sea, and the waves dashing the little boats about so much that one of the *Antarctic*'s was stove at the first attempt they made to take anyone off, and another just as night was coming on.[12]

The boats, originals and replacements, made five trips before nightfall came, transferring 32 soldiers and two sailors to the *Three Bells*, and another 52 passengers, mostly troops, onto the *Antarctic*. The provisions were lowered by a whip rigged on the *San Francisco*'s bowsprit, and the drinking water was poured into bread casks and thrown over the side to be towed over to the *Thee Bells*. Finally, with the dark setting in, and with a gale blowing up again, it became much more difficult to use the whip on the *San Francisco*, and so the *Three Bells* and the *Antarctic* hoisted up their boats.[13]

---

9. Winder, 1883.
10. Winder, 1883. Actually, the smallpox case died aboard the *Three Bells* three days later, on January 6.
11. Auchinleck; McDougall; Winder, 1883.
12. Mellus account; Wickham; Gretton; Buel, 1872.
13. *Three Bells* log; McDougall; Mellus account; Wickham; Gretton. No provisions were transferred to the *Antarctic*.

The 32 soldiers taken aboard the *Three Bells* were divided into three watches to work the pumps, a great relief to the long-suffering crew and passengers, who were pretty much all in. But now, with the pumps in better working order and the leak stopped, it was easier to keep the water down, and whereas early that day there had been two feet of water in the main hold compartment, now there was only about 12 inches.[14]

At 8 p.m., the *Three Bells* passed close by the *San Francisco*, but two hours later had beaten back and was lying not far away, burning a blue light in order to avoid a collision. Also relatively close by was the *Antarctic*, showing three blue lights. During the night the wind was steady at west northwest, but it was ameliorating now, and the sea was going down fast, so much so that both ships were able to lie by the steamer throughout a night that was quite moderate and pleasant, and offering the prospect of a fine day on the morrow. But anything could happen out there in the violent and unpredictable Atlantic, as the 30 women and children and those of the men still remaining aboard the *San Francisco* knew only too well. For them, would tomorrow ever come?[15]

---

14. McDougall.
15. McDougall; Gretton; Mellus account; Wickham.

Wednesday
January 4

The last thing those on the *San Francisco* wanted was a repeat of the week before, when they had drifted away from the *Kilby* during the night. Now, all through the dark hours the crew fired their guns continually, while the men on the *Three Bells* and the *Antarctic* burned blue lights. In this way, and with the wind remaining mercifully calm, the three vessels were all able to stay close to each other until morning came.[1]

Daylight ushered itself in clear and beautiful, the sun shining bright and the gentle wind puffing only slight ruffles on a relatively smooth and calm ocean. The wrecked steamer was lying so still in the water that the *Three Bells* was able to put out not only the boat they had been using the day before but also the long boat, which until now they had held back as being crucial to their own future safety. As for the *Antarctic*, she had only one boat left—or, rather, oars enough for only one boat—but she lowered it. The three small vessels were able to get alongside the *San Francisco* with no difficulty, and at 7 a.m. they began again the process of transferring crew members and passengers: Men, women, and children. Given that the *Three Bells* was still short of water and provisions, those particularly invaluable commodities were also shipped over, biscuits going across wrapped in blankets.[2]

The women, children, and sick were slung over the stern of the *San Francisco* in bed clothes and bags, with those who were well enough being dropped into the boats as quickly as possible. Notwithstanding the danger of loading in this manner, and the still more hazardous mode of getting them aboard the two rescue ships, not an accident of the least consequence took place, although three died in the boats as they were being transported from the steamer, and several were brought aboard both the *Antarctic* and the *Three Bells* in a dying state. Private Ernst Northman of Company H and musician Thomas Mulholland, for example, had no sooner boarded the *Antarctic* than they died.[3]

---

1. Mellus account; Wickham; McDougall.
2. Mellus account; Wickham; McDougall; Gretton; *Three Bells* log; Auchinleck.
3. Wickham; Mellus account; McDougall; Army enlistment records; Gretton. The entire Mulholland family was on board the *San Francisco* that chilly December day: James, hospital steward; Mariah, his wife; Thomas and Ezekiel, their sons, both soldiers; and their daughters, Adelaide Jane, aged 9; Matilda, aged 4; and Lizzie, aged 2. James, Adelaide, and Lizzie were taken off by the *Antarctic*. The others all died.

As soon as the passengers were brought aboard their two new homes, accommodation was made for them and they were carefully attended to, especially the sick, who, for example, were accommodated in the cabin of the *Three Bells* along with Major Wyse and Lieutenant Bill Winder.[4]

The latter part of the early morning was quite moderate and pleasant, with a gentle breeze coming in from the west and a few squalls. Come noon, with the weather much the same, the transfer was coming along very quickly.[5]

The boats were kept going all day, until an hour after sunset, when it was considered too dangerous to press on. About 120 persons had been carried to the *Three Bells* that day, and a good number to the *Antarctic*. By the end of the exercise it was estimated that there were just over 30 men still on board the *San Francisco*, Commodore Watkins preferring to remain with his ship until the morning. The night continued moderately pleasant.[6]

At the approach of midnight, land time, the *Maria* arrived at Liverpool, Nova Scotia, the first ship in to port with news of the *San Francisco*. It had been nine days since her encounter with the doomed steamship. Captain Freeman immediately sent a dispatch to Halifax, dated that day, January 4, 1854. Very soon the eyes of an anxious world would be riveted upon the news stands.

---

4. McDougall.
5. Mellus account; Wickham.
6. McDougall; Gretton; Mellus account.

Thursday
January 5

About 150 soldiers, firemen and sailors were grouped around on the deck of the *Three Bells* early in the morning. It was a gloomy gathering. Several enlisted men and some women had died on board during the night and more were dying every hour. However, by 7:15, with the day coming up beautiful and clear, and the wind moderate from the west southwest, the *Three Bells* maneuvered toward the *San Francisco*, preparing to launch her lifeboat to begin yet again the process of transferring water and provisions from the steamer. Commodore Watkins saw every officer, every sailor, every fireman, and every Negro waiter safely in the boats, and by half past 10 the *Three Bells*'s little boat set out on its last short trip back from the *San Francisco*, carrying a further supply of water and the last of the crew, the last, that is, with the exception of three men: Commodore Watkins, First Officer Mellus, and Chief Engineer Marshall. It was noted that during the drift between Christmas Day noon and 10:30 a.m. on January 5, the *San Francisco* had drifted 480 miles in an east half north direction, magnetic, for most of that time having been pushed along by a wind blowing strong from the westward. The distance traveled, over a period of 10 days, 22 hours, and 30 minutes, meant that the steamer had traveled at an average speed of one and five-sixths knots.[1]

A few minutes later, with smoke still coming out of the *San Francisco*'s smoke pipe, Mr. Mellus and Mr. Marshall went over the side into one of the *Antarctic*'s lifeboats, and then, finally, Commodore Watkins bade farewell to his doomed ship, lowered himself down the side by a rope, and the boat pulled away. They had decided to leave a number of dead bodies lying in different parts of the steamer, not thinking it necessary to bury them, as they knew the ship, having been scuttled, would go down in a short time after they left her. So, every living soul—man, woman, and child—was now off the *San Francisco*.[2]

Mr. Mellus and the engineer were hauled up onto the *Three Bells*. The commodore, however, after yelling out his thanks to Captain Crighton, was rowed around the ship at precisely eight minutes before eleven o'clock, and as he bobbed about in

---

1. Mellus account; Wickham; McDougall.
2. Mellus account; Wickham; McDougall; Gretton; Auchinleck.

the water the men on the deck above him gave nine lusty cheers. "He waved an adieu and cried like a child; he couldn't speak. His whole ambition had been to get [his] ship into port." A few minutes later, Watkins boarded Captain Stouffer's ship, which he had chosen to go on in order to look after his passengers as they went to a foreign land.³

About 11 a.m., having received all the crew and passengers from the wreck that they could take, the men on the *Three Bells* hoisted the boats in.⁴

These seem to be the figures of those taken off on the *Three Bells*: Two Artillery officers, Major Wyse and Lieutenant Bill Winder; 140 enlisted men; 89 crew members; and an unknown number of women and children. Of the crew there were two officers, Mr. Mellus and Mr. Gretton. There were the four quartermasters, Osier, Gallagher, Hooker, and Kelley, as well as the storekeeper, Mr. Wickham, and Dr. Buel. In the engine room or the fire room worked 41: these included Chief Engineer Marshall, First Engineer Auchinleck, Second Engineers David Dunham and James Crosby, and Third Engineers B. Donaghan and C. Hoffman. The rest were assistant engi-neers and firemen, but the only names we have are Arthur Henry and Walter Wat-kins. There were 26 waiters, stewards, etc., taken off, the only named ones being Mr. Sanford, the Negro head steward; John Logan, the Negro cook; William Scofield, the steward; the waiters Isaiah Carter and Walter Heath; the Negro waiters Wil-liam Fields and William Evans; Levi Heath, the steerage steward; and Catherine Livingston, the stewardess. There were also 14 seamen, all unnamed. Of the camp women and children we know only Sergeant Joe McIntyre's wife and two boys.⁵

The latter part of the morning saw a gentle breeze from the west, and squally weather, and from every vantage point the hundreds of people whom fate had conspired to bring together in this particular part of the Atlantic Ocean were intently watching the once mighty steamer as she settled deeper and deeper into the water. The *San Francisco*, which had been an agonizing prison for two weeks, night and day, went down almost immediately.⁶

Was this decision to scuttle the *San Francisco* the correct one? A reliable source claimed that "...at no time was there over two and a half feet of water in the vessel; and had they been aware of the fact that vessels had been sent to their relief, the ship's company would not have abandoned the *San Francisco*."⁷

About 2 p.m., the *Antarctic* headed out to sea, bound east for Liverpool, while the *Three Bells* hauled all sail and began to move away from the sunken wreck in the direction of New York, 600 miles away. Her progress toward that city would be slow

---

3. McDougall; Auchinleck. The quote is from Auchinleck.
4. *Three Bells* log; Gretton.
5. Second Officer Gretton says that 140 were taken off on the *Three Bells* and 250 on the *Antarctic*. The *Brooklyn Daily Eagle* of Jan. 14, 1854, gives us the number of 41 engineers and firemen and the number of 26 stewards, waiters, etc. Burnside, writing on Jan. 16, 1854, says, *"The Three Bells took off about 185 persons in all, some 30 or 40 of whom died before reaching New York, and one since."*
6. Wickham.
7. According to the reporter who wrote Mr. Marshall's account in the *New York Tribune*, Jan. 16, 1854.

as she encountered a lot of northeasterly wind, but by evening she was on the right course, with a light breeze south by west.[8]

It was this morning that the *Maria*'s dispatch of the previous night was sent on from the American consul in Halifax to the U.S. Secretary of State in Washington, where it started a ruckus. Senator Gwin, of California, received the news at 5 p.m. Of course, unaware of events out at sea since the *Maria* had left the stricken *San Francisco*, Gwin immediately applied to the Secretary of the Navy to send a government vessel out. Unfortunately, there was not one to be found. He then applied to Secretary of War Jefferson Davis. Mr. Davis visited the home of Quartermaster General Jesup in Washington, handed him the original dispatch from Nova Scotia, and ordered him to take the most prompt and energetic measures, in other words to dispatch a steamer, at public expense, to go the relief of the *San Francisco*. Jesup proceeded immediately to the telegraph office in Washington to send a message to Colonel Swords in New York, instructing him to go and see W.H. Aspinwall, with the object being to charter a steamer from that port. Mr. Aspinwall had already learned about the wreck, but he was having trouble finding a suitable steamer to go out, so the Secretary of the Treasury was then applied to, and that evening he also telegraphed New York, giving orders for all his disposable revenue cutters to proceed on the same service: The *Washington* to sail immediately from New York, the *Walter Forward* from Wilmington, Delaware, the *Campbell* from Norfolk, Virginia, and the *Jefferson Davis*, from Charleston, South Carolina, even though the last was not quite yet ready for sea service. Of course, unknown to anyone in North America, the rescue had already been effected.[9]

---

8. *Three Bells* log. It was McDougall who said they were "more than 600 miles" from New York when the *Three Bells* parted from the wreck.

9. *New York Times*, Jan. 16 and Feb. 8, 1854.

Friday
January 6

With the crew of the *Three Bells* busy repairing sails, the soldiers tucked into their thrice-daily ration of biscuit, water, and one piece of bacon. "It is hard fare but the best that can be afforded them at present." Those who manned the pumps, for the prescribed period of an hour at a time, would be issued something stronger than water, whereby they were able to keep their spirits up. But several people gave up the ghost during the night and day, including Walter Watkins in the engineers' room, and the soldier with smallpox who had transferred over three days before in the small boat with Bill Winder. Mr. Sanford, the Negro head steward, was disturbing those in Mr. McDougall's berth. He fancied the persons around him were plotting his death. "All I want is a chance," he said. Mr. Sanford's "exertions on the deck were unremitting."[1]

"Rain and wind came on, and our good ship goes like a duck at a rapid rate."[2]

The *Maria*'s dispatch appeared in the *New York Times* of January 6, but the *Boston Atlas*, for example, of that day, was still totally ignorant of what had happened out there in the Atlantic. Those two were morning dailies, but the evening newspapers of that day had learned more about the incident. The *Star*, published in Washington, D.C., gave a report of what they called the terrible gale of the twenty-third of December, in which they had the *San Francisco* off the coast of Virginia, a little north of the latitude of Norfolk, with 514 officers and men aboard, along with about 200 women and children, and others; a total of 715 persons.

On the *Kilby* those out on deck spotted a ship in the distance, standing to westward, but that was where it remained. Captain Low tried all he could to attract their attention. He had the remains of a flag run up with the union down, indicating a ship in distress, and then, getting into his little boat, he rowed out some distance. But nothing worked. The ship disappeared over the horizon. This was a crushing blow, of course, but the Reverend Cooper, as he led prayers in the hold, undoubtedly provided the right, comforting answer to his flock. The Almighty had sent them a death ship and then taken it away, in order to show them how bad things could really get.[3]

---

1. McDougall.
2. McDougall.
3. Eaton.

When Captain Low got back to the *Kilby*, he found Colonel Gates, Lieutenant Fremont and some of the other officers in the cabin. They had inked in the original contract, which had been written in pencil, but had inserted certain clauses without young Low's agreement. They had decided that "[t]his noble officer has done nothing for himself," and so they had added $1,000 bounty for him, and inserted a 5 percent primage on the charter. They tried to press this new contract on Low, but as his only concern at the time of the original contract had been to protect himself with his owners, he rejected this new one, and would ultimately return to Boston without it. As he would write to Fremont on January 18, 1854, from New York, "I did not work for gain. I want it withdrawn. The primage I get from my owners—I do not want it twice."[4]

After the excitement of seeing the other vessel, things settled down on the *Kilby*, and routine took over. Colonel Burke, Mr. Graham, Lieutenant Van Voast, and Doctor Wirtz all slept in the hold, considering the cotton bales preferable to the cabin floor. This gave everyone in the cabin more sleeping room, the floor now being taken by Lieutenant Frank Murray, Lucia Eaton, Lieutenant Loeser, Mrs. Chase, Vallie Merchant and her two little sisters, while Mrs. Cooper and three of her children slept at the entrance to Sarah Loeser's tiny state room. Captain Judd's bed was on the starboard side of the bark, about four feet from the bulkhead, between Colonel Burke and Dr. Satterlee, both damaged men. Captain Gardiner's was against this bulkhead, about eight feet from the starboard side.[5]

After taking their tea and crackers, just after sunset, Lucien Loeser would take a broom and sweep the cabin floor clean. He then spread down the thickest blanket for their bed, then a carpet bag that he had saved for a pillow, and there he and his ladies would lie, a lone candle burning during the night, until morning broke upon them.[6]

Lucia Eaton did not always sleep, as the hard boards and the incessant rolling of the bark often prevented such a luxury, and so she would sometimes sit up for hours, even though she was exhausted. There was a piece of iron fastened to the floor near them, and Lieutenant Loeser would keep hold of it all night, telling Lucia to take a grip on his arm, which she did, to prevent herself from interfering with her neighbor's sleep. The cabin door was constantly being opened by persons coming in and going out, and one night Lucia took a violent cold. The next day she lost her appetite, developed a serious chill, and couldn't get warm. This was not good, for if she got really sick the two doctors aboard would be able to do little for her as there was no medicine. Lieutenant Loeser insisted she get into the little bed with her sister, head to toe, toe to head. This did the trick, that and a little stiff alcohol that her brother-in-law gave her. Next morning she was up and about and went back to the floor of the cabin. Her throat was still very sore, but that was an affliction shared by

---

4. Fremont.
5. Eaton; Graham/Kilby; Judd. One hundred bales of cotton had eventually been broken out of the hold since Dec. 28, and it was on those remaining that several people would spend two of the longest weeks of their lives. Dr. Satterlee would soon move down to the hold.
6. Eaton.

all the ladies. It was from drinking tea boiled in a copper kettle. It was a dull red color, and tasted bad, very astringent. The steward cleaned the kettle that day. "Now the water was getting low in the barrels each person was allowed but two gills a day, one in the morning and one at night. For a day we were obliged to give up having tea as we were using the water too freely. One biscuit and two slices of bacon a day. The latter being a small piece about an inch square after being fried. The officer of the day came in and said we will have a famine if we are not more provident." They prayed.[7]

"It was truly distressing to hear persons calling for water," wrote Lucia Eaton who, luckily, could go from meal to meal without drinking. It wasn't so much food they craved—they really couldn't care about that—it was water. If only they could have a glass of water. They didn't care how stale it was, as long as it was water. And when it finally came they would clutch the glass and drink as though it were the last drop of water they would ever have. Unfortunately, because they were so thirsty, no matter how much they had it was too little, and so increased their thirst. The children would call, "Mother, will you not give me a drink of water? I am so thirsty." Mrs. Gates had her three little children with her all the time, as they were not feeling well. Julius, the middle one, was only four, and was recovering from the measles. As he was feverish he was always calling for water, but "his poor mother could not give it to him." The younger of the two girls, only three years old, had also had the measles, and, like her sister and brother, would not leave her mother's side, just wanting to be in her mother's arms. Mrs. Gates was a model of patience.[8]

Mrs. Fremont, a "pious and excellent lady," was worn out, and quite distressed. Despite everything she had done, her sick baby was simply not getting any better, her three-year-old boy was down with the measles, while the eldest, who was only four, was complaining of not feeling well and was obliged to lie down upon her hard bed. "The helpless little babe would look up into its mother's face and moan most piteously, but nothing could be done to make it better." Then word was brought in that they had floated back into the Gulf Stream, and Mrs. Fremont gave up in despair, bursting into an agony of tears and moaning, "I have lost all hope, we will never get to land and my poor little babe will die." Lieutenant Fremont, who was beside her, and who had shared in the care of their little ones, was much distressed and tried to soothe his suffering wife, telling her not to give up, there was still hope. Lucia Eaton sat next to her and tried to calm her by getting her to tell her life story.[9]

On this day, Friday, January 6, 1854, W.H. Aspinwall sent a telegraph to his agent in Washington, W.H. Davidge: "The *Alabama* can be had at a thousand dollars a day—same as paid by underwriters recently for the *Marion*—can be got to sea early Sunday morning—*Northstar* [sic], *Jamestown* and others could be got—fog thick to

---

7. Eaton.
8. Eaton. The three Gates children were Louise Anita, known as Loulie, aged 6½; Julius Granville, coming up for 5 the following February; and Ida Wellington, originally called Norma, aged 3.
9. The Fremonts' baby was Mary Lawrence Fremont, aged 1; Richard Langdon was 3; Ellen Mae was 4.

day—If charter is to be made, let written orders come by mail to Swords—Nothing more from Halifax. W.H.A."

And so the *Alabama* was duly chartered that very day, by direction of Lieutenant Colonel Swords, the quartermaster in New York, and it would, indeed take two days to get her ready to sail. A message to Quartermaster General Jesup from Colonel Swords of that day: "The *Alabama* is engaged—she will start Sunday morning. The steam tugs are not adapted to the service—the '*Illinois*' did not see the '*San Francisco*'—the opinion of practical men is very favorable as to her safety."

Several dispatches were sent by Aspinwall to Swords, and vice versa, and instructions were repeated by telegraph, to send a large steamer to relieve the *San Francisco* should she still be afloat. Communications passed between Jesup's office and the owners and agents of steamers in Philadelphia, but none could be got ready sooner than, or as soon as, the *Alabama*.

Saturday
January 7

During the night, as she fought her way toward the American land mass, the *Three Bells* was tormented by a gale from the northwest, forcing the crew to shorten sail and lie the vessel to. In the cabin five refugees from the *San Francisco* lay on their death beds. Levi Heath, the steerage steward, would not make it to daylight. Arthur Henry of the Engineer Corps died in the morning, just after the *Three Bells* had passed another wreck. The other three, all enlisted men from Company A, struggled throughout the day, but cholera would get them all before they saw another sundown. Corporal William Bennett was one of them. Private George W. Park was another. Only 116 days earlier, Park, a laborer from Pittsburgh, had been at the recruiting station in Toledo, signing a five-year contract, the first step in an exciting new career that would take him out to the new western frontier. Two days later Clark Wallace walked into the same recruiting office. Originally from Madison, New York, and two years older than Park, Clark had made his way to Toledo after a spell in Lafayette, Indiana, as a boatman on the Wabash. Before they knew it both young men were on board the *San Francisco*, heading for California. Now, as they lay dying of cholera in the cabin of the *Three Bells*, the great adventure was over.[1]

Meanwhile, that morning in Boston, two vessels of consequence arrived in port. The brig *Napoleon* was the first, and Captain Strout reported that they had fallen in with the *San Francisco* on Christmas Day, in coordinates 38° 04' N, 69° 30' W, and that the great steamer had been in distress. The masts all above deck were gone, they said, and the sea was making fair wreck over her. Strout stated that the steamer had been making water very fast, and that when the *Napoleon* spoke her there were about 200 persons on her deck. Commodore Watkins had requested the *Napoleon* to lay by her, which the brig did. Next morning the *San Francisco* was not to be seen, having drifted to the eastward. This was reported from Boston at midday on January 7 as a telegraphic dispatch expressly for the *Evening Star* in Washington, D.C.

---

1. McDougall; Army enlistment records; 1850 U.S. census. Bennett, from Pittsburgh, was a veteran of the Mexican War. On November 1, 1853, at Fort Columbus, he enlisted for a fourth term, at the age of 35. Enlisting with him in Company A was his nephew, William Lock Bennett, who also made it onto the *Three Bells*. An Englishman, who happened to be born in Montgomery, Wales, in June 1836, young Bennett came over to Pittsburgh at the age of six, and at 14 followed in the family footsteps, as a miner.

The second ship to arrive at Boston that morning, at ten o'clock, was the steamer *Alabama*, up from Savannah, under the command of Captain Schenck. As the crew was helping to discharge a thousand bales of cotton the last thing that would have crossed their mind was that their ship would be at sea again the following day, on a mission far different from their usual type of run.

Other things were happening that morning which related to the *San Francisco*'s plight. There was a report in from Boston, received earlier in the day from Liverpool, Nova Scotia, via Halifax. Captain Freeman, of the *Maria*, stated that when he saw the *San Francisco* the day after Christmas—the very day after the *Napoleon* had spoken the wrecked ship—her engines were not working, her smoke stacks were gone, and her decks were swept of everything. He saw at least 150 persons on board. Just as in Captain Strout's story, Commodore Watkins of the doomed ship had requested the *Maria* to stay by him, and Captain Freeman had obliged. But, again, in a story very similar to the one told by Captain Strout, a gale sprang up during the night, increased to hurricane force, the *Maria* laid to, but the storm drove the two ships out of sight of each other. When daylight came Freeman could not find the *San Francisco*, but he thought she might have foundered.

A press report went to London, and from this report, published in England a few weeks later, it is clear that a lot of people did not believe the stories they were hearing. But their skepticism was ill-founded, based, as it was, on ignorance. They had trouble believing that a passing ship would fail to render assistance, no matter how bad its own condition or the state of the weather, and they failed to comprehend how the *San Francisco*, if hit by such a storm and as damaged as the captains of the *Napoleon* and the *Maria* claimed it was, could still be floating.

All this Saturday the *Three Bells* had been lying to out in the ocean, but at eight o'clock that night, with a light but favorable wind behind them, they got underway again. The crew threw over a further quantity of cargo so that there was now an abundance of room for all below.[2]

Mr. Aspinwall, and his agent in Washington, Mr. Davidge, were untiring in their efforts to aid the War Department in the attempted relief of the *San Francisco*.[3]

---

2. McDougall.
3. Quartermaster Jesup, letter of Jan. 23, 1854, to Jefferson Davis.

Sunday
January 8

It was midnight, and New York City was rolling over into the Christian Sabbath, when there was a late knock at the door of the splendid house of millionaire W.H. Aspinwall, the owner of the *San Francisco*. Standing outside was Mr. McCarty, the mate of the *Napoleon*. He had been eight hours on the road from Boston, and was here to give the great man his report in person. After listening to the mate's story, Aspinwall sent a report to the government in Washington, D.C., and the government duly sent it up to the *New York Times*, who published it on January 9. "His story is consistent and intelligent," Aspinwall said of McCarty in the article. The mate goes on to tell that the *Napoleon* had passed within 30 yards of the *San Francisco*, that Commodore Watkins had plenty of provisions at that time, but had lightened ship. There were no men at the pumps and the steam pumps seemed to be working. McCarty claimed he saw 20 male passengers come from the upper after-cabin. The hurricane deck forward of the wheels was standing, the damage being mainly in the upper works amidships. The wheel houses were gone, whereas the wheels were entire, both guards were in good order, and the rudder was all right. The foremast was gone above the deck, but the mizzen mast was standing, and while the smoke stacks were gone the hull looked to be in good order. The gale was heavy from the northwest that night of the twenty-fifth, according to McCarty, and they saw the steamer the next day, in relatively good shape, and there was now strong reason, said Aspinwall, to hope that the *San Francisco* was still safe.[1]

That day, Sunday, January 8, on the *Three Bells*, the wind was south, and it was almost a dead calm, all sail being set. The crew filled a large case of rain water, in case it should be needed, especially for the sick, who were being attended to by Major Wyse and Dr. Buel. But the precious liquid would not be needed by Walter Heath, one of the waiters taken off the *San Francisco*. About 7 p.m., the wind freshened, and increased to a gale. The sail was shortened, and several heavy seas came fore and aft that night.[2]

---

1. *New York Times*, Jan. 9, 1854.
2. McDougall. Walter Heath was not a close relative of Levi Heath, the steerage steward who had died the day before, despite the fact that both were from Haverhill, Massachusetts.

Meanwhile, back in the States, rescue attempts were underway. The newspapers were already aware that morning that the War Department had chartered the steamship *Alabama*, then just arrived in port at Boston, and that the Secretary of the Navy had directed two naval officers, Lieutenants Gansevoort and Boggs, to proceed aboard her to seek out the *San Francisco* and render assistance. Of course, at that point in time there was no one on land who knew that the *San Francisco* was now just an uninhabited hull lying at the bottom of the Atlantic. That morning the *Alabama* took on 450 tons of coal, fresh provisions and water for a fortnight's consumption, ample stores, cables, life-boats, smoke-pipe, etc., and left her dock at noon. By 1 p.m. she was out of the harbor, heading out into the ocean.

The War Department had also chartered two other vessels that morning, for the same purpose. The sloop-of-war *Decatur*, at that moment in the yard in Boston, fitting for sea, was to proceed in the search, if, in the opinion of the commandant of the yard, she was in a condition to be of service, and the Secretary of the Navy ordered up Commodore Vanderbilt's steamer *North Star*, then at New York.[3]

It was on or about this day, "After we had been on board of the bark ten or twelve days," that someone aboard the *Kilby* spotted a sail, in the distance but close enough so everyone who had run excitedly up on deck could see her hull. What remained of the *Kilby*'s poor old flag was instantly run up union down and all sails that were of any use were set. But the strange vessel kept away. At sunset she was still in sight but evidently steering away. Lieutenant Van Voast made a torch of oakum, cotton and old rope dipped in tar, and, setting it on fire, he held it on the deck until it burned out. Although it gave off a very brilliant light that must have been seen for miles, the vessel disappeared with the night.[4]

---

3. It was later rumored that Cornelius Vanderbilt twice refused the use of his steamer, *North Star*.
4. Southworth.

Monday
January 9

Charles Sanford, the colored steward who had gone insane and been placed in the charge of half a dozen men, somehow managed to break free in the early hours of the morning. Pursued not only by his keepers but by demons as well, he zigzagged wildly across the deck of the *Three Bells* yelling, "Save me, Oh, Save Me!" But no one could save him now. Although he managed to elude the more human of those chasing him, the evil ones caught up with him just as he was sprinting along the very side of the ship. There was a splash. It was Mr. Sanford. He was never seen again.[1]

A coarse, blowy morning wind, north by west, annoyed those on the *Three Bells* that morning. Captain Crighton was laid up, very unwell, suffering from the effects of exposure, want of rest, and over-exertion. An observation taken during the course of the day showed that the vessel was one and a half degrees south of New York, but still 350 miles from their destination. As they battled their way west, they passed the wreck of two vessels, one of them having a part of her stern burned.[2]

Meanwhile, back in Savannah, the *Daily Morning News* shared with its readership the unfounded fear that all aboard the *San Francisco* had perished. Those written off, they said, included Georgia notable Major George Taylor and his wife. Major Taylor's parents lived in Macon, and would soon be reading this tragic news, which, in this particular anyway, just happened to be right.

Things were happening in Boston too, that afternoon, on the rescue front. The steamship *Union* arrived from Charleston, and was chartered by the War Department.

As for the *Kilby*, they were alone again on the very hostile ocean. Their water was getting very low, but then came a shower of rain and they caught a barrel full. Painfully aware that there was no immediate prospect of their getting into port, they had to do something about rationing the food. While the bacon allowance was not lessened, they were obliged to limit themselves to half a cracker per person day, since that valuable commodity was going very fast. Sometimes, when she thought about it too much and began to loath the very idea of the cracker and bacon, Lucia Eaton couldn't eat. On those occasions she would put a portion away and have it later when

---

1. McDougall; *New York Tribune*, Jan. 16, 1854.
2. McDougall.

she was very hungry and not disposed to dwell on how disgusting it all was. It was surprising how good it tasted then. Captain Low found half a barrel of molasses and had it brought to his passengers in tin plates or in cups or tumblers. At first it was quite a treat, but the human stomach, even that of a dying man, will adamantly refuse to accept anything more than the merest sampling of straight molasses, and so they would dip their crackers into it and eat it that way. Even then, the effect was to make everyone thirsty and sick. As Mrs. Gates says, "[F]for two days we feasted upon sea biscuit and molasses," and then this new addition to their diet gave out. There was more molasses, but they couldn't get to it, as it was lying beneath the cotton in the hold. And it wasn't long either before the crackers were stopped altogether, except for the ladies and the sick.[3]

It was not only the crackers that were giving out, it was the bread too, and the gentlemen and soldiers were obliged to give up their share to the females. Some good news was needed, and it was to come in the form of corn. Captain Low told them he had one part of the hold filled with bags of the stuff, and they might be able to use it. The bags were opened, with anyone being able to take if they pleased. But it was the large yellow corn such as horses eat. How to cook it to make it palatable? Lieutenant Murray decided to experiment. He and a little boy spent all morning pounding some of this corn into what, after all that effort, proved to be a disappointingly small mess, then, mixing it with bacon, fried it up in a skillet. It was not pounded very fine, but it tasted good, especially when well-roasted or parched. Dr. Satterlee offered the suggestion that the corn would be more healthy if cracked, but it was not the kind to pop, and so it didn't crack.[4]

The trouble was that there no proper order and method in cooking for the troops, and this was having a bad effect on the men. The main problem was that the galley would get crowded, and not everyone could always get in. And so a new regimen had to go into effect. At breakfast and tea time the commissary sergeant would call the roll, and each soldier answering his name would come forward and receive his handful of parched corn, and slice of bacon, and then their allowance of water, and the same basic routine was followed by the other passengers.[5]

Then there was tea to wash it all down, green tea, of the very best kind. Every few moments a dish, tumbler, or broken cup would be handed to the people, containing their allowance of tea. They would take a sip and then hand it on to their neighbor. However, the sugar had long since given out and, without it, the tea tasted awful. But, as bad it was, it was better for the passengers than water, as it seemed to give them strength. And it would have been more palatable if it had been weaker and not boiled, but the steward reasoned that as everyone on board was having tea, it had to be made strong, and the last to receive their portion would find it weak.[6]

All you could hear, all over the ship, day in and day out, from early dawn until

---

3. Eaton; Mrs. Gates.
4. Eaton; Graham; Gardiner.
5. Eaton; Gardiner.
6. Eaton.

late at night, was the pounding of the corn. Officers, civilians, soldiers, and sailors, pounding, pounding, pounding, tying the life-giving substance into a cloth and, using a piece of wood, smashing it into its next incarnation. It would take them all of one day to get enough to fill a pan. The job was tedious, too tedious for some—Colonel Gates and Lieutenant Lucien Loeser hired a couple of soldiers to pound for them and their families—but those who pounded worked with a will. Their lives depended on it. It was, in the end, quite a fine meal.[7]

Then someone dreamed up the idea of a corn cake. Even under normal circumstances, there is something quite exciting about eating a vegetable cake, whether it be potato, pea, or corn, and this feeling is greatly heightened when one is facing starvation. While mixing up the cake they seasoned it with salt water, there being no actual salt aboard the *Kilby*. The cake was very good. However, a corn cake doesn't last long when so many sets of teeth are sinking gratefully into it, and so the pounding continued, and the galley became filled with men baking new batches of the delicacy. The steward would stand by the door, looking down upon the passengers as they sat on the floor, a bit of corn cake in their hand and a slice of bacon in the other.[8]

A group of people found an old coffee mill, and nailed it up against the post near the door in the little passageway which led into the cabin. Then they threw in the corn and started to grind. After one person had ground their portion, another would take the mill in hand. With constant use, it didn't take long before the wear and tear had its effect, and the mill broke down. Someone tried grinding hot corn in the mill, and that broke the handle, which couldn't be fixed. It was back to the wood and pounding.[9]

After the mill broke, they could have corn cake only once every two or three days, as well as a mush made with a portion of salt water. Soon after the corn cakes had taken the place of crackers, the officer in charge came into the cabin and told everyone that the water was getting very low in the barrels. The corn cakes and mush took a good deal of water to mix them up, and it was ordered that they must be dispensed with. They had to give up the tea as well, and it was back to two gills of water per day. Many a person would say, "Oh, what would I not give if I could have a good, cool glass of water." Early in the morning, the commissary sergeant would come in and bring them their portion of water in bottles. For their morning allowance the Merchant family, for example, would have one full bottle, there being seven in the family.[10]

Every pleasant day Captain Low would take an observation. Sometimes their nearest port would be Charleston, sometimes Newport, sometimes Boston and then New York. Dr. Satterlee thought it advisable to put into a Southern port as everyone was so exhausted and thinly clad, it being winter. As soon as an observation was taken, if the wind favored, all sail would be set and their course directed for the

---

7. Eaton; Gardiner.
8. Eaton; Judd.
9. Eaton.
10. Eaton.

closest land. But soon the wind would go down, or adverse winds would spring up, then the sail had to be taken down and they would have to lie to. Everything they had gained by a favorable wind during the day would be lost at night. If only they had had good sails, they might have made a port.[11]

The only fire on the *Kilby* was in the galley, which was generally filled with soldiers and sailors, so the survivors of the *San Francisco*, too thinly clad for a winter's day outside, would often wrap blankets around themselves, then leave the cabin to go up on deck, where, braving the cold wind, they would get together and chat among themselves, especially on an agreeable day. Some of these discussions were pleasant, but just as often depression seeped into the group.[12]

One evening, while they were sitting engaged in conversation on deck, they heard Captain Low call to the seamen to put up all sail, a fine breeze having sprung up. Immediately the crewmen were in the rigging, singing merrily as they unfurled the sails to the breeze, everyone hoping that this stiff wind would carry them to Sandy Hook. The bark was finely underway, making several knots, and with Captain Low and Lieutenant Frank Murray making every effort to get her to port when, all at once they heard the sail tearing. The sails were very old, and the wind had wreaked havoc on them. Captain Low then gave the order for all sail to be taken in, or they would be destroyed. But they had managed to make a few miles on their homeward course.[13]

At one time, after taking an observation, Captain Low said they must be near the Isle of Shoals, and a sounding taken soon afterwards proved him right. They had to go back out to sea, fearing that the vessel would founder on the shoals. They were actually on Georges Bank, 62 miles east of Cape Cod and south of Nova Scotia, but lack of visibility prevented Low from ascertaining this. Since leaving New York on Dec 22, they had encountered 13 storms, all of them severe.[14]

---

11. Eaton.
12. Eaton.
13. Eaton.
14. Eaton; Stackpole.

Tuesday
January 10

The *Three Bells* awoke to a fine, mild morning out at sea, and with the wind light and favorable, they were able to set more sail, but the happiness that should have brought was tempered somewhat by the death in the cabin some hours earlier of Sergeant Joe McIntyre's wife and older son. By 11 a.m., the sun was shining bright, with the wind freshening and men, women, and children crowding the decks. But again this good news was offset, this time by mathematics. It was calculated that their water would not last more than three days at the present rate, and so the daily allowance for all on board had to be further curtailed, to one pint—one third of what it had been.[1]

By midday the *Three Bells* had gone 80 miles since the day before, but only half of that distance had been on their actual course toward New York, the Gulf Stream having carried them 40 miles to the south as well. There was a ring around the moon that evening, and seamen were saying it betokened stormy weather. Despite that prediction, the ship went on smartly through the night.[2]

Aboard the *Kilby*, Lieutenant Frank Murray and Captain Low often held consultations. Low was always cheerful, and if he saw any of the passengers depressed would always comfort them by assurances that they were safe on his bark, and that the vessel was getting along as well as could be expected. Murray, of course, was always the epitome of cheerfulness. But it was difficult to lighten the load of the Merchants. Mrs. Merchant had been confined to bed for about 10 days, sick, each day getting weaker and weaker until finally, with the tea being so bad and because she couldn't eat the bacon and hard bread, she lost her appetite and became very ill. Major Merchant and the children were all very much distressed, of course. Fortunately, Dr. Satterlee had brought a bottle or two of port wine from the *San Francisco*, and he gave Mrs. Merchant a small portion of it, together with a little brandy. Thus she was kept alive. She gave no trouble and was very patient, and it helped that she and Lucia Eaton had many pleasant chats.[3]

---

1. McDougall; Winder, 1883. Joe McIntyre's younger child, a boy of three, was adopted by the regiment.
2. McDougall.
3. Eaton.

Whenever they were in the cabin, the passengers would sit on anything that would afford them a seat. With the exception of the old sofa, and one trunk, everything had been taken out of the cabin to make room for the passengers, so the floor served as their seat during the day and their bed at night. Sometimes Miss Eaton would sit on the floor with her blanket around her, and her arms folded, and at other times the ladies would get together on a pleasant evening and sing. Mercifully, during their last few days aboard the *Kilby*, the water restrictions were relaxed.[4]

That evening, after dark, there came a cry on board the *Kilby*. Someone was shouting that the lights of Sandy Hook were in sight. Captain Low took a look, and declared that it was impossible, that they couldn't be so near land. George Aspinwall suggested that they must be the lights of a steamer, but Low thought that highly unlikely as steamers generally carried three lights, whereas they could only see two. But Aspinwall was sure it was a steamer, with one light deliberately blacked out in order to attract attention.[5]

One of the passengers came into the cabin where Lucia Eaton was, and said, *"We are inside of Sandy Hook; the sailors have seen the lighthouses!"* But Miss Eaton knew that it was impossible that the ship could have crossed the Bar without a pilot. Her brother-in-law, Lucien Loeser, also knew it had to be a false report.[6]

As it turned out, it was a steamer, probably the *Alabama*, which had been sent out from New York a few days before to look for the *San Francisco*. But there was the rub; the *Alabama* was looking for a large steamer, not a bark. If the people on the *Kilby* had only had lights to show, or gongs to beat, or rockets to fire, they might have been noticed and thus rescued. But so destitute were they, indeed, of light, that had they not brought some candles on board from the *San Francisco*, they would have been in total darkness.[7]

And so ended January 10 aboard the *Kilby*, and with it passed George Woolsey Aspinwall's fortieth birthday. It would be his last.

---

4. Eaton; Gardner.
5. Aspinwall.
6. Eaton.
7. Eaton; Aspinwall.

Wednesday
January 11

A stiff breeze from the southeast came up to help the *Three Bells* on her way to New York. At about 3 a.m., the wind chopped around to the northwest, and back to fair wind. The ship's bosun died early that morning, and was put overboard; he had been showing exactly the same symptoms as the dying soldiers—crying for water, cramping and vomiting. Under other circumstances, they would have read a prayer over his remains.[1]

By 1:30 in the afternoon the *Three Bells* was 240 miles from New York, and they saw several ships going north or northeast. All who were well were on deck, enjoying the fine weather. There were no fresh cases of sickness, and Major Wyse informed Mr. McDougall that his men were improving. In the evening they saw some coasters.[2]

The *Three Bells* was not the only vessel helped by a favorable wind springing up during the morning. Captain Low, skipper of the *Kilby*, having taken an observation, found that they were about 70 miles from Sandy Hook. All sail was immediately put up, which enabled them to make many knots. Lucia Eaton wrapped a blanket around herself and joined her friends on deck, where they ate parched corn with real pleasure, and spoke of their absent friends. The day passed very pleasantly. The sun didn't set very clearly that evening, but they all figured they would be at Sandy Hook the next morning. Captain Low, however, looked troubled. Something was going on.[3]

Miss Eaton's party sat on deck till quite late, when dampness drove them into the cabin for the night. After tea, the Rev. Mr. Cooper prayed for all on the *Kilby* and for those on the *San Francisco*, although of course, for almost a week now, there had been no one on the *San Francisco*. In fact there was no longer any *San Francisco*, not above water anyway. The good reverend and his flock went off to bed.[4]

Unknown to those on both the *Three Bells* and the *Kilby*, further rescue efforts were underway. The steamer *Union*, under the command of Captain Adams, and with Commander Hudson and several officers of the Navy on board, left New York City, carrying six metallic life-boats.[5]

---

1. McDougall.
2. McDougall.
3. Eaton.
4. Eaton.
5. *New York Times*, Jan. 14, 1854.

Thursday
January 12

During the night and early hours of the morning, the *Three Bells* was traveling through the sea at a rate of about 12 knots. During those dark hours a man died, and come morning they found themselves enveloped in a dense fog with rain pouring down in torrents. "Beans and bacon served out today." At 11:30, with the weather now hazy, the *Three Bells* was in a mere 35 fathoms of water, the distance from Sandy Hook being calculated at between 20 and 30 miles. The sail was shortened to keep off shore, but at 2 p.m., it cleared up after a slight squall, and more sail was set. By later that afternoon they were off soundings near New York, but by evening the weather grew thick, and Captain Crighton decided to stand off until morning.[1]

The ocean had been very rough on the *Kilby* during the night, and in the early part of the morning, the wind having changed, they were forced to take the sails in. With the vessel rolling fearfully, and their supply of water almost exhausted, there was no choice but to lie to until the winds favored them. The passengers woke up that morning to the same thick fog that was enveloping the *Three Bells*. It was so dense they couldn't even see the bow of their own ship, and the crew kept the bell ringing constantly so other vessels wouldn't accidentally run into them. But any misgivings about the weather were dispelled as soon as they saw the rain and snow pelting down through the fog and filling the large water barrel on deck. Soon they had not only replenished their vital drinking supply, but now had enough water to wash their face and hands in with something other than salt water, which had been making the skin feel very dry and disagreeable. Other good news was that the *Kilby* was still strong and, even though there were no comforts aboard, there was still plenty of corn, and the bacon had not given out. God was, indeed, looking after the Reverend Cooper's flock and, as they all sat on the floor and took their breakfast as usual, they expressed deep gratitude to their Heavenly father.[2]

They didn't get their tea until quite late that evening and, after prayers they took their usual places on the floor. The sea was very rough that night, and for the second

---

1. McDougall.
2. Eaton; Graham.

night in a row Lucia Eaton slept very little. Every few minutes she would sit up as the bark rolled about fearfully. Thus was passed their last night on the *Kilby*.[3]

But elsewhere on the *Kilby*, unknown to Lucia Eaton and the other passengers other things were happening, more menacing events were threatening the safety of the ship, and, indeed, it was beginning to look as if the bark may never make it safely to shore.

The *Kilby* was standing in for Sandy Hook that evening, with the crew uncertain as to exactly how close they were to the coast. About 10 or 15 miles, they reckoned. A violent nor'wester was then blowing, and the skipper, fearful of being driven onto the Long Island coast, had no option but to pull out to sea again. The crew, already discouraged by their continually fruitless efforts to reach the coast, were now openly muttering threats of mutiny unless Captain Low pulled into land immediately. It was just this sort of eventuality that had been causing the skipper anxiety for some time now. Lieutenant Fremont didn't help the situation at all when he went into the galley and found two sailors there. Under normal circumstances, this was strictly against the rules, as only two appointed cooks were allowed in there while two guards were stationed outside the door to prevent anyone getting in. Fremont, being officer of the day, ordered the sailors to leave, they refused, and so he tried to throw them out. They pulled their knives, and Fremont called the corporal to bring some guards up. He then instructed the ship's skipper to place the two offenders under arrest. However, Captain Low knew that if these men were put in irons, the crew would, indeed, mutiny, and there would be no one to man the ship. Whereupon Fremont armed himself with a club and tried to beat the sailors out of there but, just as Captain Low had predicted, the crew joined in, on the very point of open rebellion. Four of the sailors went up to Captain Low and told him they intended to run the bark on to Barnegat, at the northern tip of Long Beach Island, half way down New Jersey's Atlantic coastline. Low tried to reason with them, promising that come eight o'clock on the morrow, he would pull into the nearest land regardless of consequences, but it was useless to try to pacify men who were so worked up. Lieutenant Murray, being an experienced seaman with knowledge of such things, went to the mutineers and said, "My men, if you run this bark on Barnegat not one person will escape with their life. You will not be safe for the bark will go to pieces instantly, and you will not be able to get on shore." Murray talked to them for a long time, and finally succeeded in quieting them down for that night. But they were still determined that if the next day's weather proved unfavorable, they would seize the bark. Lieutenant Fremont had to back down.[4]

All night long the passengers lay upon the cotton bales, waiting for morning, while the crew maintained a nervous vigil on the tinderbox that was the *Kilby*.[5]

Meanwhile the *Lucy Thompson*, after battling her way toward New York, had

---

3. Eaton.
4. Graham; Eaton; *New York Times*, Jan. 16, 1854, using Mr. Aspinwall's report. Miss Eaton only learned of the incident a few days later from Frank Murray.
5. Eaton.

been blown far off her course by the tremendous gales, and now found herself enshrouded in dense fog. Captain Pendleton thought it best to anchor out until it cleared off, as he wished to get up to Sandy Hook as early as possible the next morning. When he retired, utterly worn out after three days of no rest or sleep, he told his mate that he was going to catch a nap on the transom, and that he was to call him at six the following morning, when he would see about changing the course.[6]

---

6. Graham; Eaton; E.H. Pendleton. Pendleton tells the story somewhat differently from Miss Eaton, who claims to have gotten her version from Pendleton himself. In this other version the skipper tells his mate to wake him at eight bells—midnight.

Friday
January 13

For the entire night the crew of the *Three Bells* could make out two lights in the distance. The Scottish ship was only about seven miles from land now, and, with little wind and clear weather conditions, the dark hours presented a glorious scene. With all sail set, Captain Crighton was expecting to reach firm ground by daylight. But they were not out of danger yet. Crighton, anxiously watching the signs of the weather, was apprehensive. "I think the wind will soon be northwest, and if so, we shall be blown off the coast without water." It was a critical moment in the lives of scores of passengers who had had more than their fair share of such moments, for they were down to their last pint of water.[1]

But it seemed to all that Captain Crighton's forebodings had been groundless. The morning rose bright and fair, especially, perhaps for Major Wyse, whose forty-third birthday it was today, and the *Three Bells* signaled for a pilot. At 11 a.m., the steam tug *Jacob Bell* hove alongside, and the pilot came aboard. But then, all of a sudden, minutes after the tug had taken her charge in tow, the wind came into the northwest, just as the skipper had predicted, and by the time they were crossing the bar, it was blowing quite a gale, which increased to a hurricane. But they managed to get in, and between 4:30 and 5 p.m., the long-suffering bark arrived at anchor off New York Battery. Her trip from Glasgow had taken 45 days, with merchandise and unexpected passengers, most of whom, now, at their moment of greatest rejoicing, could not even go ashore because they had too few clothes. A *New York Herald* reporter went aboard and got the news that 240 had perished on the *San Francisco*. He also managed to obtain an interview with Edward Osier, one of the *San Francisco*'s quartermasters, and another with Bill Winder, an interview that was peremptorily cut short by Major Wyse.[2]

Of course, eventually they got off the *Three Bells* onto dry land. Observers noted that some of the soldiers and crew displayed a marvelous amount and style of luggage for their station. These were the thieves, the pirates, spewing out of the ship with

---

1. McDougall; Winder, 1883.
2. McDougall; Winder, 1883.

their stolen goods, already making their way with profit aforethought from the *Three Bells* to the Three Balls.³

At six o'clock that morning Captain Pendleton got his wake-up call on the *Lucy Thompson*, just as he had ordered. He should have gotten up immediately, but was so tired he fell asleep again, something he had never done before.⁴

At daybreak, a few minutes after six o'clock, with the sea rolling very heavily, the *Lucy Thompson* was sailing under a double reef at the rate of some 12 to 15 knots, 60 miles southeast of Sandy Hook and "about fifty miles east of Fire Island." Suddenly, they spotted the wretched *Kilby*, emerging from the fog like a ghost ship. At that moment, James Lorimer Graham was on the deck of the *Kilby*, with many other passengers when he heard the cry that a ship was lying close by them. Captain Low immediately hailed her, and to the relief of everyone on the *Kilby*, a light was seen passing along the deck of the *Lucy Thompson*. The passengers on the *Kilby* tumbled out of their berths, in all states of array, to see what was going on. Someone came into Lucia Eaton's cabin and said a ship was in sight. It was Friday the Thirteenth.⁵

Captain Pendleton finally awoke at seven o'clock and hove to as speedily as possible, finding the *Kilby* in sad distress, with sails torn, and the remains of a flag with the union down, indicating a ship in trouble. "Thus this unusual fact that he had overslept that morning had saved us, for had he not seen us at that time he would have sailed, and as we were without sail we would have drifted back into the Gulf Stream."⁶

Pendleton sent the message, "Send your boats alongside," but the officers on the *Kilby* could not decide who should man the small boat to go over. Lieutenant Murray offered his services, but whoever went over had to be empowered to offer a contract to the *Lucy Thompson* on behalf of the United States Government, so it had to be Lieutenant Fremont, the quartermaster.⁷

With a gale still blowing, and the ocean rough as usual at this time of year, the crew of the *Kilby* duly lowered their quarter boat carrying Fremont, Captain Low, and a couple of other officers. Having boarded the *Lucy Thompson*, they made arrangements for the trans-shipment of the *San Francisco* survivors then being carried by the *Kilby*. The *Lucy Thompson* lowered two of her own boats, and the three vessels rowed back to the *Kilby*. The passengers went down a rope ladder on the side of the *Kilby*, taking hold of the ropes, a man holding on to the ladies to prevent them falling. Because the sea was running very high from the southeast, care had to be taken as they stepped from the ladder into the small boat. And sometimes the waves would

---

3. *Presbyterian Magazine*; Brown account. Sergeant Brown says he lost everything, including $1750 in gold, "*which was taken from my trunk. Every trunk was broken open before it was thrown overboard.*"

4. Eaton. This anecdote, or at least a version of it, was later told to Miss Eaton by Captain Pendleton himself. E.H. Pendleton says that the skipper got his midnight call but slept through it, finally waking up at 2 a.m., when, about to reprimand his mate for allowing him to sleep in, he suddenly saw, just as the moon broke through a rift of cloud, another ship close by, and in distress. The evidence is heavily in favor of Lucia Eaton's version.

5. Huston; Eaton; Graham. The quotes are from Huston, and it is he who gives the time of this first encounter at 6 a.m. Graham puts the time at 4 a.m.

6. Huston; Eaton. The quote is from Eaton.

7. Huston; Eaton; Murray; Fremont.

send the little vessel off a great distance from the bark, and there would be a frustrating delay before it was able to return.[8]

The first boatload over included Lucia Eaton, her sister, Sarah, and Sarah's husband, Lieutenant Loeser; Mrs. Wyse and her infant daughter; George W. Aspinwall; James Lorimer Graham; Captain and Mrs. Judd; the severely disabled Colonel Martin Burke; and Marianne Sauer, the bandmaster's wife, and her three children. When they got to the *Lucy Thompson*, Mrs. Sauer and her daughters were the first to be taken up by the rope ladder. Mrs. Judd was next, followed by Lucia Eaton and Lieutenant Loeser and his wife. But then the waves carried the lifeboat to the bow of the ship, and they had to try again. It took several attempts before they were all up the rope ladder and onto the *Lucy Thompson*. Mrs. Merchant was brought up in an exhausted state, and a mattress was brought for her to lie on. Just as Mrs. Wyse was being hoisted up the ladder, her baby girl slipped out of her blanket and fell. A man in the boat below caught her before she plunged to her death.[9]

Captain Pendleton was watching all this activity and threw a large rope down, letting the men tie it under the arms of the passengers as they came up the rope ladder, women and children being dashed against the sides by the rolling of the vessel. It was lucky none of them were killed. Watching these devastated people struggling for their lives and unable to do anything more for them, Pendleton left the side of the ship, overcome with emotion. The emigrants who had been on board since Liverpool crowded to the side of the ship to see the people coming aboard, exclaiming "Poor things!" And they were poor things. Their blankets were half off them, hats hanging off, and hair getting loose and hanging in wild disorder. Completely exhausted.[10]

Colonel Gates was among those who went over in the second boat. As for the Rev. Mr. Cooper, before leaving he offered up prayers of thanksgiving to his god for his goodness in protecting them while aboard the *Kilby*, and for this new deliverance.[11]

There came a point when Captain Pendleton ordered the transfers halted for the day. It had now begun to breeze up and, after three successful crossings, he felt it would be unsafe to attempt any more. However, Lieutenant Fremont told Pendleton that it was Colonel Gates's wish that everyone under his command be transferred, and so Pendleton agreed to one more trip. He decided to send over the largest of the *Lucy Thompson*'s life boats, one which his first mate had told him had ample room to take off all the remaining survivors. So, Pendleton's last order to Mr. Huston was to bring all those who wanted to come. When the mate got to the *Kilby* he found, much to his surprise, that not everyone wanted to get off. Frederick, the *San Francisco*'s Portuguese cook, had decided to stay, as had Madame Alex Besse and her ser-

---

8. Eaton; Pendleton; Huston.
9. Eaton; Pendleton.
10. Eaton.
11. Eaton; Huston; Gardiner; Pendleton. Captain Pendleton says that Gates went over in the third or fourth boat, but, in fact, it was in the second.

vant, as well as the Brazilian contingent, consisting of the consul and his servant, and Senhor Abrio and wife.[12]

Lieutenant James Van Voast was the only Artillery officer left on the *Kilby*, and so was having to supervise the transfer of the remaining soldiers. When the *Lucy Thompson*'s boat arrived for its last pick-up of the day, First Mate Huston told Van Voast that he had to come over to the *Lucy Thompson* on this trip, orders of Colonel Gates, and that they had to leave a certain number of soldiers on the *Kilby*, to help Captain Low keep the mutineers in check and to get the vessel back to port. This would leave enlisted men on the high seas, in a potentially explosive situation, with no officer to command them, but fortunately Sergeant Joe McIntyre of Company K volunteered to lead the men, and so he was placed in charge.[13]

So, fighting an increasing wind, the lifeboat beat its way back to the *Lucy Thompson*. When Lieutenant Van Voast got aboard he found Colonel Gates, and advised him that he had brought over with him the worst enlisted men and left behind the best, to which Gates replied: "I approve of your conduct, Sir."[14]

All in all, in those four boat trips, they took off 85 "of the starving human beings" in six hours. And it was not just people making those four trips. In order to complete the work of rendering assistance to the *Kilby*, provisions had to be transferred by boat from the *Lucy Thompson* to the *Kilby*, to last all on board from three to four weeks. Mr. Huston, the *Lucy Thompson*'s first mate, selected not only sails and ropes, but four casks of sea biscuit, two barrels of beef, a barrel of pork, a hundredweight of sugar, two barrels of flour, and a cask of fish, as well as a good stock of water, some of the best brandy, some arrow root and oatmeal, bread, and various other necessaries.[15]

On entering the cabin of the *Lucy Thompson* the survivors found a delicious meal of bread and butter which had been delivered by the steward, along with tea, while the ship's doctor brought them an abundance of port wine, which quite restored them. The doctor said to Lucia Eaton, "Miss, you look worse than any of them," to which she replied, "I have not suffered more than the other passengers, although I may look frailer." The cabin was very clean and roomy, airy and light, and as Lucia looked around it she saw Colonel Burke, Captain and Mrs. Judd, and the Loesers,

---

12. Van Voast; Huston; Southworth; Eaton; Pendleton. The *New York Herald* of Jan. 15, 1854, quoted Fred Southworth as saying that Mrs. Wyse stayed on the *Kilby*, being so nervous from exhaustion that she could not trust herself to climb down the side of the bark. But this was a misquote, and was cleared up by Southworth in a letter he wrote that day and which was published in the *Herald* of Jan. 16. It was Mrs. Abrio, not Mrs. Wyse. Mrs. Abrio remembered only too well her torturous crossing from the *San Francisco* to the *Kilby* a few weeks before, and refused to do anything like that again. The other citizen passengers who remained on the *Kilby* did so to keep her company. Southworth calls the Abrios "Dr. and Mrs. Labrade."

13. Van Voast; Huston; Southworth; Eaton; Pendleton. The fifteen who stayed behind under Joe McIntyre were Corporal Charles Reidt and Private Patrick Molloy, both of Company A; Privates Isaac N. Sleeper, Patrick Lilly, and Moses Eldridge, all of Company D; Henry Filce, of Company H; and the rest privates from Company I: Warren Adams, John Murphy, William Kelley, John Lund, Condy Conneghan, Robert J. Boylan, John Cavaugh, William Walsh, and John Dwyer.

14. Van Voast.

15. Huston; Eaton; Pendleton; Graham. The quote is from Huston. We know the names of only two seamen on the *Lucy Thompson*—Robinson Miller and William McDonald.

this sextet having been among the first to board the *Lucy Thompson*, and the same six who had been placed together in the *San Francisco*'s galley that tragic Christmas Eve morning so long ago.[16]

Captain Pendleton and the mate stood watching them as they ate. Pendleton had put the sufferers on short allowance that first day as he feared they would become sick. He turned to the ladies and said, "I have been a sea captain for more than twenty years and never in all that time have I seen as much of the horrors of the sea. I have never been wrecked. You have seen in the space of three short weeks more than I have in all my twenty years experience."[17]

As the *Lucy Thompson* had plenty of room, the new massive influx of *Kilby* passengers was not a strain on her. After the transfer was done, Captain Pendleton made sail about noon direct for New York.[18]

The *Kilby* too was going to try to make New York City. Huston, the first mate of the *Lucy Thompson*, was worried about the *Kilby*'s future prospects as she "did not seem to be in a seaworthy condition, as she was leaky, in consequence of being considerably racked by heavy gales of wind" on her voyage from New Orleans. Captain Pendleton promised to arrange for a tug to be sent out to tow the *Kilby* into port. The truth was, though, that despite her sails and rigging being disabled, her hull was sound, and she was safer than she looked.[19]

Lucia Eaton says that at sunset the joyful cry, "Land! Land!" was heard, and they soon came in sight of Sandy Hook. Miss Eaton went out on deck to look at the lighthouses on the highlands, thinking how many times she had seen those same lights from her own home in Brooklyn.[20]

At 5 p.m. the *Lucy Thompson* arrived at anchorage outside the bar, where they spent the night.

As for the *Kilby*, at about 6 p.m., with a heavy, squally west wind blowing, the pilot boat *Phantom* (No. 17) of New York, pulled alongside her off Fire Island, and Mr. Richard Decker, pilot, went aboard and took charge of her. Captain Low reported that he was 68 days out of New Orleans and had U.S. troops on board that he had taken off the *San Francisco*.[21]

During the night the west wind freshened into a severe gale, and somehow the *Kilby* got separated from the pilot boat and floated off into the night, position unknown. Unknown that is to the outside world. In actual fact she went 19 miles south of the Highland light, and got blown 50 miles east of Barnegat.[22]

On the *Lucy Thompson* that evening everyone retired quite early and met in the cabin, some going into their state rooms, some dropping on the floor mattresses being spread for them, one or two on the sofa, and one in the rocking chair. Before

---

16. Graham; Eaton.
17. Eaton.
18. Huston.
19. Huston.
20. Eaton.
21. *New York Tribune*, Jan. 16, 1854.
22. *New York Tribune*, Jan. 16, 1854; *Kilby* log.

they went to sleep the Rev. Mr. Cooper led the prayers, in which they thanked their fickle god for his goodness.[23]

By this date several vessels had been sent out to look for the *San Francisco*. The steamships *Alabama* and *Union*, from New York; the revenue cutter *Washington*, also from New York; the revenue cutter *Walter Forward* and two pilot boats from Philadelphia; the revenue cutter *Jefferson Davis* from Charleston; and one each from New London, Wilmington, and Bermuda. On the morning of this day, the thirteenth, the sloop-of-war *Decatur* and the U.S. revenue cutter *Morris* sailed from Nantucket Roads on the same mission. The *Morris*, under the command of Commodore Whitcomb, cruised for several days in and about the latitude and longitude in which the *San Francisco* was last reported, and found nothing but a floating bale of cotton, probably one of those thrown overboard from the *Kilby*.[24]

---

23. Eaton.
24. *New York Tribune*, Jan. 16, 1854; *Evansville Daily Journal*, Indiana, March 8, 1854.

Saturday
January 14

It was the fearful blowing of the wind that awoke Lucia Eaton at midnight aboard the *Lucy Thompson*, that and the creaking of the giant masts and the ropes rattling against them. The ship had dragged its anchor and the sailors were putting out another one to prevent them from being pulled onto land. With all this noise going on, everyone got up quite early and found breakfast already prepared for them. The steward allowed them to sit at the table, ladies first, and the gentlemen waited upon them. Their bill of fare that morning consisted of hot rolls, salt mackerel and crackers, tea and water, their first "able breakfast" in 20 days. They begged Captain Pendleton not to laugh at them as they tore into it like savages. "It gives me pleasure to see you all so happy," he said. "I like to look at you all seated around that table, and think it has been in my power to make you so happy." After breakfast, they engaged in prayer.[1]

That morning, General Wool and his aide-de-camp, Lieutenant James H. Hardie, of Company H, left Troy, New York for Manhattan, in order to begin the long job of replacing lost personnel of the Third Artillery.[2]

Meanwhile, unknown to the outside world, as the steamship *City of New York* was making her regular run between Boston and New York under the command of Captain Matthews, she fell in with the *Kilby*, and at 10 a.m. took the battered and long-suffering bark in tow.[3]

About eleven o'clock that morning, the *Lucy Thompson* was reported fighting her way toward New York, battling a gale from the west-northwest that was blowing dead against her. The steam tug *Titan* came near and spoke her, but couldn't come close enough to offer anything more, and so returned to the city. However, by noon, with the weather having eased off considerably, the *Lucy Thompson* reached the Sandy Hook Bar. The trouble was, they couldn't cross the bar into New York Bay because the water was too low, and so they threw over the anchor and waited. As there was plenty of vacant space aboard, all of the rescued sufferers were quite comfortable,

---

1. Eaton.
2. *New York Tribune*, Jan. 16, 1854; Army post returns.
3. *Kilby* Log.

and the next few hours were spent quietly. The steward brought the passengers a fine dinner at one o'clock.[4]

Various steam tugs tried in vain to approach the *Lucy Thompson*, and by mid-afternoon this telegraphic dispatch, sent at 2:30 p.m., reached the offices of Messrs. Howland & Aspinwall: "The ship is still at anchor. There have been tugs near her during the day, but they could not communicate. No tugs near her now."[5]

Finally the pilot tug *Mary Taylor* got close enough to send a man over to act as pilot, to guide his charge through the shoals. It was only when he scrambled aboard with the morning's newspapers that over 100 survivors of a fantastic maritime disaster first heard the names *Three Bells* and *Antarctic*, and learned of the safe arrival of the former in New York the day before. As for the crew on the tug, they knew nothing of any bark named the *Kilby*, and consequently had no idea that any survivors had transferred from that vessel to the *Lucy Thompson*, just assuming that the people they were now looking at on the *Lucy Thompson* had been transferred from the *Antarctic*.[6]

At 3:30 that afternoon, just as a dispatch was being sent to Howland & Aspinwall—"*The weather is moderating. There is a tug—has got a bark in tow—going in the Hook*"—a large meeting was convened at the Rotunda of the Merchants' Exchange, in New York City. Over 1,000 merchants and businessmen were called to order by Colonel James Lee, who moved that Mr. George Griswold should take the chair. This was carried unanimously. At the conclusion of the meeting, Mr. Mellus, the first officer of the *San Francisco*, got as far as the Portico of the Exchange, when he was immediately surrounded and cordially congratulated on his escape.[7]

About 4 p.m., Messrs. Howland & Aspinwall sent the *Titan* back out to pull the *Lucy Thompson* into harbor, hopefully before night. The *San Francisco*'s owners had thoughtfully placed aboard the *Titan* a large supply of warm clothing, for both males and females, blankets, and plenty of fresh provisions, with a note telling all the sufferers that they were welcome to stay with each and every member of the firm in their homes as long as they wanted.[8]

Someone from the *Titan* yelled out to ask if there were any *San Francisco* survivors aboard, and, on hearing that there were, the crew of the tug yelled out cheers of joy. On hearing that the *Titan* was here to take them back to port, it didn't take long for the passengers on the *Lucy Thompson* to get ready. All they had to do was put on their hats and wrap their blankets around themselves. That was all they had. Bidding Captain Pendleton adieu, they transferred to the *Titan*, where they were taken down below, to find the blankets and shawls that had been sent out from the city, and that a fine supper had been prepared for them on board the tug. They also

---

4. *New York Tribune*, Jan. 16, 1854; Eaton.
5. *New York Tribune*, Jan. 16, 1854.
6. *New York Tribune*, Jan. 16, 1854; Eaton.
7. *New York Tribune*, Jan. 16, 1854.
8. *New York Tribune*, Jan. 16, 1854; Eaton.

found W.H. Aspinwall, who, with a copy of the day's *New York Herald* in his hand, had come along in the *Titan* to meet his friends and to read them the news.[9]

Not all the survivors who were at that time on the *Lucy Thompson* were taken off on the *Titan*. Lieutenant Van Voast approached Colonel Gates to ask permission to transfer to the tug along with the others, and while he was at it he brought up the subject of the troops. However, Captain Pendleton, the skipper of the *Lucy Thompson*, had already broached that subject with the colonel, requesting that the troops be allowed to remain on his vessel overnight, to help with the anchor in the morning. Gates dithered—"Shall I, shan't I?" When Van Voast first talked about this with Gates, the colonel had reached the point where he was inclined to transfer the men to the *Titan*, but then he changed his mind. Then he changed it back again, and then again, feeling that the men should stay aboard, that they would be more comfortable there than ashore, at least until morning.[10]

Van Voast waited for Gates to detail an officer to stay with the men, but no instructions were forthcoming, from the colonel or anyone else. Finally Van Voast had to ask Gates for orders. *"I thought it was my duty to have some instructions, and I went to Colonel Gates just as he was leaving the vessel, and asked him if I should stay with the troops or not."* Gates replied in the affirmative, and so, as he and all the officers and their wives got on board the steam tug, Lieutenant Van Voast found himself stuck on the *Lucy Thompson* that night, in command of the men.[11]

About eight o'clock that night the *Titan* returned to the City, carrying, among others, Colonel Gates, his wife and three young children; the severely wounded Lieutenant Colonel Martin Burke; the disabled Major Merchant, his wife, two grown daughters, two younger daughters, and grandson; Captain Judd and wife; Lieutenant Fremont, wife, and children; Lieutenant Lucien Loeser, his wife, and Lucia Eaton; the disabled Dr. Satterlee and Surgeon Wirtz; Captain Gardiner, the dragoon; Lieutenant Frank Murray, U.S. Navy; George W. Aspinwall, the brother of the owner of the late steamer, *San Francisco*; the Rev. Mr. Cooper, his wife, and family; Mrs. Major Wyse and child; Fred Southworth; and James Lorimer Graham.[12]

Among those waiting at the pier to welcome the survivors were Captain Robert B. Coleman and Charles A. Stetson, owners of the country's most famous hotel, the Astor House. These two gentlemen threw open their establishment for the long-suffering passengers of the *Titan*—only the officer class, mind you—and conveyed them to the magnificent building on the corner of Broadway and Vesey Street, where

---

9. Eaton; Van Voast.
10. Van Voast.
11. Van Voast; Eaton; Gates testimony.
12. *Weekly National Intelligencer*, Jan. 16, 1854; Eaton; *New York Tribune*, Jan. 16, 1854. The *Intelligencer* lists Lt. Van Voast, disabled, as among the passengers brought into the city on the *Titan*. Van Voast was not disabled, and, of course, he remained on the *Lucy Thompson*. The same newspaper says that "about 100 soldiers" also came in on the *Titan*. They did not. They remained aboard the *Lucy Thompson*, under the command of Lt. Van Voast. And besides, there were only 31 soldiers aboard the *Lucy Thompson*, 16 having remained on the *Kilby*. The *Tribune* says that the *Titan* pulled into New York at 10 o'clock that evening, which is wrong; it was 8 o'clock; Miss Eaton says: "The tug arrived at the pier at eleven o'clock on Saturday morning, January 14." She must have meant Saturday evening, but the hour was still wrong.

they were all well ensconced by 10:30 p.m. Those who registered included: Captain Judd and lady; Lieutenant Fremont and family; Major Wyse, lady and child; and Lieutenant Frank Murray, U.S. Navy.[13]

As for Lieutenant Loeser, his wife Sarah, Miss Lucia Eaton, and their servant woman, when they disembarked from the *Titan* they took the ferry boat to Brooklyn, taking off their blankets so as not to attract attention, and soon arrived in a carriage at the Eaton home.[14]

Colonel and Mrs. Gates, and the infant, along with Mrs. Gates's sister, Miss Carter, all spent the night at the residence of G.G. Howland, while Major Merchant and family, along with George Woolsey Aspinwall, were lodged at the rather magnificent house of Mr. W.H. Aspinwall. J. Lorimer Graham went to the home of his father, General Nathan B. Graham. Young Mr. Graham was emaciated from illness, exposure and starvation, and had only the clothes on his back. He had lost all his possessions, including his extensive and valuable autograph collection. However, he had managed to save one beautiful opal stud, which still glistened on his dilapidated shirt front.[15]

The severely damaged Colonel Martin Burke was accompanied by Surgeon Wirtz and other army survivors to Fort Wood, on Bedloes Island, in New York Harbor, and went straight to the hospital, where he would languish for a few months. Wirtz himself seemed "to have sustained the terrible mental and physical [strain]" to which he had "been subjected wonderfully well," although he was still complaining "of the nervous reaction from such fearful tension of both mind and body, continued throughout the lapse of more than a fortnight." Lieutenant William A. Winder, in command of a number of other survivors who had come in the day before on the *Three Bells*, also left that day for Fort Wood.[16]

---

13. *Weekly National Intelligencer*, Jan. 16, 1854. This newspaper mistakenly has Mrs. Chase and child being swept overboard from the *San Francisco*. They also have Fremont as a captain.14. Eaton.

15. *New York Daily Times*, Jan. 16, 1854. The *Weekly National Intelligencer* of Jan. 16, 1854, mistakenly has the Merchant family staying at the Astor House.

16. Army post returns; Wirtz account. The *Weekly National Intelligencer* of Jan. 16, 1854, mistakenly has Col. Burke and Surgeon Wirtz staying at the Astor House. The Fort Wood post return for January 1854 says, "The detachment of recruits for Companies B and L from the wreck of the *San Francisco*, 42 in number, was broken up, and assigned to the different companies at the same time." The return also says, "The command (recruits excepted) arrived at this post from the wreck of the steamship *San Francisco*, Jan. 14th, 15th, and 20th, 1854." It also says, "Companies A and K, 3rd Artillery, left for Fort Lafayette, Jan. 28, 1854."

Safe

At three o'clock in the morning of Sunday, January 15, while the *Three Bells* lay moored at Pier 32, in the East River, a colored waiter, name unknown, who had suffered from exposure during the wreck of the *San Francisco*, died of exhaustion and general debility. He was about 25. That day Coroner O'Donnell performed the inquest.[1]

He was not the only one to die on the *Three Bells* that day. That afternoon, Matthews, their colored head cook also succumbed to exhaustion. In life he had been a strong, powerful man, and in death he left a wife and two children in New York City.[2]

In the morning, after a reunion with his wife and child at the Astor House, Major Wyse proceeded to Fort Wood, where he immediately assumed command of the post, taking over from Captain and Brevet Lieutenant Colonel Edward J. Steptoe.[3]

People started calling at the Astor House to see the sufferers who had come in on the steam tug *Titan* the night before. As for the *Lucy Thompson*, she had made her way to Staten Island, where, at noon, Second Lieutenant James Van Voast, in command of all those troops and camp women who had remained on board, rapidly transferred his charges to the quartermaster's steam tug which had been sent to pick them up and take them to Fort Wood. As they approached Bedloes Island, and drew up alongside the pier at 1:45 p.m., they found a crowd waiting, women, children, and uniformed soldiers, many of them who had come in off the *Three Bells* the day before, and now with their eyes anxiously riveted to the incoming tug, searching the vessel for familiar faces, for relatives who had boarded the *Kilby* all those days before, who had then been transferred to the *Lucy Thompson*, and who may, or may not, now be on the quartermaster's tug. Amid joyous shouts the passengers were landed on the pier with all possible dispatch, and everyone found each other. Then the place emptied of people, all except one woman, still standing on the promenade deck with a baby in her arms, looking for her husband whom she had been informed had been on the *Kilby*. With tears in her eyes she asked if he had made it. He had, but he had been taken off on the *Antarctic*, and was now on his way to Liverpool.

---

1. *New York Tribune*, Jan. 16, 1854.
2. *New York Times*, Jan. 16, 1854.
3. Army post returns, Fort Wood, Jan. 1854.

On Bedloes Island, that afternoon, Major Wyse, with Lieutenants Winder and Patten, went to the hospital, where they found a number of the troops lying in bed with dysentery, rheumatism, and injuries received on the *San Francisco*, but being very well looked after by the ordnance sergeant of Bedloe's Island, Thomas Sanborn. Bill Winder himself was far from well; in fact he had been sick from the moment this adventure began the previous December. As Major Wyse wrote in a letter to Colonel Sam Cooper, the adjutant general of the army, "The other officer with me, Lieutenant. Wm A. Winder, was sick nearly all the time, and that prevented him from rendering the services which otherwise he would have done."[4]

Somehow the number of troops on the *Kilby* got misquoted as 100, and this, along with the news that the bark was leaky, crippled by the storm, and rather short of provisions, was reported at the office of the commissary general that afternoon, and immediate measures were taken to dispatch a steamer in search of the *Kilby*. The steam tug *Leviathan* left New York at 4 a.m., under the command of Capt. Hazzard, to look for the *Kilby*. At 9 a.m., 60 miles SE of Sandy Hook, she spoke the steamer *Thomas Ellis*, from Cape Hayti bound for New York. At 11 a.m., 75 miles east southeast of The Highlands, she spoke the bark *St. Andrew*, from Mobile for New York. At noon, 85 miles east by south of The Highlands, she spoke the brig *R.H. Moulton*, from Richmond, Virginia, bound north for Boston, and at two o'clock that afternoon, 15 miles north by east of Fire Island, she spoke the brig *Marinam*, heading up from New Orleans to New York. Finally, at 4 p.m., 50 miles east by south of The Highlands, she spoke the *Kilby*, which was still being towed by the steamer *City of New York*. Captain Hazzard offered to take off the *San Francisco*'s remaining passengers, but Captain Low, skipper of the *Kilby*, politely declined, saying he would take them on to Boston. At 6 p.m., 20 miles east of The Highlands, the *Leviathan* spoke the bark *Overman*, bound from Rio Grande for New York, and at eight o'clock that night the *Leviathan* returned to port in New York City.[5]

The *Kilby*, towed by the *City of New York*, passed the village of Holmes's Hole on the morning of Monday, January 16, 1854, and the next day, at about 6 a.m., arrived safe at Boston as expected. Those survivors of the wreck of the *San Francisco* who had elected to stay aboard the *Kilby* rather then be transferred to the *Lucy Thompson* were reported in good health, and at the earliest opportunity were taken to the Tremont House and well looked after. Some of the ladies of Boston were on hand to render assistance to the sufferers. From the Tremont House the 16 enlisted men led by Sergeant Joe McIntyre made their way to Fort Independence, in Boston Harbor. On the nineteenth they were carried by steamer to Governors Island, in New York Harbor.[6]

---

4. Wyse to Cooper, dated Fort Wood, New York Harbor.
5. *New York Tribune*, Jan. 16, 1854.
6. *Boston Herald*, Jan. 18, 1854; Army post returns, Jan. 1854; *New York Times*, Jan. 17, 1854. Holmes's Hole is now known as Vineyard Haven, and is to be found within the town of Tisbury, Mass.

At 10:30 on the morning of January 17, at Grace Church, in New York City, with Dr. Vinton officiating, the officers of the Third Artillery who had been rescued by the *Kilby* and then the *Lucy Thompson*, met, with their families, to offer up their united thanksgiving for their safe deliverance from death. It was a joyful act of praise and prayer to Almighty God, for His abundant and great mercies, and the officers requested all their fellow sufferers of the army, as well as citizen passengers, to join them. The sacrament of the Lord's Supper was administered to all who were devoutly disposed to receive it. the Rev. Mr. Cooper was especially welcome.

Scurrilous stories started to spread beginning on Wednesday, January 18. This from various newspapers: "The *Napoleon* made no attempt to lie by the unfortunate vessel; no attempt to relieve her; but this is what she did; she hovered around her long enough to fish up some of the barrels of pork and other provisions which the *San Francisco*, in her necessity, had been compelled to cast overboard, and then leaving the wreck to the mercy of the furious waves, went on her way, rejoicing!"

The *Boston Atlas* of January 19 reported that Captain William Strout of the brig *Napoleon* had been arrested on the charge of brutal conduct toward Daniel Davis, the ship's cook, but that he was out on bail. Three of the *Napoleon*'s crew had apparently sworn that Strout deliberately left the stricken *San Francisco* because he feared his vessel would be swamped by passengers. However, these same three men also claimed to have seen 70 men swept overboard from the *San Francisco*. The only time a large number of men were swept off the *San Francisco* was in the morning of December 24, and the *Napoleon* did not encounter the steamer until noon on the twenty-fifth. On Friday, January 21, Strout was examined by U.S. Commissioner John Rand, at Portland, Maine. It transpired at this hearing that Strout struck Davis three times, but with justification. He was discharged.

On January 16, Major Wyse was ordered to Washington, D.C., thus leaving Fort Wood without a commander. On January 21, First Lieutenant Romeyn B. Ayres, who had not been on the *San Francisco*, joined Fort Wood. He was of Company B, but had temporarily taken command of Company I, which Lieutenant Colonel Martin Burke had relinquished when he arrived sick at Fort Wood a week earlier. On January 22, Captain and Brevet Lieutenant Colonel Edward J. Steptoe arrived as commander of Company H, Third Artillery, and to take command of Fort Wood, but on the twenty-fifth, Major Wyse returned to resume command. However, he was not there long. The following day an order came in that he should repair to Washington again, as quickly as practicable.

By Monday, January 23, 1854, Colonel Swords had paid $15,000 to the owners of the *Kilby*, per the contract made between Captain Low and Lieutenant Fremont, for rescuing a portion of the survivors of the wreck. $250 had also been paid to the crew of the *Kilby*, as well as $100 for provisions used. The *Kilby*'s owners were also claiming for the cotton that had been thrown overboard to make room for the 108 survivors they took on board, but the government could not settle until an accounting was done in Boston and they could figure out how much was owed. The consignee of the ship *Three Bells* was claiming $25,000 for their rescue services, regardless of a lack of contract. In his letter of this date, January 23, Quartermaster Jesup wrote to Secretary of War Jefferson Davis that the Artillery's lost camp equipage and clothing, which must be replaced, came to $26,590.28. In addition, the officers and men had lost everything, including the proceeds of six months advance pay. Jesup had not yet received an account of the loss of the Quartermaster's stores, nor had he any information on how much he was going to have to pay the owners of the *Antarctic*, which was approaching Liverpool as he wrote. This was turning out to be very expensive for the American tax payer.

The General Assembly of Maryland, on January 24, 1854, officially tendered the thanks of the state to Captain Crighton of the *Three Bells*, to Captain Low of the *Kilby*, and to Captain Stouffer, of the *Antarctic*, "for their noble and humane conduct in rescuing so many valuable lives from the wreck of the ill-fated steamer *San Francisco*." Various native Marylanders were thanked: Captain James T. Watkins, "the noble and heroic commander of the unfortunate steamship *San Francisco*," and Major Wyse, Lieutenants W.A. Winder and Charles S. Winder, and Lieutenant Frank Key Murray, "for their courageous and gallant bearing during those trying scenes." It was also resolved that Maryland's senators and representatives in Congress be "requested to use their influence to procure the passage of a law granting assistance to the widows and families of the officers and soldiers who perished during this distressing occasion."

Discarded items from the *San Francisco* were found floating in the Atlantic from time to time. On February 1, 1854, Captain John McKenzie, of the ship *Amelia*, who had just arrived at the French port of Havre, wrote a letter to the owners of the wrecked vessel, telling them that in latitude 30° 12', longitude 56° 05' W, he had picked up a case marked "Lieutenant L. Loeser, U.S. Army, steamer *San Francisco*," containing a dozen cane-bottomed chairs; another case containing several articles of clothing; and on the same day a bale of New Orleans cotton, with a quantity of loose cotton bales.[7]

---

7. *New York Times*, March 3, 1854.

The Voyage of the *Antarctic*

About 162 soldiers were taken off the wrecked steamer by the Liverpool-bound *Antarctic*, including the band and non-commissioned staff. Second Lieutenants Charlie Winder and J.G. Chandler were the only officers, Winder taking his servant. William G. Rankin, the regimental sutler, made the transfer, as did 65 camp women and children. As far as can be ascertained, 27 of the *San Francisco*'s crew went aboard, including Commodore Watkins and his servant, Purser Schell, Third Officer Barton, Fourth Officer John Mason, and Washington Duckett, the ship's carpenter. All of these seem to add up to about 255. Not all of them would make it to England.

They had a good quarter of fresh beef hanging in the rigging, and Captain Stouffer directed the cook to make it into soup, so the first thing the sufferers got when they got on board the *Antarctic* was a substantial basin of good, warm soup, and were put immediately into dry berths.[1]

On January 7, as the *Antarctic* headed east through the Atlantic bound for Liverpool, Sergeant Edward Jakel, of Company A, became the first soldier to succumb to cholera since the ship had parted company with the wreck. It had been almost three years since he and William T. Johnson had signed on at Philadelphia, and now, for the former weaver from Saxony, it was the end of the road. He was 32. Eighteen more soldiers, 22 of the *San Francisco*'s crew, and 18 from among the camp women and children would be struck down by the dreaded specter before the *Antarctic* had completed her run across the Atlantic.

During the evening of Monday, January 23, British time, Captain George Close Stouffer negotiated the final stretch of the Mersey Estuary and brought his packet ship *Antarctic* safely into dock. The troops were not allowed to come ashore during their stay in Liverpool, but that didn't stop about a dozen of them jumping ship, to be swallowed up in the wynds and alleys of the great port city. Such desertions were inevitable, after what these men had been through, and, with only the two second lieutenants on board to maintain army discipline, it is surprising that there weren't a lot more who went overboard. Commodore Watkins, of course, had no authority over the soldiers, but Charlie Winder did. As soon as she *Antarctic* docked, Watkins, Winder and several passengers made straight for the Waterloo Hotel, where

---

1. Stouffer.

the commodore immediately wrote an official letter to the U.S. Consul in Liverpool, giving an account of the tragedy. "Sir, I have the painful duty to report to you the loss of the U.S. mail steamer *San Francisco*, under my command..."[2]

The U.S. consulate at Liverpool had been the first mission of its type ever established overseas by the fledgling United States of America, in 1790, and by 1853, although an underpaid position, the consulship there was considered a prestigious posting for an American citizen, second in Britain only to that of the U.S. ambassador in London. The consulate occupied two dreary rooms on the first floor of the Washington Buildings on the lower corner of Brunswick Street, near the docks. The consul at the time was as much a Yankee Doodle boy as anyone could be, having being born in Massachusetts on July 4. He was now 49, and had been appointed to his Liverpool post owing to a campaign biography he had written for the successful presidential candidate of 1852, his old college friend Frank Pierce. The biography wasn't his only book, by any means. Nathaniel Hawthorne was an unusual consul.

Following up on Watkins's letter, the Commodore and Lieutenant Winder went over to the consul's office on Brunswick Street, where they told Hawthorne that they wished to obtain passage to America for themselves and their charges, and asked if the consul could provide them with the necessary clothing and sustenance while they remained in Liverpool. Mr. Hawthorne had no power to send the troops home, but he would telegraph to James Buchanan, the U.S. ambassador in London, to see if he would like to take over the case, or, failing that, to sanction any action Hawthorne might take. In the meantime, out of his own money, Hawthorne advanced Winder $2,000 to pay for the necessities. Before Hawthorne received Buchanan's reply, Watkins headed down to the British capital that evening. Buchanan demurred, but did recommend to Messrs. Baring that they provide a line of credit for the soldiers. And so Charlie Winder drew $400 to pay for the supplies, charging it to the U.S. Government.[3]

Then came the matter of the ship to take them back to America. As the *Antarctic* had not yet actually docked, it was considered hugely inadvisable to do so, as they feared mass desertion. As Hawthorne says, a number of these cases had already been reported. A few shipping lines offered their services, but it wouldn't be until a week or more from that date, and that was too long to wait.[4]

The Cunard screw steam ship *Alps* arrived at Liverpool on the morning of January 26, after a most excellent run across the Atlantic from New York. She brought news that the *Three Bells* had arrived in New York with 230 troops and passengers from the *San Francisco*.

In London, Commodore Watkins was conferring with the American minister

---

2. Army enlistment records. Captain Stouffer says he landed 176 passengers at Liverpool, which may or may not include the dozen or so men who deserted. But if it didn't, and if the death toll of 59 is accurate, that means the *Antarctic* took off about 250 from the *San Francisco*.

3. Hawthorne; Hawthorne to Ticknor. Hawthorne wrote in his letter to the State Department that 152 soldiers, not including the two officers, arrived at Liverpool.

4. Hawthorne.

as to the best way to get his *San Francisco* survivors back to the United States. Through the efforts of Mr. Charles McIver, the British and North American Royal Mail Steamship Company very generously offered for charter the *America*, their 2,138-ton Glasgow-built Cunard steamer. The price was $6,500. Charlie Winder signed the contract.[5]

On Tuesday morning, January 31 the *America*, under the command of Captain W.J.C. Lang, left Liverpool bound for Boston, carrying those survivors who had been plucked off the *San Francisco* by the *Antarctic*, minus, of course, those who had died on the transatlantic crossing or deserted in Liverpool. Still in the Mersey Estuary, she passed another ship coming in, the *Pyramid*, just arrived from New Orleans under the command of Captain Henderson. Another steamer passed them coming into Liverpool. They supposed it to be the *Andes*, which had left Liverpool on the eighteenth, and was now putting back into port. Off the Bell Buoy, they saw, about to enter the Mersey, the ship *Morning Star*, Captain Foster, 22 days out from New Orleans, setting a new record for the quickest passage between those two ports. The following day, at 11 a.m., off Waterford, the *America* passed the steamer *Baltic*, Captain Comstock, from New York for Liverpool.[6]

At 8 a.m., on the morning of February 16, 1854, the *America* arrived at Boston, bringing back the last of the *San Francisco* survivors. All 157 were in good health: Lieutenants Charlie Winder and John G. Chandler; Winder's servant; William Gorham, the ordnance sergeant; William G. Rankin, the sutler; James Mulholland, the hospital steward, and his two daughters, Adelaide and Lizzie; Commodore Watkins and his servant, and four other members of the crew: Purser Schell, Officers Barton and Mason, and Washington Duckett, the carpenter; 13 women, seven children, and 126 enlisted men of the Third Artillery, including five band members. Corporal Clayton's wife, Adeline, was with him; Private Miles Coffey had his wife Margaret and their child along; Private Patrick Foley was accompanied by his wife, Margaret; Private Patrick Lilly was aboard with his wife, Catherine, and their two children; and Recruit John McKernan had his wife, Ellen, and their three children. Mrs. Ellen Delany was also aboard. Her husband, Private Fenton Delany of Company D, had died on the *Antarctic* two days after having been rescued from the *San Francisco*. Also aboard the *America* were five women whose identities remain something of a mystery: Mrs. Barbara Forster; Mrs. Jane Knap; Miss Margaret Gramon; Mrs. Mary A. Smith; and Mrs. Jane Davidson, with her daughter. Not survivors from the *San Francisco*, but still on the *America*, were a couple from Ellsworth, Massachusetts—Captain Isaac Lord and his wife, survivors from the schooner *Ozark*, which had been wrecked in the Atlantic on December 29. Not all of Mrs. Lord had survived the disaster. Her finger had been jammed while the gale was at its fiercest, and during the seven days they floated on the doomed *Ozark* at the mercy of the elements, the digit had taken a turn for the worse. Within an hour after being plucked off by the

---

5. Hawthorne.
6. *Boston Daily Atlas*, Jan. 17, 1854.

Philadelphia ship *Tuscarora*, that vessel's surgeon had amputated it, and thus, Mrs. Lord found herself arriving in Liverpool, and then coming back to the United States on the *America*.[7]

The U.S. Government had ordered all the passengers to be amply supplied with clothing upon their arrival at Boston, and in the afternoon the men, under the command of Lieutenant Charlie Winder, were marched to the Old Colony depot, and from there took passage to Fall River on their way to Newport, Rhode Island, where they would remain for the present in order to recruit.[8]

On February 22, from New York, Commodore Watkins wrote a letter to Messrs. Zerega & Co., the owners of the *Antarctic*, and on the evening of the following day, at 5:15, as the tug *Lewis* was towing the *America* out of Boston Harbor, the wind was blowing a gale from the northwest, and the seas were so rough that Captain Lang couldn't discharge the pilot, Ben Tremere, who got a free ride to Liverpool, in company with 11 passengers, a much smaller manifest than the one the *America* had made out only a week before when she brought in the last of the *San Francisco* survivors from England. The *America* would arrive in Liverpool on March 7.

---

7. The *America*'s manifest shows 157 *San Francisco* survivors coming back to the U.S.A. Captain Stouffer claimed he landed 176 passengers at Liverpool. Allowing for the dozen or so men who deserted at Liverpool, that leaves a small handful unaccounted for. But perhaps there were a few more deserters than we know, or it may be that Captain Stouffer's estimate of 176 was a little off.

8. *Boston Daily Atlas*, Feb. 17, 1854; *Boston Evening Transcript*, Feb. 17, 1854; *Newport Mercury*, Feb. 18, 1854.

The Inquiry

The *New York Herald* of January 16, 1854, published a letter from "An Old Soldier" who had been on the *San Francisco*. This anonymous correspondent called upon the paper to "hold up to public indignation the officers of the government that drove us on board of a steamer to send us on a voyage of fifteen thousand miles, instead of the direct route across the isthmus of Panama." The government, he said, claimed it was cheaper, and besides, if the men went across Panama some of them might desert, "which was adding insult to injury." The writer complained of the inhumane treatment and that most of the troops had lost everything. The "monstrous outrage that has been perpetrated in our case should consign for all time every government officer who managed the matter to eternal infamy." He called for justice, and for the punishment of the guilty parties, "no matter how high their position, whether it be the Secretary of War, or the Navy, or both," and demanded a proper investigation of all the facts.[1]

Whether or not this letter to the *Herald* was read by anyone in high places, that same day the U.S. Senate adopted a resolution, requesting that the Secretary of War lay before them all the information which he may possess in relation to the wreck of the steamer *San Francisco*, and the loss of life and property occasioned by that disaster; the means employed by the War Department and otherwise, for the rescue of the vessel and passengers; the number and condition of the survivors; and the nature and extent of the relief required by their calamitous condition. The ball of inquiry was beginning to roll.

Colonel Gates was, of course, fully aware that he might be in for a very bad time. His first plan of action was to sit down that very day at his regiment's headquarters in New York City, and write a report to Colonel Samuel Cooper, the adjutant general in Washington, D.C., setting down, for the record, an account of his arrival at New York with a remnant of his command. "I embarked on the 22nd of December last, with eight companies of my Regiment, on the steamship *San Francisco* for California." He goes on to say that on December 24, when about 300 miles from New York, the engine gave way, and then the storm broke. The entire upper cabin was swept away, taking with it four officers and about 200 men, as

---

1. *New York Herald*, Jan. 16, 1854.

well as Mrs. Major Taylor, Gates's own eldest son, and a number of citizen passengers.[2]

Then came his testimonials, designed to get as many of his officers on his side as he could: "I consider it my duty to speak of the meritorious conduct of Major Wyse, Capts Judd and Fremont, Lieuts Chandler, Loeser, Charles Winder, Wm Winder, and Van Voast. Their conduct is above all praise, and I think that, at least, they deserve the thanks of the Government, for the safety of all on board depended greatly upon their untiring and incessant services."

Captain Gardiner of the Dragoons had survived the wreck of the *San Francisco*, no thanks to Gates, and on January 22 he wrote a letter to Captain Irvin McDowell, on the staff of the general-in-chief, impugning the reputation of Colonel Gates and his conduct throughout the trying episode in the Atlantic.

Within a very short space of time, Captain McDowell had brought this vilifying report to Gates's attention, at which point the Colonel found himself with a decision to make. But that decision was bound to be influenced by certain factors. The first was that time 17 years ago when he was court-martialed for cowardice.

Cowardice is cowardice, even though, for reasons of explanation or excuse, it may be sub-divided into different genres, physical cowardice and moral cowardice, to name but two. A man may run from a fistfight but not from artillery shells exploding all around him. He may be able to stand up to a crowd of mutineers, but not to his wife. Every man knows better than anyone else whether he is a coward or not, and he has to live with that, for good or bad. But at that stage of the argument it is merely internal, and will probably lie dormant, pushed by necessity to the back of the mind. It is when the issue comes out into the open, for example when a man is accused publicly by another man of being a coward, that things start to happen. Such an accusation may lead to a duel, which the accused man may win. The world may or may not form its own opinion of the survivor, but that opinion has nothing to do with the cowardice of the man. It is just a matter of who won the duel. However, if a professional soldier is up before a court-martial, accused of cowardice, and found not guilty, then officially he is not a coward. But, like the winner of the duel, he will know the truth. Now, here, in 1854, Colonel Gates was facing the charge all over again. He was facing not just his accuser, but himself.

The second factor that was going to influence his reaction to Gardiner's accusation was a legalistic variation of the duel. Demand a trial; let the truth come out at a court of inquiry. Colonel Gates could have just ignored Gardiner, let the thing take its course, whatever that course turned out to be. Of course, that course might have led to a court of inquiry, but it may not have done. It might have been better, therefore, to let sleeping dogs lie. But then Colonel Gates had this new, young wife,

---

2. The colonel's inaccuracies can be gauged from just these short extracts. The storm did not break after the engine gave way. On the contrary, the engine broke while trying to get through the storm that had already been attacking them for some time. And Gates must have known that his figure of 200 men was wildly exaggerated, since by January 16 he would have been informed, either directly or indirectly, by his company sergeants, of the true figures.

Louise, whose bad influence over the old man had already been exercised more than once. It is reasonable to picture in one's mind Louise exhorting her husband, "Clear your name, Bill, clear your name!" And maybe she was right; who knows?

Either way, any way you look at it, Colonel Gates was, fully or partially, responsible for what happened to him next, and what happened happened in a hurry.

On January 23 the *New York Times* published the testimonials part of Colonel Gates's report to Sam Cooper, and the next day the impugned Gates wrote to the adjutant general again, asking for a court of inquiry to clear his name of Captain Gardiner's charges. In effect, this would be a public court-martial. Within a few days, Gates's request was on the desk of the President of the United States. Mr. Pierce directed his Secretary of War, Jefferson Davis, to have the War Department draw up an order for such an inquiry. On January 26, Mr. Davis, as required by the resolution of the Senate of January 16, wrote to President of the Senate Pro Tempore David Rice Atchison—the man famous as being president for a day—including all relevant material on the wreck. Davis, in summing up his letter, says that the strength of the command upon setting out was estimated at 501, that 164 perished, and that of the survivors 146 were taken to Liverpool.

On Friday, January 27, 1854, Special Order No. 17, signed by Jeff Davis, was issued, authorizing the court of inquiry.

On February 2, 1854, Secretary Davis, asked J.C. Dobbin, his counterpart at the Navy Department, to send him copies of the inspection report made of the *San Francisco* back in November and December of 1853. The following day, Dobbin complied with the request. In his covering letter to Davis, Dobbin wrote: "The Department did not accept the steamship *San Francisco* under the contracts for mail service." In order to explain this rather sinister-sounding declaration, Secretary Dobbin had to admit that the steamer "sailed from New York before the report reached the Department, an explanation of which was required before I could consent to accept."

On the morning of February 6, 1854, in New York City, the court of inquiry was convened at No. 114 West Eleventh Street, the headquarters of General-in-Chief Winfield Scott, who was to act as president of this special tribunal. The purpose of the court was to investigate the circumstances attending the loss of the *San Francisco*, to examine the causes of the failure of the expedition, and to uncover all facts concerning the conduct of Colonel Gates, his officers, and men from the time of the embarkation of the regiment in December to the present. There would be no fewer than 17 days of inquiry, which seems a lot until one realizes that, far from being a hard nine-to-five grind, each working day consisted of merely a relaxed few hours, and sometimes no hours at all.

That first morning, after a secret session of the court, the doors were thrown open to the public, and the press boys were given a table at which they could take notes. While they all waited for the principal villain of the piece, Colonel William Gates, to show up, the star of the show, General Scott, the old hero of the Mexican War—actually, he was only two years older than Colonel Gates—sat at the head of the inquiry table, looking well enough but still showing on the right side of his face the impression of the Fifth Avenue flagstone he had tripped over seven months before. Beside him lay the splendid sword that bore the inscription: "Presented by the people of the State of Louisiana to General Winfield Scott, for his gallantry and Generalship exhibited at the Siege of Vera Cruz, in the battles of Cerro Gordo, Contreras, Churubusco, Molina del Rey, Chapultepec, and his final entry into the city of Mexico."

Next to General Scott sat two of his old comrades-in-arms from the Mexican War, both now in their late fifties: Brevet Brigadier General Henry Stanton, assistant quartermaster general, to his right, and to his left the recent military governor of New Mexico, Lieutenant Colonel and Brevet Colonel Edwin Vose Sumner, of the First Dragoons. Bullhead Sumner sounded like a roaring bull even in his quieter moments, but that wasn't why he got his nickname; at the battle of Cerro Gordo a musket ball had literally bounced off his skull. Despite already having been an officer for 35 years, Sumner's great army days were still a decade in the future. The foot of the inquiry table was occupied by Brevet Major John Fitzgerald Lee, 40 years old, the able and learned judge advocate of the army, acting as recorder and conducting the investigation on the part of the government. In effect, Major Lee was to be the state prosecutor in the case. These four men formed the court of inquiry.

And then Colonel Gates came in. Everyone in the room knew his career was on the line, seriously on the line. Dressed in the undress uniform of his grade, Gates took a seat on the right of the judge advocate. The court then rose and took the oath administered by Major Lee, who, in turn, was sworn in by General Scott.

Colonel Thomas Swords, the quartermaster general of New York, was first to take the stand, as a government witness. His testimony and presentation to the court of a series of letters set the scene for what had led up to the expedition. Swords's time on the stand took up the first day of the inquiry.

On Tuesday, February 7, the second day, Colonel Gates was again present, and asked leave of the court to introduce Captain Hamilton L. Shields, of Company H of the Third Artillery, an acting judge advocate, former aide to General Wool, and a distinguished veteran of the Mexican War. Shields would, later this very year, 1854, resign from the army to become a farmer in Vermont. Seven years later, he would, despite his impeccable service to his country, be persecuted by the Lincoln administration because of his Southern roots. Now, though, at the court of inquiry, he was, in effect, Colonel Gates's attorney.

This day and the next five days saw several witnesses come and go: Lieutenant Fremont, who summoned up the energy to offer a modicum of praise for Gates's conduct during the wreck; Colonel Lorenzo Thomas, who was in a hurry to get back to Washington, D.C.; Doctors Buel, Wirtz and Satterlee; Lieutenant Murray of the Navy; and Captain Judd, whom the court quizzed about discipline, short allowances of food aboard the *Kilby*, and then—and now the court was getting down to it— about Colonel Gates's behavior.

The question was put to Judd: "Did any matter of neglect, disorder, or irregularity occur on the *Kilby* to your knowledge," at which point General Scott ordered Major

Lee to add these words, "which could have been prevented by the commanding officer of the troops."

The court was trying to press Judd to incriminate Colonel Gates. The banal and relatively inconsequential subject came up of how the corn was cooked aboard the *Kilby*, which shows the lengths they were prepared to go to nail the colonel of the Third Regiment of Artillery rather than have the War Department placed under scrutiny for negligence.

"Please to answer the question," demanded the judge advocate. So Judd did. Yes, Colonel Gates could perhaps have prevented the irregularity of cooking the corn.

"Do you mean to impute any fault or neglect to him, or was it the best he could do?," asked Judge Advocate Lee.

"Better arrangements could have been made," replied Judd, "and were afterwards made for the uniform parching of the corn for the whole command."

On the sixth day, February 11, Lieutenant Van Voast was examined by Major Lee. The judge advocate was once more out to get Colonel Gates when he asked Van Voast about the colonel's orders for getting the men to aid the officers in the work parties aboard the *San Francisco*. "*I heard of no instructions given by the commanding officer*," replied Van Voast, in his most honest yet damning manner. The only instructions Van Voast ever received were from Major Wyse, and then there were his instructions from Lieutenant Fremont to board the *Kilby* with 10 men. Major Lee asked if the orders given him by Fremont were in Fremont's role as adjutant for the colonel, or simply because Fremont was Van Voast's superior. Van Voast said he assumed the former.

Captain Gardiner, the dragoon, was then called to the stand, and examined by Major Lee. Asked about what orders Gardiner heard Colonel Gates give between the twenty-fourth and the twenty-eighth of December, Gardiner claimed he heard no orders given to the service, only to the servants of the ship, and occasionally to the troops, to bring him food and water. Gardiner felt that there had been an utter want of system, with Gates failing to assume command or to give orders.

Colonel Gates then asked if it was proper to have put on the record that which Captain Gardiner had only heard and not seen. General Scott then replied that courts of inquiry are not so strict on this matter as courts-martial, but if Gates wanted it excluded from the record, then it would be.

On Monday, February 13, 1854, the seventh session of the court of inquiry opened, as usual, at 10:30 a.m. The star event of the day's show was the return of Major Wyse. The essence of his complaint against Colonel Gates was that he had not given the necessary orders for bailing and lightening the *San Francisco*, and that he had failed to look after his command. Wyse goes on: "I would further state that had he been a citizen passenger, he could not have taken less interest in that command than he appeared to do." And again, "I did not notice a single particle of duty done by the commander," meaning Gates. Specific complaints made by Major Wyse about Colonel Gates were: That when Commodore Watkins came into Gates's cabin to let him know the *Kilby* was there, the colonel failed to set his quartermaster and commissary to getting out water and provisions from the hold of the ship and transporting them to the rescue ship. The next complaint was that Gates neglected to have a minute inspection of the command to determine those of the sick and invalided who should have been brought to the quarter deck for transfer to the *Kilby*. He also neglected to retain Captain Judd on the *San Francisco* at the very time that Judd was in command of two companies of raw recruits and was much needed. Gates neglected to retain on the *San Francisco* the Regimental Quartermaster, Lieutenant Fremont; the Commissary of Subsistence, Lieutenant Loeser; and the assistant surgeon, Dr. Wirtz. He also failed to inform the next senior on the wreck—in other words, Major Wyse himself—that he, Gates, was about to leave the *San Francisco* and go over to the *Kilby*, nor did he turn over authority to that next senior in any way. Aside from the two companies of recruits now without an officer, that is Companies B and L, there were two other companies, A and K, whose officers had been swept overboard on the twenty-fourth. These companies too were without an officer, and Company I was without a permanent commander, as Lieutenant Colonel Martin Burke was very sick. Thus there were, left on the wreck, five companies without a commander or an officer. Wyse felt that, of the officers who transferred to the *Kilby*, Captain Judd, and Lieutenants Fremont and Loeser should have been left behind on the *San Francisco*. That would have been three more, and would have made life easier. Those three should have not have gone over to the *Kilby*; their staff duties required that they remain on the *San Francisco*, at least according to the vehement Wyse.[3]

Wyse had nothing by unstinting praise for Lieutenants Charlie Winder, Chandler and Van Voast, but he was not so kind to Bill Winder, whom, he said, "I believe, was on the sick report; I am, however, not positive of that, but he was constantly complaining of being sick; he was on the sick report after we parted from the *Kilby*; but before that, whether he was on the sick report I do not know; I do not know of any other who was sick." This statement, true or not, would have repercussions later in the inquiry.

Later that Monday, February 13, Colonel Gates wrote a letter to Major Lee, the judge advocate at the ongoing court of inquiry. It was not so much the letter itself that was of importance, it was what the colonel enclosed, which was a complaint brought by six of the men against Captain Gardiner, and had to do with the brandy and biscuit issue aboard the *Kilby*. The general charge against the dragoon officer was "disgraceful conduct," and had been brought to Colonel Gates by the six signatories: Sergeant Joe McIntyre, of Company K; Privates Isaac Sleeper, Patrick Lilly and Moses Eldridge, of Company D; and Privates John Murphy and Warren Adams, of Company I. All of these soldiers had been part of the contingent of 16 that had stayed behind on the *Kilby* after the *Lucy Thompson* had taken off most of the survivors.

The specific charge against Gardiner revolved around an incident on the *Kilby*

---

3. Lieutenant Chandler had taken over Company I when Colonel Burke was incapacitated.

which took place several days after the bark had separated from the *San Francisco*. With the *Kilby* unexpectedly still at sea, and with a port nowhere in sight, one fact above most others was pressing itself upon everyone aboard—not enough provisions had been transferred from the wreck to satisfy the 108 hungry and thirsty mouths that had so suddenly and unexpectedly swarmed aboard the *Kilby*. If they were to be out on the ocean for any further length of time, and if they were to survive until they made land, then strict rationing would have to be imposed. And so, with the officers and men undergoing a reduction of bread and meat rations and a limit of half a sea biscuit a day, Captain Gardiner took 10 or 12 biscuits from the depository that held the entire biscuit supply for all the men, women and children aboard the bark. He then secreted them near his sleeping place This act was committed without the permission or knowledge of Colonel Gates or Captain Low, skipper of the *Kilby*. They called it theft, and that was the written charge brought by the six men to Colonel Gates, and relayed by him to Major Lee.

Major Lee received Colonel Gates's letter and enclosure that same day, February 13, and immediately informed Captain Henry Judd of it. Judd was then in New York, on the point of returning to South Carolina, but, upon receiving word from Lee, he found time to go straight to Colonel Gates, from whom he learned that the charges against Captain Gardiner would be withdrawn or suspended. Judd was outraged over the matter. It is not that he blamed Gates, rather the enlisted men who, for reasons of their own, had pressed this scandalous story upon the colonel. Judd made a statement to Gates there and then. The following day, February 14, Judd would write this all down in a letter to the judge advocate.

First of all, Judd explained that for the two or three days after the *Kilby* separated from the *San Francisco*—while they were still in the frustrating process of trying to find the steamer again—and for the next few days following that, the allowance of biscuit was not restricted to the amount afterwards established, but each person received from between one and one and a half, morning and evening.

Mrs. Judd suffered from dyspepsia at the best of times. For several days now she had been without appetite, and Captain Judd himself was little better off. However, they did take their allowance, and stored it away, thus accumulating a fair pile of back biscuit. Their intentions were, of course, the noblest, to give them to some needy soul at some future date, if such a case were to present itself, that is if the Judds themselves hadn't already eaten their stockpiled supply. By and by they amassed a total of about five or six crackers, no more, and those were stored in a trunk belonging to the captain of the *Kilby*. There was no key to this trunk. Judd seemed to think that this cache was fairly common knowledge, and there the crackers remained for a week or 10 days.

Then came the moment Judd removed his wife to the *Kilby*'s hold so she could get some rest. As for the crackers in the captain's trunk, the trunk with no key, Judd went to remove them, to take them down to the hold, and found only four there, where previously there had been five or six. He did not say anything, but he definitely knew one or two had been taken by someone. He and his wife continued to draw their allowance of biscuit, which had now been reduced, but, always thinking of others less fortunate than themselves, they continued to stockpile, living all the while as best they could on the parched corn. Those then were the biscuits found in the hold, and that's how they got there.[4]

As for brandy, the only brandy Judd heard about was that introduced by the surgeon as hospital stores, and only issued as such. The head of each family of officers, Judd himself excepted, received a little of this, as medicine only, and the remainder was reserved for use among the men and other officers in case of sickness. Many cases of diarrhea had made their appearance, and it became necessary to husband this small supply of brandy with extreme care. A portion of it, all that remained in one bottle, the last bottle, as a matter of fact, was given in Judd's charge by Surgeon Satterlee, to be issued whenever and to whomever Satterlee directed. The surgeon, being disabled and suffering greatly, could not take care of the disposal of the brandy himself. Judd did not believe that any brandy was found on board the *Kilby* after the transfer of personnel to the *Lucy Thompson*, for only about a gill remained in this last bottle, which Judd, at the surgeon's suggestion, took with him when he transferred to that ship. It would be given to the fainting and exhausted ladies, as they would be the first in need of it.[5]

Judd finished his letter with, "With a heart overflowing with gratitude to Almighty God for our preservation, and in full charity with all men, I never dreamed of being requested to explain the most trifling incident of our perilous trials to remove from a fellow sufferer [he means Captain Gardiner] such an imputation."

The truth is, Judd had not explained the incident at all. He had not even come close to explaining it. In fact, he hadn't even addressed the charge.

Sooner or later Major Lee would have to present these letters to the court of inquiry, along with the original charge by the six enlisted men, but, as it was a side issue, he would have to wait until a suitable lull in the action before he was able to do so with any justification. That moment would not present itself until February 21.

While all this was going on in the inquiry room that Monday, things were happening outside, on the streets of New York City. A colored man, John Logan, who had been a cook on the *San Francisco*, was arrested by Officer Baldwin of the 8th Ward police, on suspicion of having stolen a quantity of surgeon's lancets, which he was now offering for sale at a hardware store. He was taken before Justice Stuart and committed to await examination. It was said that he had been seen with a valuable gold watch and chain in his possession, but that was not found at the time of his arrest.[6]

About the same time, William Evans the black steward and William Fields, the black waiter, were also caught in the act of trying to sell merchandise for 75 percent of its value. A lot of this was jewelry they had stolen from passengers' trunks while

---

4. Judd.
5. Judd.
6. *New York Evening Post*, Feb. 14, 1854.

the legitimate owners had been going through hell on the *San Francisco*. The two men confessed to that, and to more—that they had continued their depredations after having been taken off the wreck by the *Three Bells*. Other Negro stewards and waiters were involved, William Scofield for one. Lieutenant Fremont had a gold chain and breast pin worth $65 taken from his trunk. Sergeant Oppenheimer lost two gold bracelets, which were subsequently found in the possession of Evans. A diamond chest pin with gold chain attached and a pair of earrings belonging to Major and Mrs. Taylor were found in the possession of Fields, and identified by Mrs. Taylor's maid, Margaret Parker, of 25 London Terrace, 23rd Street.

An officer found a large gold locket with a middle-aged man's miniature on one side and hair on the other, of the style of 30 years earlier, and a modern gold pencil attached. The thief died soon after being compelled to give it up. It could be rescued by the surviving friends of the wearer at the offices of Howland & Aspinwall, 54 South Street.[7]

Captain Shields, Colonel Gates's counsel, opened day eight of the inquiry proceedings on Tuesday, February 14. Referring to Major Wyse's complaints of the previous day, Colonel Gates wished to state that Captain Judd, Dr. Wirtz, and Lieutenants Fremont, Loeser, and Van Voast were all on the *Kilby* by his orders, so any criticism by Major Wyse of these men in that regard could be clarified. Gates also wanted the court to know that if Major Wyse felt that he had automatically assumed command of the *San Francisco* by virtue of the fact that his superior officer, Colonel Gates, was not aboard any longer, but on the *Kilby*, then he was mistaken, because the two ships were still connected by a hawser. Gates was, therefore, until the *Kilby* actually separated, still in command of all troops on both ships, at least according to him.

Mr. Mellus, the first officer, was then examined by the court. Asked about the character of the storm in which the *San Francisco* was wrecked, he replied that, in 20 years at sea, it was the "heaviest I have ever seen in the Atlantic." After being quizzed about times and events aboard the ship during that fateful day of the wreck, he was asked if the steamer would have weathered the storm if the engine had not broken. Mellus, being a good employee of the Pacific Mail Steamship Company, was guarded in his response. He felt it was "questionable." Then came the inevitable question, one Mellus could not evade: "What was the breaking—what part?," to which the good mate had no option but to tell the truth, "The air-pump piston rod."

Major Lee, the judge advocate, then exhibited all the correspondence relating to the board of examination and the inspection of the *San Francisco* prior to her departure. The main concern was the small air-pump in the engine which had been called into question by Mr. Shock, the inspector who had written the board's report on December 19, 1853. First Officer Mellus was asked if that was the piece of machinery that had failed, and, again, he had no choice but to admit that it was.

On Wednesday, the fifteenth, day nine of the inquiry began at 11 a.m., with sev-

---

7. *Presbyterian Magazine*.

eral witnesses in attendance, including Captain Pendleton of the *Lucy Thompson*, Major Merchant, Lieutenant Van Voast, and Dr. Horace Wirtz. According to Wirtz, Major Wyse spent most of his time in a cabin with the ladies. Then Lieutenant Bill Winder presented his letter to the court, one he had just written that day: "Sir, Conceiving that I have been very much injured by the testimony of Major Wyse, (in saying that I did no or very little duty on the wreck) I respectfully request that the Court will permit me to introduce testimony to rebut that of Major Wyse, and to vindicate my character as an officer. I have but few questions to ask. I am, Sir, very respectfully, your obedient servant, William A. Winder, 1st Lieutenant, 3rd Artillery."

Day 13 of the inquiry, Monday, February 20, produced a shock—literally. William H. Shock, Chief Engineer of the U.S. Navy, one of the members of the naval board who had made the official inspection of the engine and machinery of the *San Francisco* before she sailed. He was here to testify before the court in regard to the loss of the *San Francisco*, so far as concerned her machinery, which he had found very strong and well built. Then it came down to the piston-rod of the air-pump, which had broken. Shock had been unhappy with this rod during his inspection, and, as he had written in his official report, he found it novel. It wasn't the novelty of the part which disturbed him so much, it was that he discovered some irregularity in the motion caused by that very part. Because it was an experiment, Shock had felt obliged to bring it to the attention of the Navy Department. But, again, in principle, he found nothing to object to, and certainly found the parts to be strong. Of course, it was here, at this very piston-rod, that the engine broke on that fateful day. He then produced a model, and gave the two reasons why the piston broke: A defect in the iron, and the tremendous strain put upon the engine. As for the extraordinary pressure put on the engine, the engine had been tested, according to the steamboat laws, for 40 pounds of steam, and rated and approved for 30 pounds, but in contending with the storm the engine exerted a greater portion of steam than it was intended for. It was the press of steam, and the defect in the iron, that broke the rod, according to Shock. Defective iron cannot be detected, so that part of it was no one's fault. However, as to the novelty of the contrivance, because it was new in the U.S.A., and, Shock thought, worthy, the engineer of the *San Francisco*, not being familiar with it, needed time to get to know it, time he never had.

Day 14 of the inquiry looked to be a big day when the court opened at noon on Tuesday, February 21. Commodore Watkins, who had been having trouble getting to Manhattan, had finally arrived in New York, and the vicious dragoon, Captain Gardiner, was back. The first thing Colonel Gates did was get Watkins up on the stand and examine him before he could disappear. The questions were limited to those that would show the colonel in as good a light as possible, which was only fair, as Gates was fighting for his life.

The court asked Watkins an interesting question. If those traveling on board the *San Francisco* had all been citizen passengers, and he had had the same amount of freight, would he have quartered the freight and passengers in the same way Colonel Gates had done. The answer was an unequivocal yes.

Watkins, just like his first officer Mr. Mellus, had never gone through an Atlantic storm so great. These two experienced sailors, then, were in accord on that issue, which is more than can be said of the next question posed by General Scott, the President of the court of inquiry: "To what cause or causes do you attribute the loss of the *San Francisco*?" Without hesitation, the Commodore replied, "To the stopping of the engine during the storm."

Now, this was quite a different response to the one given only a week before by Mr. Mellus, who, when asked by the court if the steamer could have weathered the storm if the engine had not broken, replied that that was questionable. It may have been questionable for Mellus on February 14, but by February 21 Mellus's superior, Commodore Watkins, did not find it questionable at all.

General Scott now went for the jugular. "But for the breaking of a part of her engine, do you think that the *San Francisco* would have weathered the storm?" Again, Commodore Watkins's reply was immediate—"I do, Sir."

The fact is, if the *San Francisco* had ridden out the storm, Watkins would have taken her to the nearest suitable port—Norfolk, perhaps—to have her refitted.

It was now Tuesday afternoon. Colonel Gates wanted until Saturday to present a written statement, but the court could not adjourn that long. However, Major Lee, the judge advocate, had something else to fill the time, and that was the exchange of letters concerning Captain Gardiner's theft of the sea biscuits while aboard the *Kilby*.

Lee presented the letters to the court, and one other one, written by Colonel Gates to General Scott and the Gentlemen of the Court. The letter said that Gates, upon learning of the charge by the six enlisted men, had taken measures to find the cook of the *Kilby*, Frederick Lincoln, a man he knew to be well acquainted with the circumstances of the case. The cook had flatly sustained the accusations against Gardiner, and had done so in front of witnesses outside the court room. Accordingly, he was requested to appear in court on the twentieth to give his testimony. The cook duly arrived outside the building, where he was accosted by Captain Gardiner, who informed the man that he would not be needed that day. According to what Gates had heard, Captain Gardiner then gave the cook some money and told him that he would be called when needed. Gardiner and the cook then disappeared to a hotel together, and despite strenuous efforts on the part of Colonel Gates to find Lincoln again, he had been unable to do so. "It is my belief that Captain Gardiner is informed of his whereabouts, and I therefore request that he may be required by this Court to produce the witness."

Now, in the court room, Gates stated that he had no knowledge of the facts stated in his complaint against Captain Gardiner, but was merely bringing the original charge to the attention of the court.

Gardiner wanted this charge investigated, and said that the cook was now present. However, the cook, who had indeed been hiding, was singing a different tune now, and Gates had no option but to withdraw the charges against Gardiner. However, Gardiner didn't want the charges dropped unless Gates admitted publicly that they were groundless. Gates couldn't do that because he didn't know the facts of the charges. Mr. Lincoln was then called as a witness.

Colonel Gates objected to the cook being called, but was overruled. Lincoln was a native of Madras, and his English was, to put it kindly, bad. According to him, he had not been given any money by Gardiner. Gardiner had taken his gloves out of his pocket, not his purse. Lincoln said he had already told Gates that. Nor did Gardiner try to dissuade Lincoln from coming to the court, nor to hide himself from Colonel Gates. The furious Colonel Gates refused to cross-examine a witness he found unreliable.

Captain Bucker of the Commissary Department was next up. Bucker had been at Captain Gardiner's room at the Metropolitan Hotel on Friday, February 17. In going into Gardiner's room, Bucker had noticed Lincoln hanging about in the hall outside. Then Lincoln came into the room, and told Gardiner he didn't want to be called as a witness. Gardiner told him he must appear, if called, and not to worry, to tell the truth no matter whom it might hurt, even including Captain Gardiner himself.

Wednesday, February 22, was the fifteenth day of the inquiry. General Scott announced his regret that they should have to sit on Washington's birthday, but bigger things were at stake, he felt. One of those bigger things was not Major Charles S. Merchant's birthday, which, in the court anyway, went by unobserved.

Private Isaac Sleeper, of Company D, was first up. He was one of the signatories against Captain Gardiner in the case of the biscuit theft aboard the *Kilby*. When asked by the court if Gardiner took from the public stores and hid biscuits on the *Kilby*, Sleeper replied that he did not. All he knew was that some were found down in the hold, between decks, nearly in the center of the hold, on the right hand side of the hatchway, going forward, nearly halfway from the hatchway hold to the side of the vessel and about four or five feet from the side of the ship. Sleeper himself saw nine whole biscuits and some pieces. He did not know who put them there or how they came to be there.

Colonel Gates then asked Sleeper where Captain Gardiner's bed was, and if the biscuits were found in the vicinity. Sleeper said he couldn't say where Gardiner's bed was, that Gardiner changed the place of his bed several times, "if my memory serves me right."

Privates John Murphy and Warren Adams, both of Company I, were the next witnesses, one after the other. Questioned briefly by the court, they also knew nothing of the matter, but they had heard rumors. Then Private Lilly, of Company D, was called, but General Scott was tired of this. He didn't wish to have a parade of witnesses called merely to prove rumors. Private Moses Eldridge, of Company D, was then called. Colonel Gates, seeing which way the wind was blowing, had no wish to interview him. Those were five out of the six signatories requested as witnesses by Gates, and they had all let him down. There were two more, not present—Sergeant Joe McIntyre, at that moment, was at Fort Lafayette, in New York Harbor, and, with the ice moving, communications with the shore were probably impossible. Gates had found another private, Henry Filce, of Company H, who was, as that time, absent on pass and couldn't be found.

Gates then read a letter he had just written to the court. The "bread," as he calls the crackers, had reportedly been found by the beds of Captain Gardiner and Captain Judd. This had come to Gates's attention, and he felt it deserved investigation, the same way Gardiner's charges against Gates had demanded investigation. Now Gates wanted to drop the charge against Gardiner.

But the court wanted to know what Colonel Gates expected to get out of Sergeant McIntyre and Private Filce, if and when they showed up in court. Gates expected McIntyre to prove that Gardiner gave money to Fred Lincoln, and that Gardiner ordered Lincoln away from the court room, telling him that if he needed him he would call him. Gates also expected McIntyre to verify that he was head of the 16 troops left on the *Kilby*, and that he reported to Colonel Gates the circumstances of the crackers being left under Captain Gardiner's bed. From Private Filce Gates expected to prove that Filce himself found the crackers in the place just occupied by Gardiner. Gates then exhibited Sergeant Joe McIntyre's letter of February 10, written from Fort Wood to Colonel Gates. It was a brand new piece of evidence. It read, in part: "The men that knew about the finding of the biscuit on board the *Kilby* after the officers left, are…," and then he names himself, Sleeper, Murphy, Adams, Lilly, and Eldridge. "The man who found the biscuit is our purser. Any further information you require, I can give, if required."

The court decided that Filce's testimony, merely to prove that crackers were found in the hold of the ship, and nothing more, could not be of any consequence in the inquiry, and declined to wait for an absent witness for such testimony. Indeed, even if the witness had been present, the court would have regarded such a testimony as quite useless. The court directed the judge advocate to have Sergeant McIntyre in attendance the following day, at 10 a.m.

Although Sergeant McIntyre didn't make it to the inquiry for Day 16, the affair of the crackers dragged on. All of Colonel Gates's witnesses had betrayed him in his effort to discredit Captain Gardiner, and now Sergeant Horne did the same. Gates then left the court. Lieutenant Van Voast was then recalled as a witness by Captain Gardiner. Apparently Gates had gone up to Horne at the Astor House, to see if he knew anything about the biscuit affair. Horne didn't, and told the Colonel that. Gates then told Horne that 10 or 12 biscuits had been found between Gardiner and Judd's places on the *Kilby*, and that he found Judd a very conscientious man.

The seventeenth day of the inquiry opened at eleven o'clock in the morning of Friday, February 24, 1854. The first witness called was Sergeant Joe McIntyre, of Company K, for Colonel Gates. McIntyre knew nothing of Gardiner trying to keep Lincoln from testifying, and never saw the dragoon captain giving Lincoln any money. However, the day before—February 23—a little before two o'clock, McIntyre heard Captain Gardiner tell Lincoln not to be afraid to appear before the court, but that he would not be required that day.

Captain Gardiner was then asked if he had anything to say, but he didn't, except to say that he didn't have anything to say. The court then went into secret session.

Upon return to public session, the highlight of the day's events, at least for Colonel Gates, was the reading in court by his lawyer, Captain Shields, of a written argument prepared by Gates himself. The colonel would have read it himself, but he was suffering from an indisposition. "In less than one short month, after enduring shipwreck, suffering sickness and starvation, I find myself here, not to receive the sympathy and kind offices of friends which my distressed condition calls for, but to be arraigned before this Court, charged with being the author of more direful outrages than were ever attributed to the many-headed monster Peloponnesses." Of course one feels sorry for Gates, but not sympathy. After all it was the colonel himself who pressed for such an inquiry. He goes on, in words of purple: "I am depicted as the wretch in human form who would spread a deadly contagion among his fellows, regardless of all remonstrances and appeals; as the selfish and heartless tyrant who was rioting in stately and luxurious apartments while those claiming his care were freezing in the wintry blast; as the sluggard who, in the hour of danger, when, by his neglect, hundreds were swept into the seas, and when the utmost efforts of all were needed, folded his arms and refused all advice and assistance—deaf alike to the appeals of men and to the cries and entreaties of women and children. I am further accused as the heartless tyrant who stealthily seizes the first opportunity of escape from danger, and after reaching the rescuing ship in safety, set sail and left his comrades to perish in the deep; as the gluttonous wretch who, while faring sumptuously every day, clutches the only remaining sack of corn, drags it to his cabin, and, sullenly refusing the entreaties of his starving men, invokes curses and imprecations upon their heads. Such, gentlemen, is scarcely an overdrawn picture of the crimes which my accusers have sought to establish against me. Thank Heaven they were unsustained by proof, and I sincerely believe that their unhallowed shaft will prove harmless when I recall the facts, and review the testimony before this court."

The subjects he addressed were his child's measles; the efficiency of the embarkation; his purported lack of command on the steamer during the voyage; and above all the accusation of cowardice.

The court went into secret session and then came back merely to adjourn sine die. That was it. The end of the tribunal. The testimony taken over the 17 days was sent to Washington for the correct action to be taken by the appropriate department.

Finally, on June 5, 1854, the results of the inquiry into the behavior of Colonel William Gates on board the *San Francisco* and the *Kilby* was concluded in a written report by the court, and published in the *National Intelligencer* of June 12. Basically it accused him of cowardice, by transferring onto the *Kilby* as soon as he could. Yes, the army admitted, he had had an interesting son washed overboard, but that did not seem to prevent him from being cool and active on foot. But it was his state of mind, which left him alive to the immediate wants of himself and wife and remaining children, looking for the first accidental avenue of escape. All this led him to neglect nearly every high duty imposed by his rank and circumstances. In short, he failed to go among his men to cheer and animate them. He failed to organize the men in pumping, bailing and lightening the ship. He failed to organize all the officers fit for duty. He failed to regulate the transfer of persons and supplies to the *Kilby*. He failed to organize the labor on the *Kilby* and to issue of bread and water on that vessel. He was the first to go aboard the *Kilby*, instead of running the show from the *San Francisco*. All of this led to junior officers being forced to assume this load, on both ships. He was also found guilty of taking a measles case on board, against the advice of the doctor. It was a devastating indictment of the Colonel.

On February 18, 1854, about 20 of the leading merchants in Boston threw a dinner at the Revere House, with Robert B. Forbes presiding. At Mr. Forbes's side sat the guest of honor, Commodore James Watkins, skipper of the ill-fated *San Francisco*. Next to him was the first mate, Mr. Mellus, then Captain Lang, commander of the British steamship *America*, which only two days before had brought back from Liverpool the survivors of the wreck who had been taken off by the *Antarctic* on January 5. The first thing on the agenda was a testimonial of respect made to Commodore Watkins, and then they all tucked into a magnificent repast. Speeches were made by Mr. Forbes, Captain Watkins, Father Taylor, and others.[8]

The *Three Bells* left New York on February 22 for the return to Glasgow. She got a 21-gun salute from Fort Columbus as she passed Governors Island on her way down the harbor, and arrived in Glasgow on March 10, the quickest trip ever made to that date.[9]

On March 27 an act of Congress was passed for the relief of the United States troops who had suffered in the wreck of the *San Francisco*. Each officer, non-commissioned officer, musician, and private, as well as Lieutenant Francis Key Murray of the U.S. Navy, was awarded a sum equal to the amount of his pay and allowances for 8 months. If a man had died, either in the wreck or consequent to it, then his widow or minor children got six months pay and allowances, as well as a pension just as if the man had been killed in battle.[10]

---

8. *New York Times*, Feb. 20, 1854.
9. *New York Tribune*, April 4, 1854; *New Hampshire Statesman*, April 8, 1854.
10. Army musicians fell into one of two categories. Each company had its own musicians, usually a fifer and a drummer, for basic reasons, such as marching. Others who were more musically trained, were not attached to a company; they belonged to the regiment, and played songs as a band.

The *Falcon* and the Trial of Major Wyse

On April 5, 1854, two companies, B and L, of the Third Artillery sailed out of New York Harbor in the notoriously filthy and uncomfortable *Illinois*, on the first leg of their journey to California. For the most part these were men who, until very recently had been raw recruits. They might not yet have had the opportunity to come up against the Indians in battle, but they all knew what it was like to fight for their lives. They had survived the wreck of the *San Francisco*. They were now a brotherhood. This steamship, the *Illinois*, would take them to Aspinwall, the town on the Atlantic side of the Isthmus of Panama. They would cross the isthmus by train as far as the rail went, and then continue on by mule to Panama City, where they would pick up another steamer to San Francisco.

Ten days later, Lieutenant Edward Day, who had not been on the *San Francisco*, left Fort Wood in the company of Lieutenant William A. Winder, to seek out the mail steamship *Falcon*, which had been chartered by the War Department for transporting four other companies of the Third—D, G, I, and K—down to Aspinwall, to follow Companies B and L. The rest of the regiment—Companies A and H, 180 men all told—planned to go overland to California, via the Plains a few weeks later. They would first make their way to St. Louis, and then take to horses, taking advantage of the first grass.

On the eighteenth, the *Falcon*, under the command of Lieutenant McKinstry, made ready to leave her moorings in New York Harbor. Aboard were 255 enlisted men plus Lieutenants Day and Bill Winder, Lieutenant James Van Voast, Adjutant Lieutenant Charlie Winder, Mrs. Sarah Loeser, Miss Lucia Eaton, and a few other passengers.

However, something strange happened only minutes before the men were to board the *Falcon*. Major Wyse had been ordered to command this contingent, but right at the last moment he refused to go, considering the *Falcon* unseaworthy, or at least unfit for the transportation of troops. By order of Major General Scott, he was placed under arrest at Governors Island, and the embarkation and future command of the regiment on board were left to the various lieutenants, with Lucien Loeser at their head.

Corporal John Crawford of Company D, a native of Edinburgh, had been a laborer when Major Wyse enlisted him at Boston on December 16, 1852. Immediately after the wreck he was promoted to sergeant, and now just a few months later, aged 28, he was faced with another sea voyage, on a vessel Major Wyse had deemed unfit. He pondered this. One of his privates, Dublin-born John Dooling, had transferred from Company A just before the *San Francisco* sailed, and he too gave great consideration to his upcoming voyage on the *Falcon*. Musician William Schmidt, of Company I, like Crawford and Dooling, had been posted to Fort Wood after the wreck of the *San Francisco*, and now, as they were preparing to board the *Falcon*, the three men fell into a serious discussion after which they decided that this new sea voyage was not for them. And so they lit out. However, the very next day Crawford and Dooling were caught, as Schmidt was the day after that, and the trio were sent back to Fort Wood, and thence, on April 30, to Fort Columbus, where Crawford was busted to private.

Four days out, in heavy seas off Cape Hatteras, it became apparent that the *Falcon*'s engines were quite out of order, and the following morning, Sunday, she had to put in at Old Point Comfort. They decided to turn back rather than try to press on south to Aspinwall, and, by the twenty-fifth, as they were hugging the Virginia coast on the upward route to New York, the *Falcon* was in real trouble, and put in at Norfolk, where everyone was safely landed at Fortress Monroe. On the twenty-seventh, the ship arrived back at New York, to have her machinery repaired.

That Major Wyse was absolutely right in his assessment of the *Falcon* didn't stop his court-martial from going ahead, and proceedings began at Fort Columbus, on Governors Island, in New York Harbor, on May 3, 1854. The main specific charges against Wyse were disobeying the order to lead his troops on board the *Falcon*; relinquishing his command just before the ship sailed, on the pretense that the vessel was unseaworthy, and thereby abandoning his men to a supposed danger to which he was unwilling to expose himself; and giving no time for a substitute officer to replace him The general charge was conduct unbecoming an officer and a gentleman.

The president of the general court-martial was Brigadier General Henry Stanton, the assistant quartermaster general, while Major John F. Lee, the judge advocate general of the army, was the prosecutor. Wyse had last encountered these two gentlemen at the court of inquiry in February. On May 4 the prosecution wound up its case, and witnesses for the defense were heard. Lieutenant Loeser, who had come to New York from Norfolk for the trial, was the first witness, and he testified as to the condition of the ship, and told the court that on the way down from New York the *Falcon* had had to stop twice to fix its engine. One witness said that, compared to the *Falcon*, the *San Francisco*, even in a perfect storm, was a palace. All the witnesses confirmed that the *Falcon*'s reputation among nautical men was bad.

On May 5 the *Illinois* left New York Harbor. It had been a month to the day since she had last left this port, taking Companies B and L down to Aspinwall. Now, quite unexpectedly, she found her self re-chartered by the government to take down the four companies who had failed to get there on the *Falcon*. Aboard, against their wishes, were the three men who had deserted on April 18. They had fled one ship, only to exchange it for another. Their little escapade had been an entire waste of time.[1]

On Monday, the eighth, at Major Wyse's trial, additional testimony was being taken by the prosecution in regard to the seaworthiness of the *Falcon* and the condition of her boilers and engines. Various witnesses gave evidence favorable to the judge advocate's case: One of the firm who built the vessel, the boiler maker, the engine maker, and the person who put the engine in the ship. Captain McGowan, of the steamer *Empire City*, testified to the sea-going qualities of the *Falcon*. None of these witnesses were what might be called impartial, nor were those who testified the following day: Mr. M.O. Roberts, agent, and Mr. Skidmore, engineer, both of the steamship company to which the *Falcon* belonged, and each one of them radiantly extolling the good qualities and condition of the vessel and her machinery. And impartial can hardly be the word to describe the persons who superintended the repairs of the *Illinois* prior to her ill-fated voyage of April 5, or Lieutenant Schenck, who was in the service of the company, and who had been offered, and intended to accept, the command of the ship. He believed the *Falcon*'s seagoing qualities to be excellent, or so he said. Lieutenant McKinstry, the actual commander of the ship during her latest, disastrous, voyage, gave evidence to the effect that the failure of the recent trip was wholly owing to the defect in the valves of the port engine. In every other respect, he said, she was a good vessel. Undoubtedly money had changed hands.

After hearing some additional evidence for the defense, the court adjourned the case on Thursday, the eleventh, until Monday, in order to afford the defendant, Major Wyse, time to prepare a written statement.

On Saturday night, May 13, the men who were still being lodged at Old Point Comfort boarded the *Illinois* and set sail for Aspinwall, which they reached on the seventeenth. From there they crossed the isthmus to Panama, catching the *Yankee Blade* which would take them up to San Diego.

On Monday, May 15, the trial of Major Wyse came to an end. His defense essentially consisted in the argument that every officer, whatever his rank, must not obey blindly and unreasoningly, but has the right to exercise some private judgment. The proceedings of the court were sealed up and forwarded to Washington. The upshot was that they found him guilty only of disobeying orders, dismissed him from the service, then recommended that he be taken back. His case went to President Franklin Pierce, who sent it on to Jefferson Davis, the Secretary of War, who concurred in everything, and also agreed to Wyse being taken back with a six-month suspension of command, rank, and pay. The verdict came down on June 3, along with Jeff Davis making a very big point about the safety of transport ships.

---

1. Crawford actually went out to Fort Cascades, in Washington Territory, made sergeant again, was re-enlisted by Major Wyse in 1857, transferred to the Fifth Artillery, and got out of the army at Baltimore in 1862. Dooling was 21 and a laborer when he enlisted at Philadelphia on September 24, 1853. He deserted finally on May 21, 1854. Schmidt, from Württemberg, was 24 when he enlisted at New York, four days after Dooling. He got out of the army in 1858.

On May 29, 1854, the *Yankee Blade* pulled into San Diego, where two companies were put off to join their new post, which at that point in time was commanded by Captain Henry S. Burton of Company F of the Third Artillery. For Bill Winder, in command of Company G, although he would have no way of knowing it then, this was more than just his first day in California; it was the start of a new life. For his cousin Charlie, who stayed with the ship as it left San Diego at 6:30 that evening, it was the beginning of a long, gradual process which would transform him from the genial, well-loved young lieutenant who had been one of the heroes of the wreck of the *San Francisco* into one of the most hated men in the army. Charlie arrived in the town of San Francisco on May 31.

Epilogue

This article from the *Richmond Daily Dispatch* of June 17, 1854, was titled "Old Fogies," and reads: "The evidence before the court of inquiry to inquire into the conduct of Col. Gates, on board the steamship *San Francisco*, shows the necessity of a retired list from the Army—the unofficerlike, selfish and inhuman conduct of Col. Gates can only be accounted for on the ground that he is superannuated. That the Court failed to expel him at once and ignominiously from the Army is owing, undoubtedly, to his former long and faithful services. There ought to be a retired list, with adequate pay, on which old, infirm, or imbecile officers could retire, and leave the honor and efficiency of the service in young and vigorous hands."

Gates was so upset about bad press like this, not to mention the outcome of the court of inquiry, that he called for a court-martial, a real court-martial of himself, that is, as distinct from the court of inquiry. However, the army simply put him on the shelf, pretended he wasn't there, until 1861, when he was 73, at which point he was given his first active assignment in seven years—command of Fort Trumbull. He was transferred to Fort Constitution in 1864, from which place he finally retired in 1867, after having been in the army for 66 years. He died on October 7, 1868, in New York, where his wife, Louise, died on July 24, 1895.

Of the Gates's three young children who survived the wreck of the *San Francisco*, Julius Granville Gates followed partly in his father's footsteps in that he was court-martialed and dismissed from the army in 1880. He later became a clerk in a railroad office in New Haven, Connecticut, married, and had several children. He died on February 6, 1911. His sister, Ida, married in 1885 to salesman turned bookkeeper Dunbar Paul Robertson, and lived in Manhattan. She died in Brooklyn on October 6, 1934, aged 84. As for the eldest Gates girl, Loulie, she survived the infamous Atlantic storm, but only for two years, dying of a spinal disease in Boston on July 15, 1856, two months past her ninth birthday.

If Lieutenant Colonel Martin Burke had not recovered well enough in the wake of the *San Francisco* disaster, he certainly got a boost in 1861, when he married the widow Eliza O. Perkins—enough of a boost to fight in the Civil War. He died in New York City on April 24, 1882.

Major F.O. Wyse also went on to fight in the Civil War, and retired as a lieutenant colonel, dying at Pikesville, Maryland, on January 21, 1893. His wife, Mary Eliza, died on December 26, 1925, and their daughter, Florence Eliza, the baby almost lost to the sea during the transfer to the *Kilby*, married Eugene Thomas, a salesman, in 1881, and died on June 16, 1918, in Manassas.

Major Charles Spencer Merchant survived his fall down the hatch, which is surprising given how far he dropped and that he was almost 60 years of age. He was promoted to lieutenant colonel, but that reward came at a cost, for his health suffered for many years afterwards. In 1865 he was awarded his brigadier general's brevet, and died in Carlisle, Pennsylvania, on December 6, 1879. His wife died on February 3, 1884. Their four daughters had suffered with them through the *San Francisco* disaster. Vallie married Colonel William M. Penrose in 1858, and died in 1909, aged 82. Sallie Chase married again, in 1855, at the age of 30, to Frederick H. Wolcott. Her son, Leslie Chase, also on the wreck, died in 1919, in Atlantic City. Virginia married Mr. Maben, and was buried in New York on May 4, 1920, and Lydia married George W. Bowman, and died of chronic myocarditis in Carlisle on January 18, 1927, aged 80.

Captain Judd was on sick leave for a mighty seven years after the wreck, and the opening year of the Civil War found him at Benicia Barracks in California. On November 1 of that year he was promoted to major, and 20 days later retired from active service, citing disease and exposure brought on during the line of duty. He stayed in the army, but behind the scenes, and died on July 27, 1892, at Wilmington, Delaware, aged 73. His dyspeptic wife, the former Elizabeth Cox Bonneau, of Charleston, South Carolina, died on December 10, 1899, aged 75. They had no children.

Lieutenant Fremont resigned his commission on April 5, 1854, and went to live in Smithville, North Carolina. On December 30 that year, Mary Elizabeth gave birth to their fourth child, but this joyful event was severely tempered by the death of the younger of their two daughters to survive the wreck—Mary Lawrence, who was not yet quite two years old. On July 17, 1856, the Fremonts' next daughter was born, but again tragedy struck on November 26 of that year when their eldest daughter, Ellen Mae, one of the other Fremont survivors of the wreck of the *San Francisco*, died, aged seven. In 1858 their last child was born, and they named him after Francis Murray, their Navy friend aboard the *San Francisco*. As for Fremont himself, he was superintendent of various Southern railroads, and fought for the Confederacy during the Civil War, being arrested on April 3, 1865, by his former West Point classmate, William T. Sherman. Richard Langdon Fremont, the son who had also survived the wreck in 1853, grew up and went to the University of Virginia. However, after two years there plagued by ill health, he died on July 20, 1871, aged 21. Fremont's wife died on September 28, 1885, and Colonel Fremont himself died in Memphis on May 1, 1886. As late as September 1887 the Fremont claim against the government for losses on the *San Francisco* was still going on.

Lieutenant Lucien Loeser, after serving out west and being promoted to captain, resigned from the army in 1858, and moved to Brooklyn. The Civil War brought him back into the fight, and he wound up as a colonel. His wife, the former Sarah C. Eaton, died suddenly at her home in Brooklyn on January 26, 1882, aged 56, and his sister-in-law, Lucia D. Eaton on April 16, 1896, two months short of her seventy-fifth birthday. On her tombstone in Green-Wood Cemetery, in Brooklyn, can be read the words, "He shall give his angels charge over thee," an entirely suitable epitaph for Miss Eaton. Colonel Loeser himself died on March 6, 1897, aged 79.

Come the Civil War, Lieutenant William Andrew Winder was the only member of the infamous Winder family to remain loyal to the Union, but, bearing the unfortunate name he was not considered trustworthy enough to hold a command in the field. Instead he was sent out to command the prisoner-of-war camp on Alcatraz, an irony indeed when one considers the roles his father and brother Sid would play at Andersonville later in the war. Bill Winder resigned from the army in 1866, left his wife and child, tried mining and other ventures, and settled in San Diego, eventually becoming a doctor and a well-known painter. On New Year's Day 1883, a reporter from the *San Diego Union* paid a visit on one of that city's great citizens. "We had heard Captain (now Doctor) W.A. Winder, of this city, relate some years ago his experiences in the 'wreck of the *San Francisco*,' and it occurred to us to make our old friend a New Year's call and try to induce him to 'tell the story o'er.'"

The reporter found Dr. Winder comfortably seated in his room, surrounded by a medley of medical works, oil paintings, surgical instruments, and fine engravings, which made one doubt whether he was in an artist's studio or a doctor's office; while a sabre hanging on the wall and various military books in the bookcase were calculated to further puzzle the strange visitor as to the inhabitant's profession. *"Our friend has fairly earned his diploma in each of three professional fields."*

The reporter brought the subject back to Captain Crighton, *"Yes,"* said Dr. Winder, *"That man saved my life, very near this time thirty years ago. He was a splendid fellow."*

Bill showed the reporter a tin box. This box contained a parchment roll. It was the letter of commendation from the state of Maryland, dated February 17, 1854, thanking Lt. Wm A. Winder and others for their services.

Dr. Winder's last years were spent as an Indian allocating agent at the Rosebud reservation in South Dakota, and he died of cancer of the tongue at the Millard Hotel, in Omaha, on March 6, 1903.

On April 4, 1854, not long after the wreck of the *San Francisco*, Bill's cousin, Second Lieutenant Charlie Winder became adjutant of the Third Artillery. The following day he became a first lieutenant, and on March 3, 1855, he was promoted to captain, and headed out west. He went South in 1861, and became a brigadier general. Something had happened to the genial, affable, and amiable Charlie Winder over the years since the wreck, and he was now possibly the most hated man in the Confederate Army. If he hadn't been killed at Cedar Mountain on August 9, 1862, he would probably have been shot by his own men.

Following the wreck, Lieutenant J.G. Chandler arrived at Fort Wood on February 25, 1854. He was breveted a colonel during the Civil War, and retired as a brigadier general on April 23, 1904. He died in Los Angeles on January 21, 1915.

Lieutenant James Van Voast spent much of the Civil War in San Francisco, as provost marshal of that city. He retired as a brigadier general, and died in Cincinnati on July 16, 1915. His son was in the French Foreign Legion during the First World War.

Mrs. Elizabeth R. Smith was in receipt of a regular widow's pension, her late husband, Lieutenant Richard H. Smith having been swept overboard from the *San Francisco* that fateful Christmas Eve morning in 1853. Now, a dozen years later, in early 1866, her claim for property lost in that wreck was judged in a Senate hearing. She itemized her losses: wardrobe: $150; two gold watches, $200; silver plate, $200; two carpets, $75; library, $350; china, $50; sword and epaulets, $50; wardrobe of Lieutenant Smith, $400; jewelry ornaments, articles of vertu, etc., notes (interest not included:) $750. Total: $2,468. The claim was denied.

Of the three surgeons aboard the *San Francisco*, only Dr. Satterlee would become a general. He died in his sleep in November 1880. Horace Wirtz, the assistant surgeon, crossed the Plains after leaving Fort Wood in April 1854, serving at Fort Yuma and in Washington Territory. He fought with the Union during the Civil War, joining General McClellan's staff. He rose to major in 1862, was captured by Confederate general Earl Van Dorn, and in 1865 won his lieutenant colonel's brevet. He continued in the army, and, while serving in San Francisco, died of cancer of the face on January 28, 1874, survived by his wife Carrie, who died in 1912. After the wreck, Dr. Buel, the ship's surgeon, continued to work for a year or two for the Pacific Mail Steamship Company on their steamers plying between New York and the Panama Isthmus. In 1855, backed up by a letter from Major Wyse, he claimed against the U.S. Government for medical services performed on the *San Francisco* and the *Three Bells*. The claim was referred to the Committee on Military Affairs, who awarded Buel $500. The good doctor lived for 15 years in Litchfield, Connecticut, and then became a surgeon in Brooklyn, where he died in 1888.

Corporal Lewis Smith of Company G continued on in the army, progressing steadily through the ranks, and in 1865, after the Civil War, was commissioned an officer. In 1897 he had been in the army 46 years and they made him a major. Two months later he married Agnes Ruth Lange, daughter of an old comrade in arms. He was 69. She was 20. The bride cut the cake with the major's sword. He retired in 1900 and went around the world with his new wife. In 1904 they made him a lieutenant colonel, and he died in Washington on April 22, 1907. He was buried in Arlington Cemetery.

No one could have guessed at the recruiting office that day in New York, in September 1853, that a future Medal of Honor winner had just come in the door. But, indeed, one had. Owen McGough was 25, a laborer not long in from county Monaghan. They put him in Company G of the Third Artillery. He survived the wreck of the *San Francisco*, and fought heroically at Manassas in 1861, something for which, 36 years later, the army awarded him their highest tribute. He died in Troy, New York, on January 5, 1908.

An Irishman from a good family, Stanger James Tate arrived in the U.S.A. from Dublin in September 1851. At six feet tall he looked a lot older than his 17 years. It took him no time at all to get a job as a groom in Staten Island, and no time at all to quit the job, enlisting at Newport, Rhode Island, on November 19. It took him no time at all to make sergeant in Company H of the Third Artillery. After the wreck he went to Oregon Territory, where he was discharged in 1856. He drifted down the coast and got a job with the San Francisco and Pacific Sugar Company, becoming their deputy manager in 1865. Two years later, just as he was going places in local Democratic politics, a very popular man with wife, child, and mother-in-law, he got so behind in gambling debts that he bilked his company out of $150,000. They began to close in on him, and on September 3, 1867, he rushed aboard the P.M.S.S. steamer *Great Republic* just as it was about to sail for Yokohama. Who should he meet on board but Commodore Watkins, the old skipper of the *San Francisco*, who was heading out as a passenger to Japan. From Singapore, with telegraphic dispatches catching up with him, Tate fled for Hong Kong, and then on to Manila and Batavia, bilking as he went. On January 9, 1871, he was convicted of forgery in London, and sentenced to five years in Brixton Prison. Between May and September of 1886 he served two sentences at hard labor in New South Wales, for embezzlement and stealing, and he died in Sydney in 1907.

"Lieutenant" George Washington May, the poster recruit who had once distinguished himself in Mexico, was put into Company L just before leaving New York on the *San Francisco*, and, with the Third's need to provide guidance to the new recruits, was given a temporary promotion to sergeant. After the wreck he transferred to Company G, but deserted on March 5, 1854. He surrendered himself on May 20, and was escorted to Fort Columbus, where he was confined in the stockade. He was court-martialed and discharged, on June 7, but re-enlisted on July 26, at Fort Niagara, serving as a private in Company H of the Fourth Artillery, at Fort Ontario, New York. He was discharged on November 28, 1854, with ordinary disability, and died on January 8, 1860, in New York.

Darius Klemm was born on April 3, 1824, in Pausa, Saxony, to well-off parents. Educated at Heidelberg, he learned to read and write Latin, French and Greek, as well as how to wield a sword, with which he engaged in many a duel, all of which he won. This activity did not fit in too well with the ministerial curriculum he was following, and so he was offered the usual choice. He took the point and went to college with Carl Schurz. The two young men naturally got tangled up in the revolution of 1848, and when things turned sour, they both escaped. Darius fled to the U.S.A. in 1849, became a painter and then, on Feb. 11, 1850, in New York, enlisted in the Third Artillery, becoming a private in Co H. An accomplished viola player as a teenager, he was a natural for the regimental band, and that was where he wound up. Mr. Schurz arrived in the U.S.A. in 1852, and would go on to become a great figure in American history. Darius Klemm lost partial use of his feet as a result of the *San Francisco* nightmare, but he lived, being taken to Liverpool on the *Antarctic*. Returning to Boston on the *America*, on February 16, 1854, he arrived at Fort Wood on March 10, 1854, sick, and remained there until May 1, 1854, when he transferred to Fort Columbus. On May 25 he went on leave for 20 days, to Boston, to get married to an Irish girl several years younger than himself—Ann Hartnett. He completed his five-year term in 1855, and the following year he and his wife moved to Dedham, Mass., where he bought a saloon, being the first man to sell beer in that town. In 1861 Darius, still in Dedham, built the Reunion Hotel, and died of pleurolysis, or brain disease, on Dec. 1, 1884, two weeks after his wife had died of cancer.

Upon his arrival at Fort Wood on January 20, 1854, Sergeant Joe McIntyre, sick and devastated after learning that his wife and son had died on the *Three Bells*, went into the hospital, and the following month traveled with Maj. Austine to Fort Lafayette, along with Drummer Stewart and a handful of privates who had not been on the wreck. He got out of the army on a pension certificate in 1856.

Captain Gardiner, the vicious dragoon, married on July 5, 1854. On October 26, 1861, toward the end of the first year of the Civil War, he was with the Second Cavalry when he was promoted to major, but disease and exposure forced him to go on the retired list less than three weeks later, and for the next three years he was provost marshal general in Augusta, Maine, for which service he was breveted lieutenant colonel. He died in Gardiner, Maine, on September 27, 1879.

Lieutenant Frank Murray, U.S. Navy, was promoted to commander on July 16, 1862, retired as a captain in 1867, and died on July 11, 1868, leaving a widow and son.

On January 25, 1854, Senhor Falcão, the consul, wrote a statement in Portuguese, for circulation in Brazil, that attacked the conduct of the officers aboard the *San Francisco*, saying that when ships hove to alongside the stricken steamer, the officers told him that, as the ship had been chartered by the army, citizen passengers had to take second place in the rescues. Falcão said he would never trust himself to another American ship. Well, at least he got off on the first ship, the *Kilby*, and didn't have to wait for the *Three Bells* or the *Antarctic*, an opportunity not afforded some of those officers he maligned. The ungrateful consul died in 1878, at the age of 80.[1]

On February 6, 1854, Howland & Aspinwall wrote to the Secretary of State asking for a new passport for George Woolsey Aspinwall, who had lost his old one in the wreck. Two days later the document came through, and on the ninth George left for Havana, and thence to Southampton. He didn't know it for sure, but he strongly suspected that there was another passenger traveling with him, there just to keep an eye on him, a dark, shadowy figure with whom George had an appointment in Philadelphia a few months hence. After his stay in England, George left Liverpool on the *Arctic*, but the ship ran into difficulties and had to put back to port. For a moment there, George had figured his number was up. They tried again, and George was finally able to make it back to Philadelphia, where he kept his appointment on June 19, 1854.

The Reverend Cooper was so shattered by his experience on the *San Francisco* that he was released from his church commitment, and, instead, served at various places in the U.S.A., and in the 1870s was a missionary in Mexico. He died on July 4, 1892, aged 75, in Chicago, and was buried there, at Graceland, with his wife, who had

---

1. *New York Herald*, May 14, 1854.

died four months earlier. Of the six Cooper children who survived the wreck, Ellen became a teacher in Waukegan, Illinois, but her ultimate fate is unknown, as is that of William and Isabella. Sofia married Stedman Hanks Hale in 1865, and died in Chicago on May 14, 1891, 10 days short of her forty-sixth birthday. Josefa married George Keating Dyas, and died in Los Angeles on May 21, 1927. James Warburton Cooper worked for the railroad in Chicago, married Charlotte but had no children, and died on February 5, 1912.

James Lorimer Graham, a notorious practical joker, had a joke played on him by the storm gods. His health was ruined by the wreck, and after some years as a U.S. consul in Italy, he died in Florence, on April 30, 1876, at the age of 41.

Nina Cole, the orphaned daughter of citizen passengers Howard M. Cole and his wife Louise, went to live in Philadelphia with a relative, Hannah Burnham. Soon afterwards, Mrs. Burnham was appointed a matron in the army, and went out west, taking with her the child, now known as Nina Burnham. In 1872 Nina married a riverboat captain, James A. Emmons, and they lived in the Dakotas until 1885. Emmons gave his name to Emmons County, North Dakota. The couple later moved on to Nebraska, and from there to Oklahoma, where Nina died in 1916.

Lizzie Andrews, the girl in Massachusetts who was waiting for news from her beau Ned Tenney, married in 1862 to Samuel Cook Oliver, and died in Salem, Mass., on March 15, 1922.

Fred Southworth, the inventor who had deserted his wife and family, continued on in South America, mostly Brazil, and died in Santa Clara, California on August 23, 1861. His wife, overcoming monumental hardships, went on to become the famous novelist, E.D.E.N. Southworth.

There was no snow on the streets of Spokane the day after Christmas as Badge 38 walked his beat. Not that Mike Tynan had any previous winter to compare it with in that respect, as this was his first year on the regular force, having only a few months before been a railroad flatfoot.

The old man coming toward him was confused. A dude, you could tell that by his attire, stiff white collar, tie, and black suit. The big white mustache was impressive. Mike Tynan had seen mustaches like that on old bareknuckle boys. Mike was a nice guy. He knew what it was like to be alone and uncertain in a big town, in a new country. The old man was looking for the Colman Docks. But there were no docks in Spokane. Spokane was a long way from the sea. The Colman Docks were in Seattle. Fred Sherwood he said his name was; claimed to be the mayor of Colville—the old Fort Colville, that is—upstate a bit. Only 10 days before he'd had his seventy-eighth birthday, so he said. Didn't know what the hell he was doing in Spokane. How did he get here? It was the Colman Docks he wanted. The young cop found it hard to believe some of the things the old boy was telling him. His story seemed just a bit far-fetched. Only four feet four inches tall when he'd joined the army at the age of 12, enlisted by Lieutenant Martin Burke as a drummer boy. Shot in the head at the age of 13 while fighting the Mexicans, and left for dead. His new life on the ocean wave at 17, as a ship's engineer, crisscrossing the world, and then his career as a naval attaché which came to a head on—what day is today? The twenty-sixth of December 1910? Ah, 57 years ago today he was on his way from New York to California, along with almost the entire Third Regiment of Artillery, aboard the brand new luxury steamer *San Francisco*, when suddenly he found himself fighting for his life, far out to sea, in the most demonic storm the Atlantic had ever thrown up. Hundreds of men, women and children swept off the deck by waves the size of mountains. The Third Artillery decimated. Cholera on board. The ship tossed about for two weeks at the mercy of the wind and waves, engines gone, sails gone, masts gone, all hope gone, a floating coffin. Finally other ships started to pass by, and the survivors were taken off in the *Kilby*, the *Three Bells*, and the *Antarctic*, and so young Fred got back to America. He was one of the lucky ones. No wonder Officer Tynan couldn't really swallow all this, but he humored the old man, and tried to help him. The hardest thing to believe was the story of the wreck. Surely such an incident would be famous for ever. But Mike Tynan had never heard of it.

In the July 27, 1912, edition of the *Colville Examiner*, Samuel Frederick Sherwood, former mayor of the town, received a big obituary. It seems he had died at Fort Steilacoom. In subsequent editions of the paper the Masons lamented the death of one of their brothers, and everybody in Colville was sad. However, reports of Fred's death had been exaggerated, but not greatly, for in October he finally died. This time he got a smaller obit. If Officer Mike Tynan, in Spokane, had read that obituary, and he might well have, he would have shaken his head and said, "Well, blow me down! Everything the old man told me that winter's day was true." On June 24, 1916, Officer Tynan was investigating a homicide when the suspect shot him in the back. Mike was 36.

Commodore James T. Watkins continued on as a sea-going man. In 1865 he ran the first mail steamship to China, and on September 3, 1867, he left San Francisco as a passenger on the *Great Republic*, bound for Japan. On his return trip, he left Nagasaki on November 12, 1867, as supercargo on the *Costa Rica*, and at dusk of that first day out fell to his death through an open hatch.

Mr. Mellus, the first officer, was skipper of the *Antelope* when he died of a brain fever at Foo-Chow-Foo, China on August 11, 1856.[2]

Third Officer Charles Barton later made captain and died in Boston on November 7, 1872, aged 37; "supposed die of kidneys & heart," said the death record.

John W. Marshall, the *San Francisco*'s chief engineer, died in Shanghai when the boiler exploded in the American ship *Union Star*, on June 18, 1862.

The stout chief engineer sat on the deck of the *William H. Seward*, engaged in conversation with his fellow officers while their revenue cutter found itself moored off Key West for the evening. They were, in their own "three drams" way, celebrating the ninety-ninth anniversary of the founding of the United States of America. At six o'clock, Mother Nature sent a sudden squall of rain in a vain attempt to alleviate the stinking July heat of southern Florida she herself had created, and everyone went

---

2. *Boston Daily Atlas*, Nov. 15, 1856.

below to put on flannel. Everyone, that is, except the chief engineer, who remained on deck until he was seized with a chill. The next morning he was brought to the marine hospital on shore during a light shower of rain, and at eleven o'clock on the night of July 8, 1875, Alex Auchinleck died of yellow fever. The body was embalmed, but, as the Collector of the Port at Key West told Mrs. Auchinleck in Buffalo the following day in his message, the body couldn't be moved until the colder weather came.

After the wreck, in 1854, Theo Schell became purser on the *Golden Gate*, again serving under Commodore Watkins, and in 1856 he was on the *John L. Stevens*. Just before the Civil War he quit the sea, took up residence in Sonoma, California, and became very successful as an importer of pianos. He died in December 1877.

William H. Wickham became the eighty-first Mayor of New York City, 1874–76, being chiefly responsible for the downfall of the corrupt Boss Tweed. He died in 1893, of heart disease.

Washington Duckett, the ship's carpenter, died in his home town of Philadelphia in 1891, aged 60.

Catherine Livingston, the stewardess, continued to live in Brooklyn, even after her husband died in 1869. She and her two children stayed on in the house until she died on October 19, 1877. She was buried five days later, with her husband.

In the immediate wake of the incident, Captain Edwin Low, of the *Kilby*, was so sick with an inflammation of the throat that the January 21, 1854, edition of the *Boston Daily Atlas* reported that he couldn't speak. By a few days later he was getting better, and expecting his new wife to visit from their home in Baltimore. In late December 1854 he took command of the *William and John*, and on November 20, 1855, arrived in New York from Glasgow as skipper of the new barque *Helen Mar*. In early 1857 he and his wife left New York on the *Helen Mar*, bound for Bombay, where Low was to engage in the East India trade. That fall his wife died and was buried in Penang. Two years later two of his crew brought charges, claiming that his brutal treatment of his wife was what led to her death. The American consul in Bombay tried to arrest him and have him sent back to the U.S.A., but the American Government wanted none of that. Captain Low was dead by April 1864.[3]

Seaman Robert Gibson Garthley, from Dundee, was 18 and a seaman on the *Kilby* when he encountered the wreck of the *San Francisco*. Not long after the incident, he married in Boston on October 24, 1854. He stayed at sea for years, eventually returning to Dundee, where he married again in 1875. In 1890, now a grocer, he claimed a medal for the heroics he had performed while saving, at peril of his own life, the passengers of the *San Francisco*. He died on August 15, 1902, two weeks short of his sixth-sixth birthday.

Robert Crighton, the old skipper of the *Three Bells*, continued to ply the seas as captain of various ships. About 1860 he was presented with a medal in Charleston, and six of the soldiers at the fort there were men he had saved on the *Three Bells*. In

---

3. *New York Times*, Nov. 9, 1860 and April 16, 1864.

1872 he moved to Antwerp as marine superintendent of the Red Star Line. He died there on December 17, 1882, aged 61, and that made the news.

Alexander McBeath, a crewman on the *Three Bells*, died of over exertion during the great event. Later in 1854 Captain Crighton had a whip-round for McBeath, and another crewman who had suffered a similar fate, and their families back in Scotland eventually received 17 pounds 6 shillings and sixpence.[4]

William Ewing McDougall, the passenger on the *Three Bells*, and the source of a good deal of the material for this book, was married in Brooklyn on April 9, 1855, by none other than the Rev. Henry Ward Beecher. McDougall and his wife Fanny moved out to Christchurch, New Zealand, where Mr. McDougall became a grain merchant, dying on July 17, 1903, aged 78.

George Close Stouffer continued on for years as skipper of the *Antarctic*. In 1866 he and Captain Low of the *Kilby* were recognized by the award of the Congressional Life-Saving Medal. Stouffer died on May 6, 1873, in Brooklyn, aged 51, survived by his wife, Margaret and two children.

Charles Pendleton remained master of the *Lucy Thompson* until 1862, when he retired from the sea to go into business in New York City. He died in Brooklyn on Christmas Day, 1882.

In 1855, William H. Aspinwall would be listed as one of the 19 millionaires inhabiting New York City, up there with John Jacob Astor, Commodore Vanderbilt, A.T. Stewart, the merchant prince, and—at a mere $800,000, and therefore not quite on the list—P.T. Barnum. Mr. Aspinwall was one of the founders of the American Society for the Prevention of Cruelty to Animals, in 1866, and of the Metropolitan Museum of Art, in 1869. He died on January 18, 1875.

Miers Coryell, the designer of the *San Francisco*'s engines, died in New York City of a paralytic stoke on June 5, 1902. He was 77.

William Henry Webb retired from shipbuilding at the age of 53, and died on October 30, 1899, in New York.

Colonel Swords, the quartermaster so instrumental in chartering the *San Francisco*, died a brevet major general in New York City on March 20, 1886. His boss, Thomas Sidney Jesup, died in 1860, still quartermaster general after 42 years.

General Winfield Scott was breveted a lieutenant general in 1855, and died on May 29, 1866.

There had been other vessels called the *San Francisco* before this one, and several others would bear the name in the future, but they did so at their peril. On February 8, 1854, a brand new clipper ship, out of New York, sank in San Francisco Harbor On May 16, 1877, the Pacific Mail Steamship Company, determined to overcome what looked as if it might become a jinx, saw the loss of their steamship *San Francisco* during its regular run from Panama to the city of San Francisco. Everyone was saved. On the morning of May 17, 1921, a U.S. mine-laying cruiser bearing the fateful name, bound from Boston to Newport, Rhode Island under Captain Reginald Belknap,

---

4. *Sabbath Recorder*, May 25, 1854.

grounded on Nantucket Shoals during a gale in 41° 22' N, 69° 46' W. She was released four hours later. It was thought at first that there were several fatalities, eight members of her crew in a whaleboat, but that proved to be untrue. The seven-year-old United States Steel Products Company steamer *San Francisco* left Marseille on October 4, 1921, and Lisbon on November 3, bound for New York. On November 13 she caught fire in 35° 20' N, 52° 03' W, 700 miles south of Cape Race, and 1,100 miles southeast of New York City. She finally made it into New York on November 20.[5]

---

5. *New York Times*, March 13, 1854.

Appendix:
Those Aboard the *San Francisco*

These are the people who were on the *San Francisco*, at least those whose names we know. There are three lists: the crew, the passengers, and the soldiers.

Reports indicate that there were between 100 and 150 crew members on board the *San Francisco*, probably closer to the latter figure, but as there are no lists it is impossible to be any more definite than that.

We have the names of most, if not all, of the citizen passengers, but some of them, notably a few in the Brazilian contingent, are simply unfindable, either because there is not enough to go on or because the newspaper accounts have botched their names out of all recognition.

We know all the regimental "ladies," because they were officers' wives, but only a few names of the "women" have come down to us, simply because they were the wives of enlisted men. Similarly we cannot identify many of the "laundresses," i.e., the camp followers belonging to the regiment, who were there for the use of unmarried officers and men. We know the names of even fewer children, except those of the officers.

The number of citizen passengers, added to that of the known regimental wives and children, comes to 68, but there were probably quite a lot more than that.

There seem to have been 455 Artillery men in Companies A, B, D, G, H, I, K, and L, as well as 13 bandsmen, and six non-commissioned staff, making a total of 474 enlisted men who went on board. Add to that the 17 Artillery officers and we have 491. Possibly in addition, as we shall see when we come to the end of the enlisted men section below, there were a dozen others who may well have made the trip. That might make a total of 503. All in all, then, there must have been about 750 people aboard the *San Francisco* when she sailed out of New York on December 22, 1854, just as the newspapers reported, and as Commodore Watkins estimated.

The Crew

Captain: Commodore James Thomas Watkins
1st Officer: Edward Mellus
2nd Officer: George Gretton
3rd Officer: Charles Frederick Barton
4th Officer: John Mason, Jr.
Chief Engineer: John Woolsey Marshall
First Engineers: Alexander Auchinleck, Jr., James Farnsworth
2nd Engineers: David Dunham, James Crosby
3rd Engineers: B. Donaghan, C. Hoffman
Ship's Surgeon: William Peter Buel

>Storekeeper: William Hull Wickham
>Quartermasters: Edward Osier, John Gallagher, Leonard Hooker, Kelley
>Purser: Theodore L. Schell
>Head Cook: Frederick (a Portuguese)
>Cook: John Logan
>Stewards: Charles Sanford, William Scofield
>2nd Steward: William Evans
>Steerage Steward: Levi Heath
>Stewardess: Catherine Evelina Livingston
>Head waiter: Johnson
>Waiters: Walter Heath, William Wilson, Louis Testador, Brooks, Isaiah Carter, William Fields
>Steerage Waiter: Franklin Duckett
>Firemen: Arthur Henry, Walter Watkins
>Barber: (a negro)
>Carpenter: Washington Duckett
>Seamen: Alexander, Anderson, Kelly

Mr. Marshall tells us that there were 16 seamen aboard, and that under his command as chief engineer there were about 40 assistant engineers, firemen, coal passers, etc. As Marshall says, "At one time only did the firemen desert their post, which was in consequence of the increase in water in the fire-room; they returned immediately, however, by request of Mr. Marshall."

We don't know how many waiters, stewards, etc., there were, but 26 were taken off by the *Three Bells*, and none by either of the two other ships. However, if "etc." includes cooks, then Frederick, the Portuguese cook, who got off on the *Kilby*, would make 27, and allowing for a few of the crew who died, then we must say there about 30 all told who would fall in this general category. The report that came in on the *Three Bells* on January 13, 1854, says that there were 11 deaths among the crew of the steamer from the time she was disabled up until January 8, including two who were washed overboard.

Another man must be mentioned. Amos Burgess. A colored ship's cook from Detroit, he made the news in 1879, being one of the sailors scalded when the dome of the steamer *Alaska* exploded. The next time he appeared in the papers was in 1883, following the death of Captain Crighton in Holland. A reporter from the *Detroit Free Press*, having heard that Burgess had been the chief cook on the *San Francisco* back in 1853, sought him out and interviewed him. The story ran in the January 6, 1883, edition of that paper. Yes, Burgess had been the head cook on the *San Francisco*, or at least that's what he confirmed to the reporter, and he had plenty of story to tell, including the fact there were about 860 passengers. As for biographical details, it seems he was born in Kentucky in 1829, and died in Detroit in 1900. He was married about 1849 to Sarah Monroe, and they had several children. The question is, is his story true? Nothing he tells in the newspaper interview is of such individual character that it can be offered up as friendly testimony; on the contrary, pretty much everything he recounts is a rehashing of the newspaper accounts of 1854.

The Passengers—68

We have the names of 68 passengers: Senhor and Senhora Abrio; George Woolsey Aspinwall and colored servant; Mr. Baker; Mme Alex Besse and servant; Miss Rebecca Jane Slater Belton; Miss Carter (Mrs. Gates's sister); Mrs. Sallie Chase and Leslie Chase; Mrs. Adelaide Clayton; Mrs. Margaret Coffee and daughter; Howard M. Cole and his wife, Mrs. Louise Cole;

the Rev. Mr. Cooper, his wife, and their six children; Mrs. Jane Davidson and daughter; Mrs. Ellen Delany; Miss Lucia Eaton; Antonino Jose de Miranda Falcão and servant; Mrs. Margaret Foley; Mrs. Barbara Forster; Mrs. Fremont and three children; Capt. Gardiner, 1st Dragoons, and servant; Mrs. Gates and infant; Charles Gates; A nurse for the Gates children; James Lorimer Graham, Jr.; Miss Margaret Gramon; Mrs. Catherine Higney; Mrs. Judd; Mrs. Jane Knap; Mrs. Catherine Lilly and two children; Mrs. Sarah C. Loeser; The Loesers' female servant; Mrs. Ellen McKernan and three children; Mrs. Sarah Merchant; Miss Vallie Merchant; Miss Virginia Merchant; Miss Lydia Merchant; Miss Adelaide Mulholland; Miss Eliza Mulholland; Lt. Frank Murray, U.S. Navy; Mariana Noland; William G. Rankin; Mrs. Mary Ann Sauer; Samuel Frederick Sherwood; James Stockwell; Ned Tenney.

The Artillery Officers (17)

Four were washed overboard from the *San Francisco* on Dec. 24: Maj. and Lt. Col. John M. Washington (no company), Maj. George Taylor (Co A), 1st Lt. and Capt. Horace B. Field (Co I), 1st Lt. Richard H. Smith (Co A)

Nine were saved on the *Kilby*: Col. William Gates (no company), Maj. and Bvt. Lt. Col. Charles S. Merchant (no company), Capt. and Bvt. Lt. Col. Martin Burke (Co I), Capt. Henry B. Judd (Co B and Co L), 1st Lt. Sewall L. Fremont (no company), 1st Lt. Lucien Loeser (Co K), 2nd Lt. James Van Voast (Co D), Surgeon Richard S. Satterlee, Assistant Surgeon Horace B. Wirtz

Two were saved on the *Three Bells*: Maj. F.O. Wyse (Co D), 1st Lt. William A. Winder (Co G)

Two were saved on the *Antarctic*: 2nd Lt. Charles S. Winder (Co H), Bvt. 2nd Lt. John G. Chandler (Co I)

The Enlisted Men

With the then current records of the Third Regiment of Artillery being destroyed in the wreck, the list below had to be compiled the hard way, to a great degree from newspaper reports of the day, Army enlistment records, and Army post returns. In addition, we have the manifest of the *America* upon coming into New York from Liverpool on February 16, 1854, listing those who had been taken off by the *Antarctic* minus, of course, those who had died aboard that vessel and those who had deserted in Liverpool. All these sources had to be painstakingly examined and understood, then compared, one with the other.

Almost as soon as the first survivors were landed in New York from the *Three Bells* on January 14, 1854, the company sergeants gave the press boys a "Correct list of the names of the U.S. troops lost and saved." The *New York Tribune* published this list on Page 5 of their January 16, 1854, edition, and beneath it "A muster roll of the companies of the Third Artillery, taken at Bedloc's." This muster roll is basically what Major Wyse used when he sent in his report to the government on January 14, and, as far as can be ascertained, this is the only such muster roll ever officially published. The most useful newspaper list is probably that published in the *New York Semi-Weekly Courier and Inquirer* of January 16, 1854.

A difficulty with this list, and others like it, is that the spellings as published are often so wrong that many men are, at first glance, unrecognizable. It is only by using imagination, logic, and the process of elimination that a researcher can deduce who is meant. But it can be done, and it was, using the Army post returns and, especially, the enlistment records as a control. However, these lists were not as "correct" as the newspapers claimed. For one thing, the men who promulgated them, the company sergeants now safe in New York, could not possibly take into account the fate of the passengers aboard the *Antarctic*, which, even as the lists were being published was making her way to Liverpool. But there are other difficulties with this list, much more serious.

A problem, rather than a difficulty, and again one that has been almost completely overcome, is the fact that the only muster rolls the sergeants had were out of date. Many men on those rolls had, for one reason or another—desertion, sickness, transfer—not left New York on the *San Francisco* at all, and so some of the lists are drastically out of keeping with reality, not just in names but in numbers.

On January 18, 1854, the *National Intelligencer* in Washington published its list of those known to have perished in the wreck of the *San Francisco*. For the most part the list is accurate, spelling mistakes notwithstanding, but there were two types of error that must have caused unnecessary anguish for relatives when they read the paper. The first is that the list claims several men as dead when, in fact, they got off on the *Antarctic* and survived. The other is that using the out-of-date regimental rolls given them by the sergeants, the *National Intelligencer* also compiled a list of those men not accounted for, but feared dead, including, they reckoned, 15 or 20 who, at the moment the ship sailed, were detached on account of illness. "Most of these have no doubt perished." Today this would be considered irresponsible journalism, but the reporters were men in a hurry to get to print. Another thing that makes the researcher's work difficult is that, while names on the list are attached to companies, sometimes the wrong company is given. Therefore, with all this, the list and the roll cannot be taken seriously, except in the case of Companies A, D, H, and I, which are all absolutely accurate. Companies G and K are slightly off in certain regards, and, as for the two companies of recruits, B and L, they are hopelessly at sea.

Company A (54)

Three privates died of cholera on the *San Francisco*:
Dec. 29. Karchen Schank
Jan. 3. Zebediah P. Knapp, Abraham Workman

Five died of cholera on the *Three Bells*:
Jan. 6. Pvt. Francis Miles
Jan. 7. Corp. William Bennett, Pvt. George W. Park, Pvt. Clark Wallace
Jan. 9. Pvt. Johan Miller

Six died of cholera on the *Antarctic*:
Jan. 7. Sgt. Edward Jakel
Jan. 8. Pvt. Henry McCann, Pvt. Anton Goebler
Jan. 10. Pvt. Patrick Ward
Jan. 14. Pvt. Michael Burke
Jan. 16. Pvt. Alvin Aleshire

Two were saved on the *Kilby*:
Corp. Charles Reidt
Pvt. Patrick Molloy

Eighteen were saved on the *Three Bells*: First Sgt. Joseph Clay, Artificer Richard Whitehead, Drummer Charles Sanders, and the following privates: Charles Bayer, William Lock Bennett, Samuel Cunningham, Charles Dulkiewitz, George H. Emerson, John Hary, George Hermann, John Hyland, Peter King, John Lecount, John Mack, William G. Mills, Theodor G. Rost, John Sullivan, Walter W. Wyatt.

Twenty were saved on the *Antarctic*: Sgt. Ross McIntyre, Sgt. Thomas L. Young, Corp. Thomas Hoare, Corp. Michael McNamara, and the following privates: John Bergin, William E. Briggs, John Brown (deserted at Liverpool), Lawrence Carroll, Georg Kleinlein, James Cooper (deserted at Liverpool), Benjamin Hughes, George Hughes, Samuel S. Johnson, William T. Johnson, William Power (deserted at Liverpool), Patrick Savage, Hiram Tuttle, John Walsh, John Walsh [*sic*], Pvt. Welsh

COMPANY D (56)

One private was washed overboard from the *San Francisco* on Dec. 24: David Sullivan
Six privates died of cholera on the *San Francisco*:
  Dec. 30. John T. Salmon
  Dec. 31. John Downing
  Jan. 1. Joseph Trumper
  Jan. 2. Patrick Graham
  Jan. 3. Edward Higney
  Jan. 4. Stephen Spillane

Three died of cholera on the *Antarctic*:
  Jan. 7. Pvt. Fenton Delany
  Jan. 12. Artificer Francis N. Rimal
  Jan. 17. Pvt. Martin Fox

Nine privates were saved on the *Kilby*: William P. Belton, Patrick Costello, John Dooling, Moses S. Eldridge, Henry Hart, Patrick Lilly, Anthony Millar, Isaac N. Sleeper, John Wiseman

Twenty-five were saved on the *Three Bells*: Sgt. George W. Duncan, Sgt. William Harpur, Sgt. John Meehan, Corp. John Crawford, Corp. John B. Dailey, Corp. Elias Sprague Trask, and the following privates: Hugh Bart, Oliver H.P. Cross, John Dulling, Paul Duncan, Henry Fisher, James A. Gardner, Michael Healy, Nicholas Higgins, Hubert Kirwen, Lorenzo McBride, Henry Marshall, Henry Moore, Timothy Murphy, Daniel O'Connor, Henry O'Hara, Joseph Power, Louis Pulfermuller, Albert S. Rice, James W. Twaddel

Twelve were saved on the *Antarctic*: First Sgt. George Hogg McLoughlin, Sgt. Thomas Dwyer, Musician John A. Feig, Artificer Miles Coffey, and the following privates: James Best, Thomas Bulger, Patrick Foley, Albert Hooper (deserted at Liverpool), Charles Miller, Hough O'Neil, William Pfeifer, Robert Stevens

COMPANY G (57)

One private was washed overboard from the *San Francisco* on Dec. 23: Charles Heinrich
Six were washed overboard from the *San Francisco* on Dec. 24: Drummer John Smith, and the following privates: Jacob Bossart, Henry Hillan, John H. Phillips, Henry Smith, George W. Wallace
  Five died of cholera aboard the *San Francisco*:
    Dec. 29. Corp. James Smith, Pvt. Charles Campbell, Pvt. John Greenway
    Jan. 1. Artificer John Donnelly
    Jan. 2. Fifer Leonard Karg

  Four died of cholera on the *Three Bells*:
    Jan. 4. Pvt. Carl Meir
    Jan. 5. Corp. John P. Fisher, Pvt. Richard Walsh
    Jan. 6. Pvt. William H. Davis

Two privates died of cholera on the *Antarctic*:
  Jan. 5. Frederick Aberle
  Jan. 8. Joseph D. Sawyer

Three were saved on the *Kilby*: Corp. Lewis Smith, Pvt. William Gleeson, Pvt. Daniel Sullivan

Thirteen were saved on the *Three Bells*: 1st Sgt. Elijah R. Brown, Corp. Alfred McDonald, and the following privates: James Brennan, Thomas Hogan, John Henry Kobbe, Owen McGough, James Moore, Robert Nixon, James Sinnot, Henry Sippel, Michael Smith, John Tampleton, Anton Zinglar

Twenty-three were saved on the *Antarctic*: Sgt. Emery W. Sawyer, Sgt. Joseph Summers, Sgt. George Swan, Musician Alexander Berkler, and the following privates: Archibald Martin Dallas, William Dinsmoor, George Furst, John Haverty (deserted at Liverpool), Charles Herzog, Christian Kramer, Hugh James McEvoy, Michael Moloney, Henry Moses, Louis Muhlemann, James Murphy, John Myer, John Phelps, John W. Pope, Jacob S. Roof, William Sallmann, Philip Shirrer, Charles H. Sweeney, Thomas Turner

Company H (52)

Seven were washed overboard from the *San Francisco* on Dec. 24: Musician Richard Connoly, and the following privates: William Cameron, Marcus Clanton, John W. Denny, Charles Gerk, Patrick Malady, Thomas Moran

Five died of cholera on the *San Francisco*:
  Dec. 27. Sgt. Richard Hopley
  Dec. 28. Pvt. Edward P. Ballard
  Dec. 29. Pvt. Michael Rogan
  Dec. 30. Pvt. Dennis Healy
  January. Pvt. James Henry

One private died of cholera on the *Three Bells* in January, probably Jan. 6: Richard Coghlan

Two privates died of cholera on the *Antarctic*:
  Jan. 4. Ernst Northman
  Jan. 8. Jean Florentine

Two were saved on the *Kilby*: Corp. Charles Frederick Taylor, Pvt. Henry Filce

Twelve were saved on the *Three Bells*: Sgt. Samuel Bennett, Musician Joseph H. Ricketson, and the following privates: Charles E. Bowling, Patrick Clark, Jacob Adam Dubach, Philipp E. Eggley, Frederick Krueger, John Martin, John Molony, Joseph Mooney, John Tracy, John Wilson

Twenty-three were saved on the *Antarctic*: Sgt. Stanger James Tate, Corp. Theodor Augustin Blanckhardt, Corp. William B. Devere, Corp. Edward Eylsom, and the following privates: David Adams, Joseph Broswell, Karl Duerr, Robert Wilson Dunn, George Haug, Joseph Higgins, Joseph Kelly, Herman Kirsch, George Mack, Cormac McCarty, James McDonald (deserted at Liverpool), Michael McLoughlin, James Nowlen, David Saxton (deserted at Liverpool), William Steinert, Christian Friedrich Uhrback, John Werssal, James Wharton, Samuel Zolnay

Company I (46)

One private died of cholera on the *San Francisco*, on Jan. 3: Henry Drechsel
One private died of cholera on the *Three Bells*, on Jan. 6: Adolphus Haage

Two privates died of cholera on the *Antarctic*:
Jan. 5. Adolph Ehrhard
Jan. 7. August Winter

Twenty-nine were saved on the *Kilby*: Sgt. James McKinley, Corp. George R. Proudfoot, Musician John Costello, Musician Louis Blumenreich, Artificer Robert John Boylan, and the following privates: Warren Adams, Johan Bauer, Patrick Buckley, John Cavaugh, James Collins, Condy Conneghan, John Corry, John L. Dwyer, John Glassel, Michael Kelleher, William Kelley, William H. Kelly, John Knowles, John Lund, Simon McGill, John Murphy, Edward O'Hara, James Oliver, Robert Redmayne, Alp Reiners, William Walsh, William Watson, Dennis Whelan, Horatio Winship

Twelve were saved on the *Three Bells*: First Sgt. Reuben Twist, Sgt. Daniel Casey, Corp. Michael Murphy, Musician William Schmidt, and the following privates: John Bennis, James Cruise, Thomas Dunn, Julius Fromme, John Kemp, Carl Schmitz, William Smith, Anthony Van Sanford

One private was saved on the *Antarctic*: John Ahearn

Company K (55)

Twenty-eight were washed overboard from the *San Francisco* on Dec. 24, 1853: Corp. William Lee, Corp. Elbridge Gerry Ingham, Corp. Adolph H. Meincke, Lance Corp. William Graham, Artificer James Carter, Fifer Edmund Gardner, and the following privates: Charles F. Bond, Richard Carland, Anthony Fleck, James Galligan, Patrick Gordon, Antoine Gross, Charles Heinicke, Harvey Royce Heller, James Hillock, James Keiley, Michael Kennedy, Thomas Kernen, John McLane, Thomas McManus, Thomas McNamara, John Mitchell, Peter Murray, Seth Rowland, Joseph Schurmann, Patrick Sheehan, Fred Smidt, Philip Ward. Note: Several newspapers had two John McLanes dying, and list them as John McLane (1) and John McLane (2). However, only one of them died. There was indeed another John McLane, and, oddly, he was also in Co K, but he deserted before the *San Francisco* sailed.

One private died of cholera aboard the *San Francisco*, in the first week of January: Dietrich Brauer

One private died of cholera aboard the *Three Bells*, on Jan. 7: Frederick Heine

Two were saved on the *Kilby*: Sgt. Joseph S. McIntyre, Pvt. Samuel S. Thompson

Twelve were saved on the *Three Bells*: 1st Sgt. James McKenzie, Drummer Robert Stewart, and the following privates: William Dowling, Herman Funk, Jacob Girnar, Joseph Mit, Gottlieb Ott, Henry Rumpel, Franz M. Stautenmeir, Amos R. Thomas, William Turner, John Whalen

Eleven were saved on the *Antarctic*: Corp. William Clayton, Lance Corp. John Brenan, Musician James Fox, and the following privates: Carl Christiansen, Oscar C. Gartig, John Gloker, John Mines, Wilhelm Friedrich Mutschler, John Quirk, Charles Simon, James Smith

Company B (84)

Twenty-one were washed overboard from the *San Francisco* on Dec. 23: Sgt. John Scheerer, Corp. William Meyers, Corp. Henry Myer, and the following recruits: Charles Engel, Heinrich Engelbach, William S. Graeff, Frank Griffith, Alexander Hart, Peabody Herkimer, James Knowlton, Abraham Lawrence, Patrick Lynn, Michael McAllister, Lawrence MacAuliffe, Peter McGuire, William McLaughlin, Carl Meyn, Abraham Moore, Christopher Poman, Conrad Steinman, James Wallace

Fourteen recruits were washed overboard from the *San Francisco* on Dec. 24: Levi H.

Bentz, Wilhelm Buchholz, George Calbe, Frederic B. Clifford, Thomas D. Cooper, Jacob Falleegger, John Fried, Charles Mayer, Constantine Schweitzer, Gebhard Shmit, Henry Shultz, John Smith, John Wendt, Charles White

Eleven recruits died of cholera on the *San Francisco*:
  Jan. 2. John Button
  Jan. 4. Charles Rooney
  January. William Fauerback, John H. Koedecke
  Date unknown. David Brindle, John Haag, Hugh McLaughlin, Martin Mixel, Michael Morgan, Christian Peters, Andrew J. Powell

Two recruits died of cholera on the *Antarctic*:
  Jan. 7. Theodore Shirley
  Jan. 11. Leonard Boody

Fifteen were saved on the *Three Bells*: Sgt. Charles Frederick Otto Skobel, and the following recruits: Thomas Doran, Granville D. Frost (real name: Joseph Woodbury Frost), William Gerry, Denis Leonard, Reuben Libby, William McBride, Thomas Matthews, Frederick Merkel, James Murray, Solomon Ridenour, Frederick Schnell, Charles H. Shuter, John Friedrich Ludwig Upmann, John Wright

Twenty-one recruits were saved on the *Antarctic*: Francis Burke (deserted at Liverpool), John Cashman, Joseph Clyde, John Denis (deserted at Liverpool), Jonathan English, Michael Geoghegan, James Hartney, Washington Kain (deserted at Liverpool), Michael Kelly (deserted at Liverpool), William Krause, Henry Laux, Richard Lilley, John Loyd, Timothy O'Connors, Thomas Patchel, John Paul, James Ramsay, Charles Stevens, John J. Stone, William Wallace (deserted at Liverpool), Patrick White

Company L (51)

Five recruits were washed overboard from the *San Francisco* on Dec. 23: William Ballard, James Cord, William A. Dillingham, George Walsh, Wesley S. Day

Three died of unknown causes on the *San Francisco*:
  Dec. 25, 1853. Corp. Michael Welsh
  Date unknown. Recruit Barny Clancy
  Date unknown. Recruit John Diehl

Two recruits died of cholera on the *Three Bells* in January: James Currie, Joseph Sullenberger

Two died of cholera on the *Antarctic*:
  Jan. 5. Corp. William Morris
  Jan. 7. Recruit Dennis Corbett

Fourteen were saved on the *Three Bells*: Sgt. William King, Sgt. David Oppenheimer, Corp. Patrick Coffy, and the following recruits: Charles Boyle, John Brady, Peter F. Gebhardt, Drew Goodridge, John Hill, Michael Kane, John Lee, Morgan McElligott, Francis R. Page, Benjamin F. Parsons, Charles Strauss

Twenty-five were saved on the *Antarctic*: Sgt. George Washington May, Corp. John S. Zimmer, and the following recruits: Robert Allen (deserted at Liverpool), Patrick Brennan, John Bridgeman, John Carey, William J. Clark, Stephen Conway, Louis Darque, John Deacon, Denis Driscoll, John Dunn (deserted at Liverpool), John Franks, James Gilgon, Richard Gilmore, James Hannelly, Lewis Jackson, John McKernan, John Malone, Michael Reedy, Ferdinand Rettelbusch, John Rush (deserted at Liverpool, but apprehended there), Fatlin Saib, Budolph Smidt, Karles A. Zoeller

THE REGIMENTAL BAND (13)

Two privates died of cholera on the *San Francisco*:
 Jan. 1. Ezekiel Mulholland
 Jan. 4. Thomas Mulholland

One private died of cholera on the *Three Bells* on Jan. 4: Joseph Jacob Foerster
Five were saved on the *Three Bells*: Corp. Joseph N. Horne, Corp. Johann F.P. Jensen, Corp. Francis Peter Sauer, Pvt. Damian Geyer, Pvt. John Getz
 Five were saved on the *Antarctic*:
 Pvt. John Hildel
 Pvt. Friedrich Darius Klemm
 Pvt. Carl Marschal
 Pvt. Jacob Sauer
 Pvt. John Serreier

NON-COMMISSIONED STAFF (6)

Two were taken off by the *Antarctic*: William R. Gorham (sergeant major of the command), James Mulholland
Four, all music boys of the 4th Infantry aged between 12 and 17, died aboard the *San Francisco* in late December 1853, of causes unknown, but almost certainly the big wave of Christmas Eve: Robert Crane, Joseph Black, James McCormick, George Bruse

A FEW OTHER POSSIBLES

There are also a dozen names about which one can't be sure. However, what is almost certain is that not one of these men was rescued by the *Kilby* or the *Antarctic*, and so, if they did indeed go on the trip, they were picked up by the *Three Bells*: Louis Beck (Co B), George W. Elliott (General Service), James Ennis (Co A), John McNeil (Musician, Co I), Michael Malahy (Company unknown), Robert B. Morse (Co H), George D. Paul (Co I), Mathew Quigley (Co B), Jacob Reik (Co B), Charles Reilach (Co B), James Shea (General Service), Timothy Sheehan (Co K)

A Note on Sources

The *San Francisco* was wrecked on the morning of Christmas Eve, 1853. On Christmas Day she spoke the *Napoleon*, and on the 26th the *Maria*, but, given the state of the wind and the waves, neither vessel was in a position to take off survivors. On the 28th the *Kilby*, herself in bad shape after having barely survived the same storm, rescued over 100 from the stricken steamer, and headed for Boston.

On January 4 and 5, 1854, the rest of the survivors on the *San Francisco* were taken off by two separate ships—the *Three Bells*, which was on her way to New York, and the *Antarctic*, which was going the other way, to Liverpool, in England. On January 4 the *Maria* arrived at Liverpool, Nova Scotia, bringing with her the first news of the wreck. The captain of the *Maria* immediately sent a dispatch to the American consul at Halifax. The following morning, January 5, the dispatch was sent on to Washington, D.C., and appeared in the *New York Times* of January 6. On January 7 the *Napoleon* arrived at Boston, and that morning the skipper and first mate gave their account in person to a reporter, who at midday sent his dispatch by telegraph to his home paper in Washington, D.C., the *Evening Star*. Thus began several weeks of newspaper headlines.

It wasn't until the thirteenth of January, 1854, that the first group of survivors made it back to New York, on board the *Three Bells*. As for those on the *Kilby*, most were transferred to the *Lucy Thompson* while still out at sea, the *Lucy Thompson* arriving at New York on January 14. The *Kilby* herself finally pulled into Boston on the 17th; and the *Antarctic* arrived at Liverpool on January 23. Several rescued persons on each vessel had stories to tell the press.

These eyewitnesses—soldiers, crew members, citizen passengers—were relying on memory, or, in some cases, notes or journals they claim to have kept during the incident. They were men and women who had been under tremendous stress for a long period of time, a condition that notoriously lends itself to inaccurate observation and, especially, recollection, so, for the details of the wreck and the sequence of events, several of them were forced to use the ship's log to be guided by when it came time to talk to reporters. The most notable of these cases were Mr. Mellus, the first officer; Mr. Wickham, the ship's storekeeper; Mr. Marshall, the chief engineer; and Mr. Gretton, the second officer—all of whom relied heavily on the *San Francisco*'s log, and to some extent on that of the *Three Bells*. In a story like this, if there is any type of source that can be regarded as closest to the truth, then it must be a ship's log, as presumably a log is written up on a daily basis or thereabouts by a responsible ship's officer. That is not to say that a log is infallible, but surely, of all the sources, it has to be the most trusted.

Another factor one must take into account, notably when studying newspaper articles, is that the reporters were sending their items to their editors from the very first moment that news of the wreck reached the North American coast. Much of the early coverage was therefore sketchy and ill-informed, but as the days went by fuller and better accounts were presented to the public. One will see, in those press reports, quite a bit of variation in the story, not the least being dates.

There are other sources which give us a good idea of what happened out there in the Atlantic during those fateful days in December 1853 and January 1854, perhaps the most important of these being the minutes of the court of inquiry that was held by the government in February 1854 to look into the tragedy. The major New York newspapers of the day offered what seems to be a faithful transcript of each day's proceedings at the inquiry, to which were called many of the players in the tragedy. These are the dates that the court sat (*New York Times* coverage came the day after):

Day 1	(Feb. 6)
Day 2	(Feb. 7)
Day 3	(Feb. 8)
Day 4	(Feb. 9)
Day 5	(Feb. 10)
Day 6	(Feb. 11)
Day 7	(Feb. 13)
Day 8	(Feb.14)
Day 9	(Feb. 15)
Day 10	(Feb. 16)
Day 11	(Feb. 17)
Day 12	(Feb. 18)
Day 13	(Feb. 20)
Day 14	(Feb. 21)
Day 15	(Feb. 22)
Day 16	(Feb. 23)
Day 17	(Feb. 24)

References

Following is an explanation of the abbreviated references to be found in the footnotes throughout the book. In a real sense it is also the bibliography.

Army enlistment records. Actually called U.S. Army, Register of Enlistments, 1798–1914. Record Group 94, NARA.
Army post returns. Actually called U.S., Returns from Military Posts, 1806–1916. Record Group 94, NARA.
Artizan. Vol. 8, 1850, p. 173. The *Artizan* was a monthly journal of the operative arts, published in London.
Aspinwall: After he had been landed safely in the U.S.A., George Woolsey Aspinwall, then ill and staying with his brother, W.H. Aspinwall, made a report which, through his brother, was published in the *New York Times* of Jan. 16, 1854.
Auchinleck: Engineer Auchinleck's statement, *New York Times*, Jan. 16, 1854.
Brown account: Sgt. Elijah Brown, *New York Tribune*, Jan. 16, 1854, and *New York Times*, Jan. 16, 1854.
Brown testimony: Sgt. Elijah Brown, court of inquiry, Feb. 16, 1854.
Buel, 1854: Dr. Buel wrote an anonymous account of the voyage, as a letter to the editor of the *New York Herald*, and it was published in that paper on Jan. 14, 1854, as "Statement by one of the Passengers." It was reproduced in the *New York Times* of Jan. 16, 1854.
Buel, 1872: A re-working by Dr. Buel of his anonymous 1854 account, it was published as a letter to the *New York Post*, published on Sept. 10, 1872. In this article, Buel claims that he wrote a journal as the accident unfolded, but the truth is, if he did write a journal at all, it was on the *Three Bells* after the accident, as he headed back to New York.
Buel testimony: Dr. Buel, court of inquiry, Feb. 9, 1854.
Buel, *American Journal*: Dr. Buel article, *American Journal of the Medical Sciences*, April 1854.
Burnside: Thomas Burnside's account, *New York Tribune*, Jan. 16, 1854. It is based on Mr. McDougall's "diary."
Cooper: Adjutant General Samuel Cooper's testimony, court of inquiry, Feb. 7, 1854.
E.H. Pendleton: *Brian Pendleton and his Descendants*, compiled by Everett Hall Pendleton, and privately printed in 1910.
Eaton: Lucia Eaton's Narrative [see below].
"Engineer": On Monday, Jan. 23, 1854, a letter, recalling the letter by "Justice" of the Thursday just passed, appeared in the *New York Times* from an anonymous man calling himself "Engineer."
Franklin Institute: This is an article in the *Journal of the Franklin Institute of the State of Pennsylvania for the Promotion of the Mechanical Arts* [Philadelphia, Franklin Institute, 1854, vol. 57, pp. 108–113].
Freeman: On Jan. 4, 1854, when the *Maria* pulled into Liverpool, Nova Scotia, Captain Freeman telegraphed to Halifax about the wreck. From Halifax it was sent on to Washington, and published in the *New York Times* of Jan. 9, 1854. Freeman wrote an addendum to his telegraph on Jan. 7, and it went to Washington the same way. This addendum took the form of a report, and was published in the same edition of the *Times*.
Fremont: Lt. Fremont's testimony, court of inquiry, Feb. 7, 8, 9, 16, and 17, 1854.
Fremont letter: On January 19, 1854, Lt. Fremont wrote a letter to the *New York Times*. It was published the following day. It concerned the order of leaving the doomed *San Francisco* to board the *Kilby*.ardiner: Capt. Gardiner's testimony, court of inquiry, Feb. 11, 13, and 16, 1854.

Gates account: Colonel Gates, *New York Times*, Jan. 16, 1854.
Gates testimony: Colonel Gates, court of inquiry, Feb. 16 and 24, 1854.
Mrs. Gates: The colonel's wife's account, *New York Times*, Jan. 16, 1854.
Gorham: Sgt. Maj. Gorham's testimony, court of inquiry, Feb. 20, 1854.
Graham: On Jan. 15, 1854, James Lorimer Graham, Jr., wrote a lengthy anonymous account of his adventures on the *San Francisco* and the *Kilby*. It appeared the next day in the *New York Times* as "Interesting statement of a passenger."
Graham/Kilby: There was an anonymous account called "Statement of a passenger saved in the bark *Kilby*," written to the editor of the *New York Tribune*, and published in the Jan. 16, 1854, edition of that paper. It does not seem to have been reproduced by either the *Herald* or the *Times*. It was actually written by James Lorimer Graham.
Gretton: Second Officer Gretton's account is discussed in detail in the opening paragraphs of the second part of this book—"Ship's Log."
Hawthorne: Nathaniel Hawthorne, U.S. consul at Liverpool, wrote a letter on Feb. 3, 1854, to the State Department, giving a summary of his contact with the *Antarctic*.
Hawthorne to Ticknor. A letter written by U.S. consul Nathaniel Hawthorne to William D. Ticknor, March 30, 1854.
Horne: Corp. Joseph Horne's testimony, court of inquiry, Feb. 17 and 23, 1854.
Huston: Statement of E.D. Huston, chief mate of the *Lucy Thompson*. As soon as the ship arrived at her pier, one of the *New York Times* reporters went on board and interviewed Huston. This interview appeared in the *Times* of Jan. 16, 1854.
Judd: Capt. Judd's testimony, court of inquiry, Feb. 10 and 11, 1854.
"Justice": Letter, *New York Times*, Jan. 19, 1854.
Livingston: Catherine Livingston's account, *New York Tribune*, Jan. 16, 1854.
Loeser: Lt. Lucien Loeser's testimony, court of inquiry, Feb. 16 and 17, 1854.
McCarty: Mr. McCarty, the first mate of the *Napoleon*, gave a report of the incident when he landed at Boston on Jan. 7, 1854. This account was published in the *New York Times* of Jan. 18, 1854.
McDougall: Statement of W.E. McDougall, a passenger on the *Three Bells*, published in the *New York Tribune* of Jan. 16, 1854, in diary form. He claimed he kept a journal.
McIntyre: Sgt. Joe McIntyre's testimony, court of inquiry, Feb. 16 and 24, 1854.
Marshall, Jan. 14, 1854: An anonymous article that appeared in the *New York Herald* of that date, and headed "Statement by one of the crew." It was reproduced in the *New York Times* of Jan. 16, 1854. It was actually written by Chief Engineer Marshall.
Marshall, Jan. 16, 1854: Chief Engineer Marshall's account, *New York Tribune*, Jan. 16, 1854. This is actually a narrative compiled by the *Tribune* reporter after hearing Mr. Marshall's statement. To some extent the account is based on the ship's log.
Maury: Matthew Fontaine Maury's book, *Physical Geography of the Sea*. New York: Harper & Bros., 1858.
Mellus account: 1st Officer Mellus, *New York Herald*, Jan. 14, 1854. This is in the form of extracts from the ship's log.
Mellus testimony: Mr. Mellus, court of inquiry, Feb. 14, 1854.
Merchant: Colonel Merchant's testimony, court of inquiry, Feb. 15, 1854.
Murray: Lt. Frank Murray's testimony, court of inquiry, Feb. 10, 1854.
New York Tribune, Jan. 23, 1854: "The Engines of the San Francisco," article written by the staff of the newspaper.
New York Tribune, April 4, 1854: Letter from a passenger who was on the return trip of the *Three Bells* to Glasgow after the accident.
Orders to Gates. Sept. 30, 1853, as per Report of the Secretary of War (see below).
Partridge: "Wreck of San Francisco," an article by W.E. Partridge, which appeared in the magazine, *The Rudder* Jan.-June 1909. New York: Rudder Publishing Co.
Pendleton: The testimony of Captain Charles Babbitt Pendleton, of the ship *Lucy Thompson*, was heard before the court of inquiry on February 15, 1854. He was called by Colonel Gates as a friendly witness.
Presbyterian Magazine: The article "Loss of the steamer San Francisco," March 1854, pp. 128–134.
Report of the Secretary of War, January 26, 1854: This includes all authentic correspondence held by the War Department up to that date, concerning the *San Francisco*, as well as relevant documents and letters from the Navy and Treasury Departments.
Satterlee: Dr. Satterlee's statement, *New York Times*, Jan. 16, 1854.

Satterlee testimony: Dr. Satterlee, court of inquiry, Feb. 10 and 17, 1854.
Shock: William H. Shock, Inspector General of the U.S. Navy, testified on Feb. 20, 1854, at the court of inquiry.
Smith: Corp. Lewis Smith's testimony, court of inquiry, Feb. 20, 1854.
Southworth: On Jan. 8, 1854, after having been rescued by the *Kilby*, passenger Fred Southworth wrote an account of the voyage. This was published in the *New York Tribune* of Jan. 16, 1854, in the *New York Times* of the same day, and then again in the *New York Herald*, January 21, 1854. In the *Herald* of Jan. 16 appeared a correction to certain facts, written by Southworth the day before.
Stackpole: The notes made by Edouard Stackpole as an adjunct to his transcription of Lucia Eaton's narrative.
Stouffer: Captain Stouffer, of the *Antarctic*, was interviewed in Liverpool by a London *Standard* correspondent, and the results appeared in the Jan. 25, 1854, edition of that paper.
Strout: Captain Strout, the *Napoleon*'s skipper, made a statement when he landed at Boston on Jan. 7, 1854. That statement appeared first in the *Portland Advertiser*, and was copied in the *New York Times* of Jan. 23, 1854.
Taylor: Corp. Charles F. Taylor's testimony, court of inquiry, Feb. 16, 1854.
Three Bells log: Our information from this log comes from Buel's 1872 article.
Tredgold: Thomas Tredgold, *The Steam Engine*, London, John Weale, 1838.
Van Voast: Lt. Van Voast's testimony, court of inquiry, Feb. 11, 15, 17, and 23, 1854.
Watkins dinner: Watkins gave a speech at a dinner in Boston in February 1854, and it was reported by the *New York Times* of Feb. 20, 1854, and by the Washington *Daily National Intelligencer* of Feb. 25, 1854.
Watkins testimony: Commodore Watkins, court of inquiry, Feb. 21, 1854.
Wickham: William Wickham's account published on Jan. 14, 1854, in the *New York Herald*, *New York Times*, and *New York Tribune*. Like Mr. Mellus's account, it consists of extracts from the ship's log, but is much more extensive than Mellus's, and therefore, of greater value, which is why the *Times* and the *Tribune* chose his account to reproduce, rather than that of Mr. Mellus.
Winder, Jan. 6, 1854: The first part of Lt. William Winder's account, "Ship *Three Bells*, At Sea, Friday, Jan. 6, 1854," was published in the *New York Times* of Jan. 14, 1854, but was cut short because of printing press time. The rest was printed later, and picked up by many other newspapers all over the country, under the heading, "Loss of the *San Francisco*. Statement of Lieutenant Winder, U.S. Army."
Winder, Jan. 13, 1854: Lt. William Winder's very short dispatch of Jan. 13, 1854, published in the *New York Times* of Jan. 16, 1854.
Winder interview, 1854: Lt. William Winder's account given to the reporter of the *New York Tribune* on Jan. 13, 1854, and published in that paper the following day. Winder had his Jan. 6 report in front of him as he was giving this interview, but, while much of it is copied word for word from that report, there are sufficient factual additions to make the *Tribune* interview independently worthwhile.
Winder 1883: William Winder's account, *San Diego Union*, Jan. 5, 1883.
Winder testimony: Lt. William Winder, court of inquiry, Feb. 16 and 17, 1854.
C.S. Winder: Statement of Lt. Charlie Winder, *Liverpool Mercury*, Jan. 24, 1854.
Wirtz account: Surgeon Wirtz, *New York Times*, Jan. 16, 1854.
Wirtz testimony: Surgeon Wirtz, court of inquiry, Feb. 10 and 15, 1854.
Wyse account: Major Wyse, *New York Herald*, Jan. 14, 1854.
Wyse testimony: Major Wyse, court of inquiry, Feb. 11, 13, and 16, 1854.

Four Previous Books

Given that for a while, in the first few months of 1854, the wreck of the *San Francisco* was front page news, it is odd that there have been no books at all written about it. Only four previous works, all quite obviously unedited, have even referred in any substantial way to the disaster, and, to a great degree, the essence of all four is the Narrative of Lucia Eaton, Miss Eaton being one of the survivors of the tragedy. Of the many accounts penned or told verbally by persons who made it back to safety, Miss Eaton's is the only one that can be described as "long." Her manuscript wound up in the vault of the library at Mystic Seaport, in Connecticut. The curator of the museum, Edouard Stackpole, transcribed it, and then, in order to flesh it out a bit, and to bring a perspective to it, threw in, rather too casually, 20 pages of end matter. The 79-page volume was published in 1954 by Mystic Seaport, Inc., as *The Wreck of the Steamer San Francisco: the Loss of the Steamship During the Great Atlantic Hurricane of December 1853, being an Account of the Wreck in Mid-Ocean of the New Steamship*.

In 2003 Tamara Taylor-Leigh copied Mr. Stackpole's effort word for word and titled her manuscript *Gales of War—The 1853 Shipwreck of the San Francisco*. As this was unpublishable for obvious reasons, she padded it out with over 50 pages of articles copied from mostly provincial newspapers of the day, and then added a 109-page novelette she had written about Major George Taylor, no relation despite what is claimed. This part of the book does not even begin to cover the voyage of the *San Francisco*, rather it deals with two fictional days Major Taylor and his wife spent in New York City before boarding the steamer. One must make clear that this is not the George Taylor of history; it is fiction. Five years later the completed work, with Lucia Eaton's narrative poorly transcribed, went on offer to the public as *Shipwreck! The San Francisco Tragedy*, privately printed by an on-demand company in Tennessee.

Jean Hood's book, *Come Hell and High Water*, came out in Britain in 2006, published by Conway Maritime Press, and in the U.S.A. in 2007, by Burford Books. The U.K. paperback edition, re-titled *Wreck!*, was published in 2008 by Anova (who had bought Conway). The book is a compendium of 17 maritime dramas, the *San Francisco* being one of them. Using primarily Lucia Eaton's account, but backed up by a number of newspaper reports, Miss Hood fashioned a hybrid—part novel and part narrative nonfiction.

The fourth work is *Faithful of Days: The Story of Robert Crighton, Master Mariner*, by Clare Abbott and published in 2014 by YouCaxton, apparently a self-publishing service based in Shrewsbury, England. Crighton's great great grandson, Alan Boyd, told Mrs. Abbott what little he knew of the story and she pieced it together over the course of five years. 17 pages are devoted to the *San Francisco* tragedy; the chapter "On board the rescue ships" has 11 pages; "Aftermath in America" has 14 pages; and there are 13 pages on the court of inquiry, a total of 45 pages to do with the *San Francisco*. While the author's overall understanding of the event is quite good, her grasp of the all-important details is limited, by her own admission, basically to Lucia Eaton's Narrative, two editions of the *New York Times*, and the proceedings of the court of inquiry, also published in the *Times*. However, by ignoring the accounts in the

Herald and the *Tribune*, for example, one cannot hope to get anything more than a shadow of what really happened during the voyage of the *San Francisco*. An example of her other sources is: (Anon. Undated). "An account of the Rescue of Eight Hundred and Fifty Passengers from the American Steamer 'San Francisco' by the British Clipper ship 'Three Bells' commanded by Capt. Robert Crighton, Christmas 1853." It seems there is only one copy of this anonymous manuscript, and that belongs to Mr. Boyd.

Index

Abercrombie, John J. 8, 14, 17, 41
Abrio, Senhor, and Senhora 43, 123–124, 134, 183
Adams, Captain 176
Adams, Warren 183, 203, 209–210
Alabama 164–167, 169, 175, 185
Alexander (seaman) 112
Alps 195
Amelia 193
America 196–197
Anderson (seaman) 133
Andrews, Lizzie 48, 80, 223
Antarctic 118, 145, 147, 154–157, 159–160, 187, 190, 193–197, 212
Aspinwall (town) 7, 9, 39, 72, 213–214
Aspinwall, George W. 29, 65, 74, 90, 98, 131, 134, 141, 175, 182, 188–189, 222
Aspinwall, William H. 5, 6, 19–21, 27, 29, 36, 40, 41, 43, 161, 164–165, 167–168, 187–189, 226
Astor House 189–190, 210
Atchison, David Rice 200
Auchinleck, Alexander 60–61, 73, 78–79, 85–86, 112–113, 142–144, 160, 224–225
Augusta 72
Austine, William 14, 222
Ayres, Romeyn B. 192

Bache, George 46
Bain, John 97
Baker, Mr. 134
Baldwin, Officer 205
Ballard, Edward P. 126
Baltic 196
Barnegat 178, 184
Barton, Charles F. 8, 196, 224
Bedloes Island 8, 190–191
Bell, Charles H. 28
Bell, Finlay and William 31

Bell, John 31
Belmont, Francis S. 10
Belton, Rebecca J. S. 80
Bennett, William 166
Bennett, William Lock 166
Besse, Hannah Springer Goodwin 131, 134, 183
Boggs, Lt. 169
Boylan, Robert J. 183
Bragg, Braxton 14
Brooklyn 34, 184
Brooks (waiter) 81
Brown, Elijah R. 11–12, 78, 84, 89–90, 95–96, 126, 129, 135, 138
Buchanan, James 195
Bucker, Captain 209
Buel, William P. 16, 47, 56, 62, 64, 68, 74, 77, 81–82, 87–88, 95, 116–118, 127, 139, 160, 168, 201
Burke, Martin 13, 30, 76, 86, 92, 94, 125, 128, 130–131, 133, 141, 163, 182–183, 188–189, 192, 203, 217, 220, 223
Burnside, Ambrose Everett 14
Burnside, Thomas 97, 143
Burton, Henry S. 216

Cairns, Adam, and Joseph 97
California 6
Campbell 161
Carter, Isaiah 160
Carter, Miss (Mrs. Gates's sister) 124, 134, 189
Cavaugh, John 183
Chagres 7
Chandler, John G. 13, 76, 86–88, 102–103, 112, 129, 134, 145, 194, 196, 199, 203, 219
Chase, Leslie 134, 188
Chase, Sarah Elizabeth "Sallie" 57–58, 131, 134, 163, 189, 218
Cholera 116–117, 135, 140, 147, 166, 194
City of New York 186, 191

Clayton, Corporal 196
Coal 40
Coffey, Miles 196
Cole, Howard M. and Louise 80, 223
Coleman, Robert B. 188
Coloma, California 4
Columbus 52
Comstock, Captain 196
Conneghan, Condy 183
Continent 147
Cooper, Samuel 36, 191, 198, 200
Cooper, William H. 48, 75, 96, 98–99, 109, 119, 131–132, 134, 136, 150, 162, 176–177, 182, 185, 188, 192, 222–223
Coryell, Miers 25, 226
Crawford, John 214–215
Crighton, Robert 31, 142–144, 146, 148–153, 155, 159, 177–180, 193, 219, 225–226
Crosby, James 160
Crowell, John F. 114

Dartmoor Prison 28
Davidge, W.H. 164, 167
Davidson, Jane 196
Davis, Daniel 192
Davis, Jefferson 9, 161, 193, 200, 215
Day, Edward 213
Decatur 185
Decker, Richard 184
Delany, Fenton 196
Delaware, Capes of 108
Derwanz, Senhor 43
Dobbin, J.C. 200
Dolores, Mexico 3
Donaghan, B. 113, 160
Dooling, John 214–215
Duckett, Franklin 81–82, 90
Duckett, Washington 194, 196, 225
Dunham, David 155, 160
Dwyer, John 183

Eagle 19, 34–35, 40
Eagle Wing 64, 74
East River 190
Eastport, Me. 13
Eaton, Lucia 30, 34–36, 39, 40, 43–44, 47, 49, 50, 56–60, 62–64, 70, 74–75, 83–85, 91–94, 102–103, 107–109, 112, 114, 116, 118–124, 130–133, 137, 141, 146, 150, 163–164, 175, 178, 182–184, 186, 188–189, 213, 219
Edgar 72
Eldridge, Moses 183, 203, 209–210
Empire City 215
Engineer 38
Evans, William 160, 205
Eylsom, Edward 12, 31

Falcao, Antonino J. de M. 43, 131, 134, 222
Falcon 213–215
Farnsworth, James 133
Field, Horace B. 13, 27, 80
Fields, William 160, 205–206
Filce, Henry 183, 210
Fire Island 181, 184
Fleck, Anthony 86
Foley, Patrick 196
Forster, Barbara 196
Fort Adams 31
Fort Columbus 8, 14–15, 27, 31–32, 45–46, 212, 214
Fort Hamilton 34, 57
Fort Lafayette 35, 209
Fort Wood 8, 189, 190, 192, 210, 213–214
Foster, Captain 196
Fox, Horace 13
Frederick (the cook) 133, 182
Freeman, William T. 108, 111, 167
Fremont, Mary 31, 131, 134, 141, 163, 218
Fremont, S.L. 12, 13, 30–31, 41, 45–48, 55, 58, 85, 99, 104, 110, 115, 120–121, 123, 125–127, 130, 133, 137, 138, 162–163, 178, 181–182, 188–189, 193, 199, 201–203, 206, 218

Gallagher (quartermaster) 160
Gannon, Bernard 12, 31
Gansevoort, Lt. 169
Gardiner, J.W.T. 41, 47, 86–87, 94, 104–105, 122, 125–126, 133, 138, 188, 199–200, 202–204, 207–210, 222
Garthley, Robert G. 114, 225
Gates, Charles 80, 95

Gates, Harriet Louise 16–17, 45, 47, 49, 56, 84, 123, 124, 134, 163, 171, 189, 200
Gates, William 9, 12, 16–20, 26, 30, 40–41, 45, 47–50, 55–57, 74–75, 80, 84, 94–96, 104–106, 114, 116–118, 120–123, 125–130, 133, 137–138, 147, 163, 172, 182–183, 188, 198–204, 206–212, 217
Geddes, Robert 97
Gibbs, James 97, 148
Gold 4–8
Golden Gate 72
Golden Light 8
Golden Spike 5
Goodwin, Ichabod 131
Gorham, William 106, 121, 123, 196
Governors Island 8, 17, 27, 32, 39, 41, 45–47, 191, 212, 214
Graham, James L. 65, 87–88, 90, 103, 113, 131, 134, 163, 181–182, 188–189, 223
Graham, Nathan B. 189
Gramon, Margaret 196
Grant, Ulysses S. 9
Gretton, George 35–36, 52–53, 66, 81, 107, 114, 145, 152–154, 160
Griswold, George 187
Guadalupe Hildalgo, Treaty 4
Gwin, Senator 161

Halifax, N.S. 161, 167
Halleck, Henry W. 4
Hardie, James A. 31, 45, 186
Haskell, Thomas H. 108
Hatteras, Cape 214
Hawthorne, Nathaniel 195
Hayti, Cape 191
Hazzard, Captain 191
Heath, Levi 160, 166
Heath, Walter 168
Henderson, Captain 196
Henlopen, Cape 108
Henry, Arthur 160, 166
Hidalgo, Padre 3
The Highlands 191
Hoffman, C. 160
Holmes's Hole 191
Hood, John Bell 14
Hooker (quartermaster) 160
Hopley, Richard 112
Horn, Cape 4, 5, 6, 18, 26
Horne, Sgt. 210
Howland, G.G. 189
Howland & Aspinwall 6, 8, 29, 52, 187, 206, 222
Hudson, Commander 176
Huston, Mr. 182–184

Hutchins, Stephen 53
Hyland, John 104

Illinois 72, 165, 213–215

Jacob Bell 180
Jakel, Edward 194
Jamestown 164
Jefferson 46
Jefferson Davis 161, 185
Jesup, Thomas S. 16, 18–20, 22, 26, 40, 161, 193
John Hancock 38
John L. Stevens 21, 38, 66
Johnson (waiter) 116
Johnson, William T. 194
Judd, Elizabeth 131, 134, 204–205, 218
Judd, Henry 12–13, 58, 91, 94, 99, 103–104, 121, 123, 125–126, 131, 147, 163, 182–183, 188–189, 199, 201–206, 210, 218
Judson's Hotel 45
Justice 36–38, 40, 73

Kearny, Lawrence 28, 50
Kelley, John 160
Kelley, William 183
Kelly (seaman) 133
Keystone State 38
Kilburn, Charles L. 11
Kilby 107, 114, 116, 118–120, 124–133, 136–139, 141, 146–147, 150, 157, 162–163, 169–175, 177–178, 181–185, 187, 190–193, 201–206, 208–211
Klemm, Darius 221–222
Knap, Jane 196
Knoxville 72

Labrade, Dr. 43, 183
Lang, W.J.C. 196–197, 212
Leddy, Peter 53
Lee, James 187
Lee, John Fitzgerald 201–206, 208, 214
Leitch, Agnes 97
Leviathan 191
Lightfoot 19, 33
Lilly, Patrick 183, 196, 203, 209–210
Lincoln, Frederick 114, 208–210
Linnell, Ebenezer H. 64, 74
Liverpool 160, 190, 193, 194–197, 212
Liverpool, N.S. 167
Livingston, Catherine E. 60, 65, 81, 86, 118, 134, 160, 225
Loeser, Lucien 5, 14, 30, 34, 39–40, 43, 74–75, 92–95, 99, 102, 104, 112, 119, 122–126, 128–

130, 133, 136, 146–147, 150, 163, 172, 175, 182–183, 188–189, 193, 199, 203, 206, 213–214, 218
Loeser, Sarah 30, 34, 43, 50, 74–75, 85, 93–94, 102, 118–119, 124, 141, 182–183, 188–189, 213, 218
Logan, John 160, 205
Long Beach Island 178
Lord, Isaac 196
Low, Edwin T. 114, 120, 127, 129–131, 137, 141, 146–147, 162–163, 171–175, 178, 181, 183–184, 191, 193, 204, 225
Lucy Thompson 33, 178, 181–184, 186–188, 190–192, 205, 207
Lund, John 183

Marcy, William L. 29
Maria 108, 110–111, 161–162, 167
Marion 164
Marshall, James W. 4
Marshall, John W. 50, 53, 66–69, 74, 90, 100–101, 106, 109, 113, 159–160, 224
Mary Taylor 187
Mason, John 142, 154, 194, 196
Matanzas, Cuba 31
Matthews (a cook) 190
Matthews, Captain 186
May, George Washington 13, 221
McBeath, Alexander 97, 226
McCabe, Thomas 97
McCarty, Mr. 102, 107, 168
McClusky, Francis 97
McDonald, William 183
McDougall, William E. 97, 142–143, 146, 151, 153, 162, 175, 226
McDowell, Irvin 199
McGough, Owen 220
McGowan, Captain 215
McGowan, John 97, 153
McInroy, Alexander 97
McIntyre, Joseph S. 95, 106, 133, 147, 160, 174, 183, 191, 209–210, 222
McIver, Charles 196
McKay, Donald 19, 147
McKenzie, John 193
McKernan, John 196
McKinstry, Lt. 213, 215
McVickar, John 15
Measles 48
Mellus, Edward 36, 52–54, 82, 88, 129, 143, 159–160, 206, 208, 212, 224
Merchant, Charles S. 11, 12, 30, 43, 47, 84, 103, 122–125, 133, 174, 188–189, 207, 209, 217
Merchant, Lydia 135
Merchant, Sarah 124, 174, 182
Merchant, Vallie 124, 131–132, 134, 141, 146, 163, 218
Mersey, River 194, 196
Miller, Robinson 183
Mischief 20
Mit, Joseph 86
Molloy, Patrick 183
Monroe, Fortress 214
Monterey, California 4
Morgan, Charles 7, 25
Morgan Iron Works 25
Morning Star 196
Morris 185
Morris, William W. 57
Mosquito Coast 7
Muirhead, James 97
Mulholland, James 157, 196
Mulholland, Thomas 157
Murphy, John 183, 203, 209–210
Murray, Francis K. 46, 71, 74, 78, 88–90, 100, 103, 113, 121, 123, 131, 133, 137, 146–147, 163, 171, 173–174, 178, 181, 188–189, 193, 201, 212, 222

Nantucket Roads 185
Napoleon 31, 33–35, 64, 99–102, 105, 107, 166–168, 192
The Narrows 57
New York City 168, 176–177, 180, 184, 187, 191–192, 200
New York Harbor 33–42, 191, 214
Newport, R.I. 12, 31, 197
Nicaragua 5, 7
Noland, Mariana 90, 126
Norfolk, Va. 214
North River 43, 46
North Star 164, 169
Northman, Ernest 157

O'Brien, Patrick 104
O'Donnell, Coroner 190
O'Hanlon, Philip 97
Old Point Comfort 214–215
Oppenheimer, Sgt. 206
Oregon 6
Oregon Territory 3, 8
Osier, Edward 60, 160, 180
Overman 191
Ozark 196

Pacific Mail Steamship Company 5–8, 16, 19–20, 29, 32, 52–53, 60, 152, 206, 226
Panama 5, 7–8, 213
Panama 6

Park, George W. 166
Parker, Margaret 206
Parmer, William 97
Patten, Lt. 191
Pendleton, Charles B. 33, 179, 181–184, 186–188, 207, 226
Phantom 184
Phelps, Lorenzo A. 12, 31
Pierce, Franklin 200, 215
Pirsson's Condenser 38
Plympton, Joseph 8
Portsmouth, N.H. 14
Pyramid 196

Quarantine 46–47, 55
Quintard, George W. 25

Ramsay, Albert C. 7–8
Rand, John 192
Rankin, William G. 83, 194, 196
Reidt, Charles 183
R.H. Moulton 191
Rio de Janeiro 26–27, 40, 46, 65
Roberts, M.O. 215

St. Andrew 191
Salmon, John T. 140
San Diego, California 6, 17, 32, 41, 216
San Francisco, California 4, 6, 8, 20, 33
Sanborn, Thomas 191
Sandy Hook 33, 35, 38, 57, 66, 108, 175–179, 181, 184, 186–187, 191
Sanford, Charles 65, 75, 94–95, 162, 170
Satterlee, Richard S. 12–13, 32, 45–47, 88–89, 112, 125, 127–128, 131, 133, 139, 163, 171–172, 174, 188, 201, 205, 220
Sauer, Marianne 134, 182
Schell, Theo 6, 8, 95, 111–112, 194, 192, 225
Schenck, Capt. 167, 215
Schmidt, William 214–215
Scofield, William 160, 206
Scott, Winfield 9, 14, 16, 18–19, 200–201, 208–209, 213, 226
Shand 8
Sherman, Tim 14
Sherman, William T. 4, 10, 13
Sherwood, Samuel Frederick 223–224
Shields, Hamilton L. 13, 47, 201, 206
Shock, William Henry 29, 35, 39, 49–50, 206–207
Skiddy, William T. 28–29
Skidmore, Mr. 215

Sleeper, Isaac N. 183, 203, 209–210
Smallpox 116, 155
Smith, James 133, 135
Smith, Lewis 220
Smith, Mary A. 196
Smith, Richard H. 10, 11, 80, 220
Smith, William 97, 144
Smith & Damon 6
Snow, Reuben 33
Southworth, Fred 46, 59, 64, 70, 73, 83, 134, 183, 188, 223
Sprague, John T. 14
Stanton, Henry 201, 214
Steptoe, Edward J. 12, 190, 192
Stetson, Charles A. 188
Stewart, Walter, and Margaret 97
Stewart, Walter, Jr. 97
Stockwell, James 82
Stouffer, George C. 147, 154, 160, 193–195, 197, 226
Strout, William 31, 99–102, 105, 107, 166–167, 192
Stuart, Justice 205–206
Sumner, Edwin Vose 201
Sutter's Mill 4, 6
Swords, Thomas 4, 16–21, 26–27, 40–41, 165, 193, 201, 226
Sylph 34

Tate, Stanger J 220–221
Taylor, Corporal 126, 134
Taylor, George 10, 30, 48–49, 55–56, 77, 80, 170, 206
Taylor, James 97
Tehuantepec 7
Tennessee 8, 52
Tenney, Ned 48, 80, 223
Testador, Louis 135

Thomas, Lorenzo 9, 18, 201
Thomas Ellis 191
Three Bells 31, 97, 117–118, 139–140, 142–144, 145–146, 148–160, 162, 166, 168, 170, 174, 176–177, 180–181, 187, 189–190, 193, 206, 212
Thyne, W.K. 97
Titan 186–189
Tremere, Ben 197
Tuscarora 197
Twist, Reuben 94

Unicorn 6
Union 176, 185

Vanderbilt, Cornelius 7, 25, 169
Van Voast, James 11, 30, 79, 88, 95, 112, 115, 121, 123–125, 131, 133, 163, 169, 183, 188, 190, 199, 202, 206–207, 210, 213, 219–220
Varioloid 116
Vera Cruz, Mexico 5
Vineyard Haven 191
Vinton, Dr. 192
Virgin Bay 7

Wallace, Clark 166
Walsh, William 183
Walter Forward 161, 185
Washington 161, 185
Washington, John M. 12–13, 46–48, 81
Watkins, James T. 6, 8, 21, 26, 40, 43, 52, 55–57, 63, 67, 69, 74, 77–79, 89, 91, 95–96, 98, 101–102, 104, 108, 112, 114, 117, 120–121, 129, 132–133, 145, 149–152, 154, 158–159, 166–168, 193–197, 202, 207–208, 212, 221, 224
Watkins, Walter 160, 162
Webb, William H. 6, 23, 26, 226
Westward Ho 19
Whitcomb, Commodore 185
Wickham, William H. 52, 65, 114, 145, 160, 225
Wilson, William 145
Winder, Abby 131
Winder, Charles S. 12, 30, 95, 123, 129, 134, 193–197, 199, 203, 213, 216, 219
Winder, William A. 11, 30, 32, 36, 53, 59, 76–77, 82–83, 87–88, 90, 94–95, 102–103, 105, 112, 115, 122–123, 128–129, 133–136, 155, 158, 160, 162, 189, 191, 193, 199, 203, 207, 213, 216, 219
Winder, Willy 131
Wirtz, Horace R. 11, 47, 59, 62, 65–66, 69–70, 78, 81–82, 88–89, 127–129, 131, 133, 138, 139, 163, 188–189, 201, 206–207, 220
Wool, John Ellis 18, 19, 30–31, 40–41, 43, 186, 201
Wyse, F.O. 11, 30, 45–46, 75, 88–89, 91, 93–94, 114–115, 122, 125–129, 134–135, 139–140, 144, 152, 155, 158, 160, 168, 175, 180, 189, 191–193, 199, 202–203, 206–207, 213–215, 217
Wyse, Mary Eliza 89, 114–115, 119, 123, 129, 131–132, 182

Yankee Blade 39, 216
Yankee Town 7
Yanqui Chagres 7

www.ingramcontent.com/pod-product-compliance
Lightning Source LLC
Chambersburg PA
CBHW081549300426
44116CB00015B/2818